D1570011

BRIGHT EPOCH

Women in the West

ANDREA G. RADKE-MOSS

BRIGHT EPOCH

Women & Coeducation in the American West

UNIVERSITY OF NEBRASKA PRESS | LINCOLN AND LONDON

Library of Congress Cataloging-in-Publication Data
            Radke-Moss, Andrea G.
Bright epoch : women and coeducation in the American
West / Andrea G. Radke-Moss.
            p. cm. — (Women in the West)
Includes bibliographical references and index.
            ISBN 978-0-8032-3965-4 (cloth : alk. paper)
1. Women college students—West (U.S.) 2. Women—
Education—West (U.S.) 3. Coeducation—West (U.S.)
4. Sexism in higher education—West (U.S.) I. Title.
            LC1757.R34 2008
            378.0082—dc22   2008017275

Set in Monotype Bulmer by Bob Reitz.
            Designed by A. Shahan

This book is affectionately dedicated to the educated women in my family. They have shown me dreams of education both fulfilled and unfulfilled.

To my great-grandmother Willo Muirl Dorrough Shimmin. She left a homestead in the Sandhills of Nebraska to attend two summers of the Alliance Junior Normal School in Nebraska in 1911 and 1912. She was the first to dream.

To my grandmother Mattie Elizabeth "Bee" Shimmin Radke. The Depression kept her from graduating from high school in 1935, but her dreams of reading and learning live on in her children and grandchildren.

To my aunt Muirl. She left a small farm in northwestern Illinois in 1956 to attend the Northern Illinois State Teachers College. In 1965 she was the first—either male or female—in her family to receive a bachelor's degree, and in 1985 she was the first to earn a master's degree.

To my mother, Louise, who defied family tradition and limited finances to complete the 1959–60 year at Knox College in Galesburg, Illinois. She achieved one year of partially fulfilled dreams.

To my sister, Elizabeth, the first in her immediate family to receive a bachelor's degree in 1984, when very few women studied computer science. She received a master's degree in the same field in 1986, and showed her younger sister how to dream big.

To my niece, Nicole, the next generation of educated women in our family. Now our dreams are in you.

Contents

Illustrations

Tables and Graphs

TABLES

GRAPHS

Acknowledgments

The completion of this book would not have been possible without the academic, emotional, and financial support of many individuals and institutions. From the dissertation stage of this project I would like to express thanks to John R. Wunder, whose unfailing support and energy kept this project focused, relevant, and on time. Few advisors would have provided the professionalism, attention, and speedy response that Dr. Wunder gave to me throughout the research and writing process. For other faculty mentors who provided invaluable ideas, feedback, and support, I express gratitude to current UNL history professors Dr. Timothy R. Mahoney, Dr. Carole Levin, and Dr. Benjamin Rader; to English professor Dr. Fran Kaye; and to Dr. Charlene Porsild at the University of New Mexico. Dr. Kristin Ahlberg has offered loyal friendship and support from the early research to the final stages. Danae Romrell assisted in the preparation of all statistical graphs. Finally, I am indebted to Dr. Renee Laegreid of Hastings College in Nebraska for her encouragement from the beginning to the end of this process, as she added suggestions up to the very last minute. From reading chapters and talking through ideas to sharing laughter and ginger snaps, her assistance has been priceless.

The archivists and their staffs at four land-grant universities have generously assisted me throughout the research process. Appreciation goes to Carmella Orosco and Tom Mooney of the University of Nebraska Archives and Special Collections; Larry Landis, Karl McCreary, and the staff at Oregon State University Archives; Tonya Zanish-Belcher and other staff members at the Iowa State University Special Collections Department; and finally, Bob Parson, Anne Buttars, and Daniel Davis at the Utah State University Archives. I also thank Alison Comish Thorne, whose mark on Utah State is indelible, as a professor of home economics and as the original historian of land-grant women. She graciously allowed me access to her knowledge and her collection of documents and newspapers. To Professor Thorne—I hope this work fulfills our shared dream of bringing to light the important history of land-grant women—you are greatly missed.

This book was supported financially by numerous grants and fellowships from the UNL Department of History and Graduate College; the latter awarded me the Maude Hammond Fling Dissertation Fellowship for full-time research support in 2001 and 2002. Research and travel expenses were also funded by the Landis Travel Award, the Warren F. and Edith R. Day Student Award, the Department of History Sheldon Award, and the Center for Great Plains Studies Grant-in-Aid. These funds supported research trips to Ames, Iowa; Logan, Utah; and Corvallis, Oregon, in addition to helping with photocopying and photo reproduction expenses. I received a Thomas E. Ricks Fellowship from Brigham Young University–Idaho (Rexburg) that provided some support during my academic responsibilities in the 2005–6 academic year. Also in 2005, Dr. Brian Cannon at Brigham Young University (Provo) provided a generous research grant from the Charles Redd Center for Western Studies to assist in the final revision and publication stage of this book.

I express gratitude for the patient support of my parents and family, and my history department colleagues at Brigham Young University–Idaho. I could not ask for a better professional and emotional support system. And finally, to my husband, Stephen G. Moss, who entered this process in its final stages. He has been a patient and sympathetic cheering section during a difficult and time-consuming process that he probably never bargained for. To him, I am eternally thankful.

BRIGHT EPOCH

Introduction

With the passage of the Morrill Act in 1862, many states in the Midwest and West chartered land-grant colleges following the Civil War. Because of both progressive ideologies and economic necessity, these institutions admitted women from their early beginnings. Although some historians have downplayed coeducational experiences at land-grant colleges as mere reinforcement of women's traditional roles through domestic science course work and exclusion from male clubs and activities, this study shows that women students took a much more proactive role regarding their own inclusion on these campuses. Although women students did not feel complete acceptance by their male peers and professors in the land-grant environment, many of them successfully negotiated greater gender inclusion for themselves and their fellow female students.

This is not so much the story of the access to higher coeducation as it is the practices of coeducation at land-grant colleges. Regarding the interplay between separation and inclusion for women students, this book examines various areas of contested gendered space, including course work, hetero- and homosociality, athletic and military activities, and feminist reforms such as suffrage activism, journalism, and political leadership. Rather than being venues for female exclusion, western land-grant colleges offered opportunities for women students to determine new areas of participation and inclusion for themselves within traditionally male environments. As a result, women land-grant students were able to effect change on many fronts of feminist reform by challenging gender restrictions both on campuses and in the nation at large.

Land-grant colleges in the nineteenth-century American West were among the first public institutions in the world to practice coeducation. The admission of female students was a new and revolutionary experiment, heralded by progressive reformers as a balanced and healthy educational ideal, as opposed to the gender-segregated colleges and universities of the East. Land-grant colleges began educating men and women together at a time when coeducation still endured a heavy debate, especially by critics such as Dr. Edward H. Clarke, whose anti-coeducation treatise *Sex in Education; or a Fair Chance for the Girls* (1873) argued that women could not endure the strain and stress of higher education with men because increased blood flow to the brain would deprive female reproductive organs of needed circulation.[1] The book went through seventeen printings between 1873 and the end of the century. In spite of objections by Clarke and others who believed that women were not intellectually or physically suited for mixed education, the land-grant institutions proceeded to enact coeducation with enthusiasm.

Land-grant participants accepted women's intellectual equality, at least in general, but they nevertheless struggled to work out the actual practices of mixing the sexes. In examining land-grant college environments between 1870 and 1918, one might expect to encounter either incredible progress for women or conservative attempts to limit their activities and participation to a traditional female sphere. The surprise would be in finding neither, and both. While land-grant women encountered a culture of ideological and physical separation, especially through the reinforcement of the traditional feminine expectations, these women also found ways to challenge the separation by rejecting traditional roles or simply adapting them to their own purposes. Out of this interplay between separation and inclusion, women students succeeded in negotiating new spaces of gendered inclusion and equality at land-grant colleges.

EARLY BEGINNINGS

On a windy March day in 1869, twelve hundred people met on the treeless campus of the new Iowa Agricultural College. A few buildings and the small village of Ames, population 650, served as a backdrop to the gathering of students, farmers, politicians, and reporters. Hosts and hostesses of this inaugural gathering of the college had prepared food for the visitors, but the turnout greatly exceeded expected attendance. The mood was electric as locals, visiting reporters, and politicians waited to hear Pres. Adonijah Strong Welch's inaugural address. Iowans also looked forward to meeting

Welch's wife, Mary Beaumont Welch, an educated and cultured woman who came to Ames with ideas about the need to provide women with practical and scientific education in the West.

President Welch began his speech with a recognition of the great experiment that was about to unfold at Iowa State. He committed the college to "two great and salutary educational reforms." First, instead of focusing solely on the classical curriculum of traditional European and eastern universities, Iowa Agricultural College would fulfill the purposes of higher education outlined by the Morrill Act of 1862, to teach "those branches of natural science which underlie the industries of this beautiful state."[2] In other words, this was to be an agricultural and industrial school, training students in the useful mechanical and engineering arts relative to the working classes, especially in scientific agriculture for the state of Iowa.

The other "great educational reform" was the "free admission of young women, on equal terms with young men, to all the privileges and honors which the institution can bestow."[3] Welch devoted two-thirds of his address to the topic of coeducation. He recognized women's legal right to equal higher education, and he also acknowledged women's potential for intellectual compatibility with men, once given the same opportunities as male students. In a kind of Shylockian speech, Welch asked, "Can she not see and hear, and smell and taste? Does she not apprehend and analyze, abstract and imagine, classify, generalize, judge and reason?"[4] Welch's speech called attention to the broadening ideals of feminine intellectual equality. His ideas represented an important progressive notion relative to the education of women in the new land-grant institutions. Iowa Agricultural College became one of the first schools to accept the conditions of the land-grant system under the Morrill Act. Accompanied by land-grant institutions all over the West and Midwest that also admitted women, Iowa Agricultural College was one of a handful of public, collegiate institutions in America to offer mixed education to women in the late nineteenth century.

THE MORRILL ACT AND THE WEST

President Welch's goals for Iowa Agricultural College fulfilled the dreams of Sen. Justin Morrill of Vermont, who had sponsored the original Morrill Act, and succeeded in seeing it signed into law by Pres. Abraham Lincoln in 1862. Desiring a greater democracy for a growing nation, Morrill eschewed the nonpractical and elite education of the East and sought to empower the working classes of North America through access to free and public higher education. Land-grant colleges would eventually be chartered in every state of the union, and some states would even claim more than one. Perhaps Morrill did not anticipate the great impact that his bill would have on thousands of American college women. Indeed, the Morrill Act itself made no mention of women students or their equal education. Thus, the decision to implement coeducation was left to individual states that chose to charter land-grant institutions; and many states in the West pursued this first experimentation with coeducation after the Civil War. The land-grant mission was important to western states for its ideals of providing practical and scientific agricultural knowledge to the children of rural farmers. Further, the founding of these colleges offered a regional and inexpensive alternative to sending children to distant and costly eastern schools. Land-grants could also contribute to the goals of encouraging companionate marriage and family settlement that would foster the agricultural and resource development of the American West.

This is a study of the American West, in that the institutions studied herein are located in Iowa, Nebraska, Utah, and Oregon, and peripheral references are made to other land-grants in Colorado, Kansas, California, and South Dakota. The main reason for this emphasis on American West institutions is to fill an important void in the historiography of women's higher coeducation, which has so often focused on elite colleges in the East or on the West Coast and has ignored the state institutions of lesser renown in the Midwest and West. As such, a study of these institutions allows for the voices of young western women to be heard.

This work is not trying to argue for western exceptionalism by suggesting that western land-grants were the "first" to implement coeducation, or that they did it in a more progressive fashion than eastern coeducational institutions. Indeed, they simply were not the first, being preceded by Oberlin College (1833) and other denominational colleges in the Midwest throughout the 1840s and 1850s, as well as state universities in Wisconsin, Iowa, and Michigan. This is not to say that the East made no claim to coeducational practice; for instance, even New York's own land-grant, Cornell, implemented coeducation in 1872, around the same time that its western counterparts were also going coed. However, the openness of newly founded

institutions in the post–Civil War West more easily implemented coeducation, as opposed to the greater numbers of older institutions in eastern
states that held out against the admission of women. Regarding the ease
with which new institutions were able to practice coeducation, historians
Rosalind Rosenberg and Leslie Miller-Bernal have both successfully argued
that older and established all-male institutions that had to admit women
after the fact — usually for financial reasons — often did so with resentment
and prejudice against new female students.[5]

Historian Julie Roy Jeffrey described the West's perceived progress in
coeducation, stating that in 1872 "there were ninety-seven major private and
public coeducational institutions in the country, and a majority of them,
sixty-seven, were located in the West."[6] This contrast between the gender-
segregated East and the mixed-gender West received greater emphasis with
the founding of numerous elite women's colleges as "sister" institutions
to the male-only Ivy Leagues in the 1870s and 1880s. Not even all land-
grants readily accepted coeducation, as many Morrill Act institutions in
the South and a few in the East also resisted the admission of women. The
argument for an exceptional West has more to do with how westerners
perceived themselves in relation to the East rather than quantifiable comparisons. Indeed, this book shows that western land-grant students and
administrators viewed their own experience as unique and set themselves
against the stereotypes of eastern institutions for their conservative and more
rigid restrictions on social interactions. Because western land-grants often
implemented coeducation reluctantly, they certainly were not immune from
similar acts of gender discrimination that occurred elsewhere. However,
the land-grant culture of the American West represented an environment
of acceptance and promotion of the widespread practice of state-supported
coeducation.

A few important factors led to the West's progress in land-grant coeducation. Jeffrey has argued that the "founding of new colleges and universities
was part of the frontier experience. Fears that the new society would sink
into barbarism stimulated missionaries to establish colleges as an 'important
part in Christian strategy.'"[7] The first and most practical reason was economic necessity. It was simply less expensive to educate men and women
together. Early land-grants did not require tuition fees, but the expense of
hiring staff for one coeducational institution was considerably less than

for two sex-segregated schools or classes. Larger numbers of students also brought added economic stimulus into college communities through boarding, transportation, and local consumerism. A second reason for implementing coeducation included the increasing post–Civil War demand for female teachers to fill the gaps in public education left by the war generation. Third, many administrators and reformers argued that women students' presence would be a refining and softening influence on the rough-and-tumble world of male college life. Hearkening to nineteenth-century notions of women's essentially pure and civilizing roles, educators hoped that the mere presence of women students would end the rivalries, practical joking, and interclass violence that plagued many campuses.

Finally, progressive ideology that favored legal rights for women certainly played a large part in the pioneering efforts of leaders in the West to establish coeducational colleges. Land-grant administrators often had cut their teeth at institutions in the Midwest, where mixed-gender education had already gained widespread acceptance at denominational schools. Upon arriving in the West, legislators and educational leaders found environments favorable to trying new ideas. According to Sandra Myres, "because the trans-Mississippi states were relatively new, . . . [they] had no deeply entrenched tradition of restriction, [and] it was easier to convince Western legislators to pass women's rights legislation."[8] Thus, western coeducation was imitative, especially as it borrowed ideas from a growing culture of educational reform and women's rights in America. But the West was also innovative, as western educators took the idea of coeducation and adapted it to fit their own unique needs.

The innovative impulse toward coeducation received further stimulus from the Morrill Act itself. Because the land-grant mission sought to provide scientific and practical training to the agricultural and mechanical classes, educators naturally translated this need for women to gain scientific training in their sphere of life. Domestic science education for female students fit well within the purposes of the Morrill Act, and the western environment particularly demanded a need for educated farm wives. According to Virginia Gunn, "life on the Plains worked best as a cooperative venture between the sexes."[9] Pres. John Anderson of the Kansas State Agricultural College in 1875 tried to convince reluctant easterners about the importance of a revolutionary new women's course in domestic science. According to

Anderson, eastern educators could "'purse their classic lips at the idea of including such topics in a collegiate course,' but they made sense in a Kansas girl's education."[10] A western woman needed education to help her better withstand the trials of rural western life. But collegiate expectations also determined that young women needed education for its refining effects in creating proper Victorian wives. And herein lay one of the paradoxes of western land-grant education for women: that women should be practical farm wives while also developing proper middle-class virtues of refinement and cultivated behavior. Even though westerners did not have many of the conveniences and luxuries available in the East, they still felt the importance of subscribing to dominant American cultural expectations. By combining the need for scientific domestic training with the notion of women's moralizing and refining influence, land-grant colleges provided an environment favorable to the implementation of coeducation, at least in theory. In practice, these institutions serve as important laboratories for understanding changing gender dynamics in nineteenth-century America.

INSTITUTIONS CONSIDERED

The experiences of women students at four land-grant colleges stand central to this study—Iowa Agricultural College in Ames, (referred to herein as IAC), the Oregon Agricultural College in Corvallis (OAC), the University of Nebraska in Lincoln (Nebraska), and the Utah Agricultural College in Logan (UAC). Although each was chartered as a land-grant institution, each differed in its evolution over time, especially regarding the emphasis on course work, the conflict between scientific training and traditional classical education, and the duration of time that it took each institution to implement the full purposes of the land-grant mission. In each case, these land-grants were founded by transplanted easterners from New York, Ohio, Illinois, or Michigan who brought with them prior notions of the importance of classical education that was so common to denominational colleges in the East. Even with the agricultural emphasis, many land-grants also offered students traditional education in Greek, Latin, literature, history, and philosophy, showing how the Morrill Act institutions still struggled over how to incorporate their two ultimate aims. Indeed, land-grant education required an uneasy marriage between classical education and practical agricultural or industrial training.

The impact of this tension on female students appeared mostly in how course work for women was implemented. For example, some land-grants procrastinated for decades in the establishment of domestic science courses because of more elite expectations for their female students than to aspire to the work of mere domestic servitude. Course offerings for women students in literature, French, music, and general history or philosophy displayed an implied expectation of cultural refinement that seemed to negate the land-grant mission. Thus, the conflict in land-grant missions represented the class conflicts present on the frontier as elsewhere.

Iowa State Agricultural College in Ames, later Iowa State University, was founded in 1868 with probably the most pure application of the Morrill Act's mission toward the practical education of farm sons and daughters. Drawing from the mostly rural and agricultural populations of western Iowa, the founding of the Ames school was an important regional institution for fulfilling the land-grant mission. Hence, IAC offered some of the first practical agricultural courses for male students, and for women, the first institutional domestic science (or domestic economy) course work—specifically geared toward the training of farm wives.

The Oregon Agricultural College, later Oregon State University, was also founded in 1868 and was formed out of a previously existing denominational school called Corvallis College, which had offered religious and classical schooling for local youth. This classical inheritance from the Corvallis College caused a similar conflict of mission for OAC upon its founding in 1868. Some Oregon families had roots back to the 1840s, which allowed for perhaps more connections to refinement and gentrification expected of well-established residents in the Corvallis area, and not the associations with the rough homesteading experiences of more recent post–Civil War immigrants to rural areas. Because of these imbedded middle-class expectations, the OAC founders and students also showed a great attachment to the more elite class offerings of classics. Although it was late in developing agricultural and domestic course work for its students, it eventually evolved into one of the premier agricultural institutions in the West after 1900, even inviting agricultural students from China, Japan, the Philippines, and India.

A similar conflict occurred over the mission of the University of Nebraska when it was chartered in 1869, as its students came primarily from more established communities in eastern Nebraska, many of which had been settled since the 1850s. Lincoln itself was not much older than the university, incorporated in 1869 specifically as the Nebraska state capital, which marked the city as a political, commercial, and educational center for eastern Nebraska and the central Plains, rather than as a maturing farm town. Supported more by families of politicians, businessmen, merchants, lawyers, and educators from Lincoln and Omaha, the university took on the air of a more traditional and classical institution, rather than as the distinctive agricultural college similar to its neighboring land-grants in Kansas, Iowa, and South Dakota. Indeed, members of the university community at times referred to it as the Harvard of the West, with students and professors embracing a higher intellectual standard not usually associated with the stereotype of land-grant colleges. Indeed, Nebraska even called itself a university from its earliest founding, in contrast to the other land-grants who accepted a budding "college" status. As such, Nebraska also struggled between the expectations to offer classical education and scientific agricultural training. This institutional schizophrenia affected women as well, since Nebraska was one of the last to establish a domestic science course of study for its female students and instead had a literary and general scientific emphasis. These first three institutions represent some of the earliest land-grant colleges and, because of their long histories, can provide a better sense of change over time regarding coeducational practice between 1870 and 1918.

The Utah Agricultural College, or Utah State University (1888), represents one of many land-grants founded later in the century and was attended by mostly Mormon students. Because Mormons had practiced coeducation since the 1830s and '40s in Ohio and Illinois, coeducational practice proceeded smoothly, but it also showed similar conflicts in the negotiation for gendered space as elsewhere. In the 1890s, however, Mormons still labored against stereotypes of oppressed women suffering in polygamous marriages. Thus UAC offers another unique layer of comparative analysis, since it drew mostly from among Mormon students and professors in the town of Logan and other local farm communities in Cache Valley, Utah, and southern Idaho. These land-grant colleges have been chosen to represent four important regions in the trans-Mississippi West and to show that the culture of gender separation and inclusion occurred in similar fashion regardless of the institution.

This is not an institutional history. Rather it is a study of similarities and dissimilarities in female experiences as they occurred at western land-grant institutions. Because men and women were thrown together in new environments where the sexes could interact formally and informally on a daily basis, this study offers important information about educational practices, social behaviors, and gender interaction among land-grant students who tried to mark out their gendered spaces.

METHODOLOGY

This study seeks to look at the history of women's coeducation at land-grant colleges as the story of contested gendered spaces, or areas of negotiation between men and women that played out on physical, ideological, social, and intellectual canvases. Rather than looking at the history of women students at land-grants through the lens of oppression and exclusion for women in an all-male environment, I instead suggest that women negotiated their own inclusion and separation in new environments of coeducational experimentation. At times, the separation was imposed by men, and at times it was self-imposed by women. So also the gendered inclusion was both initiated and accepted by the male power structure and also demanded by the women participants in the face of male or institutional resistance. Mary Ann Dzuback's theory of gender and education is instructive for this work, as she has argued that "*gender* is the central story of the history of higher education. We simply cannot understand the most basic and normative concepts shaping the development of formal education without analyzing for gender."[11] Further, Dzuback had called for historians to fill gaps in the history of college women by studying "how institutions resisted change to preserve gender distinctions and hierarchies and we need to study how women and men challenged those institutions to create more elastic and equal roles for men and women and less oppositional definitions for masculinity and femininity." It is to Dzuback's invitation to which I hope to respond with a thorough exploration of how women students pushed at the restrictions placed on them and then found new ways of negotiating their own inclusion with male students.

These challenges to gendered separation and power structures at land-grant institutions occurred in many arenas, including architectural spaces such as campus buildings, hallways, classrooms, quads, and chapels. Physical areas represented the jockeying for separation and inclusion, as students either kept to their separate male and female spaces or found areas where the sexes could intermingle more equally. To this idea, I am partly indebted to Gail Bederman, whose seminal work *Manliness and Civilization* described the Woman's Building at the 1893 Chicago World's Fair as a gendered space where women organizers contended for their own inclusion. While the building represented an important but limited incursion by women into the male space of the White City, it also showed the Board of Lady Managers' failure to achieve total inclusion within the masculine process of civilization that the Fair represented.[12] Bederman first invited me to think about how gendered hierarchies play out through the use of physical spaces.

Other historians of coeducation have explored examples of physical gendered separation that are useful for my study, but usually the emphasis has been on spatial exclusion rather than inclusion. Rosenberg has described campus lecture halls in which "a fairly strict pattern of segregation prevailed, with women seated on one side of the room, men seated on the other," noting how women later suffered from minority status through the lack of dormitory and gymnasium spaces built for them.[13] In examining the differences between Duke University's male (West) campus and female (East) campus, Annabel Wharton has shown how gendered hierarchies are apparent through architectural disparities consciously committed by Duke's administration and campus planners. She noted that "through the landscaping, layout, and architectural style, West Campus invites investigation and promises the excitement of discovery," thus indicating a supremacy of intellectual rigor and expectation for male students.[14] In contrast, the lack of creative planning for the East (women's) Campus showed "uneventful refinement and order," and a disregard for and inattention to women student's intellectual needs.[15] Both Rosenberg's and Wharton's studies are useful for showing how women students have been marginalized through the use of campus spaces. But rather than just emphasizing how women were restricted from male spheres, I intend to show how physical spaces on land-grant campuses became areas of gendered negotiations, where female students could contest separation and demand their own inclusion.

Beyond physical spaces, I extend my definition of competing gendered spaces to a broader inclusion of ideological, political, and intellectual spaces, especially the use of language as an arena for determining gender expectations. Again, for understanding these discourses of gendered separation and inclusion, I borrow from Bederman's use of discourse as the "ideas and practices which, taken together, organize both the way a society defines certain truths about itself and the way it deploys social power." Besides challenging the masculine physical spaces of land-grant campuses, women students could also confront other discourses of separation. Thus, the "ideas and practices" of coeducation emerged into what I am defining as a culture of the competing forces of separation and inclusion for women.[16]

This study works under a given assumption that coeducation was indeed a progressive and desirable move for women's education in the nineteenth century, especially because most of the reasons for keeping women out of colleges referred to their intellectual and physical inferiority. The acceptance of coeducation implicitly recognized that because men and women were more intellectually and socially compatible—even if not fully equal—that they should be educated together. Coeducation also rejected general ideas about women's inherent physical weakness that rendered them incapable of competing with men. This study does not seek to debate the benefits of sex-segregated education versus coeducation. Indeed, many educators and historians have argued for the validity of educating males and females separately to promote better concentration and self-esteem in an environment free of gender competition. The recent works of Leslie Miller-Bernal, in particular, challenge the notion of the superiority of coeducation over single-sex women's colleges. While I acknowledge Miller-Bernal's argument that "single-sex education still has advantages for women," I also accept the basic notion of coeducational acceptance in the nineteenth century as inherently progressive for women.[17] This work attempts to understand the complexities of mixed-gender interaction—both separation and inclusion—that affected women at land-grant colleges. Some of those effects of coeducational interaction certainly benefited women students, especially as they pushed against gendered limitations to achieve personal success on campuses and in the broader world.

Unlike other historical studies of women and coeducation—most of which have typically focused on separation and segregation—this study is not looking for gender discrimination around every campus corner. The experiences of women land-grant students do not portray a simple contrast between either outright discrimination or extreme progress and opportunity. Female experiences involved a complex interaction between both forces, and it is the purpose of this book to highlight those intricacies, and how women reacted to their collegiate cultures.

This is the first full-length book to deal solely with the experiences of women land-grant students in the American West. Many historians of women's education have examined the impact of coeducation, while often only devoting brief mention to the land-grant colleges of the West. The first significant study of coeducation in America was actually written as a novel in 1878. Olive San Louis Anderson, an 1875 graduate of the University of Michigan, wrote this fictional but semiautobiographical portrayal of Wilhelmine Elliot in 1878. Republished in 2006 and edited by Elisabeth Israels Perry and Jennifer Ann Price, the editors have found much useful historical context to women's earliest experiences at coeducational institutions. Although not meant to be a "realistic portrayal of women's experiences at Michigan," the novel represents "Will" as one woman student's challenges and successes as a female in a mostly male environment. Will's gendered encounters in course work, socialization, literary pursuits, and political ideologies—especially in her defense of the practice of coeducation—mirror the developments that other coed college women experienced in the late nineteenth century.[18]

As early as 1905 Mary Caroline Crawford celebrated American women college students in *The College Girl of America*, although her study focused primarily on eastern all-female colleges. In 1909 Helen Olin, a graduate of the University of Wisconsin, published the first work on coeducation at midwestern state and land-grant colleges. More an idealized contribution history of western women students, *The Women of a State University: An Illustration of the Working of Coeducation in the Middle West* came out of the author's personal experience with her education at the University of Wisconsin.[19] Thomas Woody wrote the first major work on the history of women's education in 1929, a two-volume work that still stands as a classic treatment of the history of female education in early America. Woody first addressed college coeducation in the second volume, mostly with the purpose of heralding the social and intellectual benefits of the system. His treatment of pro- and anti-coeducation ideologies is one of the most thorough examinations of the coeducation debate between 1870 and 1920. Writing from a distinctly pro-coeducation perspective, Woody focused on the successes of institutions like the University of Michigan (coed, 1870) and the University of Wisconsin (coed, 1870) in what he calls the West. He also lauds Cornell University (founded in 1868, coed in 1872) for its pioneering efforts in eastern coeducation.[20] Except for one chart outlining the numbers of female students at various state colleges, Woody gave no mention to western land-grant colleges in his discussion of coeducation.

By focusing on these few coeducational colleges, with emphasis given to Michigan, Wisconsin, and Cornell University, Woody foreshadowed a pattern followed by later historians of women's education, who would essentially ignore the western land-grants in any discussion of coeducation. Indeed, the only full-length work written about women's experiences at a land-grant university was by Charlotte Williams Conable, who wrote *Women at Cornell: The Myth of Equal Education* in 1977. While Conable adequately examines the implementation of coeducation in Ithaca, she also is one of the first historians to deal with practices of gender separation and segregation within a coeducational environment.[21] Later women's historians, such as Rosalind Rosenberg and Barbara Miller Solomon, would also examine the separation practices of coeducational universities. Rosenberg's essay "The Limits of Access: The History of Coeducation in America" examined the beginnings of mixed-gender education, the benefits and limitations for women, and lastly, the hiring and wage discrimination suffered by female professors at coeducational institutions. Rosenberg cited the examples of "Cornell, the University of Michigan, Wesleyan, Boston University, Wisconsin, and Berkeley" as the leaders in women's rights to equal education, but leaves out any discussion of western land-grant colleges.[22]

Solomon's more recent follow-up to Woody's 1929 study has added greater understanding to women's educational experience in America. Her work *In the Company of Educated Women* provides an excellent discussion of coeducational practice, including how coeducation realistically played out in midwestern and western state and land-grant colleges. Solomon cites examples of physical separation practices at the University of Wisconsin, the University of Missouri, the University of Chicago, and the University of California, again with only a brief mention of the Morrill Act and land-grant education. She also deals at length with the post-1900 reaction against coeducation at so many institutions, important for understanding the continuing debate and also the threat felt by male students and administrators as the numbers of women students increased in America after 1900.[23] Solomon's work stands with Woody's as a great contribution to the history of women's college education in America, but, like others, falls short in giving any significant treatment to the history of women at land-grant institutions.

Lynn D. Gordon, in *Gender and Higher Education in the Progressive Era*, has also examined the interplay between separation and inclusion at coeducational universities. Gordon focuses on women's experiences during the Progressive Era at two major coed universities, the University of California and the University of Chicago, and her chapters are significant for examining the complexities of coeducational practice. She addresses policies of separation, expectations for women, male and female interactions, and especially how women negotiated their roles within coeducational environments. Often these coeducational institutions exhibited confusion about whether or not women really belonged. According to Gordon, "Berkeley women's separatism, beginning solely as a response to exclusion and proceeding to a vision of womanly influence at the university, ultimately became a means of pushing for equality and integration." But women at Berkeley would eventually lose "their bid for campus equality, their separatist feminist vision, and their power base."[24] The most recent historian to examine coeducational experience is Leslie Miller-Bernal, whose *Separate by Degree* seeks to show the advantages of single-sex education over coeducation for women students. Miller-Bernal's study compares three colleges and successfully demonstrates some of the limitations for women at coed colleges as opposed to apparent greater access to academics and political activism at single-sex colleges around the time of the First World War. Some of her conclusions coincide with other historians' findings that many coeducational institutions after 1900 began to retreat from earlier gender successes in the 1870s, 1880s, and 1890s for women, and instead reinforced traditional gender expectations. While Miller-Bernal demonstrates some of the complexities of coeducation, she concludes with favoritism for single-sex education as more advanced and academically superior.[25]

Women's education historians like Miller-Bernal and Gordon have brought important analysis to our understandings of the complexities of coeducational practice. However, for Miller-Bernal and Gordon, as with Rosenberg and Solomon, the emphasis has sometimes been on segregation and limitation for women rather than inclusion and achievement. Further, these historians have almost overtly ignored the experiences of western women in land-grant higher education. By practicing a "fly-over" approach to women's education, focusing only on eastern academia or large urban centers in California and the Midwest, historians have left out an important part of the story of women and education in America.

This study seeks to remedy these omissions and also depart from historians' emphasis on female exclusion and discrimination, by suggesting a more complex and reciprocal interaction between men and women students in coeducational environments. Because the land-grant colleges of the West experienced gender separation and inclusion among single and marriageable young adults on a microcommunal level, this study provides an important model for understanding gender interaction both regionally and nationally. While examining primarily four coeducational land-grants, the attitudes examined here can be applied just as fully to other environments where gender mixing occurred at the turn of the twentieth century, including similar conflicts between inclusion and separation. By emphasizing institutions in the American West, this study seeks to show the West as both imitator and innovator in coeducational practice. Western educators took coeducation and then adapted factors like democratic education, militarism, scientific and agricultural training, and a progressive attitude toward women to create a unique western environment of coeducation. Whereas the mixing of sexes on western campuses conformed to larger patterns in the nation, gender interaction also departed from those patterns. Most especially, women students maneuvered within the coeducational culture of separation and inclusion and found ways to expand their own intellectual, social, and political spheres and to redefine what it meant to be a modern woman in America.

SOURCES AND CHAPTER OUTLINES

This is a history of women, but it is also a history of how women and men interacted. To fully comprehend the implementation of coeducation, the most appropriate source materials are those that speak to the experiences of students and how they reacted to coeducation. I have used student newspapers extensively because these portray the most revealing and usually honest expressions of the collective and individual personalities of students, as well as general campus attitudes. Also, literary society minutes, reminiscences, college yearbooks, and student diaries help to re-create a sense of the political and gender awareness of land-grant students. College catalogs are important sources for showing the administrative policies of the colleges and the importance of various types of required curricula, as these courses influenced student experience. An examination of these sources reveals the conflict between inclusion and separation for women students that seemed ever-present, written into the language of newspapers, course catalogs, codes of behavior, physical separation, and social experiences.

Chapter 1 presents the land-grant environment as a culture in which the discourse of coeducational inclusion was accepted and promoted as part of a larger institutional and administrative rhetoric of progressive land-grant education. At least in theory, students and administrators held up land-grant coeducation as an ideal against "monastic" gender segregation, especially as practiced in the East. Through the medium of "journalistic activism" by male and female student editors, land-grant newspapers often defended and promoted the cause of mixed-gender education as a unique experience worthy of national consideration. Chapter 2 presents an overall theory and formula for examining the experiences of women students in coeducation. Women students experienced various forms of discrimination and separation. This "culture of separation" for women included practices that kept men and women apart physically, socially, intellectually, and ideologically, especially through the use of language regarding women's separate moral and domestic expectations. Still, in spite of this culture of separation, women students challenged those restrictions by seeking greater intellectual and academic inclusiveness. The interplay between separation and inclusion will demonstrate the complex practices of coeducation at land-grant colleges. Chapters 3 through 8 will look at specific applications of separation and inclusion.

Chapter 3 addresses student literary societies as the earliest laboratories for examining the conflict between separation and inclusion at land-grant colleges. As administrators and students tried to decide the extent of gender interaction, that dynamic first played out in the literary societies, especially as these organizations were the main venues for student social and intellectual culture in the 1870s and 1880s. This chapter will show that women often negotiated their own membership in both mixed literary societies and women-only groups, sometimes even choosing female-only clubs when they had the option of membership in mixed societies. Further, within literary societies themselves, women students used the literary practices of oration and debating to find their political voice and challenge intellectual separation.

Chapter 4 examines the importance of social interaction for men and women students. The proponents of coeducation in America heralded mixed-gender education for the balanced socializing effect it had on single men and women college students. Indeed, land-grant environments focused on the importance of preparing students for life as a cooperative venture between the sexes. Thus, men and women students experienced an emphasis on marriage and family, with women treated as "wives-in-training" for educated males. However, land-grant educators still tried to restrict the extent of social interaction between the sexes. Within a culture of supervised sociality, men and women students both tried to maneuver their own opportunities for social and physical contact. Chapter 4 also examines the importance of women's sociality with other women, and the importance of female networks in the collegiate environment. Some women students even challenged the traditional expectations of heterosexuality and marriage goals by pursuing same-sex relationships.

Chapter 5 addresses the impact of women's course work on the land-grant culture of inclusion and separation. In theory, women experienced an equal education with male students, but in practice, the separate courses required for women fulfilled the need to maintain the separate female sphere of domesticity. Land-grant colleges pioneered the domestic science curriculum for women that became widespread by the early decades of the twentieth century throughout the United States. Domestic science fulfilled the Morrill Act's goals for scientifically educating the American laboring classes, and women students found a place within that scope, as they trained for domestic careers, both inside and outside of the home. Further, because women received scientific training as part of the land-grant mission, their education was not limited to cooking and sewing. Indeed, many women found opportunities for study in nontraditional areas such as botany, chemistry, biology, and even medicine and law. Chapter 5 will provide a fuller understanding of the complexities of women's course work, especially as women pushed the boundaries of their professional expectations at land-grant institutions.

Chapter 6 explores the impact of women's physical activity in mixed-gender environments. Because women found a climate of greater freedom of intellectual and social expression at land-grant colleges, that freedom translated to women's access to physical education. Women students often demanded and received access to physical culture or physical education classes, and later they asked to participate in competitive team sports like basketball and field hockey. These team sports set up an important atmosphere of physical expression and freedom, where women students exhibited masculine qualities such as aggressiveness and physicality. The public spectacle of women's physical performance in front of mixed-gender audiences helped to redefine the standards of female behavior in the late nineteenth century.

Chapter 7 provides a history of women's military activity at the land-grants. Indeed, this was truly a unique contribution of the land-grant environment. Since the Morrill Act required military training for young men, women saw this activity and demanded it for themselves. At first, women sought military drill primarily for exercise, but they expanded their activities to included rifle training, fencing, and public parading. Women's military activity on campuses helped to pave the way for their entrance into other public and political spheres, and military activity might even be linked to an expanded feminine democracy. Women's rights and woman suffrage were important contributions of land-grant student activism between 1870 and 1918. The significance of this activism at western land-grants is examined in chapter 8. To nineteenth-century feminists, woman suffrage was the final frontier of access to political equality and freedom. Indeed, the position of a women's rights chapter at the end of this study perhaps suggests its placement within a larger American feminist experience, because woman suffrage was the last obstacle in the achievement of gender equality. Equal suffrage was the culmination of decades of women's activities, as women gradually expanded their social, intellectual, and physical sphere.

Within a culture where the forces of gender separation constantly battled a move toward gender inclusion, women students worked to find their place within the changing dynamic of coeducational practice. Male and female students managed to negotiate unique gendered responses—both predictable and surprising—to mixed-gender education. In this process of challenging gender separation, women found new opportunities for success and achievement within a traditionally male environment. These included literary society participation, mixed-and same-gender social interaction and behaviors, new adaptations to traditional course work, the emergence of women's athletics, team sports, and women's military regiments, and finally, women's rights activism, especially woman suffrage. As women gained in these areas of inclusion, they helped to redefine gender expectations for land-grant college environments as well as in the larger nation.

1

Making a Welcome for Women Students

The Discourse of Coeducational Inclusion by Administrators and Students

You have done well to open the doors of the University as wide to your daughters as to your sons; and I doubt not that they will, by their scholarship in every department, abundantly justify your wisdom.

CHANCELLOR EDMUND FAIRFIELD,
"Chancellor's Address to the Board of Regents, Inaugural Ceremony, June 1876"

The land-grant experiment purposely sought to provide education as a democratic ideal, and coeducation was linked to the emerging standard for the egalitarian provision of education to men and women. When Adonijah S. Welch gave his inaugural address for the new Iowa Agricultural College in March of 1869, coeducation was still a hotly debated national topic, and much of the country, especially in the conservative East, balked at the acceptance of women students to colleges. Critics of coeducation argued that women were intellectually inferior to men and had no need for the same education in the same environment as male students. Many felt that too much education weakened women physically and mentally. Further, skeptics suggested that women distracted impressionable young men and that mixed-gender environments inevitably led to moral depravity, because young men ended up too confused to keep their minds on their studies. In the midst of this debate, land-grant administrators and students responded with overwhelmingly positive reactions to gender mixing in higher education. Thus, land-grant participants—both students and administrators—helped to foster a culture of gender inclusion through a verbal and written discourse of promoting coeducation.

The three oldest universities included in this study, Oregon Agricultural

College (OAC) in Corvallis (1868), Iowa State Agricultural College (IAC) in Ames (1868), and the University of Nebraska in Lincoln (1869), are significant as representative environments for examining early reactions to the experiment of public coeducation, simply because they were founded so early and because they were created in the midst of a heated national debate. All three were chartered before 1870, and all three admitted women students immediately upon opening. Together with Kansas State Agricultural College in Manhattan (1863) and the University of California (founded in 1868; coed in 1870), these were the earliest coeducational land-grant colleges in the West. In the 1870s, budding scholars at OAC, IAC, and Nebraska represented some of the first students in the world to experience coeducation in practice at public institutions of higher learning.

These early students, both men and women, seemed to accept coeducation—in theory—with very little protest. Reaction to the practical implementation of coeducation proved wide and varied, but western students, professors, and administrators alike defended coeducation as the ideal against the gender-segregated education of their eastern counterparts. Progressive ideology favoring advancements for women certainly had an influence on this discourse.[1] The ideas and practices defending coeducation included the voices of many supporters, especially administrators, who spoke openly and often about the importance of coeducation, as well as students, who expressed their reactions in a variety of media. These public expressions of language promoting coeducation constituted a major part of the "social capital" of women's educational reform. "Social capital," or the "organizations and connections that foster cooperation, trust, participation, the exchange of information, civil interaction, and coordinated activity in pursuit of social goals," helped to advance the knowledge and awareness regarding women's issues, especially through journalistic activism.[2] Through the "exchange of information," the land-grant culture and its arbiters sought to legitimize the coeducational experiment by spreading positive information regarding the successes of mixed-gender education. Because social capital is especially concerned with the "achievement of political democracy," land-grant commentators played active roles in trying to reconstruct a culture that accepted coeducation as preferable to the gender-segregated education of the East.

Land-grant educators and participants considered themselves the most

qualified to comment on coeducation because they actively lived the experience on a daily basis. The discourse of coeducation became a vital part of
the language of land-grant institutions because coeducation was new and
relatively untried in the national collegiate culture. Through the processes of
education, public speeches, college catalogs, books, and newspapers, land-
grant participants sought to impart the discourse of defending coeducation.[3]
These activists' purposes were twofold: first, to enlarge the public sphere of
knowledge regarding women's schooling in a mixed-gender environment,
and second, to reconstruct society's development. In other words, those
who favored coeducation hoped that critics and skeptics would change
their opinions of the system and then eventually replace outdated systems
of gender-segregated instruction.

Three areas of discourse regarding coeducation emerged in the 1870s
and 1880s. Together they represent a philosophical support system that
bolstered the land-grant coeducation movement. First, top-level administrative voices, such as land-grant presidents and chancellors, constituted a
significant part of the discourse of publicly defending coeducation. Second,
student editors of college newspapers published editorials and exchanges
regarding the progress of women's education. By doing so, these student
editors assumed an activist role and helped maintain a public dialogue on
women's rights. The printed voice of editors often represented the collective opinion of campus populations on various political issues. Third,
student literary achievement—both published essays and literary society
debates—often revealed students' reaction to coeducation. That coeducation was a frequent topic of discussion at all the universities' literary societies indicates its importance within the continuing public discourse of the
late nineteenth century. Land-grant activists—both students and professors—played important roles in expanding the public knowledge regarding
women's coeducational progress.

ADMINISTRATORS' REACTIONS TO COEDUCATION

Oregon, Iowa, and Nebraska willingly accepted coeducation in their individual charters with little debate or protest. Although the boards of regents
of the various land-grant universities disagreed on how coeducation should
be implemented, still they accepted it almost universally. The opinion of
administrators and professors regarding the acceptance of coeducation

displayed an important trickle-down influence for students' reactions to coeducational practice. Of course, students were greatly impressed and motivated by their presidents or chancellors—men who met with them daily in chapel, taught classes, and walked and talked with them during and after classes and meetings. Since land-grant institutions had sparse populations and each campus numbered no more than about two hundred students during the 1880s, administrators and professors had easy contacts and exchanges with their pupils on a personal level. Thus, these administrators' opinions on coeducation constitute important starting points for understanding student reactions in the early years of land-grant coeducation.

Many administrators' opinions on coeducation may be traced to their progressive collegiate roots. From the late 1860s through the 1880s, most land-grant administrators and professors in the West came from colleges in Ohio, Pennsylvania, Michigan, and Iowa, for example, where several small, private colleges had experimented with coeducation since the 1840s and 1850s. Western administrators and professors maintained an important intellectual exchange for framing their own land-grant experiments with their counterparts in the East. For example, the land-grant universities in Missouri, Nebraska, Kansas, and Iowa adopted charters borrowing portions from the others' charters and from other land-grants. To fill chancellor positions, boards of regents often recruited administrators who hailed from teaching and executive positions at other coeducational schools. This discourse of progress spread to the West and served an important part in molding western attitudes and reactions toward coeducation. Thus, western coeducation institutions acted as both imitators and innovators, taking progressive ideas on women's education and applying them in new and practical ways to the western environment.

Pres. Adonijah S. Welch, the first president of IAC, hailed from Michigan, where he had taught in the 1860s and where he had met his wife, Mary Beaumont Welch. She was also a staunch supporter of women's rights through mixed education, and she helped organize one of the first women's domestic economy programs in the United States. The Welches became important leaders in western Iowa for the promotion of women's education. Soon after their arrival in Ames, President Welch gave his 1869 inaugural address, which was published in booklet form only a few months later and stands as one of the best statements by a land-grant president or chancellor regarding coeducation. In addressing a national audience that he assumed might be somewhat skeptical, Welch gave a speech that took on the tone of one trying to convince a reluctant public, and perhaps even as one trying to tear down gender prejudices.

Welch heralded IAC for its admission of women. He recognized the uniqueness of this situation, which found "scarcely a parallel in history." Even though the restriction against women's higher education was a "precedent . . . honored by time," IAC now made claim to higher principles of "wisdom and justice." The justice, Welch said, was in extending to a large class of women "opportunities of which they have been . . . unjustly deprived."[4] He attacked the prejudice of centuries that kept women bound and restricted. Indeed, "the great obstacle to all reform is prejudice. . . . It is the prolific parent of obstinacy, bigotry, cruelty, and hate."[5] Nineteenth-century prejudice claimed that too much education for women was offensive to taste, morality, and "delicacy." To that idea Welch responded, "Can that delicacy be genuine which closes for woman the avenues to honorable distinction, withholds food from the craving soul, and condemns her in a thousand instances to a life of trifles? Can that be true taste which, regardless of the wide range of her intellectual and moral capacities, inflexibly assigns her place as the puppet of the parlor or the drudge of the kitchen?"[6] Welch never went so far as to negate women's natural "susceptibility . . . to moral impressions," nor their "greater natural strength of certain instinctive emotions."[7] In other words, women still held a moral influence over society and the home, but higher education could only serve to increase and stimulate this aspect of women's judgment. So, while Welch argued for an innate separation of the genders through women's moral and domestic roles, he still seemed to push for a greater inclusion regarding women's intellectual equality to men.

President Welch believed in equal education for women, but he also believed that course work for women should be specially adapted to women's particular roles in society and the home. That belief was strongly shaped by his wife, Mary Welch. President Welch was one of the first college executives to offer a public defense for coeducation. As early as 1868 in his "Plan of Organization" presented to the board of regents at IAC, Welch pronounced that "admitting girls and young ladies . . . and giving them full participation . . . has my hearty concurrence. In fact this policy is simply a recognition of their rights under the national law." He was revolutionary in his demand for equal education, not just for women but also for the member of "any race who has reached the years of discretion."[8] His published words influenced much of the thought regarding progress for women and education, especially as the discourse of defending coeducation spread through the West.

One of Welch's contemporaries was Pres. John A. Anderson of the Kansas State Agricultural College. Appointed in 1873, Anderson was the second president of KAC (1863), the first coeducational land-grant college in America. President Anderson held beliefs similar to those of President Welch — the belief in equal education for women, but also the belief that female students should pursue practical domestic training for money-earning use. Anderson participated in the discourse for defending coeducation in the early 1870s, and his public language played a significant part of the intellectual exchange by land-grant administrators in the Midwest and West regarding women's education. Anderson had read Dr. E. H. Clarke's 1873 treatise against coeducation, *Sex in Education*, and was familiar enough with the arguments against coeducation, but like Mary Welch at IAC, Anderson's wife, Nancy, was an educated woman, and they both believed in women's equal intellectual capacity.[9] In a report to the Kansas State Board of Regents, Anderson argued for course work "for young ladies who wish to fit themselves, either for earning an honorable support, or for wisely filling any position in womanly life, as the unknown future may indicate."[10]

Chancellor Edmund Fairfield of the University of Nebraska, another contemporary of Welch and Anderson in the 1870s, made a speech to the Nebraska board of regents in October 1876, in which he heralded the rise of American universities and coeducation. Fairfield recognized that "one such good thing some American universities have already adopted, in advance of these older institutions beyond the waters, [is] the admission of all who are properly qualified, without distinction of sex, thus securing a humanizing and refining influence which the universities of Europe, and especially of Germany, greatly need."[11] Here Chancellor Fairfield took the East-West comparison and expanded it to a more global contrast between Europe and North America. He further recognized the experimental aspects of land-grant universities and congratulated the regents: "You have done well to open the doors of the University as wide to your daughters as to your sons; and I doubt not that they will, by their scholarship in every department, abundantly justify your wisdom."[12]

The comments of these three land-grant college leaders in the 1870s show a clear top-down discourse on coeducation. Not only did their dialogue influence administrative policy, but it also influenced public understanding and acceptance of women's educational progress, especially for local citizens and the student bodies they represented. Although this study will not show the extent of administrators' written or verbal conversation with other college leaders, still an important ideological exchange seems to have existed at the top levels of land-grant administration.

One example of this top-level exchange on women's education occurred in the summer of 1879. Pres. W. W. Folwell of the University of Minnesota visited the IAC campus in Ames, and his visit was reported in the *Aurora*, the student newspaper. After several days' visit, he decided to hold an impromptu interview with students about the topics important to them. After a lengthy discussion about public education, at the students' suggestion, he next turned to the subject of "Co-education of the Sexes." Folwell asserted that " if no good reason can be given for their separate education, the separation should not be made." Based on his years of observation in schools, Folwell argued, "girls have shown themselves equal to any tasks which boys may accomplish." Then Folwell expressed his belief in the moral influence of women over men: "both sexes are benefited by co-education."[13]

College officials were keen to accept and promote the idea of women's "moral" influence for defending coeducation. They also used coeducation to contrast American universities' progress against the traditional schools in the East and in Europe. Land-grant administrators especially sought to defend the experiment of democratic, tax-supported coeducation against the elitist criticisms of coeducation's strongest opponents. The heads of western land-grant colleges often felt that they, like the institutions they represented, were on trial before a world of conservative traditionalists. The statements of these western administrators in print showed how seriously they accepted the mandate of portraying the success of the still-questioned mixing of the sexes. By voicing their defense, administrators gave an added legitimacy to the new practice of coeducation and the ideological inclusion of women.

STUDENT NEWSPAPER EDITORS' REACTIONS TO COEDUCATION

Land-grant students were undoubtedly influenced by top-down administrative policy regarding women and education, but the students themselves formed their own opinions regarding the mixing of sexes. Together male and female students worked, studied, and socialized, and they felt very early the impact of a mixed-gender culture. Students offered their reactions to coeducation through several media of commentary and expression, especially student newspapers. At OAC, IAC, and Nebraska, student-run newspapers appeared within a month after each institution officially opened. Student newspapers quickly became important media for campus-wide discussions of women's rights issues, and coeducation immediately appeared as a common topic.

An understanding of the organizational structures of campus papers and their editorial staffs is necessary in order to understand the importance of newspapers' influence in both representing and shaping student reactions to coeducation. There were three types of early newspaper staff organizations. Usually, as in the case of OAC's *Student Offering* (1868), a staff consisted initially of two or three members—an editor and one or two assistants (usually males). In the early years papers were small and claimed a limited budget and circulation. The second type of staff organization gradually evolved as newspapers gained greater readership, an increased budget, and expanded student participation. By the 1870s student papers like Nebraska's *Hesperian Student* (1871) were run similar to community papers, with positions such as editor, assistant editor, and other staff—each elected by the student body—in charge of the Locals, Exchanges, Personals, and Literary sections. IAC's *Aurora* (1870) represented a third type of paper organization. In that case, each campus literary society sent two members as representatives to serve on the paper's staff for a semester. From this selection of literary society members, the staff would then select students to serve in the various editorial positions.

In a natural move for the implementation of coeducation, the editorial staffs of the student newspapers included both men and women. Nebraska's *Hesperian* already had a female associate editor, "Miss" Sweet, in the fall of 1871; she was replaced by Grace G. Benton in March of 1872.[14] And at IAC, literary societies sent their representatives to serve on newspaper staffs; for instance, the all-female Cliolian Society sent two of its members to serve on the *Aurora* staff in the spring of 1871.[15] Female students showed an early interest in journalism, which was gradually emerging as an appropriate profession for women.

The newspapers' different departments allowed for various levels of participation by student staff members. The editor, an office that was usually elected by the student body, was the person with the most decision-making power. Almost always a male, the editor selected student essays, stories, and speeches for reprinting in the paper, and he also added his own editorial comments throughout the paper.[16] Finally, he oversaw the paper's final layout and decided what items from the other departments would make it to the final copy. The editor's second-in-command position of assistant or associate editor helped the editor with the major decisions of the paper. This position gradually opened to women in the 1870s and 1880s, and women could also serve as section editors in most other positions on the paper. Women were generally restricted from the business manager position, however, since financial administration was culturally a male role. Leslie Miller-Bernal has commented on this gendered "hierarchical pattern for the mixed-sex campus clubs" as a marked example of exclusion for women at coeducational institutions that occurred well into the 1960s. In many cases, this meant that female students did the work for which male figureheads took the credit.[17]

Still, in spite of women students' restrictions to "assistant" positions, their presence on campus editorial staffs helped to contribute to a larger culture of journalistic activism that included both male and female voices. Sharon Harris has argued that women's editorial activism should be examined and acknowledged on many levels, from low-level copyediting and menial tasks to "apprenticeship to influential editors" in female-run papers. Further, Harris suggests that the "most important aspect of studying women editors . . . is understanding how women wielded the editorial pen to influence public opinion."[18] Thus, even though women mostly served as assistants or as support staff to male editors, their contributions must be recognized within the land-grant culture of defending coeducation. Regarding the contributions of student editors, Lucille M. Schultz has shown that editorial activities gave female students many opportunities. These included "the opportunity to write about writing and what it meant to be a writer, a forum for shaping school opinion and engaging with other writers and thus for anticipating the adult role of public citizen, writer or editor."[19]

In promoting a discourse of supporting coeducation and women's rights, sometimes newspapers took on a genderless editorial voice, or a collective "we," that represented the editorial opinions of mixed-gender staffs. Thus, while most land-grant papers were led by male editors, they joined their activism with female assistants to support larger political rights for women.

These staffs used other subdepartments like the Literary or Exchanges columns to discuss and publicize current issues. The Literary department, for example, accepted submissions by students in literature, poetry, and fiction. The department editor worked closely with the literary societies in order to stay informed about the writing achievements of society members. Many times, essays published in the student newspapers had been originally presented as speeches during literary society meetings. Editors worked most closely with Literary editors in selecting submissions for the newspaper. Exchanges were another important part of early college newspapers, especially as they represented national political trends that held local importance. College publications throughout the United States maintained a system of exchanging articles so that fellow students all over the country could see writing samples and news items that were important to their American colleagues. For instance, the *Hesperian* and *Aurora* listed many exchanges with student papers from New England, Ohio and other Midwest states, and even Europe. In this way, the unique happenings at places such as Harvard, Cornell, and the University of Michigan often found their way into the pages of college newspapers in the Midwest and West. Likewise, writing samples and quotes from Nebraska or Iowa would appear in student newspapers back East. Editors often commented on the writing quality of their fellow students at other universities and colleges. Typically, an Exchanges editor waded through the collection of monthly subscription exchanges and chose a few items to reprint verbatim in the paper. In a "cut and paste" approach, each quote included no more than three or four sentences and usually recorded the name and location of the quote's source. Exchanges were a significant way of maintaining a nationwide collegiate discourse in which social and political issues could be discussed; this cultural discourse went beyond the boundaries of a single campus or region. Just in the act of choosing what went into an Exchanges column, male and female student editors assumed important activist roles and by keeping their fingers on the pulse of campus opion, helped to promote an "imagined community that closely approximated a real one."[20]

Student editors became representative campus voices for highlighting national and local issues, such as politics, race relations, women's rights, and education. They often chose to print information recording what they perceived to be the general feeling expressed among students regarding a particular issue. Because coeducation was immediately a topic of importance to land-grant students, the newspaper staffs took advantage of many opportunities to comment on mixed-gender education, especially in the early years of coeducational practice just after the Civil War.

The earliest student newspaper at a land-grant institution in the West was the *Student Offering*, started in 1868 at OAC. The paper was hand-written and lasted for only a few issues. Only one copy survives. Interestingly, that issue, written by an all-male editorial staff in December of 1869, offered the first reactions by students—male and female—to the implementation of land-grant coeducation. In a brief, but revealing, one-sentence commentary on women's education, the editor asked, "What do the girls of this College desire the most?" in a type of rhetorical campus survey. He then answered his own question in what seemed an enthusiastic repetition of answers he perhaps heard from student colleagues: "Schooling!"[21] This was an important early observation, simply stated, about female students' desires and motivations in a coeducational environment. The *Student Offering* of the late 1860s was the last student newspaper at OAC until the *Gem*, founded in the mid-1880s. Later, in the 1890s, OAC introduced the *College Barometer*, which continued to comment on coeducation through the early 1910s. The novelty and significance of the coeducational experiment hung in the air of the land-grant campuses, and students certainly felt this fervor of change.

Student newspapers also flourished at IAC and Nebraska from the 1870s through the end of the century. At IAC, student journalists founded the *Aurora* in the spring of 1871, just a month after the college's opening in March, and the *Aurora* became the preeminent vehicle for campus opinions and issues for the next three decades. Nebraska opened its doors in September 1871, and by October, the first issues of the *Hesperian Student*, edited by a mostly male staff, came off the presses in its upstairs campus office in the Old Main building. The first issue contained a report of Elizabeth Cady

Stanton's manifesto on women's physical and mental capacity to endure a higher education.

> Mrs. Cady Stanton is credited with making a very sensible and sarcastic reply to someone who asked her if she thought that girls possessed, as a general thing, the physique necessary for the wear and tear of a college course of study. "I would like to see," answered Mrs. Stanton, "I would like to see you take thirteen hundred young men and lace them up and hang ten or twenty pounds weight of clothes on their waists, perch them up on three inch heels, cover their heads with ripples, chignon, rats and mice, and stick ten thousand hairpins into their scalps; if they [women] can stand all this, they will stand a little Latin and Greek."[22]

The leaders of the women's movement often reacted to prevailing nineteenth-century attitudes about women's lack of physical and mental hardiness with candor and sarcasm. By printing Stanton's statement, the editor joined his sympathetic voice with a woman's to show changing notions about women's abilities; he also appreciated Stanton's humor. He added, "When one wants to have a particularly neat thing said about women, the most judicious way is to get a woman to say it."[23]

The political and ideological sympathies of student editorial staffs were readily apparent in what the editors chose to print. Although readers might expect a negative attitude from male editors regarding women's political rights, instead the discourse often showed overwhelming support. Editors also kept abreast of public discussions about coeducation. Land-grant campuses served as favorable environments for Chautauqua-like public programs of speeches and recitations on current political and social issues. Local and visiting speakers periodically presented talks regarding women's issues, including coeducation. Students attended these programs, and of course the campus newspaper editors at IAC and Nebraska chose to reprint some of these speeches. The *Hesperian* of January 1878 reported a "Mrs. Soule's" lecture to the Nebraska students about the education of women: "The co-education of the sexes were presented in an able manner, she maintains that the education of women is just as essential as that of man, and that higher education is also necessary to real success in life."[24] By the 1870s the language of defending coeducation had pervaded most aspects of intellectual and public exchange in western states, with newspaper editorials, public lectures, and administrative opinion devoted to the topic.

Land-grant students seemed the most absorbed in public and print discussions about the defense of mixed-gender education. Even into the 1880s the students themselves gave public lectures regarding coeducation, and what makes many of these speeches especially significant is that they were delivered by women students. Women became activists for female education by contributing to the public discourse of promoting coeducation. Helen Aughey Fulmer's scrapbook, kept while she was a student at Nebraska, included student newspaper clippings of public speeches, especially regarding coeducation and other women's topics. On February 16, 1886, a Miss Nora Gage gave an address on co-education, and one year later, on Charter Day, Laura M. Roberts spoke on "Co-Education in Nebraska." The paper's reporter was favorable to her speech: "She first compared the general condition of women now and two or three centuries ago, and then spoke specifically upon the young women of our own University. Miss Roberts had evidently studied her subject carefully, and was able to give statistics to prove that in scholarship and in every qualification of the good student the young woman of Nebraska is the peer of her student brother. Her conclusions were that co-education is highly beneficial to both sexes and to the University."[25] After Roberts's speech, the *Hesperian Student* recorded that the chancellor stood and "stated emphatically that the results of co-education here at least have been most salutary."[26] By reprinting the public discussions, editors brought greater general attention to the discourse of defending and promoting coeducation. Further, Miss Fulmer's inclusion of scrapbook clippings on coeducation showed a broader culture of concern for women's issues.

Many male and female students believed that coeducation was a special and significant experiment and that it made western students unique in the larger culture of American higher education. To highlight this uniqueness, the student editors sometimes contrasted themselves to the eastern "highbrow" colleges such as Harvard, Yale, and Columbia, and then derided those institutions' elitist tendencies and their exclusion of women and minorities. Another important tactic that editors used to defend women's higher education was to compare the "fair sex's" intellectual abilities with those of men. Since men's supposed intellectual superiority in the nineteenth century was already an assumed and given fact, editors and writers tried to draw attention to the rise of women's intellectual achievements by showing that they could compete with men in the same academic environments. Fulmer's scrapbook included a speech given by an unnamed professor at Nebraska to the "Annual Meeting of the State Historical Society." This professor compared the male and female members of the classes of 1879, 1881, 1885, 1886, 1888, and 1889, and he even prepared a chart to show the students' performance. He was able to show that the "average grade of the gentlemen is 88; that of the ladies is 87 and four-tenths. The figures are not at all uncomplimentary to the fair sex."[27]

Women were often on trial to see if they could rise to the standards that had been set by male performance for generations. Many editors selected essays and exchanges that approached the topic of comparing men's and women's academic achievements. Thus, the tactic of comparison—both the comparison of public, democratic land-grants to elitist eastern universities, and the comparison of female to male academic performance—served as an important activist maneuver in defending coeducation. In a broader sense, the editors' portrayal of eastern elitism versus the progress of western universities was a personification of the competition between males and females in the academic world. All-male institutions represented the conservative Old World—masculine and rigid—whereas the western universities, with their new populations of female students, were fresh, progressive, and more truly democratic. Indeed, this symbolic comparison was not lost on student editors, and newspapers carried many selections highlighting female performance as set against the male standards of the day.

In December 1877 the *Hesperian Student* reprinted a clipping from the *Detroit Free Press* about a Harvard study that portrayed women's intellectual equality while at the same time making fun of Harvard itself. According to the "report of the Harvard Committee on Examinations," the results of the exam that was the subject of the study seemed "to indicate that the ladies who stood the test have acquitted themselves honorably. The board of Examiners failed to see any defective training, or anything that would indicate woman's inferiority to man in the result of the late examination."[28] The use of the word *acquitted*, a legal term meaning to absolve or pardon from a criminal accusation, suggested women's need to defend themselves legally with evidence against accusations of inferiority. Indeed, women had endured charges of the "crime" of intellectual inferiority for centuries, and the mid-1800s movement to educate females equally with men was a significant and revolutionary step toward ending that indictment.

From Nebraska's point of view, women's education deserved more credit than the all-male Harvard was willing to allow, so the *Detroit Free Press*'s insult of Harvard was enthusiastically reprinted by the *Hesperian*: "It should be remembered that it would not take a very smart woman to get ahead of the average Harvard student in anything where the intellect is brought to bear."[29] Perhaps this was also a stereotypical insult to compare the least intelligent of women to the "average" Harvard student. Hidden inside the compliment to women's intellectual prowess were still some leftover stereotypes about women's inferiority. Nevertheless, arguments in favor of women's intellectual equality were being used to justify coeducation.

The University of Nebraska sometimes expressed the desire to be the "Harvard of the West" with comparable academic achievements; however, where the land-grants spied elitism and limitations on democratic education in the East, Nebraska students were the first to show the contrast between East and West, especially in the case of women's education. An early issue of the *Hesperian* included a "College Item" that reported certain administrative stances on coeducation: "Professor Agassiz, President Elliot of Harvard and Dr. W_____ have expressed themselves as opposed to coeducation."[30] Herein lay an example of comparing Harvard's conservative approach to the progressive cause of women's education. Although Pres. Charles Eliot was a reformer at Harvard, he was still a staunch opponent to coeducation and, as such, a representative of the traditional, conservative East. The "Professor Agassiz" mentioned was Louis Agassiz, who taught at Harvard from 1858 until his death in December of 1873.

The Exchanges department of the campus papers served well for promoting the "comparison" tactic highlighting female student achievement. Student papers carried those articles that related information and occurrences from other universities, both domestic and international. Editors waded through hundreds of pages of news and events from campuses all over the country, and the land-grant papers reprinted a surprising number of exchanges relating examples of women's educational progress as they occurred in the United States and the world.

The *Hesperian* of October 1878 gave an early report of the admittance of women to the University of London. "Next month the Univ. of London is to be opened to women. Women have been admitted for several years but they have recited by themselves. Now there are classes for women only and classes for both sexes."[31] This was a great triumph for the women students of Britain, and five years later, the *Gem* at OAC reported on the progress of those London students. In April 1883 two male editors noted that "at the last examination for the degree of Bachelor of Arts at the University of London 73 per cent. of the female candidates were successful as against 42 per cent. of the male candidates. Only 27 per cent. of the men were placed in the first division, while 68 per cent. of the women obtained that honor." The editors went on to comment on the intellectual comparison that one would expect from such percentages: "And yet some benighted people hold that women are incapable of pursuing with profit the 'higher education.' We [the editors] do not believe, as this would seem to indicate, that the ladies had greater abilities, but rather that the gentlemen trusted more in their mental powers, and were distanced in the race perhaps on account of their less energetic pursuit."[32] In other words, the men at London, relying too comfortably on their inherent intellectual prowess, had simply not studied hard enough.

Some women around the world in the 1870s made strides in areas previously dominated by men only, especially in science. Since scientific training was the "new education" practiced at land-grants and at engineering schools in Europe, women's progress in science was especially noteworthy in the 1870s. Student editors often noted these advancements. In the *Hesperian* of January 1878 the editor reprinted a "fine compliment . . . paid to woman" in the article entitled "Woman and Science."[33] And an indignant *Hesperian* editor in 1872 reported that "a lady earned the chemical prize at the University of Edinburgh over 240 competitors. Her sex, however, debarred her from receiving it."[34] Noting the prejudices against women students seemed a necessary part of trying to portray women's ascendancy into coeducational institutions. Still, for student editors, the most important message was that women were indeed ascending. This message validated the progressive role of land-grant colleges in the larger movement for women's education.

The first issue of the *Hesperian* in October of 1871 carried mention of an article in the Oberlin (Ohio) *Evangelist* from August of 1858: "We observe an article on the admittance of females to state universities."[35] It seems interesting that the paper reprinted part of an article that was thirteen years old, but to the *Hesperian*'s editor, these facts were noteworthy to Lincoln students—they were playing a significant role in the ongoing saga of women's educational progress. The "state universities" mentioned here likely referred to the Universities of Iowa and Minnesota, which had both opened as coeducational in the 1850s.

Western universities must have appreciated any recognition by their eastern counterparts. In April 1872 the *Hesperian* reported that "over one hundred women are studying law in American colleges," and repeated the same notice again in May of 1872, along with the announcement that "thirteen young ladies have asked admission to the Yale school of journalism."[36] These dispatches were related as successes to be cheered, not failures to be ridiculed, and the editor reported a few months later that "some of our [Nebraska's] lady students . . . contemplate studying law." In the same issue, the *Hesperian* noted the admittance of women students to Syracuse University and later reported on Syracuse's first female architecture student: "A young woman has begun the study of architecture in the Syracuse University. She is the first of her sex to enter upon this study as a profession, in this count[r]y at least."[37] The fervor for coeducation continued to be felt abroad, and the *Hesperian* reported in June 1873 that the "University of Zurich has one hundred and ten lady students the present semester, nearly three-fourths of whom study medicine, only one law, the rest general science and literature."[38] This information about women students at Zurich would later be important to Nebraska students: Prof. Rachel Lloyd, hired in 1887 as a professor in the Department of Chemistry, received her PhD from Zurich in 1887.

Throughout the 1870s, the *Hesperian* continued to note where progress occurred for women, as in January of 1875, when the editors, in "The Scissors and Pen at Work among Our Exchanges," reported "there are 92 ladies among the 1176 students at Ann Arbor [University of Michigan]" and one month later that "there are sixty-one lady students at Boston University."[39] The *Hesperian* editors reported two years later on Boston's male-female statistics, in the Boston "Year Book," which showed that the "whole number of students registered 665, of which 163 are women and 502 men."[40] The December 1877 issue reported that the "NY State University has at last consented to admit ladies, but they are required to recite by themselves."[41]

And in February of 1878 the "Educational Notes" of the *Hesperian* reported that the "Ann Arbor [Michigan] law school boasts of a lady in that department."[42]

The three aforementioned exchanges are significant because they were published during the tenure of one of the *Hesperian*'s female associate editors. Emma Parks served on the staff in 1877–78 with the editor, H. H. Wilson, whom she would later marry. Under her shared editorial leadership, the *Hesperian* enthusiastically reported educational progress for women throughout the country. It was during Wilson and Parks's tenure that many exchanges regarding women's achievements at other universities were printed. Perhaps these selections showed Parks's influence as an activist for women, both as an associate editor, and as a sometime literary contributor to the paper. It is impossible to determine definitively whether she made decisions on the selection of exchanges. However, if her service had any bearing on the increased number of clippings that reported women's progress that year, then Parks may indeed claim the title of activist female editor.

In October of 1878, the *Hesperian* offered a grand tally for the success of coeducation in America: "There are now ninety-seven colleges in which ladies share the honors with gentlemen."[43] Ninety-seven seems like a large number of coeducational schools by 1878, but within the context of a total number of colleges and universities that loomed around 350 nationally in the mid-1870s, coeducation was still a minority movement, and not without its loud and vocal detractors. In fact, in April 1875 the *Hesperian Student* reprinted some other newspapers' comments against coeducation. One southern student editor complained that "there are ninety-seven colleges, Academies, and Institutions in this country, in which the sexes are educated together—just ninety-seven too many.—Ala. Univ. Monthly." This exchange had made its way around the country already, and two other papers added their "amens" to the Alabaman's contempt. From the *Owl*: "Precisely our sentiments," and from the *Niagara Index*: "And emphatically ours." That the editors of the *Hesperian* had reprinted these statements did not mean agreement. In fact the editor took this opportunity to voice his or her sentiments regarding coeducation, first, with sarcasm toward the detractors: "Behold, how good and pleasant it is for brethren to dwell together in unity!" Then, with a bit of contempt: "It is just a little comical to see what wonderful unanimity of sentiment against co-education there is among the 'Colleges, academies, and Institutions' which have never tried the experiment. Those that have, take it as a matter of course and would never dream that it could be a question of dispute, if not for officious [meddlesome] outsiders."[44]

Perhaps this commentary came from George Howard, who was editor of the *Hesperian* in 1874–75 and later became a professor of history at Nebraska. Perhaps the reporter was Ada J. Irwin, the *Hesperian*'s associate editor for that term, or maybe it was a joint effort, as both seemed to stand united on the paper's role in defending coeducation. Either way, male and female editors like Howard and Irwin continued to assume activist roles in the 1870s by printing the ongoing debate surrounding mixed education.

One month earlier, Howard and Irwin had entered into a public, printed debate with the editors of the *Volante*, a Chicago newspaper. The *Hesperian* had, sometime during the 1874–75 school year, negatively commented on an anti-coeducation speech by a "Dr. Moss." Howard and Irwin, or possibly Fannie Metcalf, who was Irwin's predecessor in the fall term of 1874, criticized this speech in an issue of the *Hesperian,* which, through the Exchanges column, found its way back to Chicago's editors. Chicago responded: "The *Hesperian Student* quotes from our report of Dr. Moss's Inaugural address, putting in italics at pleasure. The critic evidently does not like the Doctor's ideas on co-education." Dr. Moss's speech was likely published in one of the missing issues of Nebraska's paper, but part of the *Hesperian*'s critique of Dr. Moss was quoted by Chicago's editors: "'His theory,' she says (for we will venture that the writer is a 'she') is just a little musty-burdened with the mildew of half a century, at least." If indeed either Howard, Irwin, or Metcalf had called Dr. Moss "musty-burdened with the mildew of half a century," there is unfortunately no extant copy of that editorial. The Chicago *Volante* editors did not know how to react, except with evasion: "Now we do not purpose to enter into a discussion on co-education—we leave that to the fair sex." While they avoided the topic of coeducation, they proceeded to insult any mixed-gender newspaper staffs: "But we cannot help remarking one thing, that 'mixed schools' furnish strangely mixed papers. It might be interesting to discover why it is that no college paper with young ladies on the staff has equaled in excellence papers published either entirely by young men or entirely otherwise." In other words, schools and their newspapers should be either all-male or all-female, but anything from a mixed institution offered intellectual and journalistic inferiority. The *Hesperian* did not dignify the *Volante*'s criticism with a negative retort, but simply challenged, "Truely [*sic*] the Chicago men might inform us why our editorial staff seems strange; he gives no reason at all."[45]

This was not the first time that one of the *Hesperian*'s editorials responded to an outsider's criticism of coeducation. In addition, not all criticism of coeducation came from all-male schools; indeed, some came from female colleges where students felt that gender mixing in higher education inevitably led to assaults against feminine morality. In March of 1874, when George Howard was editor, serving with Fannie Metcalf as the associate editor, the *Hesperian* reprinted the comments of the (all-women's) St. Mary's College *Palladium*. Its editors had read one of the western college newspapers, perhaps even Nebraska's: "We do not wish to be severe, but when a western college paper gravely informs us that the 'Junior Class embraces four ladies,' we must insist that we hear no more of the 'coeducation of the sexes.'" Perhaps the play on words was lost on the St. Mary's editors, given the serious response. In his typical humorous candor, Howard replied: "Are we to suppose by this that the young ladies of Saint Mary's School object to 'embracing'?"[46]

These intercollegiate newspaper conversations regarding coeducation demonstrate the ongoing national controversy surrounding the subject, even as western schools endorsed coeducation heartily. That so many student editors followed this national controversy by printing editorials and exchanges on the topic shows the importance of coeducation's defense to land-grant editor-activists. Further, the printing of notices about coeducation placed both female and male student editors in the role of women's rights activists—promoting the cause by publishing favorable statistics. Women's rights issues in general could be found in many local and national papers following the Civil War. However, on the specific issue of coeducation, more commentary was found in the newspapers of the schools where the newness of gender-mixed education was felt profoundly. By offering the facts about women's achievements at other institutions, and then adding their own sympathetic voices of support, male and female editors solidified their activist role regarding women's educational progress.

STUDENT LITERARY REACTIONS TO COEDUCATION

Student-run newspapers were a medium for young scholars to express their ideas and opinions about college, local, national, and religious issues. Students held fast to the right of freedom of speech; newspapers of the 1870s and 1880s were laden with student sentiment, and opinions ranged from the devout Christian conservatism of the mainly Protestant campus populations to the more radical ideals of campus intellectuals. Most students expressed some kind of political and social progressivism on various issues. Editorials and essays rang with support of public education topics; land-grant universities were climates ripe for the acceptance of democratic education for all levels of society. Like the student editors, student essayists almost universally defended equal education for women students, with some variances in the opinions about female intellectual abilities. Writers overwhelmingly heralded the democratic foundation of the land-grant experiment; they recognized and championed the unique nature of their land-grant educational experiences—especially coeducation.

Newspapers called for the submission of any editorials or essays on issues important to student writers. In an editor's note in the *Aurora* of August 1877 one editor complained of the lack of submissions due to students' timidity: "Contributors ask, 'upon what shall we write?' . . . In the first place, a college paper should be representative and express as nearly as possible the sentiments of the institution under the auspices of which it was issued. It serves at once the purpose of furnishing the students a medium through which they can express their ideas, and also make known to outsiders the conditions and workings of the students as a body."[47]

In other words, most of the editorials could represent the individual opinions of students, but they also embodied the collective attitudes of the student body. This lent an even greater significance to any campus editorials or essays about women, since student populations in general seemed to favor the progressive notions of the time related to women's access to equal education. At least students seemed to be talking about coeducation on a regular basis.

Writers and speakers often used women's "moral" influence for defending coeducation. In 1879 an anonymous author submitted an essay to the *Aurora* called, "Who Make Our Social Laws?" Although this individual claimed, "it is not our object to plead 'women's rights,'" the anonymous author, named "X," still believed that coeducation was the best system for everyone: "In the oft-repeated example of the good effects of co-education, . . . the presence of girls puts a restraint upon the young men; and it is a well known fact that in colleges where the two sexes are educated together, hazing, rushes and boisterous conduct are not so prevalent as in schools for young men alone."[48] Students most often argued for women's moral influence as a defense for coeducation, but other writers used more progressive ideals about women's intellectual equality.

Female students themselves felt the importance of their participation in a coeducational situation and seemed to desire opportunities for educational advancements. There was much female talent and intellect to be tapped, and both male and female students recognized it. Indeed, in 1872 a report called "Our Cornell" described the status of Nebraska's own land-grant, and the editor celebrated the coeducational atmosphere in Lincoln as an environment for promoting the intellectual development of women students. "Let us be encouraged," he said, "by the thought that there may be among us young men and women of great literary talent, and we know not but we will have the pleasure of reading the poems, novels, and speeches on woman's rights, etc., of some of our present lady friends."[49]

Unfortunately, even after the *Hesperian* called for female authors, women still remained relatively silent on the pages of the University of Nebraska's main outlet for student sentiments in the early 1870s. The lack of women contributors to the newspaper prompted a male editor to issue a call to Nebraska's female student authors. For coeducation truly to succeed in practice, some male students felt that women should take advantage of every opportunity for progress available to them in a welcoming environment. Indeed, land-grants like Nebraska offered the best climate for promoting women's intellectual achievements, and at times, male students expressed frustration when women did not rise up to current expectations of female success. A. W. Field, in his farewell "valedictory" as the editor of the *Hesperian* in October of 1876, celebrated the successes of the young journal: "The best was done, of which . . . we were capable." His only great complaint was to the women students: "There is much we would like to say to our lady friends. We are unable at present to recall a single article written by a lady member of the school, expressly for the *Student* during the past half year. . . . Now this is not right, it is not just. When any student male or female enters the University he or she becomes morally bound to do all in his or her power to sustain the credit of this institution."[50]

Thus, as the Nebraska campus provided a friendly atmosphere for the discussion of women's rights, then women students were encouraged to take advantage of that opportunity to portray themselves worthily. "When the abstract question of female equality is broached, the female portion of the school boldly maintain for their sex intellectual superiority. This is well, but the unanswerable argument would be to present some of the fruits of this superiority."[51] So, Field suggested, if women were indeed to prove themselves on equal footing with men in a mixed environment, they should rise to the occasion. Female timidity—especially at a time when coeducation was under a national microscope—did not help in disproving the age-old assumptions about women's supposed intellectual inferiority.

After this chastisement, a few Nebraska women answered Field's call for written expression and submitted essays to the *Hesperian*. In April 1877 May Fairfield, Chancellor Edmund Fairfield's daughter and the first female president of the Palladian Literary Society, submitted an essay called, "Paddle Your Own Canoe," in which she described the process of overcoming obstacles in order to achieve success. Besides a few male examples from history, Miss Fairfield also showed feminine examples of historical success—George Sand, Florence Nightingale, Harriet Beecher Stowe, "Mrs." Browning, and Margaret Fuller.[52] May Fairfield was one of the first women essayists at Nebraska to draw examples from great historical women to support an intellectual essay. In the years following, many women student-authors would follow suit with examples of feminist success in their essays. Already, women showed themselves as the "women of great literary talent" called for in the March 1872 issue of the *Hesperian*. To be a truly coeducational institution, the land-grant universities needed to actively promote coeducation on all levels, including the academic and literary participation of women in newspaper writing and literary societies. The *Hesperian Student* and other papers acted as mediums for student comment, serving both as a reaction to coeducation and the encouragement of women's participation in literary achievements.

It seems that some of the male editorial comments almost took a condescending tone toward women as amateur scholars who needed gentle prodding into full academic participation. At the same time, these editorials were a tribute to male contemporaries' acceptance and encouragement of co-education. Observers might have expected a general reaction and rebellion against coeducation by the young men at the new western schools. On the contrary, most accepted it with full enthusiasm and sought ways to further coeducation by highlighting women's scholarly successes in the mixed-gender environment. Thus, the encouragement of women's literary expression was in itself a method of defending and promoting coeducation.

Literary society debates also portrayed that coeducation was a topic of constant student discussions. As literary societies were the most important venue for student intellectual interaction in the 1870s and 1880s, the debates often approached the topic of coeducation, especially because of its continuing controversy. Each of the land-grant colleges supported at least two campus literary societies during the 1870s. These societies required volunteer participation, but membership was also based on a formal application process. Students usually took the initiative to organize these societies with the help of faculty members. Societies ran according to strict constitutional bylaws, and presidents, vice presidents, treasurers, and secretaries were elected. Societies met on a weekly basis and included formal activities for literary expression and participation. Members could recite essays, present written speeches, or perform musical selections.

Most society meetings ended with an organized debate on a previously selected topic related to political or social issues of the day, and these were usually reprinted in the newspapers. So significant was coeducation to the early student literary society members that they often chose it as the designated topic for essays and debates at weekly society meetings in the 1870s. IAC's literary debates offer an early sampling. The Crescent Literary Society was organized in 1871 at IAC as an all-male society. The second debate ever held by the society concerned coeducation. On April 15, 1871, six male debaters on two teams debated the topic "Resolved: That the co-education of the sexes is a failure." Since this debate session had no appointed judges, the decision was given to the society's president. He decided "in favor of the negative."[53] Ironically, during the same period, the Crescents' all-female sister society, the Cliolian Society, never once recorded a debate about coeducation. Instead, the women addressed other topics regarding women's rights issues, including suffrage. The Crescents eventually admitted females, and in 1873 and 1874 they again debated the question of coeducation, the judges ruling both times that men and women should be educated together.[54] (Literary societies, especially as environments for male-female interaction, are discussed in greater depth in chapter 2.)

Debates did not always conclude with peaceful consensus. Indeed, some societies' minutes showed that even among the students of the land-grants, coeducation could spark a heated and spirited discussion. Nebraska's Palladian held a debate on April 26, 1872, that resolved that the "co-education of the sexes should be encouraged." According to the *Hesperian*, "this was first vigorously discussed by the regular class, after which the house continued the debate in a very rigorous manner for sometime." Indeed, "vigorously" and "rigorous" are words that do not suggest calm acceptance, and one individual in particular expressed opposition to coeducation. The unnamed individual, "in the true sense of the word, threw 'red hot shot into the ranks of the enemy.'" After general house discussion, the society had to adjourn.[55] The student was a Nebraska colleague of two other male students who later offered a derisive comment on women's intellectual abilities. According to the *Hesperian*, the debate question of a June 23, 1873, Palladian Exhibition was "Resolved: That the mind of a woman is superior to that of a man's." This question "produced considerable amusement, the debaters Messrs. Street and Field, treating the subject in a humorous light."[56] Male students sometimes reacted with negative jeering to coeducation or the idea of women's academic prowess. Nevertheless, a majority of early land-grant students debated coeducation with positive conclusions regarding its place in American society. These debates continued into the 1880s and even the 1890s.

At OAC, the topics of coeducation and women's intellectual capacity were debated at the Adelphian Literary Society meetings at least once a semester between 1885 and 1888.[57] Although the society was organized in 1882, the Adelphian's recorded minutes do not begin until 1884. On November 27, 1885, four men assigned to the topic debated the resolution that "man is intellectually superior to woman." After the assigned debaters presented their prepared arguments, this particular debate was turned over to the house, or the whole society membership, for a general debate. The judges still ruled for men's intellectual superiority to women.[58]

Debates, essays, and discussions comparing male and female intelligence

were always common at coed land-grants, and many still believed in unques-
tioned male superiority. However, this did not negate a general acceptance
of the educational mixing of genders. Only seven weeks after determining
that men were intellectually superior to women, the Adelphians debated
"that it would be better for the sexes to be educated separately." The topic
was again debated by four men, but in this instance, the judges ruled that
separate education was not better. A general debate by the house showed
that society members agreed with the judges.[59] The following school year,
on September 23, 1887, the Adelphians offered a new twist to the same
question, "Resolved: That the education of gentlemen is of more importance than that of ladies." This time, it was debated and judged only by the
women members of the society. Not surprisingly, the judges ruled in favor
of the negative. Perhaps this topic caused a disturbance, because after some
discussion by the members, "the Pres. declared recess."[60] One month later
on November 4, 1887, the society gave the floor back to two all-male debate
teams to once again decide if "the mind of woman is inferior to that of a
man." And once again, the winning team decided for women's intellectual
inferiority.[61] On November 9, 1888, coeducation was again debated, with
a debate team of one male, J. C. Applewhite, and one female, Clara Avery,
winning for the side that upheld coeducation.[62] Having a mixed debate team
defending coeducation seemed the most appropriate method for validation
of the system itself.

These debates at IAC, Nebraska, and OAC readily showed that although
students still struggled over men's and women's intellectual capabilities, at
the same time they easily accepted the coeducation of the sexes. This was
likely for several reasons. First, students were influenced by the progressive ideals of their administrators and professors. Further, students formed
their own opinions about coeducation as they daily lived the experience
of gender-mixed education. As editorial comments and essay submissions
indicated, students showed a readiness to accept coeducation for a combination of many factors, especially for spreading the discourse of defending
coeducation. Students helped enhance that discourse through two main
media—newspapers and literary societies. Women student editors found a
special place within this culture and used their opportunities for journalistic
influence to spread the good news of coeducation.

When Willa Cather became the editor of Nebraska's *Hesperian* in 1893, she officiated over a paper that continued to publish exchanges and college items regarding the progress of coeducation in the United States. And although Cather herself, in her editorial position, made few comments regarding coeducation, she still recognized the benefits of gender mixing for the intellectual health of the academic community. In November 1893 Cather remarked on the disbanding of the Philomathian Literary Society. Its demise, she said, was because the "society this year was composed entirely of boys coming from the prep school." For its survival, she suggested: "Had the girls only taken an interest in the society it would not have disbanded."[63] By the 1890s most participants in the coeducational experiment recognized the benefits of having men and women attend school together. Students favored coeducation both for social reasons and for the ideals of women's educational progress. Their daily experiences of writing, studying, debating, and playing together, combined with a penetrating language of progressive activism regarding women's education, jointly helped to form a college culture of expression—in printed and vocal language—that sought to defend and promote the promise of mixed-gender education. Within that process of coeducational activism, land-grant newspaper staffs and literary society membership helped to create new cultural and ideological spaces of gendered inclusion for women students.

2

The Place of Women Students

Reading the Language and Practices
of Gender Separation

*It's terribly awkward to meet all those young ladies each day in going to and from
the sanctum without being able to speak.*

HESPERIAN STUDENT, November 1877

As the defense and promotion of coeducation became an integral part of
the land-grant ideology and culture in the 1870s, students and administrators began the long and laborious process of trying to sort out the actual
practice of mixed-gender education. Because the state land-grant charters
offered no guidelines for male-female interaction, the details of coeducational practice were left to the trial and error of the participants themselves.
In the beginning, a few major problems needed solutions; seldom expressed
in print, these questions represented a general anxiety about mixed-gender
interaction that pervaded the land-grant culture. To what extent should
men and women students interact? How much was too much association?
How would the scholarly expectations for male students differ from those of
female students? Did the sexes deserve separate standards of conduct and
behavior? These unspoken apprehensions fit within one larger question.
Newspaper editors sometimes expressed this overall concern in the rhetorical (and condescending) inquiry, "What shall we do with our girls?"[1] Thus,
even though coeducation in principle received acceptance, the presence of
women on western campuses still presented logistical challenges.

In response to these challenges, many land-grants responded with what
might be called a "separationist" ideology. With the perceived progress for
women that infiltrated newspaper commentary and student discussions,
women certainly found an environment suited to their educational progress.

As women would prove themselves under the microscope of mixed-gender education, that progressive language and practice would eventually expand. However, the western land-grants still feared the possible repercussions of women's daily associations with men, and they often responded with various practices of separation. Women students experienced forms of restriction to traditional gender roles, either imposed on them by other students and professors or self-imposed to maintain their feminine sphere. These modes of physical, verbal, and ideological separation often reinforced women's intellectual, conjugal, moral, and maternal roles, especially as they fit within nineteenth-century American expectations for women. Still, in spite of the practices of gender separation, many women and men students sought to push these boundaries by expanding the educational space for women.

The practices of gender separation and mixing were most profoundly illustrated within the environments of the literary and other societies at the land-grant universities. The practical implementation of coeducation sometimes came with great difficulties and conflict, but also with progressive and even revolutionary gender mixing. Very often, both the separation of women and the inclusion of women came because of the wishes and actions of female students themselves. Indeed, the attempts to keep men and women apart—by both men and women—showed some of the early fears about too much mixing between the sexes.

Even as students were able to sort out the extent of gender interaction in their own societies and organizations, women continued to experience other forms of ideological separation within a male-dominated educational sphere. Beyond the weekly associations of the literary societies, other methods were used to reinforce the traditional roles of women at these institutions. Practices such as physical separation, the use of language, and the expectations of social behavior were implemented to reinforce an ideological separation of the sexes. The modes of physical and verbal separation also fortified women's perceived conjugal, intellectual, moral, and maternal roles within the land-grant culture. Women themselves often encouraged this separation, but they also sought ways of pushing the boundaries of appropriate female behavior in order to fulfill their own expectations.

This chapter will examine the various practices of gender segregation at land-grant institutions. First, beyond the literary society activities, land-grants sought other means of physical separation between the sexes. Physical separation represented administrators' fears of the possible extent of male-female interaction and the larger concern for women as moral distractions to male students, or even worse, the fears of premarital sexual activity. Second, the ideological separation of women often emerged in the form of a differing language for men and women. This "language of expectation," as it might be called, represented the different intellectual and moral roles required of women. Women's roles as "civic housekeepers" in nineteenth-century American society also appeared in land-grant campus environments. Just as American women could promote moral virtue and physical cleanliness in families, churches, and communities nationally, so could female students act as exemplars of morality and virtue on land-grant campuses. Thus women students can be called "campus housekeepers," especially as the land-grant culture encouraged the civilizing influence of female students.

PHYSICAL SEPARATION

Most land-grant universities implemented similar forms of physical separation of the sexes, but some to stricter extent than others. Since coeducation gained acceptance throughout the West for both ideological reasons and for the frugality of tax-based education, land-grant administrators could not afford to give women a separate institution. Still, some conservative administrators balked against total gender mixing at their new universities. Their reluctance came from the same fears that kept early literary societies from being mixed: women were social and moral distractions for male students. Thus, administrators sought simpler and less expensive methods of keeping men and women apart.

The earliest form of separation of the sexes at land-grants was a physical, formal separation. Barbara Miller Solomon has examined physical separation at a few public universities. She found that places such as the University of Wisconsin and the University of Missouri actually formed "female seminaries" wherein the women students attended classes separately from men. In 1863 the University of Wisconsin admitted women to teacher training courses to accommodate the wartime shortage of male students. For a while, women could attend other courses, although "they were not allowed to sit down until all male students were seated."[2] University of Missouri women experienced similar modes of separation. Like at Wisconsin, women started in the Normal School and then found admission to a few college classes, but their acceptance was greatly restricted. By 1871 women were admitted to all classes, but they still could not use the library or attend chapel with the men. One University of Missouri administration required women to be "marched to class" with teachers as guards at the front and rear. Another made women wear uniforms in order to distinguish female students from regular townswomen.[3] These modes of bodily distinction and separation not only kept women students ideologically apart but also kept them physically protected.

Neither Nebraska nor IAC created separate female seminaries, but by 1866–67, Corvallis College, or what would become OAC, had a type of separate department for its women students. In 1869 the *Student Offering* described a "female seminary," with classes in "ballroom etiquette, music, dancing, [and] . . . fine arts."[4] This newspaper description is consistent with the course work listed as part of the requirements for female students in the late 1860s; and the female seminary is indicative of the expectations of refined behavior for the female pupils. The OAC catalogs of 1866 through 1871 listed the "Female Department" as part of its curriculum offerings. Women were "admitted into all the College Classes . . . [with] the same honors and diplomas as . . . young gentlemen." Besides a basic education that was the same for men, the women had the additional courses of "Music, Painting, Drawing, etc.," that again fulfilled expectations of refinement for young ladies.[5]

For those early coeducational land-grants that offered mixed classes, the most common form of separation was to have men and women sit on opposite sides of the classroom, lecture hall, chapel, or literary hall. Henry H. Wilson, a Nebraska student in the 1870s, editor of the *Hesperian* in 1877–78, and later a prominent lawyer in Lincoln, remembered that for morning chapel exercises, the "young men occupied one side of the chapel and the young women the other. This, indeed, was the almost universal rule at that time in all meetings; even in the churches the women occupied one side of the church and the men the other."[6] In the 1870s mixed seating was allowed only at literary society meetings, where men and women could attend and participate together. However, as with the Crescent Literary Society at IAC, some societies still made men and women sit apart during meetings.

Separate seating during chapel exercises was practiced as late as the 1890s at UAC in Logan, Utah. There, male and female students did not necessarily

1. UAC students in chapel, ca. 1900. Maxwell Cohn Collection, Album no. 2, Special Collections & Archives, Merrill Library, Utah State University.

sit on the opposite sides of the hall, but they sat in groups by gender. A photograph from the 1890s at UAC shows women sitting together at the front of the chapel. A couple of men sit near the aisle with the women's group, but the seating of women separate from the main body of men appears very much regulated. Separate seating was often voluntary, as groups of friends stayed together for a more comfortable exchange. In the earliest years of land-grant education, classes were sometimes so small that separation in the classroom may have been impractical and even seemed ridiculous. The Nebraska *Hesperian* noted with curiosity whether women were physically separated from men at other universities. In December of 1877 it reported that the "NY State University has at last consented to admit ladies, but they are required to recite by themselves."[7] The editors reported this type of separate recitation with some wonder, either as a comparison or as an anomaly from their own experiences.

A more radical form of physical separation on land-grant campuses was the prohibition of speaking between sexes during and between classes.

OAC instituted this regulation in 1875, when the board of regents added "College Law #6" to the students' regulations. It stated that "all communications between ladies and gentlemen on the College premises are expressly forbidden." The regulations gave no real specifics on the enforcement of this rule, but a range of five to twenty-five demerits was provided as punishment for "ladies and gentlemen conversing on college premises."[8] No doubt punishment depended on the extent of the infraction; for example, expressing a greeting in passing on campus likely brought a smaller punishment than an extended conversation, or worse, a physical or romantic exchange between two individuals. In 1882 OAC even passed a rule prohibiting any "loitering in the streets" between classes, further limiting opportunities for men and women to maintain casual contact.[9] The prohibition against male-female conversation lasted ten years at OAC, ending in 1885. There is no record of how strictly the college enforced this rule, but its repeal may have coincided with the Oregon legislature's final assumption of all control of Corvallis College. The Methodist regents of the former Corvallis College had fought to maintain its authority, even after the college had taken on the conditions of the Morrill Act in 1868 to become the Oregon Agricultural College. In 1885, however, a lawsuit was settled in favor of the state; as a federally supported land-grant, OAC could now set its own standards of gender interaction.

The University of Nebraska may also have prohibited conversation between the sexes. In 1877 *Hesperian* editor Wilson heard of a "sociable" planned for Nebraska students. "'Tis a good plan," he said. "Let's have one soon." And the reason he gave: "It's terribly awkward to meet all those young ladies each day in going to and from the sanctum [newspaper office] without being able to speak."[10] If his description was correct, he also could not even enter the music room with lady students "to gently remind them that the editor is at work on a heavy editorial and the noise somewhat agitates his weary brain." When given the opportunity for a mixed social, Wilson's reaction probably echoed that of many on campus: "Oh, yes, let's have a sociable. Yes, indeed."[11] There were likely and obvious exceptions to the rules against conversing, such as when the newspaper editorial staff had to work together in the office or when literary societies met; however, it appears that a general standard of decorum prohibited too much interaction between the sexes at land-grant colleges. How interesting that interaction was considered inappropriate during the school day, but appropriate—and even encouraged—in chaperoned social settings such as literary society meetings and weekend socials. Any rules prohibiting speaking between the sexes had probably relaxed by the 1890s; in 1893 one speaker at Nebraska reported visiting Cornell University with its "thirteen hundred male and two hundred female students," and noted with amazement that "by tacit agreement, they never speak upon the campus!"[12] That an eastern land-grant's strict gender separation brought shocked reactions at Nebraska would indicate a loosening of the standards of separation in the West.

At some land-grant colleges, men and women had separate entrances in the main building, or they had a common, single entrance, and then separated down different hallways. The IAC *Aurora* reported that a young man had to wait "by the ladies' stairway" for the arrival of his female interest, but complained because, "if it was not for the convexity of those stairs, I could see her."[13] This type of physical separation seemed to heighten the mystery and anxiety associated with the untouchable sex. IAC also set aside the front piazza of University Hall "for a retreat for the ladies who did not desire the company of gentlemen." For almost fifteen years, male students had to enter the building through the back door.[14]

Usually a ladies' cloakroom was also provided for women inside the building on the "ladies' side." Intrusion into this area by male students was unacceptable and sometimes publicly and teasingly noted in the student newspaper. The Nebraska *Hesperian* in October of 1875 remarked that "going up the stairway on the young ladies' side of the University . . . we noticed a cigar stump upon the hat rack. And has it comes to this, fair maidens?"[15] The last question suggests a sense of shock either for the fact that a man might have infiltrated the "ladies' side," or worse, that a female student had been smoking a cigar! University Hall (formerly Old Main) in 1888 showed that separate hallways for men and women students were still being used twenty years after Nebraska's opening.[16] At the end of the women's hall on the first floor was the "ladies' dressing room," and the basement had a "ladies closet" and a "gents closet" on their respective sides. Perhaps it was no coincidence that the "ladies' side" also had the music and art rooms, whereas the men's side had physics rooms and biology and physics laboratories. Interestingly, the newspaper office was also located on the men's side of the building. The expectation is that journalism and the hard sciences are for male students, while women's collegiate sphere is for the fine arts and high culture.[17]

Land-grant students in the 1870s also experienced separate study facilities, and possibly even the exclusion of women from studying in the library with the men. At the University of Missouri in the 1870s, students had separate library hours. In 1877 Nebraska women had difficulty finding a place to study. They previously had studied in one of the reading rooms in Old Main, but when a professor took over the room for recitations, the women were moved across the hall, "wherein, at leisure hours, they might peruse their lessons." The results were less than satisfactory: "The dear creatures would not be satisfied, and, instead of improving the shining hours as they ought, were given too much to hilarity and social racket."[18] The chancellor learned of the disruptions, and "one morning after chapel exercises the fair students were informed that hereafter they could not use the reception room for the purpose of studying. It wasn't the study he objected to, so much as the fact that he felt quite sure that they didn't study while occupying the room aforesaid. It's too bad, but it cannot be helped."[19]

The separation of men's and women's physical spaces varied from college to college and extended to living arrangements. At IAC, because the campus was built so far away from Ames, both male and female students lived on campus in a dormitory situation as early as 1870. The second floor of University Hall was set aside for women, while male students took the third and fourth floors. Before UAC had a separate dormitory for women, it also housed the students in one hall, with men and women on separate floors, "there being no communicating passage between the two."[20] With such separation imposed on them, students came up with creative ways of maintaining communication between floors. Students at IAC used an "airline" to pass messages on a rope tied between floors, with the notes sometimes tucked into "the toe of a bedroom slipper."[21] Students also banged on the pipes to get the attention of someone upstairs, arranged meetings in stairwells, and even took to leaning out of windows and yelling at each other. In April of 1883 the IAC administration had to move the senior girls to rooms below the museum, "to prevent their talking out of windows."[22] Efforts to breach the separation barriers were creative and often successful, but at no time could students enter the floors or rooms of the opposite sex.

Boarding-house living was a more common arrangement for female

students, especially before colleges could afford separate dormitory buildings. In the 1870s and 1880s, if there was only one dormitory in the main
college building, male students had first choice of these rooms, simply
because they were more numerous, and it was cheaper and easier to house
women in boarding houses close to campus. The boarding-house culture
was another significant form of gender separation during the late nineteenth
century, but men's and women's separate boarding situations often smacked
of double standards. Because universities took over the care of students who
lived away from home, administrators considered it an important duty to
be the guardians of young women's virtue. This was best achieved through
the use of boarding houses.

Young women lived in an individual room or a shared room with female
roommates in a boarding house that was conducted by a matron. The
matron was usually a married, widowed, or older single woman of excellent repute in the community, and one who had received the approval of
university administration. While young women were required to live under
these particular guidelines, men could live in an all-male boarding house,
guarded over by a similarly respectable matron, or choose to rent a room
on their own, also known as "batching it." It wasn't until the 1890s when
women students were allowed to live in a single, rented room outside of
the boarding-house environment, and even then it was discouraged. The
living standards were even outlined in academic catalogs; for example, the
1867–68 catalog for Corvallis College stipulated that "young ladies will be
required to board at the Young Ladies' Boarding House unless they have
near relatives who can receive them, and who are willing to assume the entire
responsibility of their government."[23] Male students could "board themselves or rent rooms," whereas females had to live with "good families."[24]
A similar double standard existed at the other land-grant colleges.

The practice of women students living at boarding houses with a ma-
tron-figure would continue well into the twentieth century, with few exceptions. Land-grants had started to build men's and women's dormitories
by the 1890s, especially as student enrollment and budgets increased.
Further, fraternities—as both men's and women's Greek organizations
were called—began to emerge in the 1880s. By 1900 fraternity and sorority houses skirted the boundaries of all land-grant colleges. Because men
made up two-thirds of student populations, women students were the last

to get their own dormitories. Women had different expectations regarding boarding conditions. Gertrude Fortna remembered that while some early Nebraska male students lived in rooms in the upstairs of University Hall, women lived in boarding "cottages," where they "cooked their own meals, furnished their own heat, carried their own water from the outside pump and their own fuel from the storage box."[25] At OAC in 1894, a new "Girls' Hall was completed, wherein women students could complete some of their domestic economy assignments within their chore duties while residing at the boarding house."[26]

Boarding-house behavior standards were stricter for women than for men. The most notable example of this was the women's curfew. At Nebraska, for example, women had to return to their house by no later than 11:00 p.m., while male students had a later curfew or no curfew at all. Strict punishments fell on those who arrived even a few minutes late, and the matron waited until each young lady came in safely. As men escorted their female companions home following a social or literary activity, it was often a mad dash to arrive before the 11:00 p.m. curfew. If men arrived home late, as when one student "came home the other night at six o'clock in the morning," these infractions were noted with some humorous disapproval: "When he said that he had been studying Latin with a fellow student, it was too thin to be believed."[27] In the late 1860s, OAC demanded that "young ladies boarding in the village or vicinity who are under the care of the faculty" could not receive visits from "young gentlemen," unless the women students had "the written consent of their parents."[28] These added protections for women's virtue showed that double standards of behavior for men and women certainly matched mainstream gender expectations. Girls should be good and virtuous, while boys were allowed more social freedom.

While the residential separation of men and women was accepted with little protest in the nineteenth century, some students protested the ideal of *in loco parentis*, and saw through the hypocrisy of requiring women students to live under the eye of a matron. One anonymous *Hesperian* editorial writer accused the university of creating an "infantile nursery out of Nebraska's noblest institution." Regarding the university's plans to erect a boarding hall for "young ladies" and "placing over them some ideal matron," the editor gave this frustrated reaction: "Now we are not discussing this with the hope that anything we may say will shield the girls from the scrutinizing eye of this ideal matron, but merely because of the principle involved. Undoubtedly there are many boys as well as girls here who would better be in a school governed in a different manner; but their presence should be no reason or argument for lowering the grade."[29]

This editorial was likely referring to any younger "prep" student who sought high school education prior to entering the college course and who required more direct supervision. Still, here was the question of whether young women needed babysitting more than young men. An alternative, suggested the editor, was that "parents now understand that if they need persons to represent them in the care of their sons and daughters, they must look these up and arrange with them."[30] Even though the editorialist claimed that young women do not "require the scrutinizing eye of an ideal matron," most land-grants continued to tighten the control over women students by appointing resident matrons to supervise conduct. At IAC in 1886 the *Aurora* complained because the university had added an extra proctor to live on the girls' floor, whereas two years earlier, they had only one. Further, the university would not let the girls pick their roommates; instead, each girl had a roommate appointed to her. Continued the editor, "It is no wonder she should prefer going to Mt Vernon or Grinnell, where young ladies are *not* treated as children."[31]

The majority of women students were required to live in a strictly chaperoned boarding-house or dormitory environment well into the twentieth century. The form of a campus maternal figure became institutionalized at most land-grant colleges and universities in the late 1890s, when various "deans of women" were appointed to supervise the behavior of all women living on or near campus. As late as 1910 OAC required that women should "live in the dormitory unless their parents reside in the city, or they are given special permission to live with relatives or friends who *assume the responsibility of their care*." Again, women students needed specialized "care" to ensure proper behavior and the maintenance of their virtue, whereas male students could be trusted to themselves, within reason. In almost the same breath, the OAC catalog allowed for men to live in conditions of "self-boarding" or "club-boarding" with other men.[32]

Physical separation at land-grant universities was an important tool for maintaining a distance and propriety between men and women students, especially since a majority was not yet married. Further, the separation of

2. "The Way We Are Separated," *The Sombrero* [University of Nebraska], 1895. Archives & Special Collections, University of Nebraska–Lincoln Libraries.

women helped to keep them at an untouchable, mysterious distance — especially appropriate for reinforcing women's roles as moral creatures. No matter how indirect the modes of separation between the sexes, the students themselves understood the subtleties of methods employed to keep them apart. One 1890s cartoon in the University of Nebraska *Barometer* yearbook is especially revealing for students' reactions to the symbolism of various physical methods of gender segregation. In the 1890s Nebraska's campus walks were two board planks set apart at a distance equal to that between wheel or tire ruts. The distance between planks was so wide that a woman could not link her arm with her escort's. Plank walks had not been built with the purpose of keeping the sexes apart. They were simply the result of the university's financial troubles in the early 1890s, which prevented the construction of anything more elaborate.

However, students viewed the sidewalk as a subtle attempt to limit physical contact between men and women, and the symbolism went even further. Note frame 1: "The way we are separated from the Co-eds at the University of Nebraska," which shows an exaggerated portrayal of two students on the sidewalk, stretching their arms to reach each other. Frame 2: "Suggestions for a much more considerate, and almost as effective a means of separation," with men and women separated by a fence, symbolic of the barrier between the sexes. It kept them apart but was open enough to allow limited contact. Frame 3 drew an important contrast between Nebraska and eastern universities: "The way they are separated at Yale and Harvard," with a thick, stone wall and door with a padlock. In other words, sidewalk separation at Nebraska was still better than the conditions at restrictive eastern universities. Frames 4 and 5 show the exaggerated results of sidewalk stretching. And finally: "Such incessant balancing must drive us insensibly though surely to this!!"[33] The "balancing" suggested in the cartoon, with depictions of tight-rope walkers carefully walking on their designated planks, represented an underlying tension that students felt as they experienced the subtle practices of physical separation.

In response to the inadvertent gender separation wrought by the plank sidewalks, Chancellor James Canfield offered an open-minded solution, with the effect of actually promoting "coupling" on campus. Nebraska alumnus Dr. E. H. Barbour jokingly remembered that partially because of the sidewalk separation, "the ranks of the 'solid couples' on the campus were being depleted." The chancellor ordered the plank walk torn up and "a new board walk substituted, to the avowed approval of all concerned." He then ordered the construction of benches along the new sidewalk, where couples could sit for social interaction. Known as "bench work," this "course was popular and the enrollment large," recalled Barbour. "These benches sagged to the elastic limit of oak, and finally had to be removed."[34] The "bench work" described here, and even encouraged by university administration, coincided with a general relaxation in the rules of gender interaction that had occurred by the 1890s. Even though some forms of social and physical gender separation lessened by 1900, the ideological separation of women still helped to maintain women's specified place in the land-grant culture.

SEPARATION IN WORD: THE LANGUAGE OF EXPECTATION FOR WOMEN

The most powerful tool of separation for land-grant men and women was the use of verbal and written language in stories, poems, and editorials. Word meanings reinforced the different moral, intellectual, and social expectations for men and women. This "language of expectation" was particularly important for female students, especially as the land-grant culture sorted out how women would fit into coeducational campus life. While the practice of coeducation itself was a method of acknowledging women's educational potential, female students experienced different expectations than men, including the stereotype of women as dull-witted and silly. Coeducation was a given institutional practice, but it was not a guarantee of women's intellectual equality or high scholarly expectations. This language of portraying women as unthinking simpletons pervaded some land-grant newspaper writing and humor stories. Papers printed jokes that received very little protest, since insulting women's intelligence was still accepted, even in a coeducational environment. These examples are revealing: "'Do try and talk a little common sense,' exclaimed a sarcastic young lady to a visitor. 'Oh,' was the reply, 'but would that not be taking unfair advantage of you?'"[35] Or when a woman was asked "Do you like Lamb? (meaning the famous poet) She cared little about what she ate compared with knowledge."[36] Sometimes jokes were reversed to highlight male stupidity, but these were noted with the uniqueness of female intelligence. "'Can you spell *donkey* with one letter?' asked a silly young man of a bright girl. 'Yes,' she answered. 'U!'"[37] This girl got the better of the man, but she was also distinctively and perhaps unusually "bright."

Male writers sometimes took a condescending tone toward women, as though they were pets or children to be cared for, coddled, encouraged, or even criticized, if the women did not fulfill men's expectations. Notice the language from a February 1874 *Hesperian* article that discusses the qualities of women college students. The editor reported, "Some of our exchanges are continually harping on the talent of their lady students. We don't say much, but we think an awful sight of what our girls can do."[38] That other universities were "continually harping on . . . their lady students" shows this culture of condescension, as though male students had to stand in judgment on women students' abilities. And comments went even further to assess the women students' physical appearance. "So far as looks are concerned, they can't be beat." Since these editorials were written by males, the contrast is significant for understanding the ideological segregation of women. At OAC, a poem from one woman student to the other women made the expectations regarding physical appearance very clear:

> They shall have no thoughts of the boys,
> Cast no sheep eyes to such human toys;
> Abstain from rough hair; dress unclean,
> Lest to the world uncomely you seem.[39]

Not only should the women "have no thoughts of the boys," but they should still make themselves beautiful. Intelligent college women were not exempt from the requirements of being visibly attractive. Of course, editorial space was rarely used to chastise men for their physical appearance, except for when a less-mature male student failed to grow a beard, and that was noted with teasing reproof as a student's failure at physical masculinity.

Men in general did not have to prove their intellectual abilities, nor were they expected to be good-looking in order to deserve schooling. Note another dialogue regarding the quality of women students. When the *Hesperian* learned that at Rutgers, the land-grant college of New Jersey, male students were displeased with the unattractive Rutgers women, the Nebraska editor's response was pity: "You have our sympathy, boys" — suggestive of a common condolence for the poor plight of male college students in America now forced to interact with "ugly" women. But not all women college students were ugly. Nebraska invited Rutgers men to see Nebraska's women: "If the exquisite gents of Rutgers would come to Lincoln, they would be relieved from their dilemma. Our girls are none of your second rate kind!" Upon seeing these charming and attractive ladies, Rutgers men would have no desire "to fling them ruthlessly aside."[40] These descriptions are almost reminiscent of how someone would have described an animal or a child—even the use of "our girls" shows a possessive attitude assumed by male students toward women. Female students were the newly invited guests in a coeducational environment and thus bore the brunt of scrutiny for their intellectual abilities and physical appearance. For the most part, women ably proved themselves as adequate and equal to the intellectual rigors of a university education. However, the language of expectation perpetuated certain assumptions about women's silliness and their need to be visually attractive to men.

The discussion above is not meant to show that all male college students spurned all college women simply because of supposed stupidity or physical appearance. Many male students actually gained and publicly expressed respect for women regarding intellectual ability and sensible friendships. Ironically, perhaps one of the most pro-female *Hesperian* editors was George Howard, who also printed some of the most stereotypical comments regarding women's physical appearance. Thus, even as women students earned regard for their mental qualities, they were still often perceived and portrayed as social curiosities or even mysterious playthings—visual distractions for otherwise occupied males.

Paper commentary displayed a sense of wonder at feminine habits, especially those habits that related to women's physical appearance, such as the application of makeup. In April 1872 the *Hesperian* reprinted a story regarding a professor's observations of two women students, who came to class "with their faces disfigured by the use of black adhesive plasters . . . an obsolete Parisian fashion resorted by those of unfortunate complexions to set off the rest of their face." The professor thought that the young ladies had facial disfigurements, but learned that the makeup was "only intended to ornament and beautify."[41] And on another occasion, "several came into chapel a few mornings ago, with their faces and hair covered with flour—some of the malicious boys said it was powder, but we don't believe it."[42] Unique feminine habits were new to young male students, and only added to the mystery surrounding women.

Printed quotes sometimes remarked on the mysterious or confusing nature of women: "'The proper study of mankind is man.' The most perplexing, no doubt, is woman. — Saxe."[43] That sense of the unknown was perpetuated by the modes of physical separation that kept women at a greater distance from male students. Even with some of the mystery that shrouded women, or perhaps because of it, men actively sought the company of women. Besides some approved social activities (supervised literary society meetings and weekend socials), women students' presence served as an incentive for male attendance at undesirable events such as chapel services. Said the *Hesperian*, "It does our soul good to see so many young ladies in attendance this term. The boys say it is some inducement to get to Chapel now."[44] Women fulfilled male students' need for visual stimulation, and editors often commented on their reactions to the closeness of women in the campus environment. The very presence and appearance of women was a strong draw for men, but they still had to keep their distance from each other.

Even though various methods of physical separation sought to keep men and women apart, the inducement of eventual marital possibilities kept students integrated. Perhaps the most important expectation for women was as potential wives for male students and single male professors. Co-education was a given now, and officials encouraged supervised gender mixing as natural and expected. Students and administrators alike thought about marriage, and gender interaction was very much an important part of the coeducational experience. And yet, within that social expectation, the women's separate role was very clearly defined. Feminine stereotypes led to some harmful portrayals of women, but those same stereotypes helped to maintain women's separate spheres. Women as silly and superficial or women as beautiful ornaments to bring visual pleasure to men — these images helped to keep women at a distance from male students. Further, the language of expectation that kept women separated from men also required women to fulfill certain professional and domestic roles.

"DAUGHTERS OF EMULATION": WOMEN'S PROFESSIONAL EXPECTATIONS

Women experienced a very different language of expectation regarding their educational and professional pursuits, including their postcollegiate professional intentions. Men were to be the professionals, and women students were the wives- and mothers-in-training. An early editorial in the OAC *Student Offering* showed examples of the different language used for men and women. In a kind of humorous essay, the writer, "Ezra the Scribe," chronicled the activities of the "Sons of Aspiration" and the "Daughters of Emulation,"[45] suggestive of the expectations for male students to aspire, endeavor, obtain, and strive for some great professional success in life, and of the expectations for female students to emulate, follow, imitate, or model appropriate behavior. The distinction is significant in showing the different word usage, titles, addresses, and language applied to women students at land-grant universities, especially regarding their expected roles in life.

Part of the practice of different language included the use of exclusive nouns and pronouns for male-only expectations. For instance, in the first issue of the *Hesperian*, the editor announced that "all young men on entering a collegiate course . . . should have some idea of the course they shall pursue later in life."[46] In a poem heralding the creation of OAC, one stanza portrays how intellectual motivation was sometimes directed exclusively toward male students:

> Thus, believing this to be the place
> For young men to receive their knowledge:
> They immediately passed an act,
> That all the counties be represented in this college.[47]

It is interesting that male students were singled out as the primary beneficiaries of the land-grant purpose at OAC.

Not all editorials and essays were addressed to men only. On the contrary, nineteenth-century journalism portrayed a surprising use of gender-inclusive language. In a century that predated any modern movement for political correctness, writers often employed the use of "men and women," "his and hers," "he and she," and so forth. Phrases like "each student should feel that upon his or her individual exertions rests the success and prosperity of the society,"[48] or "the ladies and gentlemen who have not yet subscribed should do so at the earliest opportunity."[49] As women earned their professional and intellectual laurels, some progressive authors departed from the use of gender-neutral language. This new language gave validity to women by offering them inclusion, but it also maintained a strict gender separation.

Nineteenth-century writers attempted to depart from language that gave a male-only assumption of identity. For example, the word *author* evoked a male identity in the minds of most readers. The same was true for other identifying nouns. Some writers—both male and female—sought to avoid this gender ambiguity by adding the ending "-ess" in the occasion that a typically gender-neutral word was used for a woman. In land-grant writings, for example, a female author was an "authoress"; a female victor was a "victress," and so on. Because so many words were implicitly male, women sought to make their intellectual and professional presence known by adding suffixes that distinguished their gender.[50] Land-grant students were very much aware of this language tool, and they even commented on it. At times, the method was overused to the point of absurdity, and public reaction paralleled similar modern reactions to the overuse of "political correctness." Note one student's tongue-in-cheek story regarding the abundant use of "-ess," or the "silly custom of adolescent writers and speakers":

"We think the authoress will become celebrated as a poetess," remarked the young lady pertly, with a marked emphasis on two words of the sentence.

"Oh!—ah!" replied the old gentleman, looking thoughtfully over his spectacles at the young lady. "I hear her sister was quite an actress, and under Miss Hosmer's instructions will undoubtedly become quite a sculptoress."

The young lady appeared irritated.

"The seminary," continued the old gentleman, with imperturbable gravity, "is fortunate in having an efficient board of manageresses. From the presidentess down to the humblest teacheress unusual talent is shown. There is Miss Harper, who as a chemistress is unequaled, and Miss Knowles has already a reputation as an astronomeress. And in the department of music few can equal Miss Kellogg as a singeress."

The young lady did not appear to like the chair she was sitting on. She took the sofa at the other end of the room.

"Yes," continued the old gentleman, as if talking to himself, "those White sisters are very talented. Mary, I understand, has turned her attention to painting and the drama, and will surely become famous as a painteress, and even as a lecturess."

A loud slamming of the door caused the old gentleman to look up, and the criticess and grammarianess was gone.[51]

Most of the "-ess" words failed to catch on in popular or even intellectual language, but a few have remained acceptable in modern language, such as "actress," "poetess," and "authoress." In some cases, women actually took on male titles; in the 1870s, it became common for women to write the title "Esq.," for "Esquire," following their signatures. The *Hesperian* commented on this new trend; perhaps college-educated women embraced "Esq." as a title that recognized their emerging professional role in society because, according to one author, "Mrs. is about the only high sounding title to which women are accustomed." The writer explained that "according to Webster, it [Esq.] can designate almost any profession. . . . You will find that it may be applied to all persons, which means women as well as men. This being the case, women may look forward to the time when the startling Esq. may be added to their names as well as to those of men."[52] And perhaps in another fulfillment of women's maternal and moral roles in society, the author announced that in some British circles, an unmarried woman of advanced age could be called "Mrs." Was this appealing to women students? The author suggested, "Girls, is it not encouraging to know, that when we reach an advanced age, we can go to England, and get Mrs. prefixed to our names?" It is uncertain whether the author's tone was sarcastic, but the comment suggested that most women sought "Mrs." as the highest distinction they could achieve. The "Esq." trend never caught on for women in popular culture, but the *Hesperian* author very sensibly concluded that "when you come down to the real merits of the question, it is the man or woman behind the name, and not the name itself."[53]

Land-grant student writers showed an amazing amount of gender sensitivity and inclusion in their writings, and yet, the language of expectation for women still differed in very subtle ways from the language used for male students. Any editorials regarding the pursuit of graduate studies at eastern or European universities were exclusively directed at male students. One 1889 report asked only the "boys" of the class of 1889 about their "ambitions" after graduation, because, said one commentator, "co-eds of '89 were not presumed to warrant such things."[54] It was not that women never got asked about their goals and intentions, but the differences—both in the questioning and in the answering—were significant. When the question of postgraduation pursuits was put to women students, most of the responses were predictable. Whereas men intended to be doctors, lawyers, and landowning farmers, women sought to "put their domestic economy into practice," by *marrying* the doctors, lawyers, and farmers.[55] Women as domestic economists became an understood expectation for women land-grant students throughout the nineteenth century and well into the twentieth century. By 1900 it gradually became more common for women's career intentions to receive notice in newspapers and college yearbooks, especially as women chose to pursue graduate studies in areas such as biology, pharmacology, music, and domestic economy.

One female editor, Emma Williams, who served on Nebraska's *Hesperian* staff with George Howard in 1875, wrote an essay titled "Professional Education," which showed the differences between men's and women's educational goals. Williams wrote of the necessity for students to pick a career path and stick to it without distraction, and she addressed her essay to "men (and women too when the time comes) who choose their professions in early life and adhere to it undeviatingly until they reach deserved prominence in its ranks."[56] That she parenthetically included "and women too when the time comes" in this essay is important for two reasons. First, Williams saw the need for women to be involved in a discussion of professional education and career goals—but only when it became more acceptable for women to discuss career goals; and second, women—especially college students—had not yet achieved that recognition of needing "professional education." The differences emerged elsewhere. In one 1875 essay, "The Dreams of Our Youth," the author described a "young man of aspiration" as one who, "when he arrives at this or that station, or obtains this or that degree of power, his actions shall be governed by principles of integrity. He will be generous, manly and humane. If he enters the profession of the law or politics, he will avoid its vices and perils, and try to raise his chosen profession to a higher level. He mentally says, 'I will win in the battle I have planned, but I will be victor at [no] sacrifice of . . . my honor.'"[57]

The expectations for male students are very clear regarding their entrance into law or politics, the need to be manly and to have integrity in the business or political world. Further, the evocation of military language suggests a masculine need to conquer all obstacles in reaching one's highest potential.

Notice the language difference used in the same essay for a "woman of aspiration":

The girl also resolves that she will exert the power she gains for good. She has a great mission to perform. She resolves that while she champions the restricted rights and privileges of her sex, that while she demands justice and equality from the watch-towers of the nation, she herself will realize a noble womanhood. She resolves that while she leads woman to a higher conception of her mission and possibilities in life, she will become victress at the sacrifice of no jot of her womanly grace and gentleness. How necessary that these resolutions be realized in order to attain success.[58]

Again, military language like "champions" and "victress" are implemented, but for the very different purpose of defending womanhood, grace, and gentleness. Such nobility applied to women's purposes even prompted the male author to concede amazingly that "we could almost wish that we had been born a woman." In the final analysis, both men and women should strive to achieve greatness, but for different reasons. A final paragraph was addressed to both sexes: "[F]oster the dream of your early manhood or womanhood. . . . Let your aim be noble and daring. Place your ideal self high up on the eternal mountain. . . . Seek virtue, seek power!"[59] The land-grant culture expected greatness from both its male and female students, but the difference for women was very clearly defined. The discourse regarding women's contributions to society penetrated strongly throughout the written and verbal rhetoric of land-grant culture. In addition to the defined professional and domestic expectations, women students also experienced a promotion of their elevated roles as the preservers of virtue and morality.

"CAMPUS HOUSEKEEPERS":
WOMEN'S CIVILIZING AND DOMESTIC ROLES

Women's elevated moral and behavioral roles fit within a cultural expectation that might be called "campus housekeeping." As in American society, women students were perceived as examples of morality and virtue on campus. Perhaps the *Hesperian* summarized best how society viewed feminine morality: "[Woman] has shown herself the first and foremost of [Christ's] followers."[60] Coeducation was even defended because the presence of women students could potentially temper the behavior of young men. In the May 1879 *Aurora* at IAC, an anonymous author described the main advantage of coeducation: "The presence of girls puts a restraint upon the young men." At most coeducational colleges, "hazing, rushes and boisterous conduct are not so prevalent as in schools for young men alone."[61]

The moral and feminine expectations for women at the land-grants resounded strongly throughout the college culture. The above author aptly expressed the importance of feminine morality: "When a woman becomes unwomanly, all her influence ends." Author "X" gave an example that was easily applied to student interaction on campuses: "If at any social gathering we find the company loud and rough, we will see, on looking round, that the women present are themselves destitute of the attractive graces of good breeding. But place those same men in the company of refined and cultivated women, and we will soon see how their loud voices will moderate and their rough manners soften."[62] In other words, women's most important role, to this writer, was not "legal affairs," but the "more glorious part of softening the asperities and quickening the graces of social intercourse."[63]

Newspaper writings rang with discourse directed at female students as "angels," "civilizers," and "refiners." When editors described the orations or speeches delivered by women, they used descriptions like "graceful," "elegant," "beautiful," and "fair"; whereas the adjectives used to portray male students' speeches included "strong," "manly," "commanding," and "forceful." Flattering terms applied to women actually enforced separate gender expectations. Neutral words applied to either gender included "ability," "excellence," "zeal," and "diligence." A *Hesperian* report of an 1874 high school commencement serves as an excellent example of gendered separation through speech. The productions of the ladies were "surprisingly excellent in thought, and couched in splendidly beautiful language. Every sentence seemed to sparkle with word gems and sentences of pearls." Here, the evocation of jewel imagery suggested women's decorative and refining role, even through speech. In contrast, "the young man — He showed the elements of manly thoughts, in grappling with the knotty, practical problems of the day."[64] The contrast between women's decorative qualities as gems and men's roles in the hard realities of life again emphasizes the era's strong gender expectations for its young students.

This sense of elevated and even divine expectations for women could be a detriment to female students, especially if they participated in any unrefined behavior. Sometimes, papers had to chastise the students for misbehavior on campus, and these reprimands were directed at males and females equally, such as in the sarcasm of an October 1871 *Hesperian*: "Reverent—the giggling of certain young ladies and gentlemen during chapel exercises." And, "the conduct of some of our young ladies and gentlemen during chapel exercises is becoming shameful. We are afraid it will call forth a stern rebuke."[65] This was a common scolding; in May 1874 the *Hesperian* complained again: "Regarding [the] article on 'College Buffoonery' found at other universities: We have an abundant supply of that sort of thing in our University. The young man (or woman either) who is continually trying to make others laugh by silly ogling and grimaces during service in chapel and in class, is the most contemptible object we know of. We laugh, but pity the clown who amuses us."[66]

Small infractions such as giggling and disrespectful talking were common to both men and women, and together they were called to their moral duty. Other infractions seemed particularly offensive if women broke protocol, and they were sometimes singled out for the unladylike behavior. Women's roles as campus housekeepers invited a more elevated expectation of behavior and moral example for the male students. Women were simply held to a higher standard of comportment on land-grant campuses. A few telling examples of this language of expectation adequately portray the moral separation of women students. Regarding swearing, the *Hesperian* strongly rebuked that "it is bad enough for the boys to swear and use slang phrases, but when the young ladies get into this habit it is perfectly awful."[67] And on 1870s graffiti: "Girls, don't do that! It's naughty. Those delicate little, white fingers were never made to wickedly grasp a lead pencil and mark the walls of the university. Please don't. It gives the janitor great trouble to obliterate your eccentric ideas which you write on the walls. If you must correspond with the janitor, do it bravely and in the old fashioned way."[68]

Perhaps the very worst public reprimand for a female student came in April 1877: "As we came down the street, the other day, we saw a young lady student step into a saloon. If it had been temperance, we would have remained silent. O, what will the coming generation be?"[69] A woman smoking or going into a saloon for any reason other than temperance activism

3. "Coeds Smoking at University of Nebraska," *Barometer* [University of Nebraska]. Archives & Special Collections, University of Nebraska–Lincoln Libraries.

was particularly egregious, whereas the same infractions by men received very little rebuke.

Women knew and accepted their higher position of virtue, and they took their roles as campus housekeepers very seriously, in both morality and physical cleanliness. Any possibilities to improve the civility and behavior of young men were assumed with great fervor, as when the Nebraska women kept a "'Black List' . . . for male students caught playing billiards."[70] Women tried to encourage male students to shun liquor, tobacco, and gambling; further, it was much due to women's influence that hazing activities like the infamous "cane rush"—where male students literally beat each other with canes to determine class superiority and domination—were finally ended at Nebraska in the 1890s. In some cases, the moral standard for women began to erode somewhat by the end of the century, especially as women students experimented with forbidden vices, such as smoking. Even then, the double standard was very much in place. Where cigar smoking among men was accepted and even promoted as manly behavior, women smoking cigarettes evoked disapproval and scorn. An early 1900s student editorial cartoon from Nebraska's *Barometer* showed two elegant coeds smoking in their dormitory room, with a caption that read: "It is Claimed that Cigarette Smoking Among College Girls is not Uncommon. Is it True?"

Sometimes women as campus housekeepers took on a very literal significance. Women students provided elegant decorations such as furniture coverings, flowers, and paintings for literary societies, clubs, and other student organizations. They also led the way when campuses needed beautifying. In 1874 Nebraska Chancellor Allen Benton lectured the students on neatness, and one sophomore girl "got very enthusiastic over the matter. . . . She noticed sundry marks of oleaginous digits (oily fingerprints) upon the door panel [of Adelphian Hall]. In supreme disgust, she rushed for the student office, seized a basin of water and some soap, tucked her delicate sleeves and in desperate energy applied the soap and water with her lily fingers to the obnoxious panel. You may depend upon it that door was cleaned."[71]

This cleaning spree impressed one sophomore boy almost to the point of infatuation with the girl; indeed, a woman who rushed to perform domestic duties exuded the most desirable and attractive femininity. In the 1890s Nebraska established "Dandelion Day," where students spent a Saturday

4. "Dandelion Day at the University of Nebraska," ca. 1910. Archives & Special Collections, University of Nebraska–Lincoln Libraries.

morning ridding the campus of thousands of the little yellow flowers. A photograph taken in front of University Hall shows that mostly women students participated in this day of campus weed cleanup.

Women as campus housekeepers, of course, fit very naturally within the culture of domestic economy course work practiced at most land-grant colleges and universities. As students took classes in cooking, cleaning, decoration, and horticulture, they sought to apply their training toward a more visually beautiful campus environment. At OAC, women planted flowers on campus, and other land-grant women often had to prepare formal dinners for students, professors, and administrators, complete with attractive table settings; in August of 1878 the Iowa women prepared a dinner for the entire IAC Board of Trustees, which was reported to be "gracefully spread."[72] Both men and women recognized that the principles of domestic economy taught to women students helped in "beautifying homes" and campuses, and "securing the comfort and happiness of their inmates."[73]

Women students sewed curtains and draperies for classrooms and literary societies. All students participated in campus beautification, but they maintained very separate roles in that process. For example, the Bachelor Society at IAC wanted the women Cliolians to sew carpets for "Bachelor Hall." Both could help each other, by doing their prescribed roles: "The Bachelors say, 'We will be friendly to those Clios and they will sew our carpets for us.' The Clios think, 'We will make ourselves agreeable to those Bachelors, and they will nail down our carpets for us.' Verily, a mutual exchange of accommodations is very pleasant, and often convenient."[74] The separation here is obvious: men do not sew and women do not hammer.

Women's elevated moral expectation also related directly to their separate standard of work behavior at land-grant universities. Writers sometimes applied the visual image of "white hands" or "lily fingers" to evoke this separate expectation. Women's "white hands" elicited a sense of moral purity, and they could also do more delicate and refined work. One writer described the important symbolism associated with the physical appearance of hands and the different expectations for men and women:

> *White Hands*: But why should a man desire to have white hands? Why should whiteness and delicacy in the hands be esteemed preferable to the brown, the tan, and the strength which come from exposure and use? We do not see how a very delicate and very white hand can be consistent with the masculine occupations which become a man. Whiteness of the hands may be very becoming to a woman: we think it is. Her life is comparatively indoors. The same thing in a man is indicative of idleness, and the avoidance of exposure.[75]

Interesting, that at a land-grant college, where women supposedly trained to become farm wives, the expectations of indoor Victorian refinement were still securely in place. Women students were not expected to be dirt farmers; indeed, these were middle-class wives, for whom cleanliness and moral preservation were even more important than cooking and keeping a garden. Many of these "farm wives" might eventually do something else expected of women in their class: they would hire a girl or two to help with kitchen, garden, or child-care duties.

The separate "indoor" sphere for most women was not simply an eventuality of marriage and domesticity; it was also part of women's land-grant lifestyle. Women were even discouraged from taking outside jobs during the school year to pay for college expenses, whereas most male students were expected to do so. Former student R. E. Dale recalled that "although most of the men had part-time jobs while they were going to school, the girls did not work. A girl who dared accept a position would be ostracized because it simply was not done. Of course, some girls did take positions as secretaries. If it was found that a girl had a job, she was 'looked down upon.'"[76]

Work standards for students varied from campus to campus. At IAC, men and women students participated in a campus labor system that had been implemented by Pres. Adonijah S. Welch in the early 1870s. Male students helped with heavier outdoor work, such as lifting, hauling, construction, mechanical work, and agricultural labor, whereas women participated in housekeeping, laundry duties, indoor cleaning, light gardening, cooking, and decorating. If President and Mrs. Welch hosted an important campus visitor, Mrs. Welch often called on the young women students to help prepare and present a formal dinner. Students received a small allowance for their work, but the work system was also part of campus upkeep.

Most women received some kind of allowance or stipend from home for their school-year living expenses. According to Edna Bullock, "One woman in the class of '88 had $150 a year and such provisions as she could bring from the home farm. She was thoroughly comfortable and not at any disadvantage whatever because of financial limitations."[77] By the 1890s a few women students worked as library or music assistants, like Nellie Jane Compton, who began work in the University of Nebraska library in 1897; her assistantship led to a full-time position that lasted forty years. Willa Cather worked as a part-time drama critic for local Lincoln papers between 1893 and 1895. "At a dollar a column, [she] made enough money to pay for her rented room and board and her university expenses."[78] Cather was an example of professional motivation that was not typically associated with her gender. Working while attending college was considered taxing on the female physique, and Cather herself suffered because of time constraints and exhaustion. An observer found Cather in the paper offices "standing fast asleep," and she admittedly sacrificed her studies in order to work.[79] One male student remembered delivering the paper to Cather's room and many times finding her still studying at five o'clock in the morning.[80]

The most important source of wages for female students was teaching, which was usually accomplished by taking off a semester or two from one's college courses, or by teaching in the late spring or early summer months. IAC even held classes between March and November, instead of the usual September to May, so that students could use the winter months for teaching. Of the fifteen male and female members of the IAC class of 1873, all but two had taught classes during some part of their schooling.[81] Teaching was an appropriate form of wage-earning for both male and female students. Women students especially sought teaching positions, since the expectations for women as campus or civic housekeepers overflowed naturally into their roles as educators of American schoolchildren. While land-grant education certainly gave women inroads to new professions, most female students sought the professional and domestic roles that fit acceptably within the expectations for American women.

CONCLUSION

In this new, coeducational land-grant environment, the scholastic culture came to expect greatness from all of its students—both male and female. All should succeed, all should work hard, and all should add to the civility and virtue of society. Within those societal expectations, women were required to play very separate roles. On western campuses, daily physical and ideological practices of separation reminded women of their distinct position as "other." Administrators, fearing the moral repercussions of male-female interaction, kept women separate from male students through various practices of physical distancing. Even with the forms of physical separation meant to prevent too much distraction to male students, the stereotype of women as captivating social curiosities was perpetuated. Ironically, newspaper editors drew attention to women for exactly what administrators had tried to downplay: women's distracting presence. Students, especially male students, reinforced this role by teasing, cajoling, and flattering women in print regarding their charms and physical appearance.

The most powerful form of gender separation for women was through the use of language. The language of expectation on the one hand taught women that they were the silly, unintelligent gender; on the other hand, they were the preservers of morality and virtue, and thus were held to a more elevated behavior requirement. Women certainly fulfilled those expectations as campus housekeepers through the promotion of their moral and physical cleanliness. Other practices of gender separation sought to keep women within the boundaries of their proscribed sphere. For instance, the social expectations of romancing and courting required that most women prepare for marriage as part of their land-grant experience. This was also reinforced through domestic science programs, which were pioneered at land-grant universities. In most cases, nineteenth-century young women accepted the ideological separation to which they were born, as well as the responsibilities that came with that birthright—morality, domesticity, and virtue. It was a noble pedestal, and a majority of women students enjoyed being there. And yet, many of these same women, in the midst of physical and ideological separation, sought ways to challenge the forms of ideological and physical separation placed on them, and to negotiate their own new standards of intellectual, physical, and social expectations.

3

The Early Practice of Coeducation

Literary Societies as Laboratories for Separation and Inclusion

After long and ardent pleading pro and con, [the Crescent Society] finally concluded to throw open its doors to receive the fair maids of the agricultural college who came "tapping, gently tapping" for admission.

"MEETING MINUTES, 1871–1877," Crescent Literary Society, April 2, 1873

Literary societies for male and female students emerged in the 1870s and 1880s as significant experimental laboratories for the implementation of coeducation, especially as land-grants in the 1870s struggled to define the extent of gender mixing. Coed literary societies offered what few universities possessed—an opportunity for men and women students to debate, discuss, and share their intellectual endeavors in a mixed-gender environment. As women gained admission to literary societies, either through the natural workings of coeducational progress or through their own struggle for equality of access, they helped to expand the boundaries of the social and intellectual female sphere on land-grant campuses. This broadened domain of women's intellectual activity subsequently translated into an expanded political sphere, especially as women found public space to voice their opinions through essays, recitations, and debates.

Women students were certainly not passive subjects in the process of inclusion or exclusion in campus literary societies. The process of defining literary society participation showed some of the early difficulties and triumphs in working through the forces of gender separation and inclusion. The literaries, as they were called, offered an important trial environment for women students, not only because they provided social interaction but also because they promoted students' intellectual development. To what extent women did or did not participate in these activities is important to the study of land-grant gendered relations. Sometimes women were excluded from all-male societies, but in other instances, women encountered acceptance and inclusion. They even actively settled their own membership in mixed societies, in spite of initial discrimination by male members. Even more surprising was that some women shunned mixed-gender societies in favor of female-only clubs, even when they had the option of joining the men. Thus, through literary society membership, land-grant women actively negotiated the extent of their own gendered separation and inclusion. Because of the complexity of this gender-mixing, the literary societies are a microcosm for the larger understanding of gender interaction and separation on campuses.

Once women had established their presence in literary societies—both mixed and all-female—debate proceedings in these societies became important avenues for women to develop intellectually, socially, and politically. Yet within that advancement lay subtle forces for gender segregation, through the use of language, ideology, and physical separation. Women's entrance into debate proceedings was at times gradual and reluctant, especially considering the domination of male students in this activity. And still, women debated. Debates gave women students the advantage of finding their own political voice within a mixed-gender environment, thus eventually leading them into other areas of public debate and political activism.

LITERARY SOCIETIES

Literary societies were an important part of campus intellectual life in the nineteenth century. Most college students after the Civil War considered participation in a literary society a necessity for both academic and social success. So significant was literary activity to students that almost every land-grant university claimed at least one formal, organized society within one month after the school's opening. Societies were formed according to constitutional rules, as found in various published guidebooks on organizational procedures, such as *Robert's Rules of Order* and *Smith's Diagram of Parliamentary Rules*. Founding students chartered a society, then opened it for prospective members who had to show a willingness to attend weekly meetings, participate fully in the literary activities, and be prompt and orderly. Dues were as much as two dollars per year, but expenses could be paid from members' fines for tardiness, absence, disorderly behavior, and nonperformance of duty. Each society had elected officers, including a president, vice president, secretary, and treasurer.

Literary societies met once a week, in rooms of the main university building, usually called Old Main, Administration Building, or University Hall. Societies often met on Friday or Saturday nights where students found their foremost social, political, and academic interaction. The presiding officer brought each week's meeting to order, with dues called in by the treasurer and minutes recorded by the secretary. After the business portion ended, the literary activities began, which included memorized recitations, poetry and literary readings, essays, and speeches written by the students on numerous topics. Students often wrote on political or social issues of the day, biographies of literary or historical figures, and religious tracts. Programs also included musical performances, especially piano or violin solos, vocal solos, and ensembles. Finally, but not least in importance, many literary meetings ended with a debate contest between teams of debaters (two or three), or individual debaters who had prepared arguments on a current social or political issue. Three or four judges selected from among present society members assessed the quality of the arguments and then ruled for the best team or individual debater. In cases of especially controversial topics, the president would open the debate of the society for an "open" discussion that invited audience participation. These often ended in heated debates, wherein the president might call a recess or adjourn the meeting altogether. In some cases, professors attended to mediate debates.

Student social and intellectual life centered around the literary societies, which predated the Greek fraternities and sororities that appeared at the land-grants in the 1890s. If there were more than one society, rivalries and competitions sometimes developed, but usually societies maintained friendly relationships. Literary events were a main topic of student newspaper comment, and editors often printed the written version of the previous meeting's presentations. Students felt that literaries were vital to their intellectual development at the university. According to the IAC Crescent Society, the literary societies' purpose was for "the advancement of its members in literature, science and general knowledge."[1] And one writer in the University of Nebraska's *Hesperian Student* gave an excellent description of a society's scope and purpose: "The Literary Society is a place adopted to the cultivation of our practical powers. In the university we assemble to acquire knowledge, in the society to learn the mode of diffusing it. In the one place, we collect thoughts and ideas, in the other, we learn to express them to others."[2]

Thus, the literary society existed for developing one's talents of verbally expressing the knowledge acquired through university work. It was in a student's best interest to join a society, especially if he or she had plans to go into law, politics, or teaching; for "whatever our plan of life may be we will do wisely to improve the opportunity of uniting ourselves with our literary society."[3]

Weekly literary meetings became the most important playing field for male-female interaction in the 1870s and 1880s. Further, societies practiced a maybe-we-will, maybe-we-won't approach to gender segregation, as they ironed out the extent of female participation. This process is absolutely vital for understanding the practices of gender separation in the land-grant environment. Female students were not passive victims to be acted on in the process of defining their literary club participation. Indeed, women were often the ones who enacted change, both in favor of gender segregation and in opposition to it.

THE CRUCIAL FOUNDING YEARS —
IOWA AGRICULTURAL COLLEGE

In the beginning, male students often favored all-male societies for various reasons. Many young men were simply not yet ready for an intimate intellectual exchange and political bantering with women, especially in the close quarters of a literary society room. Although it was considered appropriate for women to participate in refined oratory such as recitations, poetry readings, and musical performances, the more masculine pursuits of heated political debating, together with their accompanying images of dark, smoke-filled rooms and free-flowing brandy, were definitely outside of the feminine sphere. Perhaps the simplest reason for all-male societies was that women—even educated women—were seen as distractions for studious males. Early male students showed reluctance to female colleagues. According to one male member of the coed Philomathean Society at IAC, Dr. O. H. Cessna, "When I left home to enter college, my father warned me that here at Ames I would meet some nice girl and I would fall heels over head in love with her, and my school work would be a failure. The original literary society, the Philomethean, was composed of both men and women. I soon began to realize that my father's warning might be a reality if I continued to attend such an organization. Some other men also seemed to have similar conclusions concerning themselves."[4]

Soon after this, some male members withdrew from the Philometheans and formed two new societies, the Bachelor Society, in May, and the Crescent Society, on September 17, 1870. For the Crescents, this gender separation did not last long. "Later, it seems that the members of this new society were forced to realize the truth:—that they could not have an organization full of life and interest without the ladies. And so, for many years past, and at the present time [1920], also, the girls have been doing their very best to make and keep the Crescent Society abreast or ahead of any other."[5] This opinion seems on its face very progressive, but it obscures a much more interesting and complex narrative about women's literary participation at IAC.

The Philomethean Society had started as a mixed society sometime in 1869 or 1870, but following the formation of the all-male Bachelor and Crescent Societies in 1870, IAC soon found itself with its first all-female society. Early in the spring of 1871, a group of five women—Sallie Stalker, Hattie Raybourne, Kate Krater, Sarah Hardy, and Rowena Edson—met to form the all-female Cliolian Literary Society.[6] In the 1870s these societies' struggle between separation and inclusion made for an interesting tale of gender interaction. The Cliolian Society stands as a special challenge to the notion of strict gender separation at land-grants, simply because these women chose to separate themselves, even though they had the option of participating in the mixed Philomethean. The Cliolians remained steadfastly and doggedly all-female from 1871 until well into the twentieth century.

The Cliolian Society aptly demonstrated that even in coeducational situations, women students often maintained willing self-separation from males. It might be tempting to look at the Clios through the lens of forced marginalization of women by male students, but this was not the case. In an ironic twist of the dynamic of gender separation, four male students applied for admission to the Cliolians on May 25, 1872. The secretary reported that "four gents asked to be admitted to Society." The society discussed the matter, and "voted not to admit visitors." The same four men, perhaps in an attempt to sway the vote of the women, brought dinner to the society, which the women ate and then "returned a vote of thanks for the same."[7] The Clios reaffirmed their separation in April of 1873 and passed an amendment "that the Cliolian be an exclusive Ladies Society."[8] Nevertheless, by September of that year, a few more "gentlemen" returned and again "asked for admittance." The women postponed their activities for a few minutes to discuss and vote on the possibility "that the rules be suspended and the gentlemen admitted." Without much apparent discussion, however, the "Motion lost, [and the] Society proceeded with its debate."[9] The Cliolian minutes show no further mention of male students attempting to gain membership.

At the same time that the Cliolians were striving to maintain their feminine exclusivity, the all-male Crescent Society struggled over the admittance of women members. Between 1870 and 1873, the Crescents remained all-male, but periodically held joint sessions with the other societies, "to see what was to be seen and hear what was to be heard."[10] Literary societies — mixed, male, and female — often held joint meetings to encourage greater socialization among the members. Women and men then together participated in oratory and debates, but these were held only periodically.

The Crescents had some exchange with their sister Clios in the early 1870s, at least on an organized level. They even held joint debating sessions to discuss women's rights issues such as coeducation and suffrage. Before 1873 some women visited the Crescent meetings, and a few sought admission to the society. Finally, on April 2, 1873, the Crescents considered a resolution for the admission of women. "After long and ardent pleading pro and con," the society "finally concluded to throw open its doors to receive the fair maids of the agricultural college who came 'tapping, gently tapping' for admission."[11]

The decision might have caused some disturbance, because the vote was not unanimous. Of twelve votes recorded, three members voted to keep women out of the society, but a compromise was reached: the members carried a motion "that ladies and gentlemen should *not* be permitted to sit together during sessions of the organization."[12] Thus, even though the ladies brought "life and interest" to the society, separate seating arrangements filled a need for physical separation so often mandated in early land-grant campus interaction. Three days later, "Misses Nelson, Blodget, Aitken and Fish," were "duly elected members of the Society."[13] The Crescent Society had

coed membership for the rest of the century, and one member later noted
its successes as a mixed society: "I have yet to see a Crescent member shirk
or grumble about his or her work. All the time, the society has acted as one
person. Had it not, it could never have accomplished so much."[14]

THE UNIVERSITY OF NEBRASKA

The early literary societies at the University of Nebraska had similar interactions as those at Iowa State. Like IAC, Nebraska already had a mixed society,
the Palladian, in September of 1871. Some students remembered the events
preceding the women's admittance. "Who? . . . was the subject of some
discussion and the voices of the chivalrous against the unchivalrous waxed
strong and eloquent, as they demanded equal rights and equal privileges
[sic] for both sexes."[15] This argument that occurred among the male society
members turned quickly pointless, because a few women who attended that
day solved the question by asserting their rights to participate. In the middle
of the Palladians' fight about whether to admit women, a "few brave ladies
that stepped forward and gave their names to the secretary, silenced the
guns of the enemy and the society at once became 'mixed.'"[16] One might
imagine this a dramatic historical moment. Picture the hall that day, with a
few male students arguing at the front of the room, and the secretary seated
at a table. Perhaps the women were seated in chairs or standing at the back
of the hall, with professors and other students observing the debate. One
by one, the women students calmly walked to the front of the room and
took turns saying their names to the secretary, as the room quieted and
men ceased their discussion. Who could argue with the firm assertiveness
of these few women? The *Hesperian* pronounced women's participation
in the Palladian an "admirable success," but that statement obscured what
would turn into a more complicated history for women in the Nebraska
literary societies.

One month after the Palladian's founding, the *Hesperian* editors complained about the scarcity of women at the meetings, even though the society's first vice president in 1871 was a woman, Grace Benton.[17] The Palladian's mixed membership did not prevent some women from desiring an
exclusively female organization. In February of 1872, the *Hesperian* noted,
"We understand there is some talk of forming a ladies' literary society here.
We think this is a good project, and wish it success."[18] That plan was put on

hold, but women's participation at Palladian meetings became more active. On one occasion, the women left early because the hall was too cold. The editor encouraged them to return: "We hope they will not be discouraged by this evening as the room is now well-heated."[19]

During this time, Palladian activities in the paper were sometimes described as "rigorous" or with "much disturbance." Debates got out of hand, and male members sometimes dominated the evening with heated discussions. At other times, there were lulls in the discord, and the *Hesperian* observed that "we are glad to note the change in the behavior of the members of the society. . . . It seems to have been the purpose of some to make as much disturbance as possible." The society had held debates on such controversial topics as coeducation, abolishing the liquor trade, capital punishment, Chinese immigration, and the freedom of Ireland. Although the society took "decisive measures in order to produce good order," still the contention and disorder continued through the next school term.[20] Perhaps the masculine rowdiness intimidated the female membership, but by April of 1873, the rifts between students had grown so wide that two new literary societies split from the Palladians. First, the Palladian women withdrew and formed an all-female society, the Pierian Literary Society. A few men also withdrew from the Palladians, and formed the all-male Adelphian Literary Society. The remaining Palladians then made a decision to admit only men.[21]

The causes for the "great literary rift of 1873–1874," as it might be called, are not clear but may have stemmed from stunted male-female relations. George Howard, as editor of the *Hesperian*, had shown himself as one sympathetic to women's causes. He was also one of the Palladian deserters in 1873 who formed the Adelphian Society. Following the split, Howard's editorial notes sometimes contained derogatory comments about the Palladian men as less than refined and almost brutish. They were also younger students, many of whom were not yet university students but still in the Latin School. Perhaps the remaining Palladians were those less in favor of women's rights, whereas Howard considered the Adelphians a more progressive and sophisticated group.

Two months after the split, editor Howard publicized the Palladians' June debate, "that the mind of a woman is superior to that of a man's." This debate produced "amusement," and the two male debaters treated the subject in "humorous light."[22] One of the two male debaters mentioned was Allen W. Field, who was a year behind George Howard's class. Field would later become a prominent local judge in Lincoln in the 1890s. While at Nebraska, Field later succeeded Howard as the editor of the *Hesperian*, and during his first term as editor in September of 1875, Field learned of another group of women wanting to organize a society. His response, hearkening back to the literary rift of the previous year, may be considered, at best, sarcastic and teasing, and at worst, extremely sexist: "We will . . . venture one precaution, with your most gracious permission, fair sovereigns. Do you know that you possess one little weakness—an incapacity for self-government? Woman was never designed for a democrat. Therefore, please exercise extreme caution, or you will have your lily fingers at one another's delicate ears, in a fortnight or so."[23] In spite of his sexist disclaimer, Field confessed to be a "firm advocate of mixed societies," because women's "extreme goodness and sweetness" provided a tempering effect for "masculine savageness."[24]

Field's advocacy of mixed societies might appear inconsistent with his earlier exclusive participation in the all-male Palladians. However, even though he promoted mixing, he did so for the reason of women's inability to govern themselves. With these unabashed attitudes, likely the Pierians themselves had chosen to walk out on Field and his Palladian brothers, which is consistent with Howard's original report of the split. When Field left his editorial position in 1876, he admitted that perhaps women had refrained from submitting essays to the *Hesperian* because of his own "unpopularity with that class of students."[25] He gave no mention of the reasons for his unpopularity, but the discord was likely linked to the 1873–74 rift.

In the same column that George Howard had reported Field's infamous debate on "the mind of a woman," Howard made a less-than-subtle note that the Adelphians had "met with some women members of the Pierian for musical entertainment."[26] In a blatant snub against the Palladian Society, the Nebraska women had aligned themselves with their Adelphian brothers. Not much is known about the Pierian Society women, especially since their organization lasted less than one year. Two of Howard's associate editors at the *Hesperian* from 1873 to 1874, Fannie Metcalf and Ada J. Irwin, were Pierians. Metcalf was even elected as a marshal among the first Pierian officers. Other members of that Pierian Society were Carrie Sessions, Mary Sessions, Ada Hurlbut, Kate Monell, and Mollie Baird. A few of this group often provided musical entertainment when invited to Adelphian Society meetings. The influence of the Pierians' pro-feminine sentiments definitely emerged in the *Hesperian* literary editorials. Small in number and newly organized, the Pierians received less than their deserved recognition. The 1874 university catalog included descriptions of both the Palladian and the Adelphian Societies, but not the Pierians. Howard noted this slight in the February *Hesperian*, and as for why the Pierians had been excluded, stated, "We do not know the reason." Perhaps the exclusion had simply been an oversight, but the Pierians reacted in earnest: "The ladies indignantly assert that they will publish a catalogue of their own."[27]

The organization of the Pierian women brought much acclaim by Howard, and the Pierians and Adelphians immediately began holding joint meetings. This Pierian-Adelphian alliance was often brazenly played up in the *Hesperian*, including news of parties, social entertainments, and musical programs. The split between the "civilized" Adelphians and the less-sophisticated Palladians continued into the next school year, during which time the sister Pierians disbanded and turned their alliance with the Adelphians into full membership. In February of 1874, Howard made an indirect slam against the "brutish" Palladians when he reported on a meeting of the Adelphians and their new female members: "The union of this society with a large number of ladies, former members of the Pierian, has made this term an interesting epoch in its history. The higher and more refined tone imparted to all the literary exercises—the greater care shown in preparation and the more chaste and polished style of expression, shown in all the literary productions, attest the superior benefits which we believe 'mixed' societies always possess."[28]

Howard went on to congratulate the women on their success in the Pierian Society. "While we are a strong advocate of 'mixed' societies, we wish to say . . . [the] pleasantest hours we ever passed in the society hall, were those spent listening to the entertainments of the Pierian—which for variety, beauty of sentiment, and grace of delivery have seldom been excelled."[29] By March the Adelphians had their first female vice president, Sarah Funke, and in June the Adelphian Exhibition listed as its "bright epoch" the "hour when the fair daughters of Pieria joined the Adelphian ranks."[30]

Perhaps the literary rift ran its course, or the Palladians received some new, fresh membership. At any rate, by September of 1874 they decided to readmit women into the society. This not only helped the struggling group but also served to improve overall campus morale. Howard, still the *Hesperian* editor for the 1874–75 year, expressed his hope in renewed relations with a heartfelt compliment to his former rivals: "We sincerely hope that a spirit of brotherly and sisterly friendship which seems to be springing up among all the students this term will not grow less."[31] In November, when the Palladians officially admitted women, the paper reported that the society, in perhaps a kind of goodwill effort, had even debated the possibility of waiving women's fees. "Shall we (the gents) pay their fees or shall they have *equal* rights?" There was no mention of what "the gents" decided, but Howard offered an "Editor's comment": "Don't be alarmed or bashful, boys, they won't hurt you; we shall expect to see the Palladian prosper all the better for this innovation [admitting women]."[32] Between the 1870s and 1890s, other mixed societies would be founded at Nebraska. These land-grants displayed a complexity of gendered spatial negotiation that belies any stereotypes regarding the rejection of female presence by male students.

OREGON AGRICULTURAL COLLEGE

The Oregon Agricultural College traveled a more difficult road toward establishing mixed literary societies. Already in November of 1868 OAC had one literary society, called the Adelphian, and it was opened exclusively to male students. An editorial in the 1869 *Student Offering* called for all of the men of OAC to belong to the "tribe of the Adelphians," because "truly there is none like unto this tribe for wisdom!"[33] No such invitation was extended to the Oregon women students, and the Adelphians remained staunchly male-only for three years.

The women at OAC, however, finally gained ascendancy in 1872. During those three school years, 1869–72, there appears to have been disunity in OAC student literary and newspaper participation along male-female lines. According to the 1869 *Student Offering*, a second literary paper, the *Literary Casket*, was organized sometime in that school year with an unnamed female editor, called the "proprietress." This paper had failed in its first attempt but tried to reorganize in late 1869, and its "resurrection" was noted by the *Student Offering*. No further record of this periodical exists, but it was formed for the purposes of literary expression. The *Student Offering* editors gave a small welcome speech to the *Casket*: "This valuable little periodical has been resurrected and again launched out upon the sea of journalism. . . . We gladly welcome it . . . and earnestly wish for it a happy and prosperous life."[34] With that welcome came a word of warning against any support or promotion of women's rights. The male *Student Offering* editors cautioned their female *Casket* colleague, the "proprietress":

> Avoid advocating any of the isms of the day, but be liberal minded and public spirited. Remember the fate of the late *Casket* in other hands and profit by the lesson which it taught us, viz: the advocate of false doctrines and dogmatic isms shall surely fall. Learn from the experience of your predecessor, that Women's Rights don't pay in this age of the world. Avoid this rock upon which it split for there is danger in that direction. As a friend we give this advice to one who, we hope, will live and act so that good may be accomplished.[35]

Perhaps this argument over women's rights had played out in the literary society meetings. Disagreement over women's rights at oac somehow kept women students from full literary participation, either with the male-dominated Adelphians or in the student newspaper.

The *Gem* later described the history of female participation in the Adelphian. Seven men made up the earliest Adelphian group, but "ladies [were] not . . . originally admitted as members."[36] This segregation seemed to be the overt desire of the Adelphians' founding members, because their male-only association "fulfilled the expectations of its founder for several years," in spite of some women's attempts to gain admittance. In the fall of 1872 the "liberal or lady element gained the ascendency and as a natural result there was a change in the constitution placing the society on more liberal grounds by removing the clause restricting the roll of membership to individuals of the masculine persuasion."[37]

When women finally joined the Adelphians in 1872, this "progress" for Oregon's female students was not without its subsequent battles. The *Gem* tried to assess the impact of the Adelphians' first year as a mixed society. The admittance of women, or "that broad and liberal principle," might have been "introduced at too great an expense." For that reason, or perhaps a combination of reasons, "the society begun [*sic*] to decline soon after, and seemed to repeat the history of the Roman empire in extending its boundaries beyond its control."[38] The article gave no details of what was meant by "decline," but debates, arguments, and member misbehavior often led to discord, especially when debates covered controversial topics such as women's rights.

The specific events leading up to the ultimate decline and split of the Adelphian Society in 1873 are unclear. Perhaps the situation mirrored the literary split that occurred between Nebraska's Palladian and Adelphian Societies. The *Gem* reported a second split from the OAC Adelphian in which the "ladies, becoming indignant, drew out." It is uncertain whether the ladies formed their own society, and no OAC newspapers from the 1870s have survived to track the campus literary participation of that era. In 1873 the Adelphians reverted to their all-male membership and remained so for the next eight years. Not until 1881 would women again gain membership into the Adelphian Literary Society. The second time saw better success. An "important epoch in the society," according to the *Gem*, was "the admission of ladies [which] seem[s] to have improved the society this time, while their introduction before was immediately followed by failure."[39] The Adelphians remained a mixed society from 1881 until 1889, when it disbanded.

"RESOLVED": THE DEBATING ARENA FOR MALE-FEMALE INTERACTION

As women students participated in political debates with male students that sometimes led to vigorous expressions of opinion, these women actively changed the definition of what was considered appropriate public female behavior. Women as contestants—whether in political debates, public activism, or, as will be shown later, in athletic competition—added an important dynamic to gender interaction at land-grant colleges and universities. Proper Victorian women ventured opinions within the acceptable bounds of women's clubs and all-female parlor activities. More radical women such as suffragists, socialists, and temperance activists were considered shocking, inappropriate, and masculine, especially because they took their battles to the streets for public consumption. Through literary society debating activities, female land-grant students helped to negotiate a new culture of women's public political expression. By disputing controversial political issues in an open setting, in front of male students and professors, female students placed themselves on display. Both men and women discovered that it was acceptable for women not only to have opinions about certain issues but also to express those opinions in public.

The second decade of this study, the 1880s, was an important epoch for male-female interaction at the land-grants. By 1881 all three institutions had emerged from the gender battles of the previous decade with mixed literary societies—the Palladian Society at Nebraska, the Crescent Society at IAC, and the Adelphian Society at OAC. There were a few male-only and female-only societies at each institution, but the fact that students had the option of membership in a mixed society provided an important setting for the intellectual mingling of the sexes. Women participated actively in literary programs, especially delivering essays, performing musical pieces, and reciting poetry and literature excerpts. These types of presentations provided refinement and gentility that was important for early student organizations, especially as they modeled themselves after other nineteenth-century civic clubs. Further, poetry readings and musical numbers were acceptable methods of public feminine expressions.

Besides the feminine activities of music and poetry, women students also found ways of challenging traditional gendered expectations through literary society debating—both among themselves and with men on mixed teams. Even though women's debating occurred on a more limited scale, still this activity was an important element in women's educational and social progress at the land-grants. Debating in the 1870s and 1880s carried with it the associations of male political clubs, legislative and congressional activities, and after-hours alehouses and pubs, all venues that remained tightly closed to women on a national scale. Politics was a male arena—only in Wyoming, Utah, and Washington Territories could women vote—and since most debates argued in literary societies centered on political topics, women students' entrance into this field was slow, but still determined. The literary society meetings at land-grant universities occurred in rooms in the Old Main buildings that were specifically designated as mixed-gender space. Indeed, women students often assisted in the feminization of literary space by bringing in the physical objects of domestic refinement, such as carpets, lamps, wall decorations, and pianos. The mixed-gender space of literary society rooms also allowed women to approach a new public sphere of appropriate feminine performance and political activism.

Land-grants are significant for their role in forwarding the advancement of women's rights through mixed literary debating. Women debaters benefited from the opportunity to show male counterparts their comparable intelligence, since debating encouraged the intelligent and prepared exchange of arguments. Women were also encouraged to debate their brother literary members by those who at times took a patronizing attitude toward women and their literary contributions, as though the men needed to push the "timid angels" toward bravery of verbal expression. On the other hand, too much exuberance in debating sometimes led women to withdraw from early societies, since heated arguing was seen by "civilized" women as unrefined behavior. Perhaps at no other level in American society in the 1870s and 1880s were men and women publicly discussing current social and political issues in open, organized meetings.

While mixed debating offered some possibilities for women to be viewed on an equal playing field with male students, debate societies—both male and female members—still accepted a type of ideological separation of women within the debating process. A first example of this separation was that much of women's debating was still limited to more appropriate topics for females, such as romance, fashion, religion, and feminine moralism. They argued issues such as whether poverty is a better state than riches, whether Robert Browning's poetry was favored over that of other writers', and whether the United States should pass and enforce laws for Sabbath observance. As a second type of separation, the literary societies sometimes organized separate debate teams, so that men would only debate against men and women would only debate against women. Third, if the literary societies held mixed debates, the topics were ones that would not cause too much impassioned arguing and interaction, or the topics chosen were ones appropriate for feminine commentary. Some early mixed-team debates discussed issues important to women, such as coeducation, suffrage, temperance, and abolishing the liquor trade. This latter method was especially significant to the gender-segregated societies. An all-male literary society might invite its sister group to a special evening of a joint debate session—or vice versa—specifically to discuss issues such as coeducation and woman suffrage. A few examples of the above-mentioned types of gender interaction within debating activities are especially noteworthy.

At Nebraska in 1872 the coed Palladian Society held a mixed debate.

The topic, "that the liquor trade should be abolished," was discussed on the affirmative by "Miss [J. C.] Kelley" and C. R. Woolley; the negative was argued by E. A. Woolley, Hardy, and Tovey.[40] That Miss Kelley participated in a mixed debate with four other men is significant for the early intellectual exchange between male and female students at Nebraska. Kelley was also one of the Palladian's literary editors for the *Hesperian*. Of course, the liquor trade in America was an issue especially important to women as they joined in temperance crusades, but Nebraska women participated in other mixed debates that discussed women's issues, and many would later become important local activists in the Lincoln temperance movement.

Most debates in the Palladian and Adelphian Literary Societies in the 1870s were argued primarily by male students. As a matter of fact, the 1874 literary rift had perhaps driven some female students from participating in debates, either because discussions were too boisterous or because the women students were too timid. So when the former Pierians joined the Adelphian Society in 1874, women's participation in Adelphian activities centered around musical and poetic expression, and not so much around the vigorous debating. The Adelphians heralded the membership of their new sisters: "God bless the ladies! Without the dear girls what a cheerless, dreary waste were life! Ah! Eternal Sun, ah! Everlasting, fairy Moon, what were your enkindling rays, or wild, soul-inspiring beams, without the soft radiance of woman's smile? We have always loved the girls, alas! We fear too dearly for our spiritual welfare. They have made a polytheist of us; for in each one we see a divinity enshrined [and] . . . our adoration is certainly of the purest and most unselfish character."[41] The flowery and elevated language still used to set women apart from men shows the persistence of the ideal of women's refining influence on male societies. Even at the land-grant universities, the deification of women as the moral, civilized, and angelic gender—so common in Victorian expectations for women—kept them separate from men's so-called barbarism. And yet, even with the expectation of women's moralizing behavior, the Adelphian men still sought the participation of women in their debates.

Again, it might be tempting to look at women's lack of participation in debates as a restriction that had been imposed on them by male students or administration. And yet, in actuality, the women themselves withdrew from debates, either for shyness, modesty, or perceived intellectual inferiority, however false. *Hesperian* editor George Howard, for example, complimented the ladies for their music and essays but chastised them for lack of debate participation. "But what we want to say is this: The Adelphian society is fortunate in possessing a large membership of young ladies. Their readings, and essays, and music, to use their own sweet vernacular, are 'perfectly splendid.'" So women certainly filled the refining role, but Howard invited them out of their comfort zones: "We have a suggestion we would like to make to them with all due deference and humility. Why not join in the debates also?" The reasoning was so typical of Howard, and perhaps influenced by his associate, Ada J. Irwin: "Would not the clashing of woman's wit, the trial of her reasoning powers with man's, in polemical discourse, be mutually beneficial? Are we not here to educate our minds to meet in common the great problems which after life will bring? Will not man and woman, side by side, as never in the past, have to meet and answer all great questions of political as well as domestic economy, in the near future?"[42]

Howard's suggestion hearkened to one of the main purposes of coeducational colleges — to encourage intelligent socializing for the hopeful result of companionate marrying among students. Indeed, why shouldn't women and men "associate together in acquiring all kinds of knowledge"?[43] His reasoning for encouraging female debate participation was not simply to feed male egos, or for social amusement, or to encourage a battle of the sexes. "Do not for a moment imagine that we have the audacity to suppose, that we should come off victorious from such a combat. Ah! no, we would not hope that; we are in search of conquerors, not victims. . . . We could kiss the hands that dealt meet chastisement for our temerity."[44] Howard then expressed the hope that the Nebraska women would "take our suggestion kindly, and consider it favorably." This article echoed an earlier call to Nebraska women to submit more writing contributions to the *Hesperian Student*.

To what extent the women responded to this call for more debating is uncertain. Women students usually participated in the literary activities that were deemed more appropriate for their sex, such as poetry, music, and recitations. Many female students were more likely to volunteer for a decorating committee than for a debate team, not because of any restriction, but more because of their own sense of feminine influence and timidity. Many examples show how societies often held socials in which the female members took charge of the decorating and food preparation. For one Adelphian entertainment, the assistance of its female members was noted with language suggestive of women's roles as refining civilizers: "The hall, which is elegantly and richly furnished, was admirably and tastefully arranged for the occasion—thanks to the counsel and superior taste of the young lady members of that society. . . . For beauty, grace, wit and baking, those girls of the Adelphian may safely challenge Christendom!"[45]Further, the *Hesperian* suggested how fortunate were the "young gentlemen of said society . . . to have such providers, and they seem to appreciate their happy lot."[46] This notion of women students as "providers" of civilization and refinement seemed the more common role attributed to women in the literary societies.

Even with the typical activities of women's socializing role, many women did take advantage of the opportunities for participation in debates and other political activities. By the mid-1870s at Nebraska a few more literary societies had formed associations, including the Philomathean Society and the University Union, both with mixed membership; the former had two-thirds female membership by 1877. The women were "quite active members, doing their proportion of the society work with admirable zeal and diligence."[47] Women participated more actively in debates, including one in the University Union where the team of "Messrs. Platt and Black" debated "Mr. Field and Miss Ruth Hawley" on the question that "ambition has been productive of more good than evil." Ironically, Ruth Hawley's debate partner was Allen Field, of previous sarcastic editorial fame. The *Hesperian* gave its applause to mixed debating: "It gives us pleasure to note the interest taken by the ladies of the society in debate."[48]

Women often took action to separate themselves from male organizations as a way to preserve their feminine sphere. In literary programs and exhibitions, however, veteran women debaters still engaged in vigorous debates with their male colleagues well into the twentieth century. Women's debating continued in the Nebraska literaries throughout the 1880s, but in 1881, the Palladian Society organized a separate debating society for men, with the objective "to give opportunity for drill in debate and impromptu speaking." Two years later, a similar club was formed for the Palladian girls, called the Palladian Girls Debating Club, which met separately for female members on Friday nights. This did not restrict older women students from debating with men in exhibitions and programs; instead, it was for the "new members [who] are thus given a less embarrassing audience before which to practice the art of public speaking."[49] This act of physical separation was likely put in place by the women students themselves, as a way for the timid and modest students to develop confidence.

To allow for both separation and inclusion, some societies maintained permanent single-sex membership but still willingly met with opposite-gender societies for debating. At IAC, when the Crescents were still all-male, the Crescents and Cliolians each held their own society debate sessions, but they also held joint literary programs on occasion. Joint programs gave students the opportunity for social and literary interaction, and the chance for mixed debates. Both the Crescents and the Cliolians argued similar issues, including the truth of Darwin's theory, government control of railroads, protective tariffs, the impact of Charles Sumner on the Civil War, mandatory public school attendance, general amnesty to the Southern states, British imperialism in India, laws for Sabbath observance, an eight-hour day for workers, and woman suffrage and coeducation.

Sometimes the all-male Crescents and all-female Cliolians would argue the same topic within a few weeks of each other, and the differences in their decisions are worth noting here. In the spring of 1871 both societies held debates on whether the labor system of the IAC was a success. This work system, implemented by Pres. Adonijah Welch, required the unpaid services of students for caring for gardens, machinery, and the kitchens. Interestingly, the men ruled that the system was a failure, whereas the women ruled in favor of the work system. In June of 1871 both societies debated "that poverty is a greater benefit to a young man than riches."[50] The Crescents ruled that riches were better and the Cliolians ruled in favor of poverty. Certainly, the judges' decisions rested partially on the preparation of the debaters and the depth of the evidence presented. But decisions also depended on the political and social sentiment of the members themselves. Thus, debate topics and decisions reflected the issues important to students and how they stood on current problems.

The differences between men's and women's reactions to debates showed some of the ideological separation between the sexes. For this and other reasons, there was a measure of reaching out for political and intellectual exchange, even among the gender-segregated societies. The all-male Crescents sometimes invited their sister Cliolians to a joint session, especially to discuss women's issues. On April 27, 1872, the Cliolians were invited specifically to participate in a debate on woman suffrage.[51] Whether the Clios actually debated or they limited their participation to observation and later commentary was not mentioned in the minutes of either society. Before 1873, joint sessions were the only opportunities for mixed male-female debates. But only one week after women were admitted to the Crescents in April of 1873, the society held a mixed debate on capital punishment, argued by Emma Child and Julia Blodget. One month later, the society held an all-female debate on woman suffrage, with two teams of three women each.[52] Just like at Nebraska, once the excitement of having women members had worn off, the Crescents fell back into a pattern of predominantly male participation in the debates. Women did serve as judges in many debates, especially on women's topics, but the most heated issues were argued by men.

A mock divorce trial, argued at IAC in 1873, showed a broadening approach to women's social issues that was occurring early at land-grants. On September 20, 1873, Julia Blodget first debated corporal punishment, and then the society held a mock divorce trial. Although not as common, mock trials were an important part of early literary activity. The plaintiff-defendant relationship of a courtroom setting mirrored the negative-affirmative format of debates; students often held mock trials as an alternative to debate proceedings. In this instance, a "Jennie Kent" had sued her husband, "David A. Kent," for divorce. The judge ruled in favor of the plaintiff, Miss Kent.[53] In the mock trials, women still experienced gender separation: only male students could act as lawyers, judges, and jurors. Women students stood as witnesses, or as the plaintiff or defendant. Even with these separations, the debate format, along with mock trials, allowed for gender interaction and discussion of women's issues in a mixed setting.

Debating at OAC was of course limited to male-only participation during the time that the Adelphian Society was closed to women between 1873 and 1881. After the 1881 admission of women to the Adelphian, however, women participated in literary activities, but they entered into debating with reluctance. Between 1881 and 1885 a majority of debates were argued by men, and they argued such topics as "a lie is sometimes justifiable," "a gun is more beneficial than a dog (!)," "political parties are evil," "Indians have a right to American soil," and "scientific agriculture will increase Oregon crops." Controversial and timeless issues such as "capital punishment decreases crime" and "the law prohibiting Chinese immigration to the U.S. should be repealed," were sometimes argued two or three times in one year. Until 1885 few if any women were recorded as part of debate participation. Even the temperance issue, which was a popular feminine platform in the 1870s and '80s, was debated by all-male teams. In March of 1885 the Adelphian held an all-male debate on the question of woman suffrage. The judges for the debate were three women, "Misses Harris, Korthauer, and Newton." But on April 24, 1885, the Adelphian held a mixed debate on the question "Resolved: that the reading of novels is more beneficial than injurious to the mind." The judges were two men and one female student, Minnie Mc-Farland. The affirmative team included female student Cora Morris.[54]

Women who participated in debates achieved greater political visibility and were more likely to gain elected office within the societies. On May 8, 1885, the Adelphians held another mixed debate on whether "card playing is evil." This time the judges were all men, but Minnie McFarland argued on the negative team and Hennie Harris argued on the affirmative team. That spring, Hennie Harris was elected vice president of the society.

This same dimension of increased visibility and activity leading to expanded political participation within the societies was also true at Nebraska and IAC. Indeed, at Nebraska, May Fairfield, the daughter of Chancellor Edmund Fairfield (1876–82), contributed many essays and presentations both to the Palladian Literary Society and the *Hesperian*. She became the first elected female president of the Palladian, in 1877. Although women's entrance into debate activities was sometimes slow at the land-grants, the women who participated often did so as a route to leadership opportunities.

In the 1885–86 academic year, the OAC Adelphian had a membership of 29 males and 16 females. Even with the mixed debates of the spring of 1885, the next year saw a leveling off in women's debating. Men debated most topics, including women's topics such as feminine intellectual capacity and coeducation. Not until February 1886 did the Adelphian again hold mixed debates. In two consecutive meetings, teams of two men argued against two women, on topics such as "observation vs reading" or "dancing is injurious to the young." However, on the subject of woman suffrage, held just a week later, women were again excluded from the discussion, with two all-male debate teams arguing the issue. One of the judges, however, was Maud Hoffman. The debate became heated to the point that professors stepped in. The society extended a "vote of thanks . . . to the Professors for their attendance under such trying circumstances."[55]

That heated arguments sometimes occurred in the middle of debates might be a significant reason for women's retreat from the debating arena, or for why men and women often debated separately. One week after the woman suffrage debate, the society held an all-female debate on an unnamed topic. When men and women did debate together, the societies often chose less inflammatory issues that were meant to produce little excitement, such as "there are more curiosities in the sea than on land," which was argued on March 12, 1886, by two teams made up of one man and one woman each.

Sometimes even the mixed debate situations could not avoid conflict, and topics such as "private execution is preferable to public execution" incited disruption. This topic, argued by one team of two men and another team of one man and one woman, Mattie Burnett, became so intense that nine people were fined "for disorder." Fines of "10 cents each" were levied that evening to a group that included the debaters themselves: "Mattie Burnett, Sarah Jacobs, Francis Harris, J.H. Collins, Geo. Waggoner, Eddie Wilson, Fred Rayburn, O.U. Waggoner, [and] Harry Holgate."[56] Mattie Burnett and Sarah Jacobs were not the only women fined for disorder in Adelphian activities. One week later, the general debate was "postponed," and an election was held in which Diana Newton was elected vice president. Whether the election itself caused a disturbance was not reported in the society minutes, but three men and "Lizzie Keeser, Sarah Jacobs and Carrie Baldwin were refered [sic] to tribunal and fined 10 cents each for disorder."[57] What was this? Women students fined for disorder in literary societies? Perhaps their "disorder" was no more than speaking out of turn, or perhaps it was as extreme as disagreements, interruptions, or vocal outbursts. Still these behaviors fulfilled what some had feared in the 1870s, that women's participation in mixed debates would reduce them to the level of men's political barbarism. On the other hand, herein lay examples of women students expressing political and social opinions on a near-equal playing field. These were not the typical parlor activities of nineteenth-century ladies' societies; indeed, debates afforded women students a new way of stretching traditional gender boundaries.

CONCLUSION

Women's participation in mixed literary societies in the 1870s and 1880s showed how women sought to negotiate their own inclusion within the land-grant culture of gendered separation. Literary societies remained important to the college culture through the early 1900s when most land-grants continued to sponsor at least one mixed society. However, with the increase in student numbers in the 1890s, students more often separated into gender-segregated societies. Overall male and female student increases required more practical separation after 1900, and by 1910 OAC and UAC had as many as six male societies and six female societies. When the first intercollegiate debates in the West were held in the early 1890s, these debates were dominated by male students. Although women students continued to debate through the 1900s, and even against male students at joint literary meetings, still the intercollegiate debates saw predominantly male participation. After 1900, debate teams participated in intercollegiate debate tournaments, where sometimes mixed debate teams represented their schools. In 1905 the UAC debate team of two men and one woman defeated a debate team from the Brigham Young University in Provo. Heralded in the UAC student yearbook as the "squad that wrecked the B.Y.U.," this mixed debate team provided an example of how far male and female space could intersect at coeducational institutions.

The literary society culture of the 1870s and 1880s represented a pioneering contribution in land-grant gender interaction, especially as it laid the groundwork for women's greater public and political activity on land-grant campuses. In literary societies, women students experienced different extremes in their society participation. Most typically, they encountered the reinforcement of their traditional roles by doing standard feminine activities such as decorating and preparing food, or performing acceptable recitations, poetry, and musical numbers. But for those women who sought the expansion of female political and social expression, literary society debates were the most influential in helping to create the "New Woman" on campuses. Mixed debates also prepared the way for a new culture of student political activism for temperance, education, and suffrage throughout the late nineteenth century. Literary society participation allowed women to challenge the culture of separation and expand their own involvement in the land-grant culture.

4

Women Students' Sociality

Building Relationships
with Men and Women

It does our soul good to see so many women in attendance this term. The boys say it
is some inducement to get to chapel now.

HESPERIAN STUDENT, October 1876

This chapter will examine ways in which four land-grant institutions in
the West simultaneously sought to encourage the two opposing forces of
separation of the sexes and desirable sociality that would lead to marriage.
Most administrators attempted to maintain a strict culture of separation
between the sexes, while also allowing and even encouraging proper and
appropriate contact between young ladies and gentlemen. Not only did
this help to bridle youthful passions, they believed, but it also perpetuated
the expectations of women students as wives-in-training. Women students
overwhelmingly accepted this separate domestic expectation, along with
the social barriers placed between themselves and their male colleagues.
Nevertheless, the land-grant environment encouraged a new liberality of social interaction that allowed students to push the boundaries of appropriate
sociality and courting rituals in the nineteenth-century American West.

One of the inevitable results of coeducation at western land-grants was
the increased rate of socialization and marriage among men and women
students. For positive or negative, social contact between the sexes was an
indisputable outcome of coeducation, and both critics and proponents used
this fact to defend their respective causes. Thus, "while the enthusiastic
coeducationist was declaiming on the improved morality of the two-sex
colleges, his opponent was throwing up his hands at the prospect of dire
results."[1] A major argument in favor of coeducation suggested that since

men and women spent their lives together, then collegiate practice should mirror society's familial expectations in a healthy and natural way. Advocates stressed the "social interdependence of man and woman" and argued that "since men and women must live together, they should therefore be educated together."[2] This was not merely society's expectation for men and women. Caroline Dall, in 1861, asserted: "There is, between the sexes, a law of . . . reciprocal action, of which God avails himself in the constitution of the family, when he permits brothers and sisters to nestle about one hearthstone. Its ministration is essential to the best educational results. Our own educational institutions should rest upon this divine basis."[3]

For opponents of coeducation, socialization was a danger to the proper separate and moral education of students—especially men, who had a greater responsibility to focus on their studies, achieve professional greatness, and eventually provide for a family. Separate education also guaranteed that women would remain feminine and moral, untainted by the harsh and manly world of men's higher education. Critics mostly feared that students in a mixed-gender environment became too easily distracted and tempted by associating with the opposite sex: "Opponents of coeducation were overwhelmed with a fear of early and too many marriages," and the idea that "were girls and boys to study together, flirtations and early marriages would be the inevitable result; the girls would become masculine and unwomanly, and the boys effeminate and unmanly. Co-education would, therefore, lower the standard of morals."[4]

Supporters of coeducation claimed the contrary, that when men and women are kept apart, they develop an unnatural longing for what is mysterious and unattainable. Dall believed that where men and women received separate education, the "general abstinence from each other's society makes the occasion of re-union a period of harmful excitement."[5] And one professor at the coeducational Knox College in Galesburg, Illinois, asserted that "love between the sexes cannot be shut in or out by seminary walls" and that by keeping men and women in monastic or conventlike separation, love instead "festered and soured into lust."[6] Social and ideological separation only added to the potential for moral decline and made students "more disorderly, harder to manage, more unreasonable, and every way worse than where the two are united." Or, as the same Knox teacher so aptly put it, "Horses are known to work quietly in teams, [but] rage and neigh when kept solitary in stalls."[7] Young people were liable to be overcome with passions, especially without the tempering of calm, moral, and realistic interaction on a daily basis. Men needed education with women, without any "sentimental halo," and because "there is no disrespect and scorn of 'girls' from a youth who sees them well able to hold their own, and to stand beside, if not above, him in intellectual exercises . . . [then] both learn the true, the honest, the natural way of looking at each other, and are prepared to enter life together as they should."[8]

By the late nineteenth century, the coeducational experiment was indeed proving that mixed education resulted in more sociality and marriages among students. Coeducation supporters heralded the benefits of "companionate marriages" that were built on love, understanding, education, and a proper outlook on life, rather than wealth, social status, frivolity, and the desires of some men to have shallow ornament-wives. Thomas Woody, a proponent of mixed-gender education, argued that from coeducation, "many of the happiest marriages I have known resulted. Are we not justified in maintaining that an acquaintance of four years in the classroom furnishes as good ground for a wise choice of husband or wife as a chance acquaintance in a ball room?"[9] Thus, coeducational colleges served as the most ideal environments for a fulfilling courtship.

At land-grant colleges, administrators recognized the immense social benefits of educating the sexes together. Land-grant education inherently accepted the notion that men and women should be trained together to run efficient, civilized, and moral homes. Even with this acceptance of the positive social results of mixed education, land-grant educators acknowledged what opponents of their system feared: (1) too much moral temptation and (2) the subtle attempts to "wipe out [the] distinction" between men and women. To combat these two fears, land-grants struggled to maintain a proper balance between supervised gender separation on one hand and acceptable sociality on the other. Thus, as students worked within this sometimes ambiguous culture of competing gender separation and inclusion, they successfully maneuvered new ways of interaction with the opposite sex, especially toward the ultimate end of courtship and marriage.

LAND-GRANT COURTSHIP: HUSBANDS AND WIVES IN TRAINING

Land-grant colleges and universities became places of marital preparation and training, and unashamedly so. Women's education—whether instituted to prepare female students for teaching, domestic housewifery, or even a nontraditional career such as journalism or medicine—had behind it the intent to produce proper Victorian wives. Both critics and supporters of coeducation agreed on the fact that "romance is inevitably bred wherever young men and women come into close association . . . and when the little winged god comes in the window, study flies out."[10] To the coeducational land-grants, this was a desirable result of the mixing of the sexes, and very much encouraged, as long as it occurred within proper behavioral strictures. Marriage and courting were on the minds of land-grant students, and newspaper commentary often portrayed their centrality to the social concerns of young scholars. Very early, women students earned the distinction of potential wives for male student suitors.

College newspapers carried on a revealing and even humorous discourse about the social lives of students; because most college papers were run by male editorial staffs, the paper's comment often portrayed women students as curious and delightful distractions for the dominant male population. Certainly, the land-grants maintained a scientific and intellectual climate, but they also encouraged a culture of courting, romance, and marriage. Editorials of the time reflected the tone of the larger American issues over coeducation. Student writers often berated the older, all-male universities of the East as "monastic" and stifling, and the sister schools like Vassar, Wellesley, and Bryn Mawr as "convents" of women's separate education. When an 1893 exchange said that the "pride of the Vassar girls is that none of their graduates have ever been divorced," *Hesperian*'s editor sarcastically asked, "How many have had the opportunity?"[11]

Instead of isolating young women, western coeducation offered a more desirable alternative of preparing educated and cultured wives that were true companions to their husbands. Western women's education was distinctive, especially since the frontier conditions required marriages where men and women helped each other to survive in the harsher environment. At the inaugural ceremony of Pres. Adonijah S. Welch of IAC in March of 1869, a poet articulated the benefits of western coeducation over New York's new, all-male land-grant college, Cornell University. Prof. H. H. Parker, in "The Ideal Farmer and His Wife," noted the difference:

> Well done, O East, but not the best!
> Here in the fresh and fearless West,

We smile to think of monks and nuns.
We dare to trust our noble sons; . . .
The manly and the maiden mind
Together grow more bright, refined.
That place is holy ground and sweet,
Where earth and heaven together meet.[12]

Women readily felt the social pressures that dictated their futures as married women; through domestic economy course work, jokes about marriage, and published wedding announcements, women felt and encouraged the pressures of the culture of marriage. But men also felt the pressure to marry. Newspapers published marriage announcements on a monthly basis, and any biography of a male professor always carried a notice about whether that instructor was a bachelor and needed a wife. Paper editors wrote teasing and gossipy reports about love interests, embarrassing mishaps in romance, and reminders to students about their marital duties. In August 1885 an *Aurora* editor commented on the numbers of alumni marriages: "We see by the catalogue that nearly all the ladies are married, but have been greatly surprised at the number of bachelors. My brothers, this ought not so to be."[13]

The newspaper editors were the symbolic eyes, ears, and mouth of campus happenings. They played an important role in expressing general attitudes toward women students as lovely, enticing, and distracting curiosities for young men. Through an editor's gaze, an entire campus population could vicariously witness the spectacle of male-female socializing and romance. Sitting from their upper-floor press rooms in the Old Main buildings, or even observing while out and about on campus, editors enjoyed their view of female activities; they also reported on how other male students interacted with their college sisters. In September 1874 the new school year brought all of the students regularly to chapel, so the veterans could view the new recruits, and early fall was especially exciting for young men. Said the editor, who had noted the enthusiasm during chapel exercises: "It was very amusing to see gentlemen who attended last year watch every young lady that came in the door, to see whether she was an old student."[14] Female presence often motivated men to attend class and chapel. One editor spoke for all male students when he admitted, "It does our soul good to see so many young ladies in attendance this term. The boys say it is some inducement to get to chapel now."[15]

Morning chapel exercises—required attendance at most colleges of the time—provided additional intrigue for girl-watchers. Because men and women had to sit separately, with little or no physical contact, then the act of gazing at the women—even from a distance—fulfilled a romantic longing. Certainly, women students also gazed and stared in public places such as chapel; however, this did not get reported to near the extent that editors reported on the men's girl-watching. "Some of the Preps are complaining of their eyes being sore," said one editor. "'Tis enough to make anybody's eyes sore, to sit and stare the young ladies out of countenance during chapel exercises. Our eyes are a little weak, too."[16] Sometimes, gazing was simply not enough, and couples sought to breach the separation barriers by sending covert messages during chapel. One couple was "getting far gone when they [had] to keep up handkerchief flirtation in chapel."[17] Through nonverbal communication such as bodily movements, flirtations, and letter writing, students could break the barriers of physical separation.

Women had arrived on land-grant campuses, and no matter what activities they pursued, whether intellectual, athletic, musical, or professional, the expectation for all female students was future wifehood. One IAC student spoke negatively about the pressures placed on women students. Perhaps the experiences he recalled were typical, but the pressures on women were distinct and obvious. For those women who were "engaged to marry either students or young professors in the college," they were "a subject of unkind criticism by the young men who did not have their society." This negativity likely stemmed from jealousy, or from early stereotypes about women who went to college *only* to procure a spouse. But the other young women, "who were not engaged [or] were very diffident young women who shrank from meeting young men," also received harsh treatment from male students. "The coarse criticism to which the young women were subjected by the unrefined young men is a far from pleasant reminiscence."[18] To Frank Leverett, coeducation did *not* have a refining effect on young men; on the contrary, daily associations with young women caused too much familiarity and a loss of respect. Leverett's experience speaks to the actions of the chauvinistic few who seem to be ever-present. But these attitudes were not prevalent; on the contrary, male students seemed to have a deferential, curious, and even protective attitude toward their women colleagues.

And the students did indeed fall in love and get married: Editor George Howard, class of 1875 and later professor of history at Nebraska, married Alice Frost of the class of 1876; she later enrolled in graduate history courses while her husband taught in the department. *Hesperian* editor Henry H. Wilson (class of 1878) married Emma Parks (1880), who had served as his associate editor at the *Hesperian* in 1877–78. Educated, cultured, and even graduated—surely these were the types of companionate marriages that proponents of coeducation had hoped for. The IAC Alumni Association reported in 1880 that of the graduates to that point, "twenty-four marriages have been reported; sixteen having been celebrated where the parties were fellow students, while only eight have joined themselves to strangers to our company." This meant that "a collegian's chances of matrimony were twice as good here as anywhere else."[19] Five years later, the Alumni Association reported that of the 104 students who had graduated between 1881 and 1885, 18 of them had married already, and 10 of those were married to fellow IAC students.[20] As men and women learned to intellectualize together in literary societies and to socialize within the proper boundaries of male-female behavior, the land-grants fulfilled what the proponents of coeducation had hoped—that respect and mutual understanding would increase. After all, "it is the natural arrangement that boys and girls should be together in school as they are in the family."[21] And the land-grant purpose included the making of marriages and families.

SOCIALITY AND SEPARATION: KEEPING THE SEXES TOGETHER AND APART

Land-grant environments encouraged early sociability between the sexes, but did so with certain guidelines and restrictions. Physical separation in classrooms, chapels, and living quarters, as well as the rules that guided proper gender interaction, played a part in keeping the sexes at a safe distance. Within those strictures, students found appropriate ways to exercise their mutual sociability. In the 1870s students experienced rigid scheduling and rules regarding behavior and study. This scheduling left the young people very little time for unsupervised pairing off or inappropriate activities. At IAC in the 1870s the students' schedules began early in the morning.

At 5:30 a.m. students heard the wake-up call, and after preparation and studying, they went to breakfast at 6:45 a.m. Chapel exercises began at 7:45 a.m., lasting only fifteen minutes, although chapel exercises at Nebraska, UAC, and OAC sometimes lasted up to half an hour. Between 8:00 a.m. and 1:00 p.m., students went to their classes—entering and leaving through separate entrances—ending at 1:00 p.m. for dinner. From 1:45 to 5:45, students at IAC fulfilled their work duties—men in agricultural, gardening, janitorial, or mechanical duties, and women cleaning, cooking, and working in the college kitchen. At 5:45 p.m., students went to supper and had some free time for socializing and going back to their rooms. From 7:45 until 10:00 p.m., study hours were strictly enforced, with students "not permitted to leave their rooms during study hours except for 'unavoidable reasons,' approved by the presiding officer of each section." Lights-out was at 10:00 p.m.[22] Students were also given some recreational time in the afternoons, with men playing a game of baseball or a few men and women students playing a supervised game of croquet on the university's front lawn. No wonder students used chapel time to stare, wave, and flirt. That brief fifteen minutes, together with lunch and supper, was the only time when the whole student body could interact.

With such a restricted schedule, opportunities for socializing in the 1870s were, to say the least, limited. Female students could get permission to "promenade," or walk around with a male escort, on the front campus lawn during certain supervised hours. A young woman could ask permission to have a male student escort her to church on Sunday; and on Saturday afternoon, "couples were allowed to walk on the campus alone. At all other times there must be several together to enjoy this privilege; even then it was restricted to recreation hour, and to the limits of the campus surrounded by the drive." Students often argued about "how many individuals constituted 'several.'" Although they tried to push the envelope, they could not get away with just two; neither did three constitute an appropriate group, but "five or six was always safe."[23]

By the 1880s students argued vehemently about the group promenade rule. After one student wrote to the *Aurora* complaining about the Saturday-only rule, the editor responded, "As nearly a half day is allowed each Saturday for the young couples to while away as they wish, it does not seem very barbarous that there should exist a rule requiring them to remain in

groups during the social hours of the week."[24] This seemed generous, especially since "we all know from observation that, rigid as the laws are now,
a young couple that improves them to their extreme limits can associate
as much as any couple should, especially when in the pursuit of a higher
education." Saturday afternoons left plenty of time for proper socializing,
but not so much that couples were distracted from their studies, or worse,
tempted toward impropriety. "We cannot understand how this law can be
considered an injustice," concluded the editor.[25]

Because Iowa students lived in such close quarters during the 1870s,
their contact had to be restricted and activities strictly chaperoned. To
prevent fraternization between sexes during study hours or after lights-out,
dormitory rules forbade students from leaving their rooms or loitering in
the stairwells. Of course, students found ways to breech this barrier, but
the rules showed that administrations feared the consequences of students
being alone together in dark and hidden places. When students went on
excursions and picnics to the country or other towns near Ames, they
were always accompanied by professors and parents. For the yearly "walk
around" or "trot," students promenaded around campus under the watchful
eyes of professors and the president. It was a significant occasion, because
couples got to pair off in public: "Senior boys asked junior girls, and junior
girls invited senior men, and anyone else left could ask an underclassman."[26]
When the men went to pick up their "engagements" (dates), the particular
ritual was indicative of the kinds of unique separation practices that kept
students at a respectable distance. The young men left Old Main through
the back door, walked around to the front of the building, and called for
the young lady "at the front door where the lady on the watch went to meet
them."[27] Some of the rituals for proper gender interaction often bordered
on the ridiculous, and yet they showed the importance of maintaining strict
physical separation.

At all land grants in the 1870s, the most significant venue for student
interaction were the literary societies, which met every Friday or Saturday
evening for three or four hours. (For further information on literary societies, see chapter 2.) This was a legitimate and acceptable venue for men's
and women's pairing—it was a limited amount of time and was supervised
by adult professors and administration officials. Men could offer to escort
a female student to the society meeting and then accompany her home

afterward, as long as the woman arrived by the designated curfew. Newspapers often carried announcements about who had gone with whom to the previous week's society, or if anyone had particularly embarrassing mishaps during the evening. H. H. Wilson, of *Hesperian* fame, remembered that during the 1870s, Nebraska students were kept separate during chapel exercises and at other locales. The only place where separation was not strictly enforced was in the literary societies, "and this was the one occasion when the young man was entitled to escort a young lady." Even for this interaction, modes of formality prevailed. A student "was quite formal and might send a written invitation. A friend of mine was so precise as to ask 'the pleasure of your company to and from the literary society.' The lady was equal to the occasion and quite equal to him in the science of precision, and accepted 'for the round trip.'"[28]

Literary societies were the intellectual and social centers of students' lives during the 1870s. The *Hesperian* described how sociability occurred: "We, among the many, assembled in Union Hall, and proceeded to get acquainted with the many young ladies, who crowded around us, eager for an introduction. . . . Everybody got acquainted with everybody else."[29] One group of senior boys, "unable to bear the pressure," even asked to be relieved from their duties during society meetings so that they could have "leisure time in order to cultivate the society of the ladies."[30] Some societies required that males and females sit separately, but the meetings always ended with conversation, socializing, and refreshments. When members stayed after a meeting, the university custodian sometimes had to kick them out by 10:30 p.m. Couples had a half hour to linger together before the mad rush to get the lady home by the eleven o'clock curfew. Considering the few opportunities for socializing, students had to take advantage of what time they had together, even if that time was strictly supervised.

In the early years, dances and parties were rare, and Anna Felber remembered "There were no university dances or parties, probably because there was no place to have them."[31] In the 1870s and 1880s most land-grants forbade dancing as a potentially dangerous activity that led to moral depravity. Edna Bullock recalled that the "University [Nebraska] did not attempt to supervise the off-the-campus activities of the students. No chaperon had to put in wearisome and thankless evenings in attendance upon student dances." As a matter of fact, by the mid-1880s there were still "no student dances. . . . There was no place for dancing on the campus, and it would not have been permitted anyhow. Too many Nebraskans saw dancing as a toboggan towards the lower regions."[32] A similar prejudice against dancing existed at IAC; dancing was "entirely foreign to the purposes of this institution, . . . [and] not regarded . . . as a proper amusement for young people." In 1882 the IAC trustees "ordered that 'dancing by students upon College ground is hereby forbidden.'"[33] Dancing might be allowed in single-gender settings only; OAC offered a class in ballroom dancing for its women students in the late 1860s and early 1870s, but the class was restricted solely to female participation. Some students attended parties or dances in town, but these were not university-sponsored; literary societies remained the official form of student interaction before 1900.

Given the on-campus regulations and separation of the sexes, male and female students sought off-campus social engagements. For instance, in the 1880s most campuses organized their own local chapters of the YMCA and YWCA. These met as gender-segregated groups on a weekly basis, but at times they held joint prayer meetings. In theory, the organizations met to pray, but Edna Bullock remembered, "I have always had my doubts as to the religious urge being the motive for such attendance."[34] Men and women wanted to be together on land-grant campuses, but the public rules placed significant barriers on the extent of that interaction. Students constantly sought new ways to push against those barriers and to negotiate new means of social mixing. Students also periodically held socials or "sociables" and parties at the homes of parents and professors in town. In spite of the strict supervision that accompanied these gatherings, Bullock remembered them fondly:

> Class parties and social gatherings of various organizations were usually held in Lincoln homes. There were not attractive hotels or halls for such purposes, and if there had been, students could not have afforded the expense of such places. . . . In the Lincoln homes the parents were the hosts and were appreciated and enjoyed as a normal part of our social life. When we went to the Bonnell residence, Father Bonnell was the life of the party. It was the same way at the Barrett home and many other Lincoln homes. We knew that our elders approved our ways of life, in general, and we would have missed them if we could not have had their interest and companionship in these homes.[35]

The parents also served as official chaperones for the university, and students looked to these as surrogate parents: "We knew, too, that certain of these grand women, the mothers of our comrades, would not hesitate to let us know when our ways did not meet their approval. That sort of chaperonage worked. The parents of those days did not need to worry much about what we would do when we were out of their sight."[36] And what did students do at the sociables and parties? They played group games, sang around the piano, enjoyed refreshments such as cider, popcorn, doughnuts, and apples, and conversed over simple activities, including checkers and chess.

For formal outings that allowed a man and woman to pair off, the social protocol of the time demanded that men instigate the request. Women understood men's initiator role in social and romantic relationships and usually accepted the passive role of receiving romantic overtures. However, women found opportunities for reversing these roles. During certain school occasions, women could invite men to attend the all-female literary society socials; or, at the end-of-the-year Baccalaureate promenade at IAC in the 1870s, junior women traditionally invited senior men. Women also ritualized the reversal of male-female social roles, especially by hearkening to various classical and medieval traditions that placed themselves in the assertive position. For instance, leap year celebrations occurred whenever February 29 fell in a calendar year, as in 1880 when IAC women students threw a leap year social. On some occasions, leap year activities became part of other traditions where women instigated social events to actively pursue the men of their choice. Women claimed leap year as a special event in which all things in society became turned around or backward. Similar to Sadie Hawkins or Preference activities of the twentieth century, leap year represented a manifestation of women's social choice and power, at least for one day. The celebration was sometimes held in association with the month of May—"Flora's month in Roman times"—which "was thought to be a period in which women were powerful, their desires at their most immoderate."[37] The reference to Roman Floralia celebrations seemed to be well known by college-age men and women. Floralia festivities were held between April 28 and May 3 in honor of Flora, the goddess of flowers and blooming plants. Audiences at Floralia displays permitted actresses and prostitutes to perform openly nude—it was even expected by male audience members. These bawdy performances allowed women to show sexual expression not usually accepted in Roman society. While nineteenth-century May Day celebrations did not take feminine expression to that extent, they apparently evoked similar symbols of female power and social aggression that were familiar to students of classical history and mythology.[38] The historical roots of leap year are not as easily traced, although some cite a fifth-century Irish tradition in which women could propose to men only in leap years. Regardless of the historical or folk origins, leap year traditions were associated with an odd day in which normal social rules did not apply.

Leap year activities gave women land-grant students the opportunity to conceptualize their rights to certain feminine freedoms, with opportunities they did not have during the rest of the year. For instance, the women of IAC published the one-issue *Ladies Bureau*, "devoted to the Cause of Leap Year Privileges," for celebrating the one time every four years when women could choose the men they wanted, rather than wait to be chosen. It was only fair, after all, that "Mr. A. E. Hitchcock and L. E. Spencer were made wall flowers for the evening," because "how often have *we* been compelled to stand against the *wall* and wait in vain too." The women described an imaginary world where women had power, social choice, and political advantages. The paper called for a "Social Millennium!!" with announcements of "Glad Tidings!" and the "Great Victory!" where "Right has Triumphed!" This day was a "Golden Age" with "No More Dish Rags To Wring!" Of course, the main purpose of the celebration was "the realization of the acme of woman's fondest hopes—*the possession of a choice 'special.'*"[39]

The woman's right to choose a man, rather than to be chosen by someone undesirable or even worse—not to be chosen at all, was the special privilege of leap year role reversal. The *Ladies Bureau* reported that Cora Keith had picked "Mr. Frank Helsel," and she "seemed to border on ecstasy in her devotion to her hearts [*sic*] choice." According to regulations, all women were allowed only one man, except for "old maids above thirty-five years of age who, on account of deprivation in the past shall be given the liberty of choosing an additional man on whom to lavish the superabundance of freed affection."[40] With the new assumed position of female social dominance, women claimed other freedoms as well, such as public dancing and even woman suffrage.

A woman who vigorously acted outside of her sphere also "enriched the fantasy of a few real women and might have emboldened them to exceptional action."[41] For instance, leap year celebrations sometimes included lectures on women's rights, and all attendees were invited to "please leave their husbands at the doors." IAC's leap year celebration also included a women's "War-dance." To those "weaker sisters" who declined to dance because they "could not throw off their old foggy notions," the editors warned that "clinging to old time notions of modesty" would prevent them from "basking in the pure and free light of 'Woman's Strike for Freedom.'" "Leap Year" women succeeded in making the connection between women's social freedom and expanded political freedom. The editors announced that a "telegram was sent to Susan B. Anthony, regarding this uprising."[42]

In perhaps the most telling and humorous reversals of the leap year celebration, the female editors took on a "male-watching" role of campus social activities, similar to male editors' fascination with women students. After one Saturday social, the ladies reflected on the male subjects of their intended affections, describing them as "so *nice and sweet*," which echoed the language male writers had often used to characterize women. On one occasion, the paper completely reversed gender characteristics: "Abbie Foule . . . was proud, haughty, confident and resolute"; and "Mr. Mitchell . . . kind, noble, bending and forbearing." And Foule had succeeded in "her manner of overthrowing the King."[43] This reversal suggested that women students understood both the discourse and the separate expectations of social meekness required of them. Their place as future wives required a certain feminine demeanor and attitude. But the chance to break from this expectation in order to perform assertive roles, even if only once a year (for May Day celebrations) or once every four years (for leap year celebrations), was practiced with enthusiasm and humor. Although women had a brief window of opportunity to enact fantasies about role reversal, still the event served to reinforce their positions as wives-in-training. These activities made fun of male social dominance through the "laughter of disorder and paradoxical play," but ultimately accepted those systems they sought to attack.[44] Land-grant women, through a version of playful role reversal, experimented with challenges to the traditional gender norms of college social life.

The social climate of 1870s and 1880s land-grant campuses can be characterized as a culture of separation and regulated socialization. Certainly students were encouraged to interact in healthy and appropriate ways, but administrations went to great efforts to keep those activities within specific boundaries. Considering such limited and supervised interaction, students pursued and took advantage of every opportunity to have some kind of connection with members of the opposite sex. As students interacted socially on land-grant campuses, they often succeeded in breaking through the barriers of restricted interaction. Within the land-grant culture of gender separation, students discovered creative and unique ways to negotiate their own physicality and sociality with the opposite sex.

PUSHING THE BOUNDARIES:
PHYSICAL AFFECTION AND INTIMACY

Land-grant campuses felt acute tensions between the public world of regulated sociality among students and the private world of intimate or sexual behaviors. As much as land-grant administrations tried to restrict contact between the sexes, the coeducational environment was ideal for the erosion of social restrictions. Beth Bailey's analysis of the sexual revolution of the 1960s finds some important comparisons to the land-grant atmospheres of the 1870s through 1890s. Just as the 1960s sexual revolution "grew from . . . the tensions between private behaviors and public rules and ideologies that were meant to govern behavior," so also the late nineteenth century saw a battle between traditional standards of gender interaction and what was really taking place on campuses.[45] The tensions between public and private played out in the same medium that displayed all other land-grant tensions—the college newspapers. Of course, it is difficult to trace the occasions of sexual intercourse, out-of-wedlock pregnancies, or prostitution that occurred on or around land-grant campuses. So many students left school from semester to semester and year to year for reasons such as teaching careers, marriage, and relocation that it would be next to impossible to determine which of these departures might have occurred because of a pregnancy or so-called shotgun wedding. In truth, students were so thoroughly supervised, they had very few occasions to be alone. And yet, various degrees of physical intimacy did occur. Not only did the college papers publicly tattle—in print—when students broke the rules, but the "Local" columns were saturated with gossipy and riddle-like innuendos hinting at suggestions of students' intimate, physical exchanges.

Like the college students of the 1960s, students in the late 1800s "evaded the controls and circumvented the rules," in order to find opportunities for physical touch.[46] Students at IAC often attempted to arrange meetings in the ever-forbidden stairwells by sending messages above or below them from dormitory rooms via the "airline." They also communicated through open windows and even banged on the pipes to let the intended know they wanted to meet. When one freshman girl tried to meet with her gentleman "at the old trysting place at the head of the stairs," she was stopped, probably by the preceptress, and asked if she had permission. Suddenly caught, she had to miss her arranged meeting. The *Aurora* editor felt pity for the freshman's inexperience, because "we were all that way once," but gave sound, veteran advice for trying to secure future meetings with her beau: she could either meet him "where the stairs wind down" or learn "the secrets of the laundry window fasteners," but most important for achieving a successful clandestine rendezvous, she must "consider 'Preceptress Evasion' one of the first studies of her course."[47]

Couples were often caught pairing off by themselves, flirting during chapel exercises, sneaking away during recitations, or even kissing in secluded places around campus. One editor called attention to the two couples who continuously left their recitations to go off by themselves: "Ain't it a little transparent where some of the students go . . . especially those two young gents and ladies? If it is not repeated, we will say no more about it."[48] A few minutes alone was plenty of time to engage in kissing or more passionate embracing, and land-grants had tried to combat this with rules that intended to prevent students from pairing off in hidden places. But creative and highly motivated students sought ways to be alone, and they were often caught. No one's actions were safe from the telltale eyes and ears of college paper editors; papers reported social mishaps and improprieties almost monthly, especially during the 1870s and early 1880s. Couples' interaction was much more interesting when rules specifically intended to keep the sexes apart. The culture of separation lent a mystery and intrigue to romantic physicality, so forbidden encounters made for wonderful journalistic fodder.

Edna Bullock remembered when the campus proctor, John Green, was told that "a town couple were brazenly disregarding his code of behaviour on the front steps."[49] He marched over to the couple, "berated them roundly, flashed his policeman's star and started to the police station with them." Arresting a couple for public kissing? This scenario reveals the extent to which land-grant administrators sought to keep young students from breeching codes of propriety. As Green got ready to apprehend the guilty pair, the maiden "artfully executed a flank movement known to the sisterhood throughout the ages as almost certain to work, and began to weep." This strategic move "did not fail her." On seeing her cry, Green "tempered his wrath" and began to comfort the young woman. Just then, a group of university boys, who had been witnessing the event, shined their lanterns in the faces of the couple to reveal "the impish countenances" of two male students. Green refused to speak to the practical jokers "for some days."[50] Had the couple really been male and female, likely they would have received sound chastisement from the university administration, either for curfew violation or for the public display of affection.

Notice how a local editor described one couple, caught kissing while the young lady sat on her beau's lap in a window well: "Time—Sunday. Scene—University Building. Dramatis Personae—Two belles, admiring the campus, etcetera, etcetera, mostly and etcetera." What was the purpose in calling both the man and the woman "belles"? The suggestion was that, in principle, only two women or two men could pair off alone, and yet the humorous reality was that one of the "belles" had a "fine pair of whiskers." Belle no. 2 was "seated in lap of Belle no. 1," and with "spectators highly entertained" watching the action, the couple frantically tried to gain their composure: "Both, evidently alarmed, are frantically trying to keep each other from falling to pieces, while they prudently swap gum."[51] "Swapping gum" was a common slang term for kissing, and the implications suggested that "gum-swapping" kisses were not just simple, closed-mouth pecks. One student attended a party and claimed that he "had never *gum-sucked* so much in all his life." The editor replied, "We don't know what that means but we thought something awful was the matter."[52] All feigned ignorance aside, the editor's innuendo was plain. Students were obsessed with physical intimacy—at least to the level of kissing—and newspapers were riddled with comments about students' romantic trysts. One young lady, "upon being kissed, exclaimed, 'Now you just put that back where you got it!'" The story got "around the university" and made its way to the editor's desk.[53] The innuendos at times even hinted at unspoken sexual behavior. One Nebraska junior in 1877 approached a woman with a child in a carriage "for the purpose of petting the little one." As he came near, the child called "Papa, papa!" and the "bashful Junior, aforesaid, broke into a cold sweat, and turned from that sad place, muttering . . . such expressions as 'mistaken identity,' 'black mail,' etc."[54]

In a culture that restricted contact between the sexes, students found ways to negotiate new opportunities for physical touch. And college newspapers were always right there to report. In October 1876 the editor complained that "ye local observed one of the students with his arm lovingly twined around one young lady's waist the other day. They may be used to that sort of thing, but such proceedings are not to be tolerated by a free and independent people."[55] The commentaries of editors regarding physical interaction served as symbolic outlets for many of the sexual tensions that existed in the land-grant culture. Although administrations tried to restrict students' physical interaction, the students nevertheless obsessed with romantic contact, and it was written all over the pages. One night after a social, a couple passed the cloakroom and the gentleman "suggested that an overcoat might feel quite comfortable. 'Yes,' she said. 'I believe that I should feel better if I had a pair of sleeves around my shoulders.'"[56]

Within the bounds of appropriate contact, men and women often negotiated the occasions for physical contact to their advantage. If it was proper to take a boy's arm, then it seemed that students were always arm-in-arm. The IAC *Aurora* complained about the overuse of arm-linking: Some couples, said the editor, "get so 'spoony' as to make it exasperatingly unpleasant for all beholders." It is "sickening" to see a couple, "*every* time . . . they come to a place where the elevation exceeds one inch to ten miles, to help the other part of the couple over the elevation?"[57] Imagine the ridiculous scene, where men rushed to grab a woman's arm every time they came to the smallest hill, incline, stairs, or puddle. Women did not object to this help; they freely offered up their arms for the taking. And the reactions of those who witnessed this physical interplay? "It may be handy, but it's tiresome."[58] In 1897 the editor of the Iowa State *Bomb* joked that "the young ladies' arms are used as handles by which the young men convey them from place to place, and don't be afraid to lift too hard on the handle in taking a lady up the steps; it won't break off because it is used to it."[59] For its part the *Hesperian* reported that "the girls any more do not like to go unarmed. The young fellows will see to it that they have arms about them hereafter."[60] If one looks at arm taking through a lens of women's dependency, the practice might seem deferential to male chivalric dominance; but when looking at the practice as just one method that both sexes used to negotiate physical contact, the picture changes. Men and women together sought to maneuver the possibilities for physical touch within the culture of separation.

Sometimes the physical contact between the sexes was not directly observed, but editors loved to insinuate intimate exchanges by showing physical evidence left behind to prove such interactions. There were signs everywhere: objects such as hairpins, hairs, and cigar stubs were left in places (or on people!) around campus; these served as unspoken representations of intimate contact. A misplaced hairpin suggested the loosening of propriety, or that bodily containment had been breached. A woman's hairpin found in a man's pocket or a hair found on his jacket implied that a man had gotten close enough to a woman's bodily space for her to leave part of herself on him. In September 1874 the *Hesperian* editors warned that "young ladies should not get their heads so near young gentlemen's neckties, we saw a hairpin in a sophomore's vest pocket." And perhaps there was a nosy attempt to catch the guilty party: "The owner can have the same by calling at the student office."[61]

A woman's hair, as an extension of the female body, caused quite a stir in a male environment: "A Senior came from the kitchen to the University with a long hair clinging to his shoulder." Note that he had come "from the kitchen," thus departing a feminine place with evidence of contact with a woman. The hair "was the object of much attention and concern. It was quite a problem for the boys to solve."[62] A misplaced hair or hairpin also suggested the loosening of physical controls that kept women appropriately contained. And later, "A lock of braided hair was found in our sanctum a few days ago. Our devil fails to explain, thus casting a shadow and gloom over our once happy and tranquil office. Any information on the matter will be thankfully received by our editor."[63] The fun for students was imagining how a woman's hair got into a man's space. Not only did these reports heighten the sexual tension in a culture of restricted physical contact, but they also fulfilled the student readership's desires for vicarious romantic experiences.

Men left behind their own evidence of romance. Why else would a paper report that a cigar stub had been discovered in the ladies' closet, except to show that a male student had dared to venture into forbidden female space? A cigar might represent a romantic tryst at a gate or front door. After one student had said goodnight to her beau, the house chaperone said, "Maria! What's that strange noise at the front gate?" She responded, "Cats, sir." And the chaperone: "Cats? Well! When I was young, cats didn't wear stove pipe hats and smoke cigars!"[64]

Perhaps the most unique male object employed to maneuver opportunities for male-female sociality was a toothpick. An Iowa State *Bomb* editor described male students' artful use of after-dinner toothpicks as social diversions to secure the company of women. In an imaginary letter to a boyfriend in New York City, one fictitious IAC woman student described the importance of toothpick culture: "If you haven't cultivated a taste for toothpicks you must do so or be out of style here. . . . They form the last and a very important course of every meal. We have nice soft ones and devote the last half of the dinner hour to them."[65] These toothpicks provided a way for men and women to stay together in mixed sociality after dinner. Instead of the men separating into a different room for male conversation, smoking, or a drink, the toothpick ritual kept the sexes together in an activity that both could share. Toothpicks were "far better than an after-dinner smoke because the ladies and gentlemen can partake of them in company."[66] Then, while sitting together after dinner, "the toothpicks are passed and enjoyed at the table, [and] just before leaving the table the toothpicks are again passed and the company repairs to the entry to enjoy this second supply." Over a toothpick, students conversed, joked, and even tried "the recreation of shooting toothpicks, in which great skill is often shown."[67] Students worked on their toothpicks as long as possible to delay the end of after-dinner socialization. The Iowa woman marveled at "how many associations dear to our hearts cluster around 'The dear little toothpick, / The soft little toothpick, / The bent little toothpick, / That lies in the hall.'"

Thus, like the toothpick debris that lay in a jumbled, mixed pile on the floor, so also students managed to mix the sexes in ways that encouraged a maximum of appropriate sociality and touch. Toothpicks, hairpins, arms, and cigar stubs—these objects represented students' attempts to maneuver their own sociability, intimacy, and needs for contact with the opposite sex.

MASHING AND SPOONING: PHYSICAL INTIMACY
IN THE 1890S AND BEYOND

By the 1890s, standards of physical contact between the sexes had begun to loosen significantly. The 1870s journalistic innuendoes regarding
clandestine contact between the sexes were nearly absent by this time;
certainly the culture of separation that marked early land-grant culture had
relaxed significantly in the 1890s. Even those activities considered "covert"
in the 1870s—objectionable behaviors such as kissing, pairing off, or dancing—became "overt" and even accepted in the 1890s. The policy changes
of land-grant administrators were an important factor in this evolution. For
instance, the 1870s rules that forbade dancing, public coupling, and even
speaking between the sexes had been rescinded by the late 1880s. With
the removal of these regulations, officials encouraged a greater freedom of
interaction. For example, at the University of Nebraska in the 1890s, the
"two parallel planks . . . were so far apart that a young lady could not take
the arm of her escort nor could he reach hers."[68] Chancellor James Canfield
was disturbed because "the ranks of the 'solid couples' on the campus
were being depleted." He decided to have the plank sidewalks replaced
with boardwalks, and also installed benches, to give couples more places
for sitting down together. The "bench work," as it became known, was a
popular activity among students, and the "benches sagged to the elastic
limit of oak, and finally had to be removed."[69] This image contrasts with
the strictly chaperoned campuses of the 1870s and 1880s, where couples
paired off only under the scrutiny of university officials.

Land-grant campuses were important laboratories for social and sexual
change between 1870 and 1900. According to Beth Bailey, a sexual revolution
was more of an evolution than a true revolution; gradually, over the course
of three decades, the land-grant campuses accepted a greater liberality of
student social interaction. Just as Bailey has described the sexual revolution
of the 1960s as "develop[ing] within the protected space and intensified
atmosphere of the college campus," so also the coeducational land-grant
environments were perfect laboratories for the chipping away at Victorian
structural controls.[70] This process seemed to culminate in the 1890s.

John Higham described the importance of the 1890s as a climax in
the development of a distinct American collegiate culture that included

loosening social boundaries for women. Prior to the 1890s, American colleges had experienced their formative period when "the great reconstruction of American higher education had already occurred," but "in the nineties the structure of the modern university solidified."[71] Universities acquired more financial resources, erected more buildings, added specialized programs, hired more faculty, and enrolled more students. Because of new institutional structures and increased populations of students, "the life of the undergraduate now acquired its own glamour and took on a significance quite distinct from the official goals of the institution."[72] Students felt free to grow their own culture, complete with athletics, music, romps, pep rallies, socials, and dances. To Higham, "it was in a college setting about the end of the nineteenth century that the model of a youth culture came into being."[73]

During James Canfield's Nebraska administration in the 1890s, a group of women students decided to do away with the formal tradition of women needing escorts to attend any activities. The "G.O.I." or "Go Out Independents" had the support of the chancellor "who was always forward-looking and anxious to promote the welfare of the girl students." The G.O.I. "demonstrated that girls could attend football games, evening lectures, society programs, and other public functions, without . . . individual escorts." These changing social behaviors in the 1890s looked forward to the years just before World War I, when "college girls seem to feel free to go anywhere or to do anything, whether singly or in groups."[74] This new collegiate youth culture also meant a more liberal sociality between the sexes. Bicycle clubs, team sports, hiking, photography clubs, and dancing allowed for greater freedom of movement, expression, and unsupervised sociality, even into spaces outside of the campus boundaries. One photo of Nebraska students in 1898 shows women perched on the bicycle bar, leaning cozily against the male drivers. Students usually began an outing dressed appropriately, but by the end of a long excursion, they might end up with hats and shoes off, lounging under trees or picnicking in a field. Indeed, cycling was creating greater freedom of physical contact and familiarity among students. This caused fear among traditionalists who criticized the expanding sociality among young people, and yet the force was unstoppable.

Ralph Mueller in 1928 remembered back to his social experiences at Nebraska in the 1890s: "The terms petting, necking, and joy-riding had

5. Student bicyclists at the University of Nebraska, ca. 1898. Adelloyd (Whiting) Williams Collection, Archives & Special Collections, University of Nebraska–Lincoln Libraries.

not come into existence, but bench work, spooning, and buggy riding perhaps answered nature's purposes just as well."[75] Spooning, as he used it here, meant to snuggle or "nestle against one another spoon fashion, as to keep warm."[76] Students coupled and expressed affection more openly than they had in earlier decades. Larger numbers of students were harder for the universities to chaperone, thus making unsupervised pairing more possible. Whereas in the 1870s and 1880s dancing had been prohibited, by the 1890s "rag-time was the forerunner of modern jazz. Coon songs [as they were derisively called] and cake-walks were in vogue."[77] Students danced, played, performed minstrel shows and theatricals, and held talent contests. Beyond that, clubs, groups, organizations, and university-sponsored social activities gave students more avenues toward sociality. Group interaction occurred at football games, dances, socials, pep rallies, clubs, and the ever-present literary societies. Organized male team sports provided men and women students a centralized focus around which to celebrate and socialize together. Fans cheered at games and devotedly followed athletic activities. Women's campus organizations quickly assumed the frivolities of the football culture, and by 1900 the women's clubs, sororities, and literary societies sometimes spent more time holding socials and pep rallies for football players than they did debating political issues or reciting Burns and Longfellow.

Students even formally institutionalized their desires for socialization. In 1895 a group of male and female students at IAC formed the "Mashemology Club" for the purpose of coupling members of the opposite sex. "Mashing" meant the act of open flirting, and by the 1890s, a "mash" was "a man [or woman in this case] who makes advances in public places."[78] According to the club's constitution, "the object of this society shall be to mash the opposite sex." An "active member" included "any student at I.A.C. who shall have successfully 'mashed' three persons of the opposite sex in succession," whereas an "associate member" included only those "who shall have 'mashed' one person of the opposite sex and got no further."[79] That by the mid-1890s students openly practiced "mashing" suggests a new openness of gendered interchange between the sexes. For members of the Mashemology Club, the duties were explicit: "In bad weather to sit on the radiators, occupy the parlor and talk loudly in the halls; and in fine weather to stroll over the campus in couples, and to go to chapel likewise in couples, and at all times to flirt in the library." Male students certainly did not have a monopoly on mashing; the charter members of IAC's Mashemology Club included twelve women and fourteen men. For club activities, a "quorum" was defined as "any two members of opposite sex" who met "to transact regular business."[80]

The standards of acceptable social contact and physical interaction had relaxed even further by the first years after 1900. The term *date* emerged to signify any couple who paired off by themselves for an evening's unchaperoned social activity.[81] Because of increased physicality, the Nebraska dean of women "was growing haggard and gray, breaking up parties on campus benches where the young man's wooing was getting too *handgrieflich*, as the Germans say—too 'handgrabbish.'"[82] Students associated more freely and openly expressed more physical affection. Max Cohn, a student at UAC around 1900, kept a photographic record of his group of friends, who spent much of their free time hiking, picnicking in Logan Canyon, and playing games in the reception room of the women's dorm. One photograph, taken in the women's hall reception area, shows a comfortable presence between friends of the opposite sex. Men and women lean on each other, hold hands, have their arms around each other's waists, and touch knees and faces. This

6. Male and female students socializing, ca. 1900. Maxwell Cohn Collection, Album no. 2, Special Collections & Archives, Merrill Library, Utah State University.

public evidence of more liberal physical contact suggests that even greater sexual freedom occurred in private, for as Bailey has shown regarding the 1960s, "the myriad of rules . . . did not prevent sexual relations between students so much as they structured the times and places and ways that students could have sexual contact."[83]

CHALLENGING THE FINAL BOUNDARY: SEXUAL ACTIVITY

It is difficult to determine the extent of premarital sexual activity that occurred at land-grant colleges in the late nineteenth and early twentieth centuries, but opportunities certainly existed. Some unsupervised couples likely took advantage of private coupling and the physical games of spooning and mashing that led to sexual experimentation. A few examples portray the expanded sexual freedom among land-grant students. One UAC student, Almeda Perry, had enrolled at the college in 1897 to get over her former fiancé, Snell Johnson, who had given her up to marry another woman. At UAC Almeda maintained an active social and intellectual life and dated many young men. One beau she had met at Provo's Brigham Young University even proposed marriage, but Almeda "was still carrying the torch for Snell and could consider no one else."[84] Her dates usually occurred in group settings, and with no recorded impropriety. She soon had an opportunity, however, to bend the standards of proper social behavior.

Almeda spent the summer before her graduation with her family. While at home, Snell's sister, Pearl, invited Almeda for a buggy drive. Thinking this was a harmless renewal of an old friendship, she agreed. When they arrived at the Johnsons' home, Pearl got out and then a "man, Snell, I knew by his walk, came out from a shadow of a tree and approached the buggy."[85] Almeda tried to follow Pearl out of the buggy, but Snell "held my arm and said, 'Please, I want to talk to you.' 'There's nothing to talk about between you and me,' I said. He still held my arm and again said, 'Please.' I sat back and he got in beside me." Almeda continued: "For a while he drove in silence, then driving to the roadside and dropping the reins, turned, gathered me into his arms, pressing his lips on mine." For a moment, Almeda forgot that she was kissing a married man: "The years fell away and I felt again the rapture of his embrace, but only for an instant, then I awoke to shocked reality."[86] She pushed him away and reminded him that he had just "wanted to talk." Snell then begged Almeda to take him back; he "was ready to make a move himself after which he hoped he and I could take up where we had left off." Almeda rejected his invitation:

> I felt nothing now but shock. I told him even if he were free, which he never could be until his last child was grown and on his own, that which had been beautiful for us at one time could never exist for us again. He argued and pleaded, even threatened to ride his horse off a cliff, but to no avail. To me he had become just a phony, probably playing a part even now. I became tired, mentally, emotionally, and physically, and begged him to take me home. We drove in silence until we reached my home then he made one last plea. I could only say good night.[87]

Had she been willing, Almeda's meeting with Snell could have led to a sexual encounter. A few years after that, Almeda learned that Snell had divorced his wife.

For Almeda, even though she was a Mormon, polygamy was not a viable or legal option in 1900. Plural marriage had been outlawed in Utah since

1890, and even though some Mormons continued to practice polygamy, new plural marriages were illegal. Polygamy as a nonconforming sexual practice still had a marked impact on Utah and the land-grant culture by the end of the century. In 1899 UAC's president, James Tanner, was forced to resign his position, "on account of his being a polygamist." Alberta (Bertie) Larsen recorded the event in her diary on February 20, 1900, while a student at UAC.[88] To the UAC students, this was a significant and controversial event. Tanner was well liked and popular, and his forced resignation caused quite a stir of sympathy on his behalf. Interestingly, Bertie had recorded two separate occasions in January of 1899 in which "Pres. Tanner took all of we Club House girls for a nice sleigh-ride." One might look at Tanner's outings with female students as potential courting activities, especially since his fifth and last wife was a 1903 graduate of UAC, Lydia Holmgren, who had been a student and instructor during Tanner's tenure.

That Tanner's actions were not completely rejected by the whole UAC population showed how closely the mainly Mormon students still held polygamy as part of their shared cultural experience. According to Bob Parson, "Tanner's difficulties did not necessarily stem from his refusal to abide by the Manifesto. Utah political and religious leaders largely overlooked that. Congress, however, objected to the continuation of the practice in Utah and . . . voted to withhold all federal appropriations from the college until Utah provided proof that no polygamists were employed at the campus. The issue forced Tanner's resignation."[89]

In the same entry that Bertie Larsen had recorded President Tanner's resignation, she also noted that B. H. Roberts, the famous Mormon historian and senator-elect from Utah, "in Congress . . . was refused a seat because of his being a polygamist."[90] Any sympathy she might have felt for either Tanner or Roberts was disguised in her matter-of-fact reporting of the events. But for many Mormons, the feelings of shared persecution were still very close; threats against their culture from the outside world created a collective attitude of defensiveness.

To other land-grant students in the West, polygamy was a repulsive and degrading practice; indeed, literary societies at Nebraska, IAC, and OAC often debated the threat of Mormonism, with some societies resolving to enact plans to save oppressed Mormon women, and others deciding to completely abolish the religion. Polygamy as an aberrant and even deviant sexual practice had a different impact on different land-grant environments. William J. Kerr, who succeeded Tanner as UAC's president in 1900, also had entered into plural marriage, but he and his second wife legally divorced before he became president. He later resigned from UAC, for reasons not related to polygamy, and in 1909 he took a professorial position at OAC.[91]

Another extreme case of premarital sexual activity occurred in Corvallis, Oregon, between 1903 and 1906. In 1903 a charismatic religious leader, Franz Edmund Creffield, or "Joshua," arrived in Corvallis, claiming to be a second Christ. Creffield recruited mostly single women to join the "Bride of Christ Church," and he required them to wear their hair long and loose. A few of the women followers later claimed to have had sexual relations with Creffield. As many as thirty women may have followed Creffield, including one OAC student, Sophie Hartley, who dropped out of college to join "Joshua." She cut up her graduation dress with scissors and burned it as a repudiation of college life. In 1906 Creffield was killed by the brother of one of the women followers, and the brother was in turn killed by his own sister as revenge for Creffield's death. Some of the followers ended up committing suicide or spending time in an asylum.[92] The "Bride of Christ" cult in Corvallis was an extreme example of how college-age women might enter into extramarital sexual activities.

Land-grant colleges in the early twentieth century experienced an environment of loosening sexual activity and a greater freedom of sexual awareness. The automobile culture, often attributed to the 1920s by historians, already began to leave its mark on college campuses prior to World War I. Conservative administrators and religionists responded to the new sexual atmosphere with some reactionary fear. As one evangelist warned the Nebraska women in 1915, "Young girl, don't go with that godless, god-forsaken, sneering young man that walks the streets smoking cigarets. . . . Don't go to that dance. . . . I tell you if automobiles and carriages could talk there would be something doing."[93] Attesting to the expanding culture of sexuality, even the women's instructors began to teach sex or "hygiene" courses. Bernice Forest confided to her diary in October of 1916 that "we are having a series of lectures on Sex by Dr. Mabel Ulrich at the girls gym this week. I'm not so awfully crazy about them but as Dean Fawcett says, 'Knowledge means power.' I suppose I should avail myself of this opportunity to gain knowledge."[94]

THE CULTURE OF DATING AND SOCIALITY

For land-grant women between 1900 and World War I, most male-female social activity included group and single dating. While the experiences of Almeda Perry at UAC and the sexual cult in Corvallis certainly speak to the potential for students to have had sexual encounters, most women still maintained social interactions that fit within the prescribed standards of appropriate sociality expected of their class and gender. Most women lived in supervised dormitories or boarding halls, with little chance for sexual encounters, and instead sought traditional forms of courting. The experiences of Alberta (Bertie) Larsen at UAC and Bernice Forest at OAC serve as models for the typical land-grant woman's dating experiences in the early twentieth century.

Bertie Larsen was only fifteen years old when she first arrived at UAC in the fall of 1898. She was likable and popular and had a large circle of friends in her home near Ephraim, Utah. She also soon had the attention of many male and female friends in Logan.[95] At home, Bertie dated one young man, Ern, who called on her three or four times a week. Together they went hiking, berry-picking, and riding, and attended community dances. During one Christmas break, in 1898, she attended six dances in the ten days between Christmas Eve and New Year's Eve. She and Ern also went sleigh-riding, usually with a group or another couple. Only once did they go out alone, after which they went to a dance.[96] Typically her social outings—even when she was escorted by Ern—included many friends and family members, playing games, singing around the piano, and hiking in the canyons during nice weather.

Bertie's UAC social activities paralleled her outings at home. While in Logan, she lived in a boarding house with both male and female boarders, but all activities were strictly chaperoned by the boarding-house matron, "Mrs. Groesbeck." Many young men called on Bertie, and they had to meet her in the sitting room downstairs before they could go out. Sometimes the callers just came to talk, as on October 2, 1898, when "Arthur Tanner and John Standing came and I went down to Mrs. Groesbeck's sitting room and talked to them a while."[97] Two weeks later, Max Cohn, the UAC student photographer, escorted Bertie downtown to a college banquet. After only two months at UAC, and before she had turned sixteen years old on October

18, already four young men had called on her. She attended college balls, dinners, and socials, usually escorted by one of her male suitors. This pattern of sociality continued for Bertie throughout her two years at UAC. She later left UAC to teach school and married on December 17, 1902, in the Salt Lake City Temple.

For Bernice Forest of OAC, the events recorded in her diary in 1916 and 1917 show how early twentieth-century women students felt similar insecurities in their interactions with men as women of any age might experience. The ups and downs of Forest's dating life speak to the timelessness of social relations, especially for any who have ever sought unrequited love or received unwanted love. Bernice had many male and female friends, but one particular student, Al Meiers, courted her while they attended college. Al often escorted Bernice to social events, but she always hoped to meet someone more worthy of her affections. She simply did not like him as much as he liked her. At one college social, Bernice hoped to "meet some one nice," but feared that "I won't get a chance if Al hangs around all evening like he did at the M.E. reception last week."[98] She still went out with him, but her confusion and ambiguity made Al frustrated, because "I wasn't very polite to him when he asked and made some rude remarks on the way home." She felt angry because "I was mad at the way folks talked—and coupled our names."

It was her own fault for continuing to date Al when she did not have feelings for him. He was her most steady partner, and at least he was tolerable, whereas when Eric England began to pay attention to her, she rejected him outright: "I'd die—almost—if I had to go anywhere with him."[99] But others were more appealing. "Mr. Huffman" particularly caught her attention; he was "big, handsome, athletic and jolly. I hope I have a chance to *know* him." Indeed, he was "a *real* man."[100] She enjoyed being with Al, but she often wished that he was someone else: "I'd be a lot more excited however if it was Mr. Hauffman [*sic*]. . . . But it's silly even expecting him to look at me—altho [*sic*] I often wish he would."[101] And when Al accompanied her to church and a party, she pined, "How I wish it had been some one I really liked."

Considering her mixed feelings for Al, who paid the most attention to her, why did she continue to date him? "It's fun to have some one to take me out occassionally [*sic*]."[102] More important, Bernice felt the immense pressure to have a male companion while in college: "I think, — 'oh, what's the use of being so particular — even if he isn't up to your standards he can take you out so you won't be noticeably different from other girls.'"[103] In other words, she would rather be with someone she did not like than to have no male escort at all. She continued to see Al, because "he is nice . . . and has taken me out more than any one else. In fact, I haven't gone with anyone else at all." But throughout all of this dating for convenience and companionship, Bernice continued to have hopes: "I'm not giving up hope for '*the*' one to appear."[104] Bernice was not just seeking romantic love; she was looking for a soul mate. Dating in a western land-grant environment by the turn of the twentieth century gave women more opportunities to join themselves to men with whom they could intellectually and emotionally share life's experiences. The possibilities for companionate marriages at land-grants fulfilled what early educational reformers had hoped for the coeducational experience.

WOMEN'S SOCIALITY WITH OTHER WOMEN

Women's land-grant experiences also included important networks of female friendship and sociality. Because coeducation was a new experiment in the 1870s and because male students outnumbered female students sometimes three to one, women depended on each other for emotional support and commonalities of interest. The culture of separation that ideologically kept men and women apart also helped to nurture female friendship. Women roomed together in boarding houses and dormitories, took domestic science courses together, worked and studied together, and sat together in chapel exercises. Women shared political and social interests in what were deemed feminine issues, such as education, clothing reform, temperance, and suffrage. They also shared course work: because most women by the end of the nineteenth century chose to major in domestic economy, the shared experience of collegiate domesticity helped to further sharpen and define the feminine sphere and sociality at these institutions.

Carroll Smith-Rosenberg has examined the importance of female friendships, because "the female world of varied and yet highly structured relationships appears to have been an essential aspect of American society." Degrees of sociality varied between extremes of "the supportive love of sisters, through the enthusiasms of adolescent girls, to sensual avowals

7. Women students in front of Benton Hall at OAC, ca. 1898. Oregon State University Archives.

of love by mature women."[105] To Smith-Rosenberg, it is not necessary to divide one's understanding of nineteenth-century women's relationships between platonic friendship on the one hand and sensual love on the other. The importance lies in the "world of emotional richness and complexity" in which "devotion to and love of other women became a plausible and socially accepted form of human interaction."[106] Women's friendships flowered in the environments of women's collegiate education, and in the early years of land-grant education, newspaper editors even jokingly chided women students for their gluelike devotion to one another's company. The *Hesperian* teased Nebraska women in 1880 for their constant togetherness: "The Senior ladies now occupy two seats in chapel; we shall not say how many there are in each seat."[107] IAC had to remove the senior women from their upper-floor sleeping rooms because they spent too much time yelling at each other from open windows. The editor doubted that the removal would solve the problem, because "they are so in the habit of chatting with their neighbors, that they will get up a flirtation with the skeletons in the museum."[108]

Women needed strong feminine support networks, especially in a climate of "rigid gender-role differentiation . . . [that lead] to the emotional segregation of men and women."[109] Whatever the extent of that segregation, women always sought networks of feminine socialization. Land-grant women protectively guarded their feminine sphere in the last three decades of the century. All-female literary societies such as the Cliolian Society at IAC ardently maintained their all-female status, even when they had the option of joining mixed societies or, as the Cliolians experienced in 1873, when male students attempted to gain access. Presented with the option to admit males, the Cliolians twice voted to keep men out of their ranks.

Although the land-grants always had mixed-gender organizations — especially literary societies — they also supported many women-only societies. Even in the 1890s when students enjoyed greater freedom of sociality with the opposite sex, women still sought the associations of feminine societies. Both UAC and OAC in the 1890s had at least one major female literary society — in both places called the "Sorosis," or "Sisterhood" in Greek. Almeda Perry assisted with the formal organization of the first Sorosis Society at UAC. Together with three close friends — "Esther Evans, Blanche Cooper and Mattie Stover were most closely associated with me in class work" — Almeda, "with a number of other compatible girls organized a club — forerunner of sororities to come later. . . . Its purposes were to promote sociability and enjoyment of good literature."[110] Women enjoyed the companionship shared with other women, but they also enjoyed the chance to discuss women's issues and experiences in a nonthreatening environment. They expanded their feminine sphere through music, poetry, the decorative arts, and opportunities to act as hostesses for campus social events. A variety of women's groups helped students fulfill greater purposes of political, religious, and social reform and the perpetuation of women's domestic influence. These groups included sororities, literary societies, the Young Women's Christian Association, the Women's Christian Temperance Union, and home economics clubs.

Besides important group socialization, land-grant institutions also fostered individual female friendships, and "within this secure and empathetic world women could share sorrows, anxieties, and joys, confident that other women had experienced similar emotions."[111] Almeda Perry, feeling alone and frightened upon arriving at UAC, remembered the immense relief at meeting her first woman friend: "The second morning I started up the hill a few steps behind another girl; she turned and smiled at me; she was very pretty and her smile was like sunshine, it put heart into me. We walked up the hill together, becoming mutually acquainted as we walked. She was Esther Evans, from Malad, Idaho. Her father was a cattleman in that area."[112]

Two days after meeting, the two friends went to take the entrance examination. Almeda did well up to the arithmetic, when she "found one problem I simply could not solve." Instead of risking failure and nonadmission to the university, she decided to cheat. She looked over at Esther, who "seemed to be having no difficulty." She recalled, "Her papers were so spread out on the desk before her that it was easy to see enough of her solution to enable me to solve the problem." Fortunately, "it was the first, last, and only time I ever cheated in an examination."[113] Sure, she had abused Esther's friendship, and Almeda never said whether Esther had known. But Esther's friendship became the most important of her college career: "It began the day we entered college and lasted as long as she lived."[114] Esther and Almeda helped found the first all-female literary society at Utah State.

Considering the importance of women's homosocial, or same-sex, relationships to the feminine collegiate experience, Smith-Rosenberg warned of the danger of trying to categorize female relationships into either platonic friendship or sensual love. Women's relationships were much more complex. Indeed, the fact that women's friendships sometimes became physically affectionate should not evoke too much shock, because "such deeply felt same-sex friendships were casually accepted in American society."[115] Kissing, hugging, dancing, and sleeping in the same bed were common physical expressions of female friendship and love. Two of Bertie Larsen's best friends spent the night in her room at the Club House, and the three shared a bed. Bertie's friends wrote in her diary of the experience. Said Edna: "I guess that I had better . . . go to my repose. If repose it will be for three of us are going to sleep in one bed. Bertie in the middle and Susie and I on each side." And Susie: "Edna has given her views on the subject and now I think I shall have mine. Edna and Bertie have gotten in bed and Bertie broke the bed when she got in and Edna has all the covers on her side. It is now ten minutes to three, we have put hair polish on our hair and in the early evening we danced the hours away."[116]

Bernice Forest at OAC had a large circle of both male and female friends, and sometimes expressed her preference for dancing with women. As a freshman, Bernice disapproved of dancing: "I couldn't conscienciously [*sic*] do it as a member of the M.E. church when they disapproved [*sic*] of dancing." Her attitudes changed when her church's did: "Since then they have taken a broader view of it and do not prohibit dancing. Miss Frances dances and I can't see as she is hurt any, nor does any one think any the less of her."[117] Bernice Larsen at UAC also expressed her preference for dancing with women. "I like to dance with the girls here at the Hall but I never did enjoy dancing with the usual run of fellows who always asked me to dance. The good dancers never did ask me."[118] And on another occasion, she went to a dance with Al, because he "insisted on it so strongly that I finally consented to go." In spite of having some nice dancing, still she admitted, "I'm not very wild about it, for somehow I like to dance with girls better than boys. As a rule girls are better dancers than boys, and I'm certain Amy is a better leader than most of those boys I danced with."[119] Bernice's experiences speak to the importance of women's physical and emotional sociality with other women, as these relationships offered intellectual and social support as well as needed physical affection.

SMASHING: WOMEN'S INTENSE FRIENDSHIPS AND HOMOSOCIAL RELATIONSHIPS

While most female friendships fell within the natural expectations of nineteenth-century women's interactions, some homosocial friendships took on a more intense physical and emotional level. Called "smashing," or the pursuit of deep and earnest physical and emotional female companionship, the practice was very common at all-female colleges. In the 1870s and 1880s it was commonly feared as an unnatural result of single-sex education that kept women too closely quartered with other women and without healthy male interaction. Nancy Sahli examined the importance of "smashing" among nineteenth-century students, especially at institutions where women had contact mostly with other women.[120] In response to the women's college "smashes," some reformers expressed great criticism of the practice. Alice Stone Blackwell believed that smashing "damaged the health of girls," because of the "extraordinary habit they have of falling violently in love with each other, and suffering all the pangs of unrequited attachment, desperate jealousy etc. etc., with as much energy as if one of them were a man."[121] Blackwell was shocked at how "smashing" kept girls from studying, sleeping, and functioning as normal students. "I could hardly have believed that the things they told were not exaggerations," she said, especially in the case of one "veteran smasher" who pursued her victim, "captured her, and soon deserted her for someone else; and she used to cry herself to sleep night after night, and wake up with a headache in the morning." A student might lavish her "smash" with candy and presents; students also wrote the "wildest love-letters" to each other. "If the 'smash' is mutual, they monopolize each other and 'spoon' continually, and sleep together and lie awake all night talking instead of going to sleep; and if it isn't mutual, the unrequited one cries herself sick and endures pangs unspeakable."[122]

Critics of sex-segregated education like Blackwell saw "smashing" as a practice leading to unnatural and unhealthy female relationships. Blackwell blamed these practices on the "massing [of] hundreds of nervous young girls together, and shutting them up from the outside world. They are just at the romantic age, they see only each other, and so their sentimentality has no other outlet." At coeducational institutions, smashing was not so common because men and women maintained a more constant and natural interaction. Even Blackwell noticed the difference: "The coeducational colleges don't suffer much from 'smashes.' . . . There are plenty of cases of 'particular friends,' but few or none of 'smashes.'"[123]

Land-grant sources rarely mentioned smashing, and usually did so to report its occurrence at eastern women's colleges. It seemed to them a curious and foreign behavior, especially coming from their perspective as participants in mixed-gender education. However, although smashing was never as commonly noted at coeducational institutions and was mostly associated with the female colleges, it did occur in the coeducational land-grant environment. Women's collegiate friendships spanned a whole spectrum, from superficial acquaintances to deep attachments. For the women students who desired this passionate attachment to another female, their feelings stemmed from loneliness and the need for sympathetic companionship. Smith-Rosenberg has examined this behavior characteristic of some female friendships in college environments, who "assumed an emotional centrality in one another's lives. In their diaries and letters they wrote of the joy and contentment they felt in one another's company, their sense of isolation and despair when apart."[124] Bernice Forest at OAC experienced this type of fervent emotional devotion to her roommate in 1917:

Amy has gone to the practice house to be away for six long weeks. I don't know how I'll get along. I miss her so when she goes home just for a week-end. I don't know why I should miss her so—for she doesn't seem ever to take much notice of me. She comes and goes as she pleases and is lots more confidential with Esther and Katherine than with me. And lately—particularly since that incident a week ago Sabbath night, she has been almost open in her efforts to avoid me. And still I like her—just "*awful*." I can't help it—even tho she doesn't care particularly for me. I'll stand up for her anywhere.[125]

Her feelings seem to parallel other women college students' relationships that grew beyond friendly sociality to the point of intensity, jealousy, and perhaps even physical sensuality. And yet, while harboring an intense "smashing" for her roommate, Bernice also continued to pursue dating activities with her male friends. The complexity and diversity of these relationships experienced by land-grant women students demonstrate how these women sometimes abided by traditional social expectations and sometimes challenged them.

That coeducational land-grant colleges could be environments for homosocial activities among women students demonstrated another venue for women to challenge the prescriptions of their sex. Perhaps the most important land-grant example of a woman student who overtly challenged the expectations of femininity and heterosexual behavior is famed author Willa Cather. Historians have long debated the importance of Cather's homosocial friendships with other women and the probability of her lesbianism. Before she even came to the University of Nebraska in 1891, she had already begun to repudiate her femininity in favor of masculine characteristics, although, according to Joan Acocella, "those were the days before such sentiments placed one under suspicion of being a lesbian."[126] Cather cut her hair, dressed like a man, and renamed herself "William Cather, Jr." These qualities foreshadowed her later preference for male characteristics and female friendships while in college and beyond.[127] Sharon O'Brien extensively examined Cather's homosocial life as a student at Nebraska between 1890 and 1895. Cather continued to prefer masculine behavior and dress in college, and her classmates overwhelmingly remembered her for her "rejection of feminine dress and manners."[128] Cather never married

8. Willa Cather at University of Nebraska, 1891. Archives & Special Collections, University of Nebraska–Lincoln Libraries.

but had close relationships with women throughout her life, including with her long-term companion, Edith Lewis, with whom she lived until Cather's death in 1947.

According to O'Brien, much of what defined Cather's later lesbian relationships were her early collegiate friendships with women. Both O'Brien and Frances Kaye have asserted that Cather felt a kind of hatred for her own gender, and in Cather's writings she especially targeted the "feminine traits praised by upholders of the cult of true womanhood."[129] Those feminine traits included maternal domesticity, piety, and purity, and even women's sociality. Cather often criticized the fraternities and sororities on campus because of their elitist tendencies, and she especially attacked the sororities because of their intentions of fostering not "female community" but rather "competitiveness for male attention."[130] And according to Kaye, because of Cather's despisal of feminine behavior, "it is virtually inevitable that she would see herself as qualitatively different from other women."[131] Considering her attitudes toward women and her own feeling of "otherness," O'Brien has suggested that her intense female friendships "would have surprised" most who knew her as lonely and detached.[132]

While at Nebraska, Cather began deep and enduring female friendships and even what O'Brien has labeled "romantic" love with Cather's friend and associate, Louise Pound.[133] Willa's friendship with Pound is most notable for an application to understanding Cather's preference for female friendships, and also for her eventual "arrival at a lesbian identity by the 1890s."[134] According to O'Brien, a letter written by Cather to Pound in 1892 revealed Cather's passion for Louise, because, in O'Brien's paraphrase of the letter, Cather "described how strange it felt that she wouldn't be seeing Louise for a while and admitted to being jealous of her other friends (presumably women)." Cather also admitted how unfair it was that "feminine friendship should be unnatural, but she agreed with Miss DePue (a classmate) that it was." One year later, Cather experienced a depression that O'Brien attributed to "her doubts about Pound's love and commitment."[135] And how did Cather's intense feelings for Pound translate to an understanding of female homosocial behavior? To O'Brien, "the range of emotion Cather expresses — jealousy, worshipful admiration, insecurity, self-condemnation, depression — further reveals a turbulent, passionate attachment."[136] Although it remains unproven that Cather and Pound were sexual lovers, both O'Brien and Kaye take it as a given, especially because of Cather's admittance that female friendship was "unnatural," which, as Kaye suggests, "betrayed a self-conscious awareness, shared by her community, that women's friendship constituted a special category not sanctioned by the dominant culture."[137] In other words, Cather knew and understood that her own sexual preference was not accepted in 1890s culture. Whether or not one accepts the claims to Cather's early lesbianism, her feelings toward Louise Pound draw great similarities to the patterns of intense female sociality practiced by other college women in the late nineteenth century.

CONCLUSION

Women's friendships with men and with other women made up an important part of their social experience at land-grant colleges. In spite of some homosocial activities among women students—which probably passed unnoticed in general—the coeducational environment alleviated the fears of many educational reformers. Not only could men and women develop healthy relationships leading to companionate marriages, but also women students would not suffer the dangers of overly obsessive female attachments. By going to college with men, women earned a daily and realistic respect that was afforded an educated companion-wife. Whether or not these social ideals saw fulfillment in the mixed-gender education is debatable, but the promise of coeducation offered a sexual and social balance that gained wider acceptance in early-twentieth-century America.

To those who favored the formation of companionate marriages, co-education was indeed more desirable than gender segregation. Carroll Smith-Rosenberg saw a tendency of some women to look at men as the "other" or an "out group." Because men were "segregated into different schools, supported by their own male network of friends and kin, socialized to different behavior, and coached to proper formality in courtship behavior," those differences added greater distance between the separate spheres of young men and women. "As a consequence, relations between young women and men frequently lacked the spontaneity and emotional intimacy that characterized the young girls' ties to one another."[138] To an extent this was certainly true at land-grant colleges because of the culture of separation, which encouraged proper behavior; formalized courting rituals; and separate course work that kept women in their domestic sphere. But Smith-Rosenberg's conclusions negate some important differences for men's and women's experiences at coeducational land-grants.

Land-grants managed successfully to temper the ideological separation of men and women by allowing structured levels of gender interaction that heightened men's and women's awareness and regard for each other. Women students cherished their friendships with both men and other women; together they developed in a social network that promoted a vibrant mixed-gender sociality, as well as same-gender networks. In their diaries, Bertie Larsen at UAC and Bernice Forest at OAC mentioned almost as many male friends as female friends, and the spontaneity of their male inter-actions certainly matched that of their female relations. Many nineteenth-century young women, upon marrying, faced a "traumatic removal" from their mother's sphere when they moved directly to their husband's home. Thus, for women who came from a background of strict sexual segrega-tion, "marriage represented a major problem in adjustment."[139] Land-grant environments offered women an alternative and more positive transition from their mother's world to the married world. These colleges fulfilled the desires of educational reformers to provide a balanced social climate in which men and women developed a natural and healthy attraction for each other. Elizabeth Cady Stanton added her voice to those who sup-ported coeducation because it lessened the sexual mysteries: "If the sexes were educated together, we should have the healthy, moral and intellectual stimulus of sex . . . , without the undue excitement of senses that results from novelty in . . . isolation."[140] Land-grant colleges and universities were not simply male worlds with females invited along for the ride; they were worlds where mutual sociability was encouraged and companionate mar-riage was the inevitable and desirable result.

5

Women's Course Work

Farm Wives, Finished Ladies, or Functioning Scientists?

A few weeks of making little seams, hems, and patches, and of washing and ironing clothes . . . , I decided I was not getting my money's worth.

ALMEDA PERRY BROWN, *Memories*

The land-grant experience saw the emergence of an institutionalized form of gender separation through the new domestic science course of study. Also called domestic economy or household economics, this movement in the nineteenth century sought to train women in their separate sphere to be more efficient and productive in the home arts such as cooking and sewing. Domestic economy education for women had been preached as early as 1841 by Catherine Beecher, but the movement had gained slow acceptance. The culture of middle- and upper-class gentility saw housework as the occupation of domestic servants, not refined women, for whom domestic economy was not important as an educational course. Even those who supported coeducation often strongly opposed a female education that was based in the home arts. A shift in this feeling came with the foundation of land-grant education, where domestic economy gained acceptance as legitimate and valid course work for college women. Even with this new direction, some land-grants still felt confusion about a so-called women's course and balked at the idea of domestic training. So the development of land-grant women's course work between 1870 and 1920 demonstrates that while men and women students experienced greater inclusion through shared scientific course work, the emergence of domestic science course work also reinforced a separate sphere for land-grant women. A few women would later challenge this traditional

143

expectation by pursuing gender-neutral courses in pharmacology, law, and commercial studies.

A complete history of women's course work at land-grant colleges and universities would require a book-length examination. That is not possible here, but this chapter will consider several areas unique to women's experiences in land-grant course work. First, as the land-grants mapped out their educational scope, a conflict emerged between classical education and practical instruction, an uneasy marriage required by the Morrill Act. From this conflict came the movement for the first domestic economy programs at land-grants. Besides validating the professional tone of women's work, domestic economy course work also reinforced the culture of gender separation. Next, the separation of women through domestic science study was also linked to class expectations. In theory, these programs sought to train farm wives. However, land-grants struggled to define students as potential farm wives or as upper-class, refined women. The courses for women often reflected this ambiguity. Other developments directly fostered the growth of a separate women's course work: first, domestic economy programs began to specialize, and second, other career opportunities opened for women. The last area of emphasis for this chapter looks at the impact of land-grant education in preparing a new class of scientific women. A more inclusive role for "women as scientists" emerged from land-grant culture in fields such as botany, biology, and chemistry; these also left their important marks on women's educational environment.

COURSE WORK FOR WOMEN: THE EARLY BEGINNINGS

Although often seen by feminist scholars as the reinforcement of traditional female gender roles, some nineteenth-century women's reformers saw domestic economy as an important step in women's educational progress.[1] It validated the work that women had been doing for centuries as something worthy of scientific training, professional education, and salaried pay. It recognized the right of women, especially single and widowed women, to be able to work for their self-support, even if that work was an extension of the domestic sphere.

In spite of criticism from elitist educators who disagreed with domestic economy education on a collegiate level, a few land-grant colleges pioneered the earliest domestic economy programs for women. Kansas State

Agricultural College in 1873 and Iowa Agricultural College in 1875 initiated early domestic economy education, and other land-grant universities followed with programs established later in the century.[2] Certain factors converged to promote the introduction of this course of study. First, the land-grant mission itself encouraged the training of "scientific farm wives," or women who had the scientific and technological knowledge to bring efficiency and economy to the farm home. The Morrill Act of 1862 specifically sought the scientific and practical instruction of the industrial and agricultural classes, and women students immediately found a niche within this educational spectrum. Coeducation fostered the development of women's separate course work. Promoters of coeducation believed that since life was a joint venture for men and women, then the collegiate educational experience should also reflect the "social interdependence" of the sexes. According to Thomas Woody, "since men and women must live together, they should therefore be educated together. . . . Education must approximate the conditions of life; and this obtains only under a system of coeducation which simulates life."[3] Thus the separate expectations for men's and women's course work in college corresponded with the same pattern in American family life.

The democratic land-grant culture also fueled the criticisms toward upper-class eastern women as a "race of doll-women" — serving only as superficial and decorative ornaments for wealthy husbands. College newspaper commentary between the 1870s and 1890s condemned the frivolous education for so many women and heralded the opportunities for more practical and substantial education offered at land-grants. The influence of land-grant administrators who recognized the importance of women's practical training also helped toward the promotion of domestic science as a valid course. In the 1870s Adonijah and Mary Welch at IAC, and John Anderson at Kansas State Agricultural College were the first to encourage domestic economy curricula. They also fought for the institutional and financial support to get programs moving forward, especially because they believed that the West's environment contributed to the necessity for educated farm women. According to President Anderson in 1875, eastern educators could "'purse their classic lips at the idea of including such topics in a collegiate course,' but they made sense in a Kansas girl's education."[4] In other words, a western land-grant woman needed to know efficient methods of surviving a harsher life in the West without those conveniences and luxuries available to eastern women.

In a poem written for the IAC opening in 1869, "The Ideal Farmer and His Wife," Prof. H. H. Parker heralded a romantic notion of a farmer and his wife, who worked side by side to glean the most plentiful bounty from their land. With this ideal, he foresaw the emergence of the scientifically trained housewife, who brought comfort, efficiency, and culture to her home:

> But who the happy change may guess
> When women takes her proud B.S.?
> Smile not! She *is* in nature's plan
> Chemist and doctor to every man.
> ... O'er all her daily toil
> Science shall pour its wine and oil
> ... This and religion are the wine
> Shall make her lowly life divine.[5]

This poem captured the new mission for land-grant universities — to educate scientific farm wives. Women students overwhelmingly chose domestic economy training by enrolling in these courses and encouraging their acceptance by other students. As young women graduated in domestic economy courses, many gained teaching positions at other institutions and thus helped to spread the scientific domestic economy movement in the United States.

In spite of these stated ideals about educating farm wives, many land-grant institutions still struggled to define the scope of women's course work. Caught between the desire for both classical, literary education and scientific training, land-grants grappled to outline the range and purpose of women's education. From these discussions came the first vocal support for the practical training of women students, because while women should prepare for marriage and domesticity, they should also prepare for self-supporting careers in domestic-related fields as seamstresses, dressmakers, milliners, and boarding-house matrons.

Pres. Adonijah S. Welch at IAC very early articulated this need for practical women's education. He believed that although the sexes could receive the same scientific education, the reality of difference and separation for women came in the practical application of that background for women's separate domestic sphere. In 1868 the incumbent president outlined his plan to admit young women into all university studies, but with focused attention on their "special needs."[6] He saw the need for a specialized course of study for women, but there was no plan of action until his wife, Mary Welch, helped him to see the possibilities for feminine education. In a dinner conversation in the early 1870s, Mrs. Welch expressed the need for women to have practical training for their own economic support. One might imagine this conversation as it was recorded in Mary's personal papers:

"Why not teach the ladies as you do the men, some of the industries that directly concern them as women?" she asked.

"How can we?" he replied. "If we try to teach cooking and kindred industries they will rebel. They will say that this is not what they came to college for, that they do not expect to go into domestic service. They hope that when they marry they can afford to hire the work done."

She responded, "Do you expect all the boys who graduate from the agricultural courses to work as farm hands or even to take up farming as their life work?"

"Of course not," said President Welch.

"Then why do the men not protest because of the manual practice that is required of them?"

And in President Welch's response came the answer to his own dilemma of women's practical education, at least for Iowa State in the 1870s: "Because they realize that skill in any direction is a valuable part of training, and a marketable commodity as well, and they need the allied sciences to prepare them for any scientific pursuits."

"Just what are these allied sciences?" asked his wife, expecting certain obvious answers.

"Chemistry, botany, physiology, geology, physics."

"Are they not also allied to domestic economy?" asked Mrs. Welch.

"Yes, but . . ."

"Give me no but's for an answer. Let's present the matter to the Board of Trustees at their next meeting and see if something can't be done about it."[7]

9. Mary Beaumont Welch, ca. 1890s. Iowa State University Library/Special Collections Department.

In 1871, influenced by Adonijah and Mary Welch, the Iowa State Board of Trustees accepted a plan for a separate women's course, which in the beginning simply meant that males and females took the same scientific courses together but applied them to their different spheres in a few applied classes. For instance, the 1880 IAC catalog described a "Course in Sciences Related to the Industries" for both male and female students: "As this course is taken by students of both sexes it is given a considerable degree of flexibility to meet the wants of each." But already the IAC allowed for a gender separation in "additional studies" whereby "the course provides for the young women of the college opportunities for devoting more time to Domestic Economy and kindred subjects."[8] Thus, early land-grant education in domestic science began with offering the same sciences to both men and women students, with a few sex-specific courses gradually developing over time through the 1870s and 1880s. Mary Welch foresaw the wonderful possibilities of this training for women. If the institution graduated young women who could efficiently manage a home, "it will do a grand work for the world." She imagined the reaction when women graduates returned home. "You should each go home and astonish your Mother by saying . . . 'You shall rest, Mother dear, and I will show you what a sound, sensible practical education the Iowa Agricultural College gives earnest young women.'" Welch expected that support for the domestic economy program would increase, donations would come rolling in, and the legislature would continue to expand the college. "[A] cry would come up to us from all the mothers in our state, 'Take my daughter, and mine, and mine!'"[9]

From these ideological roots, and with good leadership, domestic science began at land-grant colleges. At first the training included lectures in basic sewing, cooking, water storage, ventilation, horticulture, training of children, and care of the sick. In the beginning resources were scarce, and instructors lacked textbooks and kitchen or sewing equipment to get programs started. As domestic economy programs expanded through the end of the century, however, land-grants established majors in domestic economy, and by the 1890s, women could earn master's degrees in domestic economy at some universities, and classes became more specialized into distinct areas of focus. Students were not offered classes in just sewing or cooking; instead, a sewing emphasis meant specific classes in cutting, pattern-making, and specialties such as men's suits and women's dresses. Cooking students took courses devoted specifically to nutrition and chemistry, the preparation of meats, desserts, fruits, salads, preparation of seafood and specialty ingredients, and later, how to run kitchens for profit. After Oregon State organized its forestry department in the early 1900s, the domestic economy department offered a class in 1910 called "Cooking for Foresters," with instruction in survival eating, cooking over the campfire, and recipes for male forestry students![10] Although men might cross gender boundaries to take a course or two in practical cooking or sewing, domestic economy continued to be a predominately female course of study during the land-grant experience.

10. OAC domestic science class, ca. 1905. Oregon State University Archives.

Besides training women to be future homemakers, domestic economy assisted women graduates who wished to be self-supporting in professional trades such as dressmaking, millinery, and hostelry management. Both President Welch and President Anderson had suggested the importance of training women, especially those "who wish to fit themselves, either for earning an honorable support, or for wisely filling any position in womanly life, as the unknown future may indicate."[11] Welch even offered the revolutionary notion that not all women desire a domestic life: "Dignified and indispensable as are the domestic duties, who does not know that there are multitudes of women to whom they do not furnish employment, and multitudes more whose intellectual needs they do not fully supply?"[12] Welch felt any woman deserved "provision for her own self-support, by a special preparation, to engage in many suitable employments on a footing equal with man, both as to the skill and the remuneration of the worker."[13] In spite of these supposed opportunities for women's professional education, graduates in the early years usually did *not* enter professional trades after graduation. Most became teachers or housewives and took domestic economy courses with the intent to put them to use in their homes. The implementation of domestic economy brought a new discourse that added professional legitimacy to women's housework. For instance, the IAC alumni reports actually gave the married female graduates the professional title of "Domestic Economist." When questioned about their postgraduate pursuits, women claimed to be "putting their domestic economy into practice." The language in an 1879 class prophecy at IAC made one graduate's future marriage sound much like a professional venture: "Miss McElyea occupies the chair of Domestic Economy in an institution near Ames, of which she claims to be one of the two founders and in the prosperity of which she is accordingly interested."[14]

Domestic economy represented both a physical and an ideological manifestation of the separation of women and men students. It also represented the institutional struggle to define a proper course of study for women in the late nineteenth century. Even as institutions like IAC and Kansas State established separate domestic economy courses for women in the 1870s, other institutions balked at the domestic focus. When President and Mrs. Welch left IAC in 1882, the domestic economy program experienced struggles through the late 1880s. OAC, after more than twenty years of coeducation, hired its first full-time domestic economy instructor in 1889. The University of Nebraska showed the most procrastination of the land-grant universities: after almost forty years of female enrollment, a domestic economy department was finally established in 1908.

For the critics of domestic economy who questioned the training of women in manual labor, what was the alternative? Traditional educators favored instead a general literary and scientific education for women that would prepare them for middle- and upper-class refinement as educated and cultured wives who would marry well and then be able to hire servants to perform domestic labors. However, a literary education did not preclude women from finding professional work, since they could become writers, teachers, or journalists—the latter an increasingly acceptable occupation for women in the late 1800s. Whether women took domestic economy to prepare for domesticity or pursued literary education for teaching and writing, the culture of gender separation was plainly manifested in land-grant women's course work.

GENDER SEPARATION AND CLASS EXPECTATIONS IN COURSE WORK

The conflict between classical education for genteel young women and practical, scientific training in household economy dominated discussions of nineteenth-century women's education. Underlying these conflicts were deep-seated class tensions and the place of women. Middle-class Americans, even those on the lower rung of the economic ladder, shunned the vulgar associations of laboring or immigrant status; thus, for the student sons and daughters of farmers, lawyers, businessmen, teachers, professors, or shopkeepers who attended the land-grant universities, the expectations of refinement were felt equally.

The concept of class, as it is used here, is not meant to suggest homogeneity among all groups who were above the laboring class, nor does it negate the existence of distinct economic and social levels in American society. Sven Beckert has suggested that there were deep distinctions within the so-called American middle class, especially between the bourgeoisie and the lower middle class.[15] For land-grant students, one would expect a stronger affiliation to the lower middle class, especially since that group "worked with their own hands [or] were masters of workshops or small factories." Women who chose millinery, seamstress work, or even farm domesticity could include themselves as part of that definition. Contrarily, a bourgeois did not "dirty his hands or his clothing," and bourgeois women "kept a healthy distance from physical exertion, recruiting a staff of servants to attain . . . cleanliness and orderliness"[16] And yet, even considering these distinctions, people of the middle classes felt similar expectations for genteel behavior. Indeed, "lower-middle-class Americans often strove to appropriate the outward trappings of bourgeois culture."[17] In order to distinguish themselves from other classes, the lower-middle class voluntarily assumed aspects of refinement through "associations that replicated some forms of bourgeois sociability."[18] Although Beckert does not include farmers as part of the lower-middle class, nevertheless the farming class was a significant group that subscribed to the same expectations of cultured behavior and materialism as other middling groups.

Whether from a land-owning farm family or the daughter of a local lawyer, businessman, or professor, every woman student experienced a similar expectation of genteel refinement and proper behavior, including social etiquette, morality, material culture, and education. Because the land-grants sought to rise above the stigma of agriculture and industrial labor, the women students—potential farm wives—often found that course offerings reflected confusion about what was expected of them. Land-grants sought to create women who could efficiently promote a better home and farm economy, but who still brought elegance to their homes. This ambiguity might have led observers to ask: did land-grants expect farm wives or finished ladies?

When women first attended the land-grants, the curriculum in the late 1860s and early 1870s was the same for all students—classics, literature, political philosophy, abstract science, and mathematics—but the different expectations for men and women soon became readily apparent. Whereas men's education could be used in law, business, or politics, women could use their background to become schoolteachers until it was time to marry. When Alice Biddle graduated from Corvallis College (OAC) in 1870 as its first female graduate *and* its first female valedictorian, she had graduated in the classical course. The classical education a woman received represented polished refinement and accomplishment, especially in music, art, literature, and the romance languages. For instance, at OAC in 1869, the basic course work was the same for men and women, with classes in Latin, Greek, algebra, geometry, elocution, classical literature, natural philosophy, plane trigonometry, and mental philosophy, among others. Indeed, the regents made certain to note that "young ladies will be admitted into all the College Classes, and will be entitled to the same honors and diplomas as are conferred upon young gentlemen."[19] Even with this acceptance of women's qualitative equality, still there were different expectations for women: the OAC women were also required to take music, painting, drawing, and ballroom dance techniques. By 1872 the separate "Female Department" had been removed from the catalog, but music, dancing, and painting courses continued to be offered for women. These colleges always set aside budget money for the fine arts, with a majority of students from among the females. These classes suggested a type of genteel finishing that was expected for proper young ladies, and not for rugged farm daughters. But ironically, most land-grant women graduates did *not* become farmers' wives after graduation. Nor did their male colleagues become farmers in large numbers. So the genteel class expectations for women students actually worked well for their futures as wives to professional men—especially engineers, veterinarians, doctors and dentists, lawyers, and professors.

After the introduction of the first domestic economy courses in the 1880s and 1890s, the descriptive discourse surrounding the purposes of domestic

11. First OAC graduating class—Robert M. Veatch, Alice E. Biddle, and James K. P. Currin, ca. 1870. Harriet Moore Collection, Oregon State University Archives.

economy was laden with class-conscious terminology. Of course, domestic science students learned the practical arts of cooking, cleaning, and sewing, but assumed within those activities was a sense of the upper-class expectations of promoting refined culture. Young women trained not only in the domestic arts but also in the arts of civilization: the "language of expectation" for women rang with words like *cultivation, refinement, culture, elevation, morality,* and *purity.* Herein lay a uniting of class and gender, since these were the expectations of women, but specifically certain classes of women as the guardians of morality and culture. It fell to women of elevated status to spread the ideals of American civilization through homemaking, education, and Christianity. Mary Welch showed how women students could fulfill these expectations: "If the Iowa Agricultural College can graduate young ladies with finely cultured minds, with hearts truly refined and womanly, and with a happy home . . . it will do a grand work for the world."[20] The OAC in 1892 suggested a similar connection between cultured refinement in the home and the salvation of American civilization. In "Social Etiquette," women learned "economic habits, cultured taste, and nobility of character . . . which go far to make and to keep the home happy. . . . Upon such homes rest the perpetuity of the Republic."[21]

An expectation of cultured refinement did not mean an unrealistic denial of the rougher circumstances for which many of these young women were destined, according to the land-grant purposes. This was still the western frontier in the 1870s, and many women students would live in an agricultural situation at some point during their lives. Malinda Cleaver (Faville) remembered the quality of life of most early IAC students: "All of us came from homes at least as good as the majority, but they would seem crude now. . . . At that time probably not 5 percent of the homes . . . had bath tubs or any sanitary plumbing."[22] Iowa homes in the 1870s still used cast-iron wood stoves, kerosene lamps, and candles, and were without screened doors or plumbing. Welch certainly did not deny the reality of simple farm living for her students, so she taught them to first seek for healthy drainage, well water, sanitation, and ventilation, before trying to refine their homes. Elegant refinement might be put on hold until a housewife had secured the cleanliness and health of her environment: "The ventilation must be provided for when the walls are going up. Better far dispense with a parlor, with carpets even, and fine furniture for a time, than neglect these. They are vital to your health."[23] She also advised students to spare no expense in having pumps and pipes installed in the house. In the less-than-civilized frontier settings, cleanliness and efficiency were the first steps to obtaining refinement.

Mary Welch recognized that many problems young wives would face stemmed from their frontier, agricultural setting, and yet that was no excuse for not seeking cleanliness and refinement. One of the biggest problems was the "swill pail," which stored food scraps for feeding pigs outside. "I have failed as yet to speak of the unsightly, often disgusting, yet necessary and omnipresent swill pail. I have been trying all my housekeeping days to get rid of it and cannot. We live in the West, we are inclined to be economical, then there is the pig. He is an undeniable, inevitable fact to every western housekeeper." Since the swill pail tended to sit rancid for days in the kitchen, Mrs. Welch suggested that housewives empty it three times a day, rinse it with hot, sudsy water, and scrub it "inside and out at least once a week."[24] After a housewife had made habits of efficient cleanliness, then she could add refining touches to her simple home with plants, furniture, curtains, and carpets. Perhaps the most important representation was the woman herself, for "the art of dressing is a fine art." To Welch, it was not sinful to seek appropriate and tasteful dress. "If she be cultivated, refined, and have the true innate womanly grace and taste that are inborn in many, her dress will evince it all."[25]

That Welch was cognizant of class expectation for young land-grant women is apparent in the courses and instruction she gave. In cooking she taught the simple, practical, and healthy meals required for all families, but she also gave instruction in fine or fancy meals, with more luxurious ingredients such as veal, oysters, and curry. Not likely found on an Iowa farm, these ingredients implied the expectations for IAC women graduates to prepare expensive and elegant meals in certain social situations. All land-grants offered cooking classes that included the art of table dressing, use of fine china, and the preparation of multicourse meals for fancier dining.

At IAC, Welch also taught a course called Managing the Help—suggestive of the fact that many of these young women should someday expect to be mistresses over household servants. Similar expectations were imposed on young Mormon women at UAC, where the students received instructions on "the relations of mistress to maid," or as in 1901–2, lessons in "the duties of mistress and servants."[26] Having at least one servant in the nineteenth century was not a luxury limited only to upper classes. Even middle-class homes could afford to keep help, especially when European immigrant girls or neighboring farm daughters could be hired cheaply. According to Glenda Riley, "Hired girls were particularly in demand during the spring and summer as domestic assistants to farm wives who were harried by such seasonal chores as canning and cooking for threshers." Some families "brought help with them from the East . . . [or] sent servants . . . with newly married daughters to the West as wedding presents."[27] Indeed, many farm wives left the menial tasks of mending and laundering to domestic servants, while saving meal preparation and house organization for themselves. At IAC, when too many women enrolled in domestic science, Mary Welch decided to abolish laundry work and sewing for her students, assuming that these more menial tasks would someday go to hired maids. This freeing of the course load for IAC women left more attention for household management, meal preparation, nutrition, and cooking.[28] It is hard to determine how many land-grant students would eventually employ hired servants, but Riley assessed the numbers of domestic servants in midwestern states in the 1870s to be 21,342 in Indiana and 42,046 in Illinois. In 1870 Kansas had 4,002 domestic servants and Nebraska had 1,285; by 1910 those numbers had reached 11,771 in Kansas and 10,760 in Nebraska.[29] The class expectation for land-grant women was clear. They certainly would not be relegated to a life of slavish farm work; on the contrary, they could expect to live a cultured life, running a proper household and partially dependent on the labor of domestic servants.

By the mid-1890s land-grant colleges began to divide more specifically the domestic science course work, showing how the separation of gender was inextricably linked to class expectations. For instance, in the 1880s many of the land-grants required horticulture classes for both the male agricultural and female domestic science students to learn the "art of budding, grafting, methods of pruning, and caring for flowers, for testing the values of vegetable products and modes of culture."[30] OAC's horticulture programs seemed at time gender inclusive, with men and women together learning the art of tree grafting, for example. The study of plants seemed a useful field for both farmers and their wives, especially for ensuring good production and preventing insect and disease invasions. By the early 1890s a subtle and important separation in this course occurred. Women's horticulture

12. OAC horticulture students with Prof. George Coote, ca. 1900. Oregon State University Archives.

course specifically included floriculture, with an emphasis on small gardens, landscape gardening, planting flowers, and beautifying the yard and home with "decorative plants." The connection between women's role in ornamental landscaping and expectations of gentility was included in catalog discourse. According to the 1890–91 UAC bulletin, horticulture was a "refined field of agriculture, [and thus] warrants the devotion of . . . young women."[31] By 1892 women students at UAC were assigned the management of the college greenhouse plants and flowers, and in 1893 the regents called horticulture a "polite art," which did not demand the hard, physical labor required of men in the agricultural classes.[32] While outdoor gardening was a "source of physical health" and induced women to work in the "open air," still women's floriculture or ornamental gardening did "not necessitate the added drudgery of physical work in the garden any further than pleasure may dictate."[33] Considering the implicit expectations for women regarding different types of work based on class, one might forecast that many female graduates would eventually be able to employ hired gardeners.

Beautifying the home physically and culturally was an important responsibility for genteel women, and land-grants fulfilled this need by offering to women courses in "Belles-Lettres," or "what is known as polite literature, including elocution."[34] Colleges also offered "Aesthetics" or the "science of taste and beauty." In 1896–97 at UAC, this course included "talks on fine china, pictures, furniture, decorations for the home, harmony of colors, taste in dress, and kindred subjects." Even the sewing classes went beyond simple cutting and sewing to include fancy work, or the kinds of needlework pursued by women of leisure, including "Roman cut-work, Spanish laid-work, drawn-work, jeweled embroidery, and modern lace-making."[35]

Music also played a major role in the level of student gentrification. From the 1860s, land-grants offered music, especially in piano and vocal instruction; and women students made up a majority of all land-grant piano students. Piano playing was a necessary pursuit for cultured women in America—indeed, musical skills were an important representation of refinement. The UAC catalog gave the best description of why music helped to promote gentility among students: "Music as a great, perhaps the greatest refiner of human nature is incontestable. Cruelty and brutality, generally the accompaniment of unmelodious races, become rare as the musical feeling grows, and music is a predominant characteristic of refined and gentle nature. Undoubtedly, therefore, music may be made a potent factor in civilization, because the tenderest feelings of men, cultured or uncultured, are awakened by it."[36] Literary societies made piano and vocal performance a requirement of society meetings and exhibitions, and colleges budgeted in order to purchase pianos for the societies and organs for the chapel. Piano and vocal music lessons were always a part of land-grant education, even if students had to pay extra for instruction. Piano lessons were not free, and not even cheap—sometimes as much as twenty dollars a semester for lessons. This depiction portrays young ladies devoting time to pursuits associated with the polite, cultured finishing of eastern women.

Language requirements showed the most striking example of gendered class expectations in course work, especially as land-grants required French instruction for women. In the early 1890s UAC made French one of its first required courses for female students. Men students were expected to take German, because of the scientific knowledge coming from Germany in the late 1800s, which in itself was not abnormal, since most land-grants required

German as part of the agricultural course. Women were encouraged to take French, partly because it was a language used in the domestic arts but more notably because French was "still the diplomatic language of Europe and that of fashionable circles."[37] Utah farm girls taking French to prepare them for "fashionable circles"? Herein lay an important example of ambiguous class expectations in land-grant course work. Until 1894 UAC used this reasoning to justify French as the women's language, but that year the college removed the words "of fashionable circles." Also that year UAC modified its requirements for both men and women to choose between either German or French, with the justification that French was the language of culinary arts and thus appropriate for domestic economy students. Eventually, all students could take either German or French, but the example illustrates the continuing struggle over women's class expectations.

A similar conflict had occurred at the Colorado Agricultural College in the early 1880s. When the regents required a teacher of "music and painting" for young women, and then substituted French for agricultural studies, a university committee of three farmers heartily protested those changes. The committee could not see any "impropriety in farmers [sic] daughters having lectures on Stock breeding or any other subject taught in this College."[38] It recommended that courses in music, art, and language *not* be mandatory for women students, but that they be allowed to take practical agricultural courses. Some educators saw the benefit of educating women in the same farm training that men received. And yet, the expectation was already in place—even if women had the option of agricultural training, it was still implicitly understood that cultural studies were more important. One contemporary chronicler of UAC struggled to make sense of the confusion: "Through all those early catalogs, the write ups of courses for women, seemed—I do not know just how to express it, should I say—torn between training a woman to be a Victorian Lady and a practical housewife."[39] Certainly, they wanted both; land-grant educators felt that one goal was not exclusive of the other. The creation of a new type of woman, one who was practical and hardworking but also culturally refined, added to the uniqueness of the land-grant experience for women. It also represented how the pressures to aspire toward middle-class refinement visibly played out on land-grant campuses.

TECHNOLOGY AND THE CHANGING
EXPECTATIONS FOR WOMEN'S SPHERE

Even with the entrenched domestic expectations for women students, new technology changes played an important role in the evolution of domestic science training. With technological advancements, the farmer's wife of the mid-nineteenth century began to see the erosion of some of her traditional domestic agriculture roles, such as canning food, milking, making butter and cheese, pumping and hauling water, and removing waste. In the 1870s Mary Welch at IAC had offered course instruction in the proper care of well water and the removal of dirty water and other waste from the house. Without modern conveniences of the later century, housewives in 1870 had to perform many of these duties by hand. Of course, some 1870s farm wives might expect to have a hired girl to help with the work, but the simple conditions in the West required most women to perform their own household labor. Malinda Cleaver Faville, an 1879 IAC graduate, remembered that most Iowa homes in the 1870s did not have any sanitary plumbing, refrigeration, or electrical lighting. Further, canned goods were rare: "Canning was done only at home. The homemakers had no screw-top or seal jars, no rubber rings. Their choice was between tin cans and earthen jars. Both kinds of containers were sealed by pouring melted wax into a groove to cover a line where the lid overlapped the jar. They expected mold and were never disappointed. Paraffin was not tried."[40]

Even the land-grant education in the 1870s and 1880s required students to participate in campus "chores" that paralleled similar tasks on farms, including cleaning, carrying water, and removing waste materials. Contrast those simple beginnings to the conditions of most land-grants by the late 1890s, where women's classrooms and buildings were equipped with electric lighting, modern plumbing, furnace or boiler heating, and even modern stoves and sinks. Land-grant students did not have to spend the time changing kerosene, cutting firewood, and drawing water, or even emptying the "swill pail" as their coed sisters of twenty years earlier had done. Some campus buildings were even equipped with telephone lines at the turn of the century. By 1910 women students could expect to have access to modern kitchen advancements, which not only offered them a more technologically savvy domestic education but also took away some of their earlier domestic roles and subsequently freed them up for more leisurely pursuits.

13. "Plumbing 101," ca. 1915; OAC students taking a House Sanitation course in the Home Economics Building (now Milam Hall). Oregon State University Archives.

Female students might graduate with the expectation of marrying a successful farmer and having access to the latest task-simplifying gadgets. While this expectation was mostly true for white female students who were destined for cultural and even economic gentility, some historians have argued that farm women were actually the last to benefit from technological advancements. If a farm family had extra money, that capital most often went to purchase men's labor-saving farm machinery rather than kitchen appliances for the female sphere. Besides the prohibitive cost of kitchen equipment, new technologies were also "slow to be embraced by women who had been socialized by the mystique of domesticity to believe that the old way was the best way."[41] Nevertheless, for land-grant women students, the expectation was clear: someday they would be housewives who possessed the financial means to afford modernities. As a reflection of this important change on domestic life, turn-of-the-century women students often took classes in modern plumbing, electrical heating, and lighting, including the proper care of cellars, drains, sinks, and electrical appliances. Technology helped with the "middling" of America, since household equipment became available to more people. An OAC catalog of 1896–97 admitted the benefits of greater home efficiency and actually listed all classes of women as benefactors of technology, including "farmers' wives, the washer-woman, the cook, the boarding-house keeper, the city missionary, the school teacher, [and] the woman of fashion."[42] In spite of this middling effect, technology still added to the stratification in society, as plumbers and electricians emerged to service those who could afford conveniences.

Perhaps the greatest example of this transition from hands-on farm wife to modern consumer housewife was the evolution of the dairy industry in the late 1800s. This transition also saw women pushed away from the more gender-inclusive and shared farm economy between husbands and wives; as the dairy industry became more mechanized and male-dominated, it eventually excluded women's dairy work. For centuries in European and American cultures, milking the cow was a significant part of the female agricultural sphere. Many women possessively guarded this realm as an extension of the home sphere, but also as a means for bolstering the household income through sales of milk, cheese, and butter. Early land-grant education respected this important part of the female farm domain, and women students were able to take classes in dairying that included instruction in making butter and cheese. At Oregon State in the early 1890s both the male agricultural students and female household economy students could take a course in dairying, including "the Babcock test, rennet tests, and curd tests, and work in the creamery." For the women students, the dairy work was "practically the same" as for the men.[43] Even with the apparent equality in this course, a distinct gender division began to emerge. As farms expanded to include larger herds and better dairy technology, milk production went from small-scale milking to larger, mechanized production for profits. With that shift, women lost their hold on this part of the farm economy, both on the farms and at the institutions that trained them. Male agriculture students took dairying with a focus on large-scale production, whereas the women's course was limited to "home dairying."

Technological developments only widened the gulf in men's and women's dairy production. After 1900, milk production in America increasingly went to the farm-factory system, and land-grant agricultural departments followed that trend by obtaining the machinery to train male students in factory milk production. With the implementation of factory dairy work, butter and cheese production also left the female home sphere. An examination

of the UAC catalogs between 1890 and 1902 shows the gender transition for
dairy work. In 1890 UAC still recognized that "butter and cheese making is a
fine art. . . . The problems involved [in milk production] are very complex
and interesting. Very decided attention will be given to this most important
field of woman's general care." The need for women to master butter making was "never greater than now, wherever butter is made on the farm."[44]
One 1894 UAC graduate, Martha Hoyt, was able to use her dairying skills
in a professional capacity as the creamery manager in Hoytsville, Utah—a
position she still held in 1904. Nevertheless, UAC, like others, recognized that
men were taking over dairying and in 1893-94 suggested that the "young
men of Utah" should focus on butter and cheese making, especially since
"factories are being started and managed by eastern experts on conditions
unfavorable to our interest."[45]

Since national dairy factorization was hurting the local industry, Utah
men needed to be able to compete in that economy. By 1897-98 there was
no listing of "Dairying" under the women's department. Briefly in 1898-99
dairying was again listed under domestic arts, but with a decidedly different characterization for women: "This subject will be treated mainly from
the home dairy standpoint. . . . In cheese-making an understanding will
be given of the best factory methods, but more attention will be bestowed
upon the manufacturing of small cheese, such as could be made up in a
few hours at the home."[46] By 1901-2 "Advanced Dairying" was listed only
as part of the Animal Industry Department, with limited home dairying
offered as an elective for women students. Women still learned about butter and cheese making, but more with the view to basic food preservation
and the nutritional and bacterial properties of milk. The transition from
home dairying to factory production on land-grant campuses paralleled a
similar national occurrence, as women gradually retreated—or were forced
to retreat—from certain parts of the agricultural sphere.

A poem, "The Passing of the Milkmaid," in the 1903 UAC *Student Life,*
aptly portrays the gender change in dairy work in the late nineteenth century; the poem also shows how land-grant students were keenly aware of
this transition as it had occurred in front of them:

But alas! How sadly the flight of times,
Has ruin wrought to the poet's rhyme;

And left us naught to tell today;
Of the dairy maid and her gentle way
For the dairy maid is a dairyman;
With bluejean pants and a big milk can;
And the old milk-house has given way;
To the modern creamery of today;
And the brimming pans no longer cool;
In the babbling stream or the limpid pool;
but the pan of today is a steel machine; . . .
For all the things of the poet's dream;
Have lost their place in this age of steam;
And the dairy maiden has had her day;
And the creamery man has come to stay;
And the next advance we look for now;
Is for some machine to supplant the cow.[47]

Indeed, the expansion of technology and industrial production in the United States worked to change gender roles by taking traditional home production away from women and placing the market control of these arts almost exclusively within the male sphere. Home dairying increasingly became perceived as a physically demanding and vulgarized activity—something that only women of the lower agricultural classes performed. Further, modern refrigeration would make the purchase and storing of mass-produced milk easier for women of means.

Sewing, dress- and hat-making, and home canning also followed similar transitions from home production to mass factory production. Women's course work at land-grants reflected these changing opportunities, and courses in sewing and dressmaking became much more specialized by 1900. Technology also shifted women's skills away from home canning. By 1900 the growth of the modern canning industry took home food production labor away from women and freed them up for other work or leisure activities. Again, technology at land-grant colleges helped to promote the separation of spheres, the cultural refinement of women, and the gentrification of domestic farm life. Both on the college level and in society, women students were not so dependent on the skills of dairying, dressmaking, and canning, so long as modern technology made products available to them through mass production and consumerism.

WOMEN AS DOMESTIC SCIENTISTS:
THE IMPACT OF LAND-GRANT EDUCATION

Women's domestic economy course work reinforced the culture of gender separation at land-grant institutions, and women themselves subscribed to the academic expectations that they should prepare for wifehood in their collegiate education. Between 1870 and 1920 most women took the domestic science course when it was available to them. In fact, when the IAC domestic economy program dwindled after 1882, the numbers of female enrollees at the college actually declined. In 1884 the *Aurora* complained about the lack of female students and called for a revival of the women's course of study: "There is need of a course of study for ladies. This is made apparent by a consideration of the rapid decrease in the number of lady students entering the college within the past few years." The reason was obvious: "We have not the course of study they desire to pursue, and hence have gone where such a course can be had."[48] In 1885 the IAC Alumni Association reported on 133 of the known 167 graduates of the college. Of the thirty-one female alumni who reported, twenty-seven were listed as "Domestic Economists" and the remaining four included a journalist, two teachers, and a clerk. The association also did a follow-up study to show the difference in numbers of domestic economists from earlier classes compared to later classes. Among the graduates between 1871 and 1880, 21 percent were domestic economists by 1885; of those from 1881 to 1884, only 12 percent were married and practicing the economy at home.[49] The difference shows that women did not rush right into marriage after graduation; indeed, before marrying, many women spent the first few years after graduation in professional work such as teaching or clerkships.

As other land-grant colleges and universities assumed more focused domestic economy programs by the end of the century, women students flocked to the course. For instance, the OAC reported that of sixty-six total women students enrolled at OAC in 1892–93, only two women—or 3 percent—majored in something besides household economy.[50] These percentages typified the numbers of women graduates in household economy for the next two decades, with only some variation, as some women pursued bachelor of science degrees in the literary, commerce, or pharmacology programs. During the 1890s and early 1900s land-grant domestic science programs flourished. Adding to this growth, domestic science programs were expanding throughout the country in high schools, normal schools, academies, women's colleges, and state universities. This led to an overwhelming demand for experienced women graduates who could establish new departments or be instructors in already-existing programs. By 1900 an emerging class of domestic scientists flowed out of the land-grant colleges, and most immediately found some kind of ready employment. Graduates from early land-grants such as Kansas State or Iowa State made their way to later land-grant programs. For example, Utah State's two founders of domestic economy, Dalinda Mason-Cotey and Abbie Marlatt, had both graduated from Kansas State Agricultural College.[51] And Iowa State's chair of domestic economy in 1896 was Gertrude Coburn Jessup, an 1891 graduate from Kansas State.[52]

Domestic science graduates made a distinct impact on the expansion of home or domestic economy at the turn of the century. Between 1894 and 1909 UAC graduated forty women; thirteen had degrees in general science, one in commerce, and the remaining twenty-six graduated in domestic science. Of the thirty-nine UAC women who graduated in science or domestic science, sixteen became instructors of domestic science in Utah high schools, Mormon academies, normal schools, or on the university level. Seven women helped to establish brand-new domestic economy departments in institutions that previously had none, and ten women taught domestic science at more than one institution.

Between 1901 and 1909, three UAC grads in succession—Lydia Holmgren (1903), Minnie Peterson (1906), and Inez Powell (1907)—headed the domestic economy department at LDS High School in Salt Lake City. At the LDS Snow Academy in Ephraim, Utah, Minnie Peterson founded the department and was succeeded by Jessie Anderson (1909). Rose Homer (1900) founded and headed the domestic economy department at Brigham Young College from 1902 to 1906; she was succeeded by Blanche Cooper (1901). Elizabeth Maughan (1900) was hired by the Utah School for the Deaf and the Blind specifically to establish a domestic economy program for disabled students. UAC graduates also took their land-grant training outside of Utah; Clara Foster (1897) became a professor of domestic science at the Agricultural College of New Mexico, and Grace Fisher (1903) went to the Polytechnic University of Pasadena (California). Two female UAC graduates worked in

TABLE 1. UAC women graduates: *A representation of postgraduate activities between 1896 and 1909*

Name	Graduation year, degree	Jobs in public schools or academies
Martha Hoyt	1894, Domestic Science	Teacher
Olla Barker	1897, General Science	Teacher (Ogden UT)
Clara Foster	1897, General Science	No
Sabina Hermoine Hart	1897, Domestic Science	Teacher and county superintendant (1906, 1908)
Victoria Lundberg	1897, Domestic Science	Teacher (Logan UT)
Mamie Smith	1897, Domestic Science	Teacher and principal (Dingle ID)
Anna Sponberg	1897, Domestic Science	Teacher (before death)
Rachel F. Maughan	1897, Domestic Science	Teacher (ID)
Anna Beers, Valedictorian	1898, Domestic Science	No
Ethel Bullen	1898, Domestic Science	Teacher (Richmond UT)
Rose Homer	1900, Domestic Science	Teacher (Logan UT and Oneida Stake Academy, Preston ID)
Elizabeth Collings Maughan	1900, Domestic Science	Utah School for the Deaf and the Blind (USDB)
Blanche Cooper	1901, Domestic Science	Teacher (Fielding Academy)
Esther Evans	1901, General Science	Teacher (Malad ID)
Almeda Perry	1901, General Science	Teacher (Juarez Academy, Mexico)
Mattie E. Stover	1901, General Science; 1902, BS (Oread Institute); 1905, BS, Agricultural Chemistry (University of California–Berkeley)	Teacher (Logan UT)
Amanda Holmgren	1902, General Science	No
Grace Fisher	1903, General Science	No

8

Postgraduate work	College-level teaching	Professional work
At UAC	No	3 years managing a creamery; married
No	No	No
No	At Agriculture College of New Mexico	At ACNM (prof. of domestic science)
At UAC	No	Taught domestic science in public schools
At UAC	Yes	Married
No	No	Married
No (deceased)	No (deceased)	Married (before death)
No	No	Married
At UAC	At UAC (Domestic Economy Dept.)	At UAC; married
No	No	Married
At UAC (food, organic chemistry)	At Brigham Young College (BYC) and Latter-Day Saint University (LDSU)	Founded domestic science dept. at BYC, 1902–1906
At University of Chicago (1907)	No	USBD; read paper on domestic science for deaf at National Convention of American Instructors of the Deaf
At Columbia Teachers College	At BYC and UAC (asst. prof.)	At BYC and UAC (asst. prof.)
No	No	Married
At University of Chicago	At BYC and LDSU (math, science)	Taught at BYC and LDSU; homesteader (Uintah Indian Reservation)
At University of California –Berkeley (nutrition, agricultural chemistry)	No	Chemist at California Agricultural Experiment Station; studied nutritive values of milk, cream, cactus; also studied irrigation
At University of Chicago, Harvard, and Columbia Teachers College	At UAC (asst. prof. of English)	No
At UAC and Columbia Teachers College	At UAC and Polytechnic Institute of Pasadena (prof.)	Head of domestic science dept. at Polytechnic Institute of Pasadena

Name	Graduation year, degree	Jobs in public schools or academies
Lydia Holmgren	1903, Domestic Science	No
May Maughan	1903, General Science	Teacher (Logan UT and Oneida Stake Academy, Preston ID)
Josephine F. Maughan	1903, Domestic Science	Teacher and principal (Greenville UT)
Geneva Egbert	1904, Domestic Science	Teacher (Salt Lake and Logan UT)
Verna Pearl Bowman	1905, General Science 1907, Domestic Science	No
Blanche Elise Caine	1905, Domestic Science	Teacher (Manti High School UT)
Eva Farr	1905, General Science	No
Hazel Love	1905, Domestic Science	No
Ella Maughan	1905, Domestic Science	Teacher (Nephi High School and Oneida Stake Academy, Preston ID)
Mary Edith Rudolph	1905, Domestic Science	No
Mildred Forgeon	1906, Commerce	Taught commerce (Richfield High School)
Minnie Peterson	1906, Domestic Science	Teacher (Snow Academy and Latter-Day Saint High School)
Inez Powell	1907, Domestic Science 1909, BS, Domestic Science (Columbia Teachers College)	No
Eunice Estella Jacobsen	1908, General Science	Teacher (Ricks Academy)
Jessie Christine Anderson	1909, Domestic Science	Teacher (Snow Academy)
Nellie Hayball	1909, General Science	No
Lizzie Odette McKay	1909, General Science	No
Ina Rosetta Stratford	1909, Domestic Science	Teacher (Brigham City High School)

Source: The Buzzer *(1909),* USUA, Logan.

Postgraduate work	College-level teaching	Professional work
No	At UAC and LDSU (dept. head)	Head of domestic science dept. at LDSU; published articles on domestic science
No	No	Married
No	No	No
No	No	Married
At UAC	At UAC and Branch Normal (Cedar City)	Head of domestic science at Branch Normal
At Columbia Teachers College	No	Head of domestic science at Salt Lake High School; wrote Education of Domestic Science page in *Young Women's Journal*
At UAC	At Weber Academy (Ogden UT)	Head of domestic science dept. at Weber Academy and Ogden High School
No	At UAC and University of Utah	Instructor in domestic science at UAC and University of Utah; extension work
No	No	Head of domestic science at Nephi High School and Oneida Stake Academy; married
At UAC	No	Married
No	No	Stenographer for Thatcher Bros. Banking
No	No	Head of domestic science at Snow Academy and Latter-Day Saint High School; married
At UAC and Columbia Teachers College	At UAC, LDSU, Branch Normal (Cedar City)	Head of domestic science dept. at LDSU, Branch Normal
No	At LDSU	Instructor of English at LDSU and Ricks Academy
No	No	Head of domestic science dept. at Snow Academy
No	No	No
No	At UAC	Instructor of domestic science at UAC
No	No	Head of domestic science dept. at Brigham City High School

typically "non-female" professions: Martha Hoyt (1894) spent three years managing a creamery, and Mattie E. Stover (1901) worked as a chemist at the California Agricultural Experiment Station.[53]

The domestic economy movement gained acceptance as a valid educational and training option, which opened even more employment avenues for land-grant graduates. Women most often chose one of two professions. As shown by the UAC graduates, most went on to teach domestic or home economics at other coeducational institutions. Graduates could also pursue the growing field of home economics extension programs, designed by the state and federal governments to take practical domestic science training to rural farm wives. Indeed, when the U.S. government took up home economics extension programs in 1914, with Pres. Woodrow Wilson's signing of the Smith-Lever Act, the first women leaders and extension agents came from among land-grant graduates. Ideally, domestic science education at land-grant universities had fulfilled what Adonijah Welch envisioned in 1868: a way for women to prepare for marriage and also for self-supporting careers. In spite of these opportunities, some historians have challenged the so-called progress of domestic science professions and instead see an American culture that limited land-grant women graduates to traditional feminized work.

Historians of women's education have responded with conflict on the ultimate effects of domestic science education in the late nineteenth and early twentieth century, with some scholars dismissing the whole venture as institutionalized sexism meant to keep women at home or in subordinate "women's work," while others have admitted that domestic science programs at least offered women students opportunities for scientific training and entrance into some professions. Historian Jill Conway argued in 1974 that the culture of gendered separation in domestic science education forcibly retrenched women into traditional domestic roles. Conway asserted that coeducation did not really create progress for women because, through domestic science, "women's intellectual energies were channeled into perpetuating women's service role in society rather than into independent and self-justifying intellectual endeavors."[54] Likewise, Margaret Rossiter has attributed the "feminization" of home economics by 1900 to "men's aversion (and inability?) to advise women on domestic matters and their willingness to let the women do it instead." Because of this aversion, home economics never achieved the same professional status of male fields of

14. UAC botany lab, ca. 1900. Maxwell Cohn Collection, Album no. 2, Special Collections & Archives, Merrill Library, Utah State University.

"medicine or religion or even the law." Instead, feminized programs kept women students and professors of domestic science relegated to academically inferior "women's work" or subordinated in lower-status (and lower paying) professorships or lab assistant work.[55]

Land-grant women's domestic science education also reflects the historical conflict over the ultimate results of these programs for women. Certainly, women experienced a separate expectation toward domesticity, as well as lessening academic standards for domestic science majors. However, critical assessments of women's education perhaps diminish the progressive opportunities that women received because of their land-grant scientific training. Women students also experienced a more equal education with men than has been recognized. Whether students took a general literary or science course, or pursued the practical training of domestic economy, mechanical engineering, or agriculture, both men and women together took a basic foundation of classes that included biology, chemistry, botany, and other sciences, as well as English, history, and business commerce courses, before separating into their gender-specific areas of study.

Although traditional expectations demanded that most women students pursue the "ladies' course," a few others felt the initiative to study alternative course work. Most women students took domestic economy as a preparation for marriage; still, the historical focus on the gendered separation of domestic economy education has also masked the numbers of land-grant women students who sought other courses of study, especially in the sciences and other, less gendered fields of study such as commerce, journalism, and pharmacology.

FINDING INCLUSION IN SCIENCE:
LAND-GRANT WOMEN SCIENTISTS

Women students found scientific study to be an area of conflicted gender inclusion and separation in land-grant course work. Since scientific education was an integral part of the land-grant mission to train the industrial and agricultural classes, male and female students alike were required to take basic science courses. Margaret Rossiter acknowledged that "by 1870, many of the state universities, especially the new land-grant institutions, were also accepting their first women students." Although not producing the numbers of female scientists as more famed eastern institutions like Cornell, the western land-grants also encouraged a female culture of scientific investigation so that "within a few decades after the Civil War the number of opportunities for women scientists at the collegiate level expanded greatly."[56] Chemistry, biology, botany, physics, and entomology were most commonly required; as land-grants grew in population and diversified their scope, they added zoology, bacteriology, meteorology, pharmacology, veterinary science, and studies in electricity. These were dynamic fields of study in the nineteenth century — constantly expanding because of discoveries coming from American and European industrial innovation. Science courses gradually began to take precedence in collegiate education, especially as so many students prepared to enter the growing fields of mechanical, electrical, civil, and industrial engineering.

In spite of the diversity of scientific course offerings at land-grant colleges, women students tended to migrate toward certain sciences that were considered either less academically stringent or simply more gender-appropriate. While male and female students experienced inclusion by sitting together in many science classes, they also separated into more gender-specific courses.

For instance, men gravitated toward what were perceived as the "harder" sciences, such as engineering, electricity, and physics, whereas women excelled in feminized sciences, such as botany, entomology, and nutritional chemistry. Since both male and female students were required to take the basic science courses before entering their defined fields of study, women also benefited from the land-grant culture of academic inclusion that encouraged their excitement for scientific study.

One UAC graduate of 1901, Almeda Perry, is an example of a land-grant woman's freedom to pursue scientific studies, as well as frustration with the anti-intellectualism of the prescribed ladies' course. Perry arrived at UAC in 1897 and enrolled in domestic science, as was expected. After starching collars for a few weeks, she found herself bored stiff: "At first I registered with home economics as my major, but a few weeks of making little seams, hems, and patches, and of washing and ironing clothes, including men's shirts with superstiff bosoms, as were in style at the time, I decided I was not getting my money's worth."[57] She considered other options for majors and finally decided on general science, since "I had not fully decided what I wanted to do after graduation, [and] general science would probably provide the best background for whatever line of work I should want to follow." In the general science course, Perry had exposure to various scientific fields: "So I waded through geology, bacteriology, zoology, mathematics, chemistry, physics, botany, horticulture, even constitutional law. I recall that while analytical geometry and calculus made me get down and dig, physics gave me the most trouble. At one term examination I stayed up almost all night studying physics then earned only a 'C' grade, which was barely passing."[58]

With a general scientific background, students were free to consider many career options. For a time, Perry entertained the idea of elocution as a career: "Since I had always 'rendered' a recitation at public functions this latter course was right 'down my alley,' so to speak." After taking private elocution lessons toward becoming a professional, she even wanted to go to New York to study with a world-famous elocutionist. The idea obsessed her and "it kept me awake nights and my lessons suffered even though I knew the idea was preposterous." She was prevented from going any further because "the professor of mathematics heard of my ambition to become an elocutionist and fairly snorted, 'A girl with your mind settling for elocution!' The scorn in his voice could be cut with a knife." Perry decided that it was in her best professional interests to stay with science, and she found that "teachers of science were in much greater demand than were teachers of elocution, and were better paid." Even though Perry had little desire to become a teacher, still she "delved into my science courses with all the enthusiasm I could muster."[59] Perry's experience in choosing a field of study speaks directly to the issue regarding women and course work at land-grants. Most women certainly felt fulfilled in their domestic science course work, but women like Almeda Perry who chose to pursue scientific studies instead of domestic economy surprisingly found encouragement—at least in this case—from supportive male faculty members.

At IAC in the 1870s, science was so much an important part of the collegiate culture that the *Aurora* had a separate "Scientific" department and editor. Students contributed scientific papers regarding all types of discoveries and new information, especially in those areas important to agriculture and mechanics. Very early, women students began contributing their papers to the Scientific column, and some women even served as the editor of the department. Women students also commonly chose scientific topics for their commencement or literary society speeches. IAC student Alice Whited gave a literary speech titled "Way in which Low Temperature Causes Death in Plants,"[60] and at the same program, Kate Carter gave a talk on "The Art of 'Electro-Metallurgy,'" regarding the 1839 discovery of manipulating softer metals with electricity. Students showed a wide variety of scientific interests, but especially in those areas that were particular to the ladies' course, like botany and chemistry. The first woman valedictorian at IAC, Ida Twitchell ('78), returned to IAC in 1880 to "take the position of assistant in chemistry." She taught chemistry and botany at the college for years, gaining great popularity for her experiments and teaching style. The *Aurora* often recorded her scientific activities, from experiments on plant evaporation to her definitive classification of ferns in the state of Iowa.[61] Twitchell later married but continued her interest in science. In 1893 she submitted an extensive botany collection for an exhibit at the 1893 Chicago World's Columbian Exposition.

In the sciences, women students seemed most attracted to chemistry, biology, and botany because of the necessity of these sciences for understanding the food chemistry, nutrition, and horticulture classes required in domestic science. In the 1870s and 1880s, before women could receive a formal degree in domestic science, a significant portion of women students received a bachelor's degree in general science. Of course, a BS often meant that the student had taken domestic science when available, but it also meant she had focused on either the classical course in science or literature. It is safe to say that scientific studies were influenced by gender expectations, since women were more likely to focus on those sciences specific to domestic economy. With that focus came less demanding expectations for women students. In fact, early land-grant course requirements had suggested a more equal academic rigor for men and women. However, by the 1880s some institutions lessened the strictness of the so-called ladies' courses. For example, a change in IAC's 1887 ladies' course gave women students who wanted to avoid science classes "an opportunity for a more thorough study of literature along with a somewhat lighter course in the natural sciences and mathematics."[62] In time, this separate academic expectation for women was firmly in place. In 1892 the IAC catalog admitted that the ladies' course was "much the same as the general course for gentlemen, except that more time is devoted to language and literature, and less to pure and applied science."[63] These lowered standards added to the negative stereotype associated with domestic science as lacking any rigor and intellectual standards, even though this representation was partly inaccurate and unfair.

This gender expectation regarding science was also apparent to the students. When one IAC chemistry class studied the analysis of soap, one junior male complained that it was merely "practical work for the ladies." But the *Aurora* editor answered back: "We see no reason why he should exclude the gentlemen in his remark."[64] For the most part, women's interest in chemistry did relate to its application in household chemistry — including nutrition, cleaning solutions, and medicine. Women were less likely to study electricity and physics — classes required for the men's course work in mechanical and civil engineering. In an outstanding exception to this rule, Elmina Wilson in 1892 was the first IAC woman student to graduate with a degree in civil engineering. Wilson went on to study the same field at Cornell University in New York in 1892 and 1893. She returned to IAC and taught drawing for the mechanical engineering department. She spent a year doing postgraduate work in engineering at the Massachusetts Institute of Technology in Boston and returned as an instructor in the IAC civil engineering department in the

1890s.[65] She was also the only female member of the Engineering Club during her tenure at IAC. Her specialty was mechanical drawing, and she earned great respect for her teaching proficiency in this field. Between 1904 and 1912, Wilson worked as a structural engineer at three New York City firms, and later traveled abroad to study engineering and architecture.[66] Wilson was followed two years later by her younger sister, Alda Heaton Wilson, who graduated in engineering from IAC in 1894. Like her sister, Alda also pursued graduate studies at the Massachusetts Institute of Technology and she later worked for architecture firms in Chicago (1898 to 1903) and New York City (1904 to 1918). She supervised the "women's drafting department" for the Iowa Highway Commission between 1919 and 1921. Both sisters also participated in suffrage activism.[67] At other land-grants in the 1890s, a few women students registered in engineering courses, but fewer still ever graduated with degrees in specified engineering.

At Nebraska in the 1880s a degree of choice for women graduates was the bachelor of science; in some degree programs, a bachelor of science still meant that the student focused on literary studies, but many students emphasized science. In 1880 Emma Parks (Wilson) — former assistant editor of the *Hesperian* — was the only female graduate that year and received the BS. Between 1881 and 1884, of the ten women who received degrees at Nebraska, six graduated in the general science course.[68] Oregon State showed a similar distribution of women graduates in science in the 1870s and 1880s. Most did not go on to a scientific career, but instead taught school, married, or did graduate work in areas such as literature or history. The land-grant environment was favorable to the healthy growth of a feminine scientific culture. The *Hesperian* in 1878 published an exchange on the success of women scientists, and one editor concluded that "it is reasonable to expect to find a woman not only fitted for the higher exercises of literature, but capable also of grasping the refinements and unraveling the intricacies of abstract science."[69]

The Nebraska regents validated woman's place in science by hiring Dr. Rachel Lloyd as a professor of analytical chemistry in 1888. Dr. Lloyd had received her PhD from the University of Zurich in 1887 and came to Nebraska where she taught until 1894. Lloyd also achieved a certain level of pioneering inclusion in her profession when she was one of the first women formally elected a member of the male-dominated American

Chemical Society in 1891.[70] Perhaps because Nebraska had a significant female role model in an area that typically lacked women celebrities, a surprising number of women students followed her into scientific studies during the 1890s. Rosa Bouton was the most notable. She graduated from the science course in 1891 and received her master's degree in chemistry in 1893, certainly under the tutelage of Dr. Lloyd. Bouton began teaching as a chemistry instructor in 1893, a position she held until she helped found the domestic economy department at Nebraska in 1908. Bouton's classmate, Edith Minerva Brace, graduated in science in 1891, and in 1894, she came back to the university to pursue a master's degree in biology.

Biology, botany, and entomology were of interest to women because of the relation to plants and insects in agricultural work and home gardening. IAC claimed its own distinguished woman graduate in botany. Emma F. Sirrine graduated in 1894 — a classmate of famous Tuskegee agricultural scientist and IAC graduate George Washington Carver. Sirrine taught for a couple of years at IAC, then pursued graduate studies at the University of Chicago. As a specialist in seeds, Sirrine worked for the United States Bureau of Plant Industry from 1906 to 1938. In 1913 she was made the assistant botanist in charge of the seed testing lab, then in 1933 was promoted to "associate botanist."[71] That she did not become the "lead botanist" during her tenure for the government speaks to a very likely discrimination against placing women scientists in head positions at governmental and research institutions.[72]

Chemistry seemed to be a science of choice for women students. At Nebraska, Mary Fossler received her BS in 1894 and did graduate work in chemistry in 1895. She later became a professor of chemistry at the university, and in 1913 she organized the first women's chemistry club at Nebraska. The purposes of Iota Sigma Pi were to "encourage good fellowship among the women students interested in Chemistry, and through a practical study obtain a more comprehensive scope of the chemical field and further the interest of women in the scientific world." In 1917 the chapter was one of only six in the country, and Nebraska's sorority had fifteen members.[73] Fossler also participated in Nebraska's peace movement opposing the United States' entrance into World War I.

Between 1894 and 1897 other Nebraska women made their mark in chemistry and other sciences: Emma J. Boose and Marietta Gray worked as assistants in the chemical lab in 1895, and Edna Bullock did graduate work in chemistry in 1896–97. Between 1895 and 1896 female students assisted in physics, botany, and zoology. This was an environment favorable to science education for women, and yet the culture still demanded an ideological separation. Female land-grant scientists represented the connection between science and the domestic science training that so many women demanded. Women like Bouton who studied chemistry could also give practical scientific application directly to women by teaching classes in food chemistry and nutrition.

The same connection between science and home economics was evident at UAC, where Almeda Perry studied general science and Mattie Stover studied chemistry, later becoming the first female director of the California Agricultural Experiment Station. At OAC, perhaps the most accomplished woman scientist to come out of the land-grant experience between 1868 and 1917 was Helen Gilkey. Gilkey graduated with a bachelor of arts in 1907 and a master's in 1911, with a focus on botany. In 1909 and 1910 Gilkey worked as a graduate assistant in the Department of Agriculture. She earned a PhD in botany from the University of California at Berkeley in 1915 and remained there for three years as a scientific illustrator. In 1918 Gilkey returned to OAC as a professor of botany and curator of the herbarium, where she served until 1951. During her tenure, she had forty-four publications on vascular plant taxonomy and tubulares.[74]

Gilkey's interest in science began with the science classes she had taken as an undergraduate in the domestic science program at Oregon State. Her interest in botany, or plant pathology, represented another area of feminized science, where the federal government, by the 1880s and 1890s, sought "to make it a regular practice to hire women as 'scientific assistants.'"[75] One might expect a successful, unmarried woman scientist like Gilkey to look down on domestic science training as useless and unacademic. On the contrary, even though Gilkey was admittedly "so far removed in my teaching from anything pertaining to Home Economics," when she was asked in the 1920s about the value of domestic economy training, Gilkey acknowledged its importance: "It has elevated woman's sphere and work, in my thinking [and] has made me realize that there are art and beauty in all work." When asked if she would want her daughter to train in home economics, she replied, "It would depend entirely upon the natural ability and tendency of the girl, but I should want her to have some work in Home Economics, no matter what profession she chose."[76]

BEYOND DOMESTIC SCIENCE:
OTHER COURSE WORK FOR WOMEN

Land-grant course work represented a culture of gender separation, in that most men studied engineering or agriculture and most women studied domestic science. Although women felt an understood pressure to conform to the expectations for their sex in taking the domestic economy courses, it is important to note that many women felt free to pursue other areas of study, and they did so. As land-grant curriculum diversified, some courses emerged as a middle ground of gendered inclusion, where both sexes shared acceptance, interest, and aptitude. Both men and women pursued journalism, pharmacology, commerce, law, and the varied sciences.

With educational equality offered to women, they prepared for college teaching, journalism, clerical and business work, homesteading, and scientific education. Not all women chose domestic economy — especially if they were not yet married. At IAC, many women taught in the public schools before marriage, but many graduates pursued careers outside of domestic economy or teaching. Mattie Locke (1872) was among the first female graduates of IAC. She not only pursued postgraduate studies at the University of Michigan and in Germany, but was also the manager of the Western Tourist Association for eighteen years.[77] Prior to her marriage, Hattie Raybourne (1873) entered political work, in various positions at the Iowa state capital during the 1870s, including "assistant in the state land office, state grange office, in two sessions of the legislature, in the Secretary of State's office, in the State Superintendent's office and . . . in the office of the Clerk of the U.S. Circuit Court."[78] The 1874 graduate Ida Smith studied art in Paris, and the 1875 graduate Lizzie Wilson was both an author and a homemaker.[79] An 1879 graduate, Alice Whited (the second IAC woman valedictorian after Ida Twitchell in 1878), followed Raybourne into politics: Whited "served several terms as county Auditor [and] rose to be State Auditor."[80] Land-grant graduates, although most became homemakers at some point in their adult lives, showed a great diversity of nondomestic pursuits, from clerical work to teaching and administration, and tried their hands at librarianships, journalism, editing, and nursing or medicine.

15. UAC commerce class, ca. 1900. Maxwell Cohn Collection, Album no. 2, Special Collections & Archives, Merrill Library, Utah State University.

Sallie Stalker (1873) pursued medicine and worked among American Indians for a time, until her marriage. Kate N. Tupper (1875) also studied medicine but gave it up for teaching and homesteading. Tupper purchased a quarter section of Dakota Territory land in 1876 and "hired it cultivated, and from it received a crop of rye and one of wheat, the proceeds of which were sufficient to pay for the land and all other expenses."[81] She was not the only IAC woman to purchase land as a single woman homesteader: Ella Hamilton purchased 360 acres in 1884; Della Neal bought 320 acres in Dakota in 1885; and Sarah E. Smith homesteaded in the mid-1880s. Fannie Wilson (1884) taught school for thirty years after graduation while also managing her own farm near Eldora, Iowa.[82] The *Aurora* seemed impressed with the numbers of IAC women homesteaders. In a tongue-in-cheek response to the truth-based criticism that land-grant students never returned to the farm, an editor asked, "Who says the IAC does not produce farmers?"[83]

Land-grant women also worked as clerks and bookkeepers. In the 1870s Estella Bebout worked as a bookkeeper in Des Moines, and Eva Paull worked in a bookstore in Dubuque, Iowa. In the early years, there was no specific course of study for clerical work, but by 1900 some land-grants began to offer a literary commerce course. This major taught business skills such as typing, stenography, bookkeeping, accounting, and banktelling. Also called the commercial course, it was popular with both sexes. The course was a predecessor to a modern degree in business, and men sometimes took it if they had long-term professional goals in business or banking. But once the course became more associated with bookkeeping and stenography, women students came to dominate the major, since these occupations were acceptable as types of professional female service work. Mildred Forgeon graduated with a commerce degree from Utah State in 1906. She first worked as a stenographer for Thatcher Brothers Banking in Logan, after which she taught commerce at Richfield (Utah) High School.

The literary course was another popular choice for women students who had interests in English grammar, literature, and journalism, and many found work after graduation as teaching assistants or instructors in university departments or as newspaper editors. The most common opportunities were in those fields of women's greatest interest: English, choral and instrumental music, languages — especially French — and some mathematics. At Nebraska, Willa Cather had originally intended to pursue medicine but decided instead to follow her literary interest. During her college career in Lincoln, she wrote articles for the student and local newspapers and served as the first female editor of the *Hesperian*. She later became an accomplished professional writer. Her friend, Louise Pound, assisted in the English department in the 1890s and later became a professor of English at the university. A large number of land-grant women graduates worked as assistants in departments or in university libraries after graduation, especially in languages, elocution, English literature, and mathematics. Some of these fields gradually became feminized at the end of the century, so that by the mid-twentieth century, English teaching and library science were dominated by women. Both Iowa State and Nebraska produced a number of women graduates in library science at the end of the century.

Course work options for women students continued to diversify. By 1920 the President's Biennial Report at OAC even bragged that "the number of women students in the technical and industrial branches of work at the College apart from Home Economics has for some time been gradually increasing." Out of 540 total agricultural students in 1918–19, 8 were women; that number increased to 19 out of 895 students in 1919 and 1920. Perhaps even more unusual were three women out of more than one thousand students in mining and chemical engineering. Women pharmacology students were 25 out of 152 in 1918–19 and 47 out of 169 in the 1919–20 academic year. Women most commonly chose the commerce or business courses, making up 232 out of 525 commerce students in 1918–19 and 282 out of 652 total students in 1919 and 1920.[84] Land-grant women graduates accepted the notion that a woman had a right to be self-supporting and to pursue professions that were outside of the traditional female sphere. And women made associations between professional education and the rights to female independence. One female essayist in 1876 complained that "from baby-hood [women] are given to understand that helplessness is feminine and beautiful, while helpfulness is unwomanly and ugly." On the contrary, all women should learn to be "self dependent," especially those "single women, who while most needing the exercise of self-dependence, are usually the very last in whom it is inculcated or even permitted."[85]

At an IAC Junior Exhibition in July 1883, Edna Bell presented an original poem called "Looking Worldward," which described a girl who wanted to leave home to "go out into the world and 'do something for herself.'" Although current thought said that a woman "should not choose a regular life work like her brother," Bell argued that a woman should "take her place among the workers as well as the stronger sex."[86] The connection between female professional independence and women's rights was a visible one for land-grant women; for example, the famous woman suffrage activist Carrie Lane (later Carrie Chapman Catt), an IAC graduate of 1880, began as a teacher, became the first female superintendent of schools in Mason City, Iowa, and later chose journalism for her profession. She worked with her husband, Leo Chapman, as a coeditor of the Mason City *Republican* in 1885. Women recognized the risks in choosing educational and professional pursuits that were outside of their sphere but still pushed for those new choices.

Alice Minick was the first woman graduate of the Nebraska College of Law in 1892. When her husband died, she decided the best way to care for the estate was through the study of law. She knew that her choice would be revolutionary, because "I felt there was an opportunity to do something for women." She remembered her first days as the only woman in her classes:

"I suppose there were from thirty to fifty young men in the class in which I entered. Of course for a woman to study law twenty years ago was an almost unheard of thing. When I would go into the classes, I would notice the smiles on their faces and the nudging each other behind my back."

In spite of the teasing, Minick "never paid any attention to that," and she later found that "before we had graduated every one of those young men was a friend of mine. A class of young women could not have treated me any better than they did."[87] Unfortunately, Minick found limited acceptance as a practicing lawyer, but she still succeeded in becoming the second woman to practice law in Nebraska, as well as the second woman to argue before the Nebraska Supreme Court and the federal courts in Nebraska. She was also the fourteenth woman admitted to practice before the United States Supreme Court. Although not extremely common, a few Nebraska women followed Minick to the College of Law before World War I.

Medicine was another field open to land-grant women. In the 1870s at IAC, Sallie Stalker (1873), Kate Tupper (1874), Ellen Harlow (1876), and a "Miss Cleaver" (1879) all spent time pursuing medicine after graduation, although only Stalker actually practiced. Nebraska founded a medical school with a two-year medical degree in 1883. Of the first class of fifteen students in 1883–84, two women enrolled—Mrs. Mary E. Case and Mrs. Tamar G. Humphrey. In the homeopathic department, three women enrolled in the class of fourteen: Emma J. Davies, Mary A. Howard, and Mary A. Lutz.[88] By 1884–85 Mary Howard and Emma Davies had stayed for the second year, and by the time Nebraska did away with the medical school in 1887, it had trained eleven women, graduating at least two female physicians, Emma Davies and Mary Alice Lutz.[89] Land-grant women recognized their own possibilities for medical studies, even though their access to medicine was curbed in the late nineteenth century. One IAC student in 1888 wrote an essay titled "Women in the Medical Profession," which argued for the need for women in medicine, because "[n]ot skill in science alone, but the wisdom and love taught by the Divine Healer mark the hand that carries . . . the greatest power for healing." Further, "women, with nothing but their own efforts between them and dependence, can scarcely afford to exercise the grace of helplessness."[90]

Between 1890 and 1899 IAC graduated from among its total female graduates three physicians, one osteopath, and three nurses, including one who served in World War I. One 1890 graduate, Kate Stevens Harpel, graduated with her medical degree in 1902 from the Iowa College of Physicians and Surgeons. Although she had married in 1892 to another IAC graduate and had one child, she spent her whole married life teaching and practicing medicine. She practiced in Boone, Iowa, from 1903 until her death in 1950.[91] The IAC class of 1893 claimed two women medical professionals. One, Jessie Hudson, worked first for the Iowa State Board of Health as a bacteriologist, and then practiced medicine in eastern Iowa from 1913 until 1927. From 1927 until her retirement in the late 1930s, she practiced roentgenology, or radiology employing x-rays, at Howard, Rhode Island. Her classmate, Lavenia Price, studied and practiced osteopathy in Des Moines, Iowa, and Los Angeles, California, from 1905 until her retirement in the late thirties or early forties.[92] Perhaps IAC's most distinguished woman doctor was Margaret Jones Monahan of the class of 1897, who went to medical school at the University of Illinois and interned at the Chicago Hospital and the Cook County Tuberculosis Hospital. She married another physician and had one daughter, but also continued to practice medicine and surgery. She became the assistant physician at the North Shore Health Resort and the superintendent of the Chicago City Contagious Disease Hospital. After 1913 she practiced ear, nose, and throat surgery and participated in much club work for the progress of hygiene, sanitation, and medical health in the city of Chicago.[93] Medicine, like other fields of study, showed how women land-grant students pursued an inclusive middle sphere of educational activities outside of traditional domestic economy. These women also opened for themselves even more professional choices and recognition for their greater intellectual and professional parity with their male counterparts.

CONCLUSION

Alice Edwards was a classmate of Helen Gilkey at OAC in 1907. Like Gilkey, Edwards began her education taking domestic science courses under Mrs. Margaret Snell, who had come to OAC in 1889. Edwards discovered she had a proficiency in science, and she found work for herself as an assistant and instructor in entomology and zoology. After graduation, Edwards taught school in Corvallis for one year, and in 1909 she returned to OAC as an instructor in zoology and physiology, a position that she held until 1915. In 1915 Edwards went to Columbia University to do graduate work in biology, and she worked as a student assistant in that department. Between 1914 and 1917 she pursued graduate work at the University of California, the University of Chicago, and the Columbia Teachers' College. She received her master's degree from Columbia in 1917. Edwards immediately found that professional opportunities for scientific women abounded. In 1917 she was hired as an associate professor of nutrition at the University of Minnesota. She remained there one year and then transferred to the University of Illinois as an associate professor of dietetics, where she remained until 1921. In 1921 Rhode Island State College hired Edwards as the dean of home economics and the dean of women. She probably would have stayed in that position for several more years, but in 1926 the American Home Economics Association in Washington DC appointed Edwards executive secretary of that organization. She remained in governmental service for ten years, during which she completed studies on high school home economics programs and also performed government-sponsored studies on nutrition, extension programs, and other work in the growing home economics movement.[94]

Edwards represented the ideal woman graduate of land-grant education. Taking advantage of the domestic science course, she had probably started her education with the intention of becoming an educated and practical housewife. Even though she never married, Edwards was able to achieve professional success with her land-grant education. While taking the science classes required for domestic science, she discovered that she also had a love of botany, chemistry, and entomology and that she could excel in those areas. Following her tenure as a successful teacher of sciences and nutrition, Edwards later chose to return to home economics as a long-term profession. Her experience resonates loudly within the context of land-grant education for women, especially considering the integral connection between science and the training of efficient housewives.

Historians Conway and Rossiter have examined the integral relationship of scientific education to women's collegiate domestic training. To Conway, "scientific education was thus to be used to bolster the traditional female domestic role, and . . . there was no effort to channel women's scientific creativity into more challenging intellectual spheres."[95] Further, the professional experiences of Edwards and Gilkey represent what Rossiter has criticized as women taking "faculty positions in a 'womanly' subject or staff jobs concerned with the women students' 'special problems.'" This marginalization consisted of doing work in "a specific, highly-sex-typed, field or location," including positions as assistants to male scientists, non-tenured (and lower-salaried) instructors, teachers of hygiene to women students, or deans of women.[96] The latter position evolved in the 1890s as a female matron to watch over the increasing numbers of female students in coeducational institutions. Not given the same professional status as male professorships, these dean of women positions showed how talented and educated women could achieve only limited professional opportunities in higher education.[97] In spite of these criticisms, the overall successes of land-grant women should not be dismissed.

Portrayals of only limited scientific education for women places these students in the passive role of accepting an institutionalized expectation of domesticity that was forced on them, without a realistic consideration for other professional options. This depiction fails to recognize the active role of women's choices toward their own professional and scientific interests, and also diminishes the diversity of women's education, especially as these women negotiated a new culture of land-grant gendered inclusion in medicine, pharmacy, law, and the sciences. Women scientists like Ida Twitchell and Emma Sirrine at IAC, Rosa Bouton at Nebraska, Almeda Perry at Utah State, and Helen Gilkey and Alice Edwards at OAC pursued scientific training for various purposes. That some of these women later put their science to use in domestic economy programs should not detract from the significance of their goals or achievements: they believed that what they did helped to empower other women—both domestically and professionally.

Domestic science course work certainly retrenched women students into their separate sphere of domesticity—either by outside cultural pressure or by their own choices—but the women's course also offered opportunities for professional satisfaction and growth. President Welch in the 1860s had foreseen a course of study that would give women the chance to work for their own living, and women like Gilkey and Edwards would later fulfill that land-grant vision. Land-grant education gave women exposure to scientific study, and many women students took advantage of that environment to pursue scientific careers or at least scientific backgrounds for other courses of study. Thus women's land-grant course work requires careful attention, not only for the impact of domestic science training on so many students but also for the diversity of educational opportunities afforded to those who sought professional fulfillment outside of the traditional domestic sphere. Women as authors, lawyers, journalists, doctors, pharmacologists, and, perhaps most importantly, women as scientists—these also must be the legacy of land-grant education for young women in late-nineteenth- and early-twentieth-century America.

6

Under the Gaze

Women's Physical Activity and Sport
at Land-Grant Colleges

And now the girls recline on the sidewalk . . . and run foot races toward the University when the bell rings. What next will our Nebraska girls do?

HESPERIAN STUDENT, May 1877

Land-grant women students experienced a favorable environment for the development of physical activity and participation in sports. Students took advantage of the relatively free and sometimes liberal culture of coeducational institutions that helped promote female sports. Further, the physical culture classes and military training offered as part of the land-grant mission helped to legitimize women's physical activity on an institutional level. For these reasons, Mary-Lou Squires has declared nineteenth-century American colleges the perfect environments for women's progress in athletics. Also, the eventual introduction of women's competitive sports in the 1890s and early 1900s "followed naturally from their initiation on an instructional level."[1] By the 1890s the "New Women" in America—independent and progressive—was usually portrayed in media images as "college educated, upper class, and fully engaged in sporting activities."[2]

Since the Civil War, the physical culture movement of the late 1800s received great impetus for both men and women; and acceptance of women's physical activity paralleled women's entrance into higher education. Both eastern all-female colleges and western coeducational institutions were favorable to the spread of women's physical culture. Ironically, the same arguments that many authorities used to promote women's physical education were also applied to the fight against coeducation in America. The famous anti-coeducation treatise by Dr. E. H. Clarke, *Sex in Education*

(1873), argued that when young women competed intellectually with young men, too much mental activity sent all of the blood to the brain, thus depriving the female reproductive organs of their blood supply. The resulting disintegration of the uterus inevitably caused educated young women to have fertility and other health problems later. That this kind of thinking was prevalent at the land-grant colleges is apparent in an 1877 obituary of a Nebraska student. Miss Lillie Fisher died because "the over-taxation of her mental faculties produced sickness, through which she was unable to pass."[3] To combat the poor circulation and ill health in young women that came from too much studying, Clarke suggested a balanced and appropriate physical regimen for women.[4] This thought pattern, although contrived to combat coeducation, ironically helped to promote women's physical activity.

Early feminist activists had called for young women to be more physically active in order to promote better health and to combat perceived feminine frailty. Improved understanding of anatomy combined with growing complaints about the use of restrictive corsets helped to increase awareness of the need for women's physical culture. The earliest acceptable feminine activities included those exercises that promoted better health and movement but still kept women within the bounds of appropriate and modest conduct. Young women were to avoid overexertion and rough, vulgar, or competitive behavior. Modesty, gentility, and grace were necessary qualities for any feminine activity, and instead of competitive sports, which educators believed were "potentially dangerous," women's physical culture began with simple calisthenics.[5] The first activities derived from Swedish gymnastics, and these concepts spread to the United States in the 1840s. Swedes promoted various movement routines to improve circulation and muscular coordination. Students used dumbbells, Indian clubs, wands, and other lifting and motion drills with arms, legs, and torsos to encourage action and mobility. Swedish drills dominated physical culture classes for women until around 1900, and these exercises were commonly used in all land-grant physical culture curriculum. Women students moved into other acceptable forms of sport, such as fencing, archery, and tennis, as long as those sports promoted feminine refinement, grace, and delicacy. Women would gradually turn to more competitive and robust sports such as basketball and field hockey, but the "culture of separation" for women students was felt strongly in athletic participation. In taking on masculine competitive sporting behavior, women "crossed over an invisible but nonetheless firm line separating gender stereotypes."[6]

Women's transition from simple and refined calisthenics to competitive team sports was an important change happening in many late-century coed and women's colleges in North America. That women's physical culture embraced many unique aspects at land-grant universities suggests a significant impact of the coed climate on the whole culture of women's educational and athletic development. This chapter examines several important aspects of women's physical activity at the land-grant universities. While not a complete history of all women's athletics at these institutions, it focuses on a few specific aspects of women's athletic participation and how women pushed the envelope of gendered behavior through sports.[7] First to be considered are the early beginnings of women's physical activity in the 1870s and 1880s, when land-grants provided a climate of greater freedom and athleticism for women. Second, women's physical activity at the land-grants occurred under the "gaze" of curious male watchers, and coed women's athletics took on what might be called a gendered exhibitionist character. Unlike their sisters at all-female colleges, coeds often performed in front of male colleagues. Men viewed their fellow women athletes as curiosities or spectacles, and in doing so, observed their sisters in the actions of defying traditional gender expectations. Finally, women athletes competed in team sports in front of mixed audiences of male and female spectators; in fact, basketball gained popularity first as a women's intercollegiate sport before achieving that status for men. On basketball courts and hockey fields, the new aggressive female play changed the definition of acceptable public behavior for women. Women students' negotiation of gender boundaries through competitive athletic play mirrored how these same women also sought an expansion of their public female roles.

EARLY BEGINNINGS: PHYSICAL ACTIVITIES IN THE 1870S AND 1880S

The first women students at land-grant campuses experienced an atmosphere that promoted more relaxed behavior and freedom of movement. Certainly, the colleges placed restrictions on all of their students in order to keep them behaving within the proper standards of conduct.

Administrations implemented curfews, prohibitions against loitering, methods of physical separation of the sexes, and the overseeing eye of matrons, professors, presidents, and chancellors to keep students behaving properly. Female students experienced the social norms that kept them erect, proper, and at a safe distance from men. Corsets, although coming under increased criticism for health reasons, stayed in use well into the twentieth century. Even with these physical restrictions, women began to act with more freedom of movement and expression, especially in the university environment. Increased social and intellectual expression naturally led the way to expanded physical activity for women. Female activity first broke from accepted patterns with simple actions like fast walking, lounging, dancing, and roughhousing.

The Nebraska *Hesperian* of the 1870s, when reporting on campus behavior, often mentioned incidences of student informality. In 1877 the paper tattled that women students were "reclin[ing] on the sidewalk in the shade of those maples, south of campus," and that between classes, they ran "foot races toward the University when the bell rings." The editors saw in these activities the potential for further laxity of behavior, for "what next will our Nebraska girls do?" Editors criticized women for their excessive noisiness during class recitations and chapel exercises: "Sit on the railing of the balcony as much as you please, but don't whisper so loud."[8] Women students had many opportunities to flirt with the changing definitions of acceptable, ladylike behavior. In the early 1880s Edna Bullock remembered that sometimes boarding-house landladies had to "lay down the law with reference to indoor etiquette and athletics." On more than a few occasions, three of Bullock's female boarding-house mates, members of the Palladian Society, would indulge in "hilarity and athletic performances" in their rooms. Bullock did not elaborate on the activities, but the houses and furniture were "not designed for such strenuous exercises." Were they jumping on the furniture, running around the room, or worse—wrestling on the floor? Whatever the activity, when the rowdiness "reached a certain stage," the landlady opened the door and told the girls "just what was what." For the onlookers, like Bullock, who watched but did not participate in the antics, the matron pronounced them "the only ladies in the University."[9] Bullock may have been praised on this occasion, but in another instance she was reprimanded by Ellen Smith, the university registrar: "I saw you sitting on the edge of a table on Friday night. Never let me see you doing that again!"[10]

Women students lounging on the grass, running across campus, sitting on tables and balcony railings, and even roughhousing in their boarding rooms—this increasing freedom of movement led to physical mishaps and injury for some students, especially as they took greater risks with increased independence and mobility. May Fairfield, the daughter of Nebraska's Chancellor Edmund Fairfield and the first female president of the Palladian Society, went riding in her "hack" one day with another student, Anna Shuckman. The horse bolted and the buggy tipped, throwing both women to the ground, with "a narrow escape from serious injury." Because they landed facedown on the road, both women suffered injury "by a rather too decided application of the campus to their faces." The girls did not ask for coddling or fawning sympathy; instead, they responded with humor to the situation, suggesting that "as soon as spring opens they intend to set out a tree on the spot where they fell, to commemorate the event." The girls wrote a poem describing their adventure. One particular stanza read, "Oh, my dress is tore and my face is black / What will the students say to that?"[11] Perhaps this poem hinted at the potential dangers of women's increasing freedom of activity—risk taking was reluctantly and humorously accepted, yet not completely condoned.

THE EARLIEST FORMAL PHYSICAL ACTIVITIES

Women first participated in formal activities with the individual calisthenics promulgated by the Swedish gymnastics movement. Arm, leg, and torso exercise was encouraged to help circulation and promote better posture. Students also took formal dance instruction, which was part of etiquette training for accomplished young ladies. At OAC in 1869, the ladies' seminary taught "Ballroom Etiquette, Music, [and] Dancing" as part of its earliest instruction for women.[12] This early dance instruction occurred in all-female classes only, without the scrutinizing glare of male students. At Nebraska, women students initiated their own first physical culture classes in 1874, when the *Hesperian* reported that "we understand that the young ladies gymnasium will be opened next month under the management of Prof. Aughey. We would like to see some of our belles swinging a ten-pound pair of Indian clubs."[13] In this, as in many cases, physical culture came by petitions from the women themselves, and not by any university policy.

Physical culture instruction continued informally at both Nebraska and IAC throughout the 1870s. Besides the typical gymnastics work, women also used the Indian clubs, barbells, and "apparatus"—which usually meant the rings, the pommel horse, or the horizontal bar. One description of this appeared in the *Hesperian*, when the editor reported that "some of the small boys were highly entertained, watching some of the young ladies perform on the horizontal bar, in the rear of the building. The girls are bound to develop their muscular powers."[14] To the male students, women doing regimented physical exercises was a curiosity, even entertaining—an attitude that suggests the separate and mysterious air that lingered around women students in the coeducational environment. Although the newness of women's athletics would eventually subside on campuses, the intrigue of feminine athletic performance continued through the end of the century.

Women's physical culture was such a new idea that educators had no preconceived notions of how to dress for it; indeed, a clothing style had to be invented. Women remained covered with long-sleeved blouses and long stockings, but athletic bloomers worn instead of skirts remained astonishing apparel throughout the nineteenth century. Although the uniform was restrictive by today's standards, the full bloomers allowed a freedom of movement not previously experienced.

Girls sometimes took their dark, conservative uniforms and feminized them with colors, plaids, bows, collars, and other accessories. Edna Bullock remembered, "There was the enlivening feature of individual choice of materials for the costume. My own outfit was red and green plaid—the first really bright colored suit I had ever had."[15] In the 1890s women students at Nebraska distinguished class groups during gymnastics exhibitions by wearing pink or light blue bows. The process of negotiating female gender through sport costume was a significant process that occurred visibly on land-grant campuses. In modern times Sarah A. Gordon has argued the importance of this process—indeed, the "physicality of newly popular sports demanded a genre of costume that would challenge prevailing ideas of decorum and women's fragility." Through physical culture costumes, women helped to "produce a new conception of what is meant to be feminine."[16] Women still wanted to be modest and private, but they also wanted freedom of movement. The new bloomered outfits allowed them both modesty and greater range of movement: "Clothing for sports functioned as a middle ground between the 'New Woman,' who was . . . physically active, . . . and older ideals of femininity."[17] Thus, as women portrayed newfound expressions of freedom and wore manly outfits, they still strived to wear visible reminders of their beauty and womanly refinement.

WOMEN'S INDIVIDUAL COMPETITIVE SPORTS

After participating in calisthenics in the separated seclusion of a gymnasium, women students began experimenting in competitive, individual sports such as fencing, archery, tennis, golf, and bicycling. All were individual sports that did not require excessive competition or aggression against an opponent, although bicycling was the most controversial for women. These individual athletic activities were important for paving the way to more competitive and vigorous women's sports. Fencing was becoming a popular sport for women, but they were restricted to "foil" fencing, or touching only the torso. The other two forms of fencing were considered inappropriate for women: "epee" allowed participants to target any point on the body, and in "sabre" fencing, opponents could target anything "from the waist up, including the head and arms." The epee was "too heavy, stiff, and dangerous a weapon for women," and sabre fencing was "too aggressive and athletic for women." For grace, beauty, and restraint, foil fencing was the most acceptable version of this sport.[18]

In 1878 Nebraska women began to show interest in fencing. And at Nebraska a few months later, a male student "procured a pair of foils and masks and now every student with duellistic [sic] propensities is learning to fence." Not just the male students followed the fencing excitement, but "even the young ladies are developing a taste for it, and some have already acquired considerable proficiency."[19] Fencing for women received a strong push in the early 1890s at Nebraska, under the chancellorship of James Canfield. His daughter, Dorothy, became an accomplished fencer at the young age of thirteen, and she often exchanged foils with some of the Nebraska women students. Fencing also became an important part of the military drill training offered to women at both Nebraska and IAC, and women even trained with the less-ladylike sabers rather than the more feminine foils. Even after Lt. John J. Pershing disbanded the women's military regiment in 1891, he continued to offer fencing drills to the women. At IAC, the "Ladies' Battalion" gained great renown in sabre drilling in the early 1890s, but this was only for exhibition and not for person-to-person contests.

Archery was another sport pursued by land-grant women. It had been a popular female sport for many centuries, with such famous archers as Anne Boleyn and Elizabeth I. Women's participation in archery did not breech any standards of propriety for young students. Archery was elegant and graceful, and women could participate outdoors, while corseted and dressed fashionably, and without having to wear the shocking bloomers. Land-grant women showed an early interest in archery, and IAC ladies formed an archery club in 1878.[20] Participation in archery and fencing offered a sense of upper-class gentility for female students, no matter what their financial background. These sports were popular with highbrow women of class in the eastern United States. It was important at land-grant colleges and universities for young women to be cultured and ladylike; appropriate ladies' sports offered physical activity within the bounds of acceptable femininity, while at the same time evoking suggestions of refinement. The women still sought "refined" games in order to maintain the "boundary between proper womanhood and 'vulgar' women of other classes."[21] Although students embraced their land-grant education, they also strove to reject the lower-class coarseness associated with "agriculture schools."

Tennis was another popular sport with land-grant women, partially because it had already gained acceptance as a genteel sport of eastern elite women. Thus, just as they had fencing and archery, women students embraced tennis as a sport of grace and good breeding. Tennis was one of the first formal sports played at the land-grants, and women succeeded notably at this sport. College women were playing tennis already in the 1870s, and the first Intercollegiate Tennis Association was founded in 1883. In 1890 the first Tennis Association was formed at the University of Nebraska, and Louise Pound was its most famous player. In 1891 Pound defeated all of her male and female opponents to become the Ladies' and Gentlemen's Singles Champion at Nebraska.[22] She also had a male partner, Emory C. Hardy, for playing mixed doubles. In 1894 IAC had a Lawn Tennis Club, with male and female officers and members. By 1895 women players at IAC participated in the matches against the University of Iowa, Grinnell College, Cornell College, William Penn College, and others. IAC was among only three colleges to have ladies' entries in the 1895 tournament, with Ethel B.

Rundall and Mary McNeill playing ladies' doubles, and Mary McNeill and Mabel Owens in singles.[23] Tennis organizations formed independently of the land-grant athletic departments. At Nebraska, tennis did not come under the jurisdiction of the Athletic Department until 1912.[24]

Bicycling became a popular leisure sport in the 1890s, but not without much controversy over women riding astride and straddling the bicycle—often while wearing bloomers or split skirts. With the invention of the drop-frame or "safety" bicycle in 1891, when both wheels were made the same size, the bicycle became much more available to the masses, and it made racing and long-distance riding possible. The bicycle, or "wheel," was to the 1890s what the automobile would later be to the 1920s. Critics feared that young men and women would ride long distances together in the country; left alone with the vulnerability of weak youthful feelings, they could fall easily into moral error. The popularity of bicycling spread rapidly and brought with it the loosening of social boundaries among men and women college students. At the land-grant colleges, including IAC, students formed mixed bicycle clubs, which increased students' freedom of mobility, physical activity, and social interaction. Student cycling groups might ride around town and meet for breakfast, lunch, and picnics, or they might pursue long-distance bicycle races in the countryside. As the popularity of bicycling spread, land-grant campuses claimed large followings of long-distance clubs. At Nebraska, Louise Pound helped to popularize bicycling; she belonged to the "Century Road Club," which required a rider to "have made 100 miles in twelve hours." She accomplished the feat with 122 miles, and was also the first woman in Nebraska to win a gold medal from the bicycle manufacturer for completing a total of 5,000 miles.[25] Both faculty and students rode on long-distance trips in the Nebraska countryside and held cycling parties and "bicycle picnics." For those who belonged to the Century Class, Pound remembered trips to Ashland from Lincoln, "accompanied by others of less endurance who returned by train." Members would begin early in the morning, ride all day to Ashland, eat dinner at the Ashland Hotel, and then return to Lincoln by early evening. One rider rode a tandem cycle so that he could pick up stragglers who lost their endurance along the way. Mrs. James T. Lees and some other students and professors' wives wore bloomers while riding. Lees recalled, "I was only one of a number of Lincoln women who found it much saner and more comfortable to ride in

16. Cyclone Bicycle Club, IAC, ca. 1892. Iowa State University Library/Special Collections Department.

bloomers on a man's wheel than in a skirt on one designed for a woman."[26] Prof. W. G. Langworthy's wife "rode a great deal, accompanied by [her husband] on horseback." Showing a similar enthusiasm for long-distance cycling, one 1883 IAC graduate, Emily Reeve, later toured the British Isles by bicycle from 1907 to 1915.[27]

Sociality and physicality were definite motivations for women to learn to ride a bicycle, and "many a timid woman learned with fear and trembling to balance on a wheel rather than to be left out of the fun of her crowd."[28] Bicycling caused women to stretch the limits of their physical endurance, and many women cyclists were capable of high-stamina riding over long distances. Cycling helped encourage the healthy, outdoor activity that was becoming so popular among both men and women college students prior to 1900. Long-distance women cyclists in the 1890s prepared the way for later generations of student hiking and mountaineering clubs. John Higham recognized the importance of the 1890s, as Americans began leaving the indoor restraints of Victorian life and seeking the spaciousness and freedom of the outdoors. The age was characterized by a "maximum of spontaneity, freedom, and vital energy."[29] In both men's and women's sporting activities, athleticism among college students reacted against the "confined and circumscribed life" of earlier decades. Indeed, through bicycling, team sports, hiking, and traveling among the country's newly created national parks, Americans were "reaching out into the open air."[30] Women students followed this pattern through vigorous attention to cycling and also by participation in aggressive, outdoor team sports.

Through individual sport activities from the 1870s to the 1890s, land-grant women increased their physicality and health, but they also began to set the stage for their entrance into more competitive group sports. Even more significant, the 1890s saw a renegotiation of women's public, social, and physical behavior space through sport. While individual sports like fencing had an influence on this movement, the sport of bicycling had a greater impact on changing the boundaries of feminine behavior. Women cyclists daringly wore bloomers in public, instead of the privacy of restricted gymnasiums. And men and women students could now socialize more freely, openly, and with greater physical contact between the sexes.

Concurrent to the expanding freedom for women through individual sport, the decade of the 1890s was also significant for the institutional formalization of women's physical culture classes. Across the United States, greater understanding of medicine, health, and anatomy led to a rapid increase in women's physical education and training. In 1893 the University of Nebraska issued booklets to all women students that echoed the growing sentiment regarding women's health and physical activity. The booklet encouraged regular exercise, discouraged smoking as harmful, and even more important, outlined the detriments of tight-laced corsets: "Now a corset is nothing but a big splint, confining the part of the body which of all others should be the most free and unrestricted. . . . The habitual compression of the waist prevents all use of the lower part of the lungs, cripples the diaphragm and compresses the large blood vessels in the waist. . . . This condition of things combined with the weakening of all the trunk muscles makes the woman ill-fitted for the crowning function of her life."[31]

Institutionally, land-grant educators recognized the benefits of women's physical culture and increased freedom of movement. Land-grant colleges and state universities were some of the first institutions in North America

17. Ina Gittings in mid–pole vault at the University of Nebraska, ca. 1906. Archives & Special Collections, University of Nebraska–Lincoln Libraries.

to create separate women's physical culture departments with full-time instructors—the University of California and Washington State in 1890, Indiana State in 1891, Illinois, Michigan, and Nebraska in 1894, and OAC in 1899, as some examples. By 1898 Nebraska was the first college or university to offer a degree-seeking program in women's physical culture; and in 1900 Alberta Spruck of Nebraska was the first woman in America to graduate with a bachelor's degree in physical education.[32]

As part of the physical education movement for women that peaked around the turn of the twentieth century, women took gymnastics, military marching, and track and field, especially sprinting, hurdling, pole vault, and long jump. Women loved the vigor of track-and-field events, the potential for individual achievement, and that they were played outdoors. The popularity of track and field escalated in the early 1900s to competition level, and many women gained notoriety for their amazing feats of athletic prowess. Ina Gittings, of the Nebraska class of 1906, and later the women's physical education director, was photographed performing major feats such as pole vaulting, hurdles, and shot put. The photograph of Gittings in mid–pole vault was subsequently published in women's physical education books and pamphlets all across North America.

Through early physical activity and individual sports, women students gradually began to expand their public physical and social space. Because men had participated in sports fairly early, women desired similar play for themselves. In most cases, it appeared that women lobbied and won the opportunities to have their own physical activities. For gymnastics work, fencing, archery, military drill, and later, competitive team sports, women students actively petitioned for their own instruction. This process—of taking male student activities and making them distinctly feminine—seemed an important part of women's land-grant experiences. Just as they had adapted literary societies, debating, journalism, and school elections for themselves, so women also sought physical activity. Eventually, they would take this process to a new level with the demand for women's competitive team sports, including basketball and field hockey.

WOMEN UNDER THE GAZE:
EXHIBITIONS OF FEMALE ATHLETICISM

Whether women were drilling on the military field or climbing ropes and swinging Indian clubs in a gymnasium, these female soldiers and players drew great amounts of attention for their athletic work. With a large stock of curious watchers—both men and women—the coeducational land-grant setting offered an added quality of what might be called "female spectacle" regarding women's athletics.[33] Women's sports created a rediscovery of female bodies for both sexes. Bodies that had been corseted and covered for decades were now uncovered and unshaped through the clothing and freedom of women's physical education. Through the methods of physical gender separation placed on students, such as separate gymnasium and class activities, administrators usually succeeded in keeping women just outside of the physical reach of young men—but not out of reach of their gaze.

In the 1870s and 1880s women's physical activity was happening in colleges around the country, but especially at all-female institutions where women students could pursue athletics in private. Coeducational land-grant colleges were unique because women's physical activity took place under the watchful and curious gaze of male or mixed-gender audiences. As much as administrators sought to keep women's physical culture classes secretive, modest, and closed to public inspection, women often found themselves—either voluntarily or involuntarily—under the observant eyes of their male colleagues. As women athletes began to exhibit athletic, aggressive, and even competitive behavior in front of men, these women pushed the boundaries of what was acceptable public feminine behavior. This "female spectacle" or "female performance" had an important impact at coeducational land-grant colleges and universities, especially as physical activities heightened the allure of female bodies.

In the 1870s male students were fascinated with watching their female colleagues lift and march and run and jump. Perhaps it was the newness of the costumes, since bloomers, military uniforms, and rifles had been unfamiliar associations with the female sex. Women's exercise was such a novel idea that women and educators actually had to invent clothing. But more than that, the movements themselves were new, alluring, and per-haps even sexually provocative, as women were more animated than male students were accustomed to witnessing. Under the gaze of male students, women's physical culture took on an exhibitionist-voyeuristic quality. Men endured great sacrifices to catch a glimpse of women's physical culture classes, which were held in secret. In two decades of women's physical culture classes, the mystery of watching women never seemed to lessen for the male students.

Male students invented creative methods for trying to watch the female students. At IAC, one creative student placed a large geranium in his window and charged other male students twenty-four cents each to "take a peep" at the women as they strolled around campus. According to the *Aurora*, these particular young men, "rather than gaze directly" at the young la-dies, found it more comfortable—and perhaps more alluring—to watch the women from behind a plant. And their reasons for hiding rather than looking at the women directly? "Either the young gentlemen of the Iowa Agricultural College are very bashful and modest, or her young ladies are dazzlingly beautiful." The *Aurora* remarked on the entrepreneur's success:

"It is needless to say that it is a profitable business for that young man."[34] When physical culture classes began at Nebraska in 1884, Edna Bullock remembered that a fourth-floor room of the university building was used, and the "course of events was veiled in secrecy," because of the mysterious bloomers rumored as the chosen apparel for the young ladies.[35] In the early years the need for modesty dictated the secrecy of physical education classes, but men still tried daring methods to fulfill their curiosity. At UAC in 1902, "the other day a number of young men were on the roof over the gymnasium watching the young ladies drill."[36] Jennie Bruce remembered that Nebraska men would "lie concealed under balcony seats, or scale brick walls and climb through windows when janitors were not watching." The best hiding place was a pipe organ. When it was placed in the Armory, "it proved to be a convenient place for boys to hide who wished to see the evening exhibition of women's gymnasium classes."[37] When the women's physical culture classes met in the 1890s, "girl watchers" often "crowded in at the doors," so Chancellor Canfield declared the entire building "off limits during the hours of women's classes."[38] However, the problem of "girl-watching" seemed ever present on land-grant campuses throughout the late nineteenth century. Administrators tried—often unsuccessfully—to maintain the culture of gender separation, especially amid the provocative new atmosphere of women's physical culture, but men were granted some limited access as spectators to the women's physical culture and gymnastics exhibitions. In the 1890s the women held exhibitions in Grant Hall, and Ralph Mueller remembered the importance of these events: "Each co-ed was allotted two tickets to give to her friends and tickets of course were much in demand." One year, an enterprising male student got hold of some of the tickets and "counterfeited" them. The resulting glut of exhibition tickets caused the gym to be "overwhelmed with men." The next year, the director of the women's gymnastics, Anne Barr, "in order to make counterfeiting more difficult," asked the printer to use a unique cut on the tickets that would be difficult to duplicate. The printer had a small selection of cuts, and so he chose one "of the Rock Island tourist in a duster, with huge binoculars to his eyes." The irony of the "Rock Island tourist" as a symbol of "girl watching" was not lost on Miss Barr; when she saw the cut, she reacted with "dismay."[39] Regarding these high-demand tickets for women's exhibitions, Fred and Adelloyd (Whiting) Williams remembered that "the

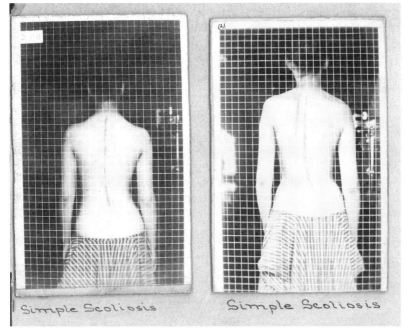

Simple Scoliosis   Simple Scoliosis

18. "Silhouetteograph" of female student, University of Nebraska, ca. 1890s. Archives & Special Collections, University of Nebraska–Lincoln Libraries.

boy fortunate enough to receive one was a lucky boy." In spite of attempts to limit entrance, male students still found creative ways to gain clandestine admission. During one exhibition, two "clever youths conceived the idea of hiding themselves in the organ during the afternoon so as to be sure to be on the inside. Unfortunately for them they were discovered and ushered out of the building before the very eyes of the early comers to the exhibition." For other hopeful spectators who could not fit inside the organ, "ladders were brought into play at the various windows and those less fortunate risked their necks and legs to get a glimpse of what was going on."[40]

Underlying this fascination with physical culture classes was a captivation with female bodies. Even the women students themselves gained a new appreciation for their bodies, through the increasing scientific knowledge of women's anatomy, health, bone structures, and reproductive systems. In the late 1890s physical educators at Nebraska and other institutions began making "anthropometric charts" of female students, first by giving each student a physical exam and measuring her body. The instructors then took a "silhouetteograph" of each woman's unclothed upper body from the front, back, and side. These special photos, also called somatotypes, could give the instructors of better sense of posture and bone deformities. With this information, instructors planned what exercises a young woman needed to improve her health. To maintain decency, faces were covered and the images kept under "lock and key," with "only women attendants present when the pictures were taken."[41] Nevertheless, herein lay another potential danger, as women increased their bodily exposure through physical education. Although for many years these charts were kept discreet, later in the twentieth century parents at the University of Washington discovered that pictures of their unclothed daughters were kept at the university. A "storm of controversy" ensued, and the university was forced to destroy more than three hundred negatives.[42]

The natural fear for parents was that any accidental public release of these photographs would compromise the modesty of their daughters. When *Life* magazine published an article about college women's athletics in the 1940s, the article included a reprinting of a naked Iowa student's silhouette, similar to the kind that had been taken since the 1890s. Critics of women's athletics were shocked; indeed, historian Susan Cahn suggested that the publishing of the photo had, "under the guise of health, cast a voyeuristic gaze on an adolescent female athlete and presented her seminude likeness to a national audience."[43] This fear of the "gaze" plagued the debate over women's athletics for years, and critics would use arguments about the danger of women's immodesty and public impropriety as reasons to combat women's team sports.

After the controversy over the Washington silhouettes, the University of Nebraska admitted that it, too, had been performing "somatotype" projects for years, but with no complaints from the students themselves or their parents. As an added precaution against the potential of the silhouettes being discovered, the university took "only positives . . . so no prints can be made."[44] Parents could request a daughter's image, in order to assist with her physical progress. Even in the 1890s women students had willingly participated in this practice, with no noted controversy or outcries from either parents or the students themselves. As young women learned more about bodily development and health through physical education, they too

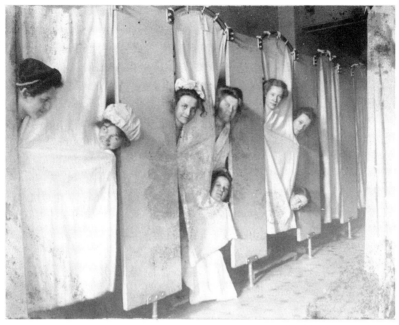

19. Adelloyd Whiting's friends in the gymnasium showers, ca. 1898. Adelloyd (Whiting) Williams Collection, Archives & Special Collections, University of Nebraska–Lincoln Libraries.

gained a fascination for self-discovery. Women students under their own gaze? In a humorous example of bodily "self-exhibitionism" in the late 1890s, Adelloyd Whiting of Nebraska took her brownie camera into the women's locker room and photographed her friends in the shower wearing only caps, as they peeked from behind thin shower curtains.

PLAYING TEAM SPORTS UNDER THE GAZE

It was one thing for men to observe women as they performed individual sports such as gymnastics. These were considered graceful and feminine, and although newly surprising to some observers in the 1890s, gymnastics allowed women some physical activity while still maintaining propriety. Newspaper reports of the exhibitions usually commented on the efficiency and skill of the gymnasts, but also on their "gracefulness" and "beauty." But female spectacle and performance took on a new dimension when women students began to play competitive team sports in the 1890s. Team sports had been dominated by men because group competition fostered aggression, barbarism, and roughness — these aspects kept cultured young ladies away from team sports. Moreover, vigorous sports were considered simply too dangerous for women. While men played baseball, football, and field hockey, women were usually "relegated to the sidelines to cheer on the men."[45] The "gaze" worked in reverse also, as women students became the most enthusiastic fans of vigorous, outdoor team sports for men. G. Stanley Hall, the president of Clark University in 1900, when he saw the "antics, cheering, and enthusiasm of the younger ladies at football games," concluded that "military prowess has a strange fascination for the weaker sex, perhaps ultimately and biologically because it demonstrates the power to protect and defend."[46] For women to experiment with team sports meant not only a revolutionary step for women's athletics but also a role reversal, as women's aggressive play came under the watch of male spectators. Through competitive sports, women could now exhibit masculine qualities in public. Thus, women's team sports came into being — accompanied by new notions of feminine independence, aggressiveness, strength, and sexual allure.

In some eastern women's colleges, such as Vassar, women had experimented with baseball prior to the 1890s, but these exhibitions had taken place in front of all-female crowds. To play team sports in front of male students added a greater dimension of "feminine spectacle" to women's athletics. Land-grant women, like most college women in America, began showing an interest in competitive team sports in the early 1890s. In 1895 IAC boasted a "Ladies' Base Ball Club" with two teams of eight members each (both teams lacked a center fielder). Instead of bats, the women hit the ball with tennis racquets. In the Iowa women's first experience playing a team sport, the concern about this being a potentially inappropriate activity was very clear from the "curious provisions" in the club's constitution: it ruled that the "diamond should not be within a two-mile radius from the college." Perhaps this stemmed from fears of broken windows in campus buildings, but there also seemed to be an underlying anxiety that women should not publicly play baseball in front of unprepared Ames residents. The possible presence of male spectators at these games created alarm also, because the second rule stated that "on no account should a lady bring with her a gentleman friend." Already at the first game of the season, campus rumors suggested that men had attended. Even though that accusation was "emphatically denied by the ladies themselves," still the likelihood was that some male students had found their way to the forbidden game.[47] The message was clear: while 1890s women might play vigorous team sports, they should not do so in front of men. And yet, male students always enthusiastically sought out opportunities to watch women's sports, and women themselves willingly accepted the attendance of men at their games.

"BASKET-BALL! BASKET-BALL!": WOMEN'S TEAM COMPETITION

Women students found the best chance for aggressive, competitive play in the form of basketball. Between the mid-1890s and 1910, basketball games and tournaments were dominated by women's teams at both female and coed colleges throughout the United States. Indeed, the "Golden Age" of land-grant women's basketball was 1896 to 1910, and women at the University of Nebraska, Oregon State University, and Utah State University played intercollegiate games with other colleges, universities, and high schools—in front of mixed-gender audiences. James Naismith had invented basketball at a Massachusetts YMCA in 1891, and the popularity of the sport quickly spread. Young women immediately took to basketball, and by 1898, all western land-grant colleges had some form of women's basketball team.

The first basketball games at land-grants took place between classes or other teams of women, akin to intramural play of the late twentieth century. Almeda Perry Brown remembered the beginnings of basketball at UAC: "Another innovation we brought into the school was the girls' basketball team, shocking some faculty members and the more sedate students by playing in bloomers."[48] In the spring of 1899 the first women's basketball games were played at UAC between two teams, the Reds and the Yellows. Bertie Larsen, a sixteen-year-old freshman, recorded in her diary the first game played on April 25, 1899. She recalled, "I enjoyed it very much."[49] For the next three months, Bertie listed the wins and losses of both teams and how often they played. Bertie herself was a Yellow, and she enthusiastically reported the times when her team won. The UAC basketball games had a spontaneous flavor, similar to modern pickup games. Between April and June of 1899, the teams of women played two or three times a week. Sometimes they would play during the noon hour, but they often played after school. On a few Saturdays, the women went to the college and played basketball all day. When Bertie could not make a game because of another appointment, she still recorded her friends' games. Bertie never mentioned whether their games had any audience. Because of the spontaneous, unofficial character of their matches, the girls seemed to enjoy the game for its low-key competition and fun, and not for impressing any spectators.

Women's basketball went to a new level of competitive play with the first intercollegiate games. Almost seventy-five years prior to Title IX legislation guaranteeing women equality in university sports, the land-grant institutions possessed women's competitive teams that rivaled men's sports teams in terms of fan support and the financial contributions from games. Between 1896 and 1906 Nebraska had an intercollegiate women's basketball team; they won often and even brought in some much-needed revenue. The women's basketball team "made so much money that the men of the campus, hard put for athletic funds, humbled themselves occasionally to the extent of borrowing from the well-filled treasury of the girls' athletic association."[50] Through intercollegiate basketball, women players gradually began to negotiate the boundaries of what was appropriate public feminine behavior. At first, games occurred in front of women-only audiences. Eventually, female spectacle had a defined impact on women's team sports, as women's basketball teams found themselves displaying competitive and aggressive behavior in front of enthusiastic male fans. The beginnings of women's intercollegiate basketball play at land-grants is important for examining how women students changed gendered boundaries regarding public displays of aggression.

The first intercollegiate women's basketball game in the United States took place between the University of California at Berkeley and Stanford University on April 4, 1896. When Berkeley accepted Stanford's challenge to play, the Berkeley women did so only under the condition not to play "before [a] mixed audience on the Stanford campus or anywhere else." To ensure greater privacy, Berkeley also wished to play on an indoor court. One writer to the *Berkeleyan* praised the conditions established, because a game before a mixed audience was not "conducive to ladylike manners and refinement . . . [and] playing in the open, before a lot of college men . . . [would] be lowering a certain standard of womanhood."[51] This important game offers some insight regarding how women negotiated their athletic play and changing standards of femininity in front of mixed-gender audiences.

An incident during the Berkeley-Stanford game is essential for portraying the various women's attitudes toward playing in front of male spectators.

During the game, one of the baskets sagged and nearly fell, so "two male laborers were called in to fix it." When they arrived in the gymnasium, the Berkeley team "screamed and hid in a corner while the Stanford girls, 'on the contrary, strutted manfully and indifferently to a convenient area, where the girls threw themselves down in various becoming postures of ease.'"[52] Here at the same game were two different reactions to the presence of males—one of modest, embarrassed, and even fearful timidity and the other of almost sassy boldness. Later in the game, a man was seen peaking through the window of the Armory Hall. The female spectators, numbering close to five hundred, "broke forth in hisses so loud and vehement that he fled in terror. The hissing of an assemblage of women is a formidable affair."[53] As the popularity of women's basketball spread in the late 1890s, so too would crowds gradually accept aggressive displays of competitiveness by women.

Detractors gave many reasons for why women should not play basketball, including the unladylike aggressive behavior on the court. Regarding the California teams' game, a local paper described the action: "The fighting was hard and the playing good. Anything to keep the ball out of the opponent's basket—anything to intercept a clever throw. The girls jumped, scrambled and fell over one another on the floor, but they didn't mind it. They were up as quick as a flash, chasing after the ball again."[54] The women's behavior on the court was such a departure from expected feminine refinement that reporters actually referred to the female players as "men." The imagined gender transformation represented what many feared—that the new athletic woman was becoming manlike. One of the players wrote of the game, claiming that the "men" of Berkeley were "inclined to foul by running and tackling."[55] The transformation from female to male took place only on the basketball court; while scrapping against other players, women temporarily assumed masculine qualities, only to return to femininity upon leaving the court. The *San Francisco Examiner* account of the game "referred throughout to the players as 'men.' . . . The bebloomered and besweatered contestants were men—real sportsmanlike men." By way of explanation, the *Examiner* stated: "When lovely woman lines up for the strain and stress of a basket ball game she prefers not to be reminded that she is a woman, and so she elected to call herself a man, which illustrates the extreme magnanimity of the athletically emancipated female."[56]

Furthermore, the players "accepted knocks and falls with the equanimity of real men," and "there were no symptoms of hair pulling." No hair pulling? Thus, by avoiding the stereotypes of women cat-fighting, these students acted like "real men." The last statement suggests the desirability of women players to take on certain acceptable masculine qualities. However, women players were expected not to discard their femininity completely, and one newspaper complimented the Stanford women as "a prettier type than a composite of the tall Berkeleyites."[57] The final assessment of the first intercollegiate women's basketball game was that it was a success. Further, "the conservative few cannot say that there was anything displeasing to the supposedly retiring nature of womankind."[58] Even though women had acted like men on the court, they still went home as women, with no permanent damage done to their femininity.

At OAC, basketball for women began in March of 1897, when "forty young ladies" joined the college athletic association. The women divided into teams and started basketball almost immediately, "two nights of each week they make the old gymnasium hum with their merry voices, and the clatter of their 'little' feet as they fly hither and thither."[59] In April of 1898 OAC began a series of its first women's intercollegiate basketball games, playing against the Chemawa Indian School of Salem, Oregon. In a *Barometer* announcement, the editors called for all of the students to show up in support of the basketball team, and women's basketball games became very highly attended by both male and female fans. In a departure from the 1896 California game played in front of an all-female audience, these early OAC women's games of 1898–99 became popular with spectators of both sexes. The first game against the Siwashes of the Chemawa School began a rivalry between these two teams that would continue throughout the duration of women's basketball at OAC. To encourage fan support of women's basketball, newspaper sports editors often invoked the language of competition—even masculine combative language—to stir the women's fighting spirit. In a later match with Chemawa, the *Barometer* in February of 1899 reported on OAC's victory: the women "went down there, met the Siwashes on their own fighting grounds and gave them a defeat that *will cause their feathers and war paint to droop and fade for years to come.*"[60] Here the language of women's competitiveness made the players into warriors. The victory of white women over their Indian opponents was celebrated and injected with the language of racial superiority that harkened back to Oregon's Indian wars of earlier decades.[61]

During this golden age of women's intercollegiate basketball at OAC, the women gained as much or more recognition as the men's football teams, for their popularity, competitiveness, and exciting games. Individual women players earned heroine status among their college fans, and some of the veteran women returned to work as game referees for later women's matches. One editor heralded the basketball team as "an organization that will be a credit to our college and one that can ably meet any basket ball team of the state, regardless of color, disposition, size or fighting qualities." The editor also invited all student fans to "encourage [the women] in their work . . . that we may be the better able to share with them in the victories they may win."[62] Monthly editions of the *Barometer* contained reports of all women's games, including those that were played at other colleges and universities. Many games had sellout crowds, and student fans from Corvallis traveled up and down the Willamette Valley to attend all games.

In a surprising fervor that rivaled fan support for modern men's sports, OAC's women's basketball team by 1900 had gained legendary status. They were the Oregon state champions, and fans treated them with the godlike regard of true sports heroes. They had soundly defeated all other teams in the state by large point margins, and the June 1900 *Souvenir Barometer* complained that "having never met their equals in this state, they endeavored to secure games with Stanford and Berkeley, but have so far failed to get their challenge accepted."[63] After one game, the freshman fans held an "entertainment," or a pep rally, for the two teams in the OAC armory. On another occasion, a literary society debate was held between the all-female Sorosis Society and the all-male Amicitia Society. The *Barometer* noted that a "large crowd was present" at the debates, "partly attracted by the basket ball game which immediately followed."[64] Women's basketball at the turn of the twentieth century was a huge draw, and the women's celebrity led the basketball team in January of 1900 to join the Student Athletic Union — previously limited to men's team membership only.

Women's basketball fans were attracted to the excitement of high-scoring, close victories by the OAC women, and they also appreciated the athleticism of especially spunky women players. In a game against Monmouth (Oregon) College in March 1900, the *Barometer* described "only one accident" during

20. OAC women's basketball team, 1900. *From left to right*: Bessie Smith ('01), Letitia Ownsbey ('00), Elizabeth Hoover ('01), Coach Will Beach ('99), Minnie Smith ('03), and Inez Fuller ('00). Oregon State University Archives.

the game. A Monmouth player tried to get the ball from OAC's Bessie Smith before the ball went out of bounds: "She slid into the stage, receiving a severe bump. In a short time, however, she revived and pluckily took her place on the team." In April 1898, Inez Fuller, the most popular OAC player, "received a black eye" that kept her from playing in the next game.[65] Most women players wore their battle wounds like trophies deserving of honor, and at Nebraska, it was "not an unheard of thing to meet at a promenade a proud coed blushing behind a black eye received in the afternoon's practice."[66] This kind of physicality only fueled the arguments of those opposed to women's basketball, since the game's detractors primarily feared the possibility of serious physical injuries to young women. An aggressive sport also inevitably led to overbearing crowd participation that encouraged such behavior.

The popularity of women's basketball games began to intensify these problems for the OAC regents. Game etiquette in 1900 — whether for baseball, football, or women's basketball — demanded refined and polite crowd behavior, and too much raucous cheering was frowned on. The college made rules that forbade "boisterous applause" during baseball and basketball games, so that players would not be "disturbed" and so that older and more conservative spectators could enjoy games without the shock of loud and unruly student behavior.[67] Perhaps because basketball was played by women, the standards of crowd behavior were especially strict for those games. Basketball fans had always been enthusiastic, but when student fans began acting inappropriately in 1900, the regents took concerned notice.

In October of 1900 the Oregon regents met to consider abolishing intercollegiate athletics. Some of the concerns included the "disgraceful tactics in the football game with Forest Grove two years ago," and "too much time wasted by, not only the participants in the games, but by their 'train of attendants.'" In other words, student fans had become obsessive in regards to game attendance and behavior. Perhaps the most revealing concern of the regents was the "behavior of those in the gallery" at the women's basketball game with the Portland YMCA.[68] Rowdiness at women's basketball games by OAC fans had become a problem. One month later, the regents voted to abolish all intercollegiate team sports at OAC.[69] Even though the regents voted again one year later to reinstate intercollegiate athletics, the conflict over boisterous crowd and player behavior was indicative of the overall debate regarding women's competitive team sports such as basketball and field hockey.

Both player and crowd behavior could potentially call into question the appropriateness of women's team competition. Responding to this debate, detractors and supporters of women's basketball offered vocal arguments for their cause. As popularity for women's basketball increased throughout the country, some physical educators sought to make the rules for women less aggressive and competitive. Although some tried to soften the rules to encourage ladylike behavior, most women's teams in the 1890s still played rules similar to the men's rules. At Nebraska, for example, "in the old days, when girls were genteel and timid, they played the game the only way they knew how—according to the men's rules." Defenders of basketball often bragged that very few injuries occurred in games. One Nebraska fan boasted that "no girl on any team was ever removed from the game because of physical injury. Not a sprained ankle, a wrenched shoulder or a charley horse is recorded."[70] Nevertheless, vocal detractors complained of women students going on long road trips, "mixing with other young people without proper supervision," and the "bad effect" that such rigorous matches had on the health of young women.[71] The dean of women, Edna M. Barkely, thought that basketball made for "less womanly conduct by the girls."[72]

After its beginnings in 1896, Nebraska women's basketball had a comparable record to that of OAC. They won almost all of their games against such teams at the University of Missouri, the University of Minnesota, the Omaha YWCA, and Haskell Indian College. As the physical culture director in the 1890s, Anne Barr (later Clapp) had learned the game at a Harvard summer camp in 1896. She brought the game back to Nebraska and was influential in its success and popularity between 1896 and 1908. She fought hard against the movement to abolish women's basketball, and arguing against the claims that basketball caused injuries to young women, Barr tried to prove that very few recorded injuries in ten years had occurred because of basketball. "Women's athletics . . . are safe," she claimed, if physical educators prepared the girls with proper coaching and gymnastics training.[73] Nevertheless, by 1908, women's intercollegiate basketball was abolished at Nebraska.

FIELD HOCKEY AND THE CONTINUED FIGHT OVER WOMEN'S SPORTS

The decline of women's basketball at land-grant colleges and universities did not significantly impede the overall progress of women's team athletics at those same institutions in the long run. However, the debate over women's team sports continued long past the demise of women's basketball. In 1910 the Nebraska women discovered the joy of field hockey, but by 1913 the introduction of this sport caused a large controversy on the Lincoln campus. Indeed, the sport excited "more comment, argument, spirited criticism and heated defense . . . than anything ever tried out by the girls of this university."[74] Parents from around the state protested their daughters' participation in field hockey, especially when they heard that it was played on a football field, because of the association with the men's more public and brutish sport. The use of physical space was an important element in the argument over field hockey. Where women's basketball could be played in a restricted and separated indoor space and audience attendance could be controlled, field hockey was played outdoors, in an unrestricted public space, open to the observations of any spectator. Indeed, women

21. Field hockey game at the University of Nebraska, ca. 1913 or 1914. Archives & Special Collections, University of Nebraska–Lincoln Libraries.

field hockey players came under public gaze; the Lincoln paper reported that "on each of these mornings there have been numbers of the curious and the interested watching from the sidelines."[75]

Field hockey was introduced to the United States in 1901 by Constance M. K. Applebee from England. It quickly gained in popularity among women players across North America. Its beginnings at Nebraska followed the national pattern, as women students embraced the game in droves: "'It's the greatest sport ever,' declare the girls who have tried it." Mothers responded less enthusiastically, and according to one mother from Fremont,

> Hockey for girls is the last straw. If our young women are required to cavort on a football field in bloomers to earn a college diploma, better that they go without it. We mothers spend years of endeavor to train our girls to be gentle women of culture, conservatism and refinement. We send them to the state university to receive the mental training and all round development which is a vital factor in true culture, only to have the

work of years painstaking undone. Our girls are taught to play rowdyish games; to romp on the football field, to shout and scream. They lose the sense of modesty which we have instilled in their minds from babyhood; they become boisterous and acquire a swagger. What can the teachers hope to accomplish by developing brute force in a girl? Let the women vote if they wish, I say, but keep them off the football field. Do we want a race of masculine women? I do not, even if the university does, therefore I forbid my daughter to play hockey.[76]

While many suffragists equated women's expanded political rights with the other freedoms of the "New Woman," this mother appears to draw the line at physical activity.

In spite of parental protest and the fear that hockey would "coarsen" their daughters, women students overwhelmingly accepted field hockey as their pastime of choice. Women athletic instructors responded to the criticisms against the sport with great vehemence, and the debate surrounding field hockey mirrored the basketball debates of an earlier decade. Ina Gittings, who had been a female track star at Nebraska in the early 1900s, was the women's athletic director in 1913 when field hockey really took hold. Gittings responded to parental protest with some frustration. Considering how far women had come in recent years, Gittings wondered why people still held objections to women playing healthy team sports. She defended field hockey as a vigorous sport that promoted "winning health, alert minds, happiness and glorious beauty in a legitimate way." Gittings asked whether parents still wanted the "wilting, wasp waisted, pale faced heroine ... [with] feminine charm made up of cosmetics and French heels." There was a healthier alternative for young women to develop natural and robust beauty based on vigorous sports. Gittings noticed that those traditional parents who objected to "athletics, higher education and political interest in femininity" were also the first to criticize the "unhealthy, languid, painted type." Parents should seek methods of "creating an ideal" of a healthy and intelligent young woman who is also feminine.[77] Field hockey encouraged the development of the ideal young woman; indeed, the "New Woman," independent and confident, especially as she thrived on college campuses.

And to those who claimed that women players assumed more masculine traits, Gittings argued that "[a] girl who plays hockey or becomes a sportsman in any line need lose none of her desirable feminine qualities, but she may and does lose many that are not desirable ... [such as] timidity, her shrinking from taking the initiative." Once again, as it had with basketball games, gender negotiation played out on an athletic field, as young women assumed more aggressive qualities. Critics claimed that competitiveness took away from feminine gentility and delicacy. To others, like Gittings, who promoted women's athletics as an avenue toward women's progress, so-called masculine aggressiveness was simply part of the necessary process of young women learning to "think for herself; to make a decision rapidly and to follow that decision with action." And how did the men students respond to their women colleagues playing field hockey, even amid the 1913 debate? "Some class to it," said one; "Bully," from another, and "Some game," said others.[78] Women students embraced the game; and as one woman remembered with enthusiasm, "we certainly did play . . ."[79] Field hockey became the most popular sport for women land-grant students in the 1910s.

When intercollegiate play was introduced in the late 1910s, university women felt the competitive pressure to win games for their college's honor. Bernice Forest at OAC recorded the intensity of one women's field hockey game against the University of Oregon in 1916. After a poorly played first half, the women's coach, Mrs. Seeley, berated Bernice and another team-mate, Katherine Howells: "She came to us just worked up—said she was ashamed of the way we were playing and we ought to be—and ought to be ashamed to wear our Letters—and if we (O.A.C.) lost the game, Mrs. Nelson had said it would be because *we* lost it, since we hadn't been faithful in practice." Bernice felt the chastisement came because "Mrs. Nelson" was "cross because we hadn't given up Y.W. and Home Economics work for hockey. If she should look at our schedules, she could see that the presidents of those organizations weren't being any less faithful than their Laws permitted."[80] By the 1910s women students' many extracurricular activities indeed caused much exhaustion, especially as women branched out intellectually and into society work, socials, and time-consuming athletics. Bernice often expressed in her diary how tired she felt. In defense of her poor play against Oregon, Bernice claimed that the coach could not see how hard she had worked because she was on the opposite side of the field, but "during the next half she praised us a good deal—but I didn't take it.

. . . It was just because we were on her side where she could see us that she thought it was better." After a hard-fought game with tired players, OAC's team won, with five goals made by the star player, Zetta Bush.

Field hockey at OAC fulfilled some of the fears that had been expressed by critics of the game — women would be prone to overcompetitiveness, exhaustion, and possible physical injury. Indeed, some of Bernice's teammates failed to play well as a team and even monopolized the ball. She complained, "I am glad I didn't have Fay as my wing, for she played out of her position most of the time and went clear into Nellie Paulson's place so that Nellie couldn't have played team work if she had been given the chance."[81] To Bernice's credit, though, "Katherine & I got along splendidly in team work for we were backed up by Ruby Thomas in the half back line and depended on her for all the balls."[82] After the end of a full day of field hockey and other school activities, Bernice "finally managed to crawl home with Al Meyers' aid — and at midnight I finally closed my eyes on the weariest day I had spent in many moons." Tired but fulfilled with the complete life of an active female student, Bernice represented a new kind of athletic college woman. She even felt a final sense of satisfaction that "during the game one of the Oregon girls hit me just above the eye with her stick and now I have a *black* eye."[83] Bernice Forest's experience speaks to the emergence of the "New Woman" on land-grant campuses — one who reveled in competitive team athletics, physical activity, and even a bit of rough play.

CONCLUSION

Land-grant campus environments of the 1870s and 1880s had allowed for greater freedom of expression by women in many areas — debating and politics, social behavior, and physical activity. The earliest physical activity for women mirrored national patterns, as the first sports practiced by women were individual, refined, and modest. At first, women students did not break from the norms of gender respectability, since they could exhibit new freedoms while still representing proper gender behavior. Land-grant women in particular sought refined upper-class sports that contradicted in some ways the agrarian and lower-class character of these agricultural schools. By the late 1880s and early 1890s, men and women college students followed national trends of seeking more vigorous outdoor activities such as bicycling and team sports, where they could exhibit freedom and spontaneity of movement. In the age of grass-roots populism and other agrarian movements, women ventured outside of the strictures of class expectations to pursue sporting activities associated with the working classes. College women began to manipulate the line between acceptable public restraint and the perceived public vulgarity of team sport competition. By making aggressive team play more permissible for women, especially in front of the gaze of mixed crowds at coed universities, land-grant women helped in the movement to redefine what it meant to be womanly.

Women students' entrance into competitive team sports symbolically marked a dilemma regarding the place of American women in public and social life. Could the "athletic girl" benefit from healthful sports without losing her femininity? According to Susan Cahn, women athletes "stood on the borderline between new feminine ideals and customary notions of manly sport, symbolizing the possibilities and the dangers of the New Woman's daring disregard for traditional gender arrangements."[84] Many saw the advantages of team sports for teaching women cooperation, fair play, and healthful exercise, but the ambiguity of women's sports was the fear of the inevitable development of unseemly masculine characteristics. Indeed, the growing freedom for women on the playing fields belied the restraint of the age, and yet women continued to push that boundary toward greater female liberty.

And how did men react to this expansion of the female physical sphere? According to Cahn, many men were threatened by the encroachment against their masculine power: "Fearing any erosion of patriarchal privilege and resenting female intrusions into a formerly male terrain, men often viewed women's athletic gains as their own loss of a clearly masculine preserve."[85] In some ways this was true for land-grant student interaction, especially as physical educators sought to preserve gender differences and separation for the protection of female virtues and influence. And yet, the experience of land-grant men and women seemed to contradict this assumption. If, as Cahn suggested, men felt threatened by new displays of female power, why then did male students flock to women's collegiate games and exhibitions, often to express the most vocal support of those events? Certainly the conduct of some male students suggested that they were indeed fascinated by the increasing sexual allure of female physicality and bodily exposure. However, since the most vocal critics of women's sport prior to World War

I were often older women—mothers, deans of women, and more traditional physical educators—then the land-grant experience of men and women students repudiates some assumptions regarding men's opposition to female emancipation. Women students were not passive subjects in this process; rather, they aggressively pursued and demanded physical sport, in spite of the objections of some maternal figures and leaders. Women students often voluntarily placed themselves and their newfound displays of aggressive and boisterous behavior in front of the observation of fellow male students. This important dynamic showed that land-grant women were actively willing to accept and broaden a more inclusive definition of "New Woman" in American collegiate life.

7

"The American Eagle in Bloomers"

"Student-Soldieresses" and Women's Military Activity

The Fair Warriors . . . demanded . . . regulation cadet muskets.
LINCOLN [NE] DAILY JOURNAL, May 11, 1888

Land-grant university environments allowed women the opportunity to take traditionally male activities—literary society debates, athletics, team sports, and school elections—and adapt these for women's participation. This process of redefining the male student sphere for women's inclusion, or better, creating a parallel female sphere, was an important part of women's land-grant experiences. As women feminized the practices and events of college education, they successfully adapted literary societies, debating, journalism, and school elections for themselves, just as they had also sought physical culture classes and team sports. In an astonishing and even revolutionary example of this process, women students sought military training in the 1870s. Land-grant colleges were the first institutions in the United States to offer military training to women in the nineteenth century, with organized companies, officers, and cadets. Female students themselves petitioned for military participation and negotiated their own participation in those regiments. Women observed the military drill that was required for male students and worked to make it their own. Thus, in an important step toward challenging gender separation, women students at western land-grants participated in organized military companies as women cadets, or "student-soldieresses."

Female military training was a significant and unique aspect of women's land-grant experiences in the West. Indeed, it was the coeducational land-grant environment itself that led to the creation of women's military regiments. Female military drill was rooted in the convergence of a few factors. First, women saw the men students practicing their military drill and wanted to experiment for themselves. Probably foremost in the minds of the women students, military marching seemed an exciting, yet appropriate way to get outside for healthy exercise. Administrators' quickness to endorse this activity for the women came because marching was considered acceptable for promoting female health. Marching was also perceived as helpful to good posture, and the importance of an erect female carriage was highlighted as a benefit in military drilling. Second, the relatively open and progressive atmosphere for land-grant women allowed for experimentation in traditionally all-male pursuits. Finally, women were inspired by a sense of military and patriotic romanticism, especially as they watched the men drilling on campus every day. The uniforms, caps, sabers, and rifles added to women's sense of curiosity and patriotic interest in military drill.

The era of student women cadets ended in 1898, and after the turn of the century, women's military participation returned to more traditional activities, especially during the wartime years of 1917 and 1918. Like women during the Civil War, women students during the First World War followed a pattern akin to the wartime support of traditional feminine war activities, including nursing, domestic production, Liberty Bond drives, and some political action. A few women on land-grant campuses even found strong political voices in protesting American war involvement. Most, however, gave their moral and political support to the war through student women groups, Red Cross volunteerism, and nursing efforts both home and abroad.

Expressions of American women's patriotism can be traced back to the Revolutionary period, but feminine nationalism got a boost from women's expanded civic and military participation during the Civil War. Jeanie Attie argued for the central importance of the Civil War in nurturing American women's patriotic involvement in the nineteenth century. Through benevolent deeds and service, household production, nursing, and other feminine wartime contributions, women began to confront the meaning of their own citizenship and participation in the Republic.[1] This sense of civic duty expanded into the political and even military realm, as some women worked as spies or male soldiers in disguise. In the wartime climate, northern women expressed political opinions and also "felt free to vent a belligerency toward the Confederacy." Many women became engrossed with displays of militarism, including marches, parades, and artillery demonstrations. Women showed a "fondness for military regalia" including swords, pistols, rifles, and cannons. One group of Maine women gained access to some artillery and presented "a salute of thirty-four guns." Women like Louisa May Alcott expressed desires to be men so that they could fight, because the "ultimate gesture of political obligation was military service" or "offering one's life for the preservation of the state."[2]

This climate of expanded political and military interest for women continued into the land-grant military culture between 1870 and 1900. Just as in the Civil War, land-grant women heartily "welcomed the sudden expansion of the emotional and physical spaces in which they could perform their citizenship."[3] In the early 1890s a renewed nationalism in the United States infiltrated the college culture as well. John Higham has linked American "jingoism and [the] deliberate cultivation of . . . military virtues," with the athleticism and combative spirit that prevailed on 1890s campuses.[4] Engulfed in this patriotic and military collegiate climate, civic-minded women sought to enact their desires for public participation. By engaging in military activity, women students took their citizenship to a new level of inclusion and republican action.

LAND-GRANT WOMEN'S MILITARY ACTIVITY

The Morrill Act of 1862 specifically required male students to participate in military training as part of the land-grant mission. The Civil War demand for a large population of trained soldiers prompted Morrill to include this requirement in the 1862 act. Even after the war, the provision remained in the land-grant mission, and all charters of the late 1860s required military instruction. Young men began military training almost as soon as the universities opened, and administrators hired younger, lower-rank military officers to direct and command these courses. Male students made reluctant and clumsy soldiers at first, but they gradually assumed the posture and culture of student-soldiers. In October of 1876 the *Hesperian* noted the newness and uniqueness of having a campus military company: "A military company is something of which every college cannot boast, consequently we are one ahead. Lieut. Dudley has displayed a great amount of energy and patience in forming the company, and although the boys are a little awkward, there is blood in their eyes, and no doubt they will make noble soldiers."[5] By the

22. IAC women cadets in front of Old Main, ca. 1893. Iowa State University Library/Special Collections Department.

end of the 1890s many of these young student-soldiers would be called on to participate in war actions, first in the Spanish-American War and later in the First World War. Some even fought in the Indian Wars of the late nineteenth century.

Land-grant military drilling preceded the Reserve Officer Training Corps (ROTC) programs of post–World War I collegiate life, and historians have yet to make a full assessment of the impact of land-grant student-soldiers during the Spanish-American War and World War I. As part of the military requirement, men marched and drilled on the campus quad, they wore military uniforms for their required school apparel, and they practiced rifle shooting, boxing, and fencing. The open-field campuses of the first land-grants offered the perfect setting for students' mass military drill. Most of this took place in the quads right in front of Old Main. Early photos show student military regiments in the parklike open setting conducive to military drilling.

Evidence of women's military drilling was first noted at IAC in 1878, and this activity was specifically demanded by the women. The May issue of the *Aurora* reported, "A petition has been circling among the ladies of this institution. It requests the Faculty to set apart a portion of land for a ladies' ball ground also that they be allowed to take military drill."[6] By the next month, the lobbying had paid off, for "the Ladies' Military Company . . . met for the first time last Wednesday evening, with about twenty members. The hour passed quickly both to those drilling, and those looking on."[7] Indeed, this was a novelty to the watchers. Like the first male soldiers, the women began somewhat clumsily: "As the warning bell rang, the orders, 'Wheel, column right, march,' were given, and they marched 'left, right, left, right,' up to the College. Here the command to form in line being given, it was quickly obeyed, but when told to 'break ranks,' not one of the twenty stirred. A second time was the order given before these military girls understood what it meant, then with one accord they broke ranks and ran—up the steps."[8]

With practice, these women soldiers would improve: "They expect to drill twice a week, and when they procure their uniforms they will without doubt, present a very novel as well as military appearance." The young women even learned their own salute, "but they touch the lips instead of the visor of the cap."[9] These early beginnings of women's military participation in the late 1870s were a rare and unique gender contribution of the land-grant culture.

In 1879 the Nebraska women also "became enthusiastic about marching and Lt. Isaac T. Webster of the military department gave the dormitory regular military drill."[10] Military drill for women at Nebraska achieved a slower start than for the Iowa women. In 1883 the Nebraska girls again petitioned for some kind of physical activity for themselves. A letter written to the board of regents on December 17, 1883, was signed by more than seventy-five women students and requested that "you will make provision in the University for giving the lady students an amount of gymnastic training that will be an equivalent for the military drill that is provided for gentlemen."[11] Whether it was military marching or simple gymnastic training, the women students sought some kind of physical activity to help balance their academic life. The petitioners went on to outline their demands: "We desire that this training should be in the form of calisthenics, that it should be given three hours a week, and that a room should be provided for that purpose."[12] Their petition was successful: in the fall of 1884, the regents granted use of the gymnasium facilities on the fourth floor of University Hall for women to pursue their calisthenics classes, with Adelaide Dearborn as the first teacher.

Women students now had the limited option to take gymnastics, but that did not preclude them from a continued interest in military drill. In 1888 Nebraska women again asked for the drill, with the help and guidance of a willing and sympathetic commander, Lt. Edgar S. Dudley, commandant of the Military Department. Dudley agreed to practice marching and saber drills with his new cadets. That the women still sought this unique military diversion even after the availability of gymnastics classes shows that factors other than a basic need for physical activity drove women to want the drill. Perhaps women simply wanted what their male colleagues had. They also wanted real guns: Lieutenant Dudley had started training them with "wooden guns," but the "fair warriors" had "disdain[ed]" their use, and instead demanded "regulation cadet muskets."[13] The women also enjoyed the striking appearance of the military uniforms, regulated cadences, and erect postures. In a culture much guided by a military spirit, women naturally sought participation in patriotic ceremonies, especially when they got to wear wonderful uniforms. The significance of this adventure was not lost on Lincoln citizens, and in honor of the students' new roles as women warriors, the *Lincoln Daily Journal* called the twenty-five cadets "Amazons."[14]

Louise Pound, 1892 Nebraska graduate, later a professor of English, and herself a member of the 1888 "Company D," suggested that exercise certainly was a motivation, especially since the women's company "used the same heavy muskets as their male rivals, and were put through something [of] the same ordeal of movements."[15] However, even more alluring for her and her fellow cadets was the "thought of a dark blue uniform trimmed with white braid, and a cap boasting two buttons and a gilt cord." Whatever the reasons for the formation of Company D, women were again the driving force behind its organization: "It had its origin in the minds of two or three enthusiastic spirits, and later was taken up tentatively and approvingly by the coed body at large."[16] Company D, formed in the spring of 1888, had the ready and active support of Lieutenant Dudley. Indeed, perhaps without the backing of a commander sympathetic to the women's desires for military training, this venture might never have proceeded. That this was true becomes apparent later, because when John J. Pershing replaced Lieutenant Dudley in 1891, Pershing "refused to sympathize with their cause so the Ladies Cadet company was deactivated."[17] In the meantime, however, Lieutenant Dudley drilled the women in rooms inside University Hall, and "the co-eds were put through the major part of the manual of arms, and encouraged to master the mysteries of the march."[18] Female officers were elected, and under Capt. Nettie Clenen, Company D prepared to take the field to show their accomplishments. In May of 1888 when the male cadets prepared to go to Camp Wymore for training, the women's company asked to go also, but their request was denied: "The matter was not looked upon with any favor by the powers that be, and the camp at Wymore will not be brightened by the presence of 'co-eds.'"[19] Gender separation was upheld in this rejection of women cadets' request to go to camp, but the women successfully managed to win an appearance at their first university dress parade, and this they would do with the men cadets.

Pound's assessment of the company's military training was not complimentary. The women's military company was "marked retrogression" in the midst of other "triumph and progress" for women. Indeed, the failure of women's experimental role as a "Military Character" showed that in this area, women would never replace men. Thus, regarding the female military career, Pound stated: "Whatever it may have been or will be elsewhere, was sadly inglorious and ephemeral." Indeed, the first military performance by Nebraska women was less than stellar: "Over our first dress parade I ought perhaps to draw the curtain of charity. To say that our appearance created a sensation would be doing scant justice. I recall vividly my extreme trepidation on finding myself, in my capacity of second sergeant, the end 'man,' of the whole battalion, with several new duties to perform of which I had not the faintest idea and all of which I got wrong. Indeed, I believe that the whole company felt greatly confused, if not pathetically rattled."[20]

The women were nervous because "there were an unusually large number of spectators present, the guns seemed unusually heavy, and the other companies seemed to take dreadfully long steps." Tired, nervous, and unprepared, the women began marching in the wrong direction and shot their rifles a few seconds too late. The women were not the only ones affected by the chaos on the field. The male cadets, fascinated by their female counter-parts, "became so interested in us as not to drill with their usual precision." The sergeant major frantically tried to get both male and female cadets back in proper order with their muskets, but the damage left him feeling defeated. Upon arriving in front of the Ladies' Company D, "he retired in hopeless desperation when he came to the tangle of musket and owner." When the D sergeant marched forward with the other company officers to report to Commander Dudley, they did so with irregular steps and their row uneven. Standing in front of Lieutenant Dudley, the young woman, in a "strangely weak" voice, mumbled "all present or accounted for."[21]

This was a unique and spellbinding adventure for the mixed audience of professors and students. Even the male cadets themselves could not con-centrate at first when the Ladies' Battalion was on the field. In spite of the obviously blundering performance, Pound remembered the "wild applause of the spectators whenever we came within reasonable distance." This was still an immense curiosity, and whether the exhibition had succeeded or failed, audiences were intrigued with the sight of young women in military uniforms marching and shooting muskets. In spite of Pound's critique, the Lincoln newspaper gave them high ratings, since their first public appear-ance had "attracted considerable attention and elicited much favorable comment."[22] Of course, the locals were enthralled with the "pretty" cadets, whose "natural charms were considerably enhanced by the blue costumes and jaunty cadet caps." The paper was forgiving of any of Captain Clen-nan's mistakes because "if there were any mistakes made in executing her orders they could not be detected by the casual looker on."[23] Observers seemed more fascinated with the women cadets themselves than whether they had succeeded during their first time on the field.

The women marched in one more dress parade after the first debacle, but interest in the Ladies' Battalion declined soon after Lieutenant Dudley left the university, and subsequent commanders showed opposition to a women's military regiment. For its part Company D got one last chance to perform. At the June 1888 graduation the male cadets accompanied the male graduating seniors, and for the first (and last) time in Nebraska's history, the Ladies' Battalion escorted the female graduates to commencement. Dudley gave his approval to the lady cadets because, "in the face of many difficulties," they still "increased healthful vigor and grace."[24] In spite of Dudley's compliments, the women students lost interest in military drill. By the autumn of 1888 enthusiasm had waned—women began skipping drill practice and uniforms fell into disrepair. The demise eventually came without any "loud regret or impressive ceremonials."[25] Pound noted that women's qualities of "persistency, brilliancy and adaptability" served well in most pursuits; however, these qualities failed "in the moment of need" for Company D. "Woman as a cadet had been quite the fad while she lasted, but there was no denying that she was not, in the strict sense of the word, a conspicuous or enduring success."[26] Perhaps this failure served to reinforce some students' prejudices against women's entrance into traditionally male activities.

In the late 1890s interest in women's military drill revived once again with Company Q under Capt. Stella Elliott. These women performed marching and saber drills, and for the first time, did so with bloomers instead of skirts as part of the uniform. Company Q lasted only a short while; it was overshadowed by basketball, tennis, and gymnastics exhibitions offered through the women's physical education department.

The Iowa State women had much more success with military drill than the Nebraska women, and women's military companies in Ames existed from 1879 through the late 1890s, with the longest period of consistent, yearly organization between 1884 and 1897. Women had first agitated for their own military company in 1879, and the interest continued because "military drill has been found to be a most healthful and enjoyable exercise for young ladies, and a Ladies' Battalion of two companies has been regularly organized and drilled during the last thirteen years."[27] Following the earliest women's military organization—first mentioned in the *Aurora* in 1879—interest in women's drill continued to grow at IAC, and eventually it became very much an accepted part of campus military culture in the late 1880s and early 1890s. In 1883 the *Aurora* reported the interest in drill to "provide exercise for the young ladies that will be of more practical value than sitting on the terrace or pacing slowly around the circle."[28] At first women trained with brooms instead of rifles or sabers, and, the *Aurora* added, "with *dish-cloth* ammunition we are informed." The women "will go forth conquering and to conquer; for her strength is the strength of ten men, because the stroke of her broom is sure."[29] This tongue-in-cheek use of the language and tools of domesticity served to evoke the image of an army of housewives. Perhaps the women's reasons for military drill activity were not completely understood, but women's separate domestic role still took precedence over these seemingly nonserious attempts to breach the male sphere. In 1886 the women still drilled with brooms and received no serious attention from the male students. In another apparent reference to using military skills in domestic chores, an *Aurora* poem chronicled the women's attempts to kill a rat:

> Girls to the right of him
> Girls to the left of him
> Girls right in front of him
> Made the rat quiver. . . .
> O, the wild charge they made!
> Ne'er will their glory fade! . . .
> Honor the Spear Brigade!
> Honor the charge they made!
> Ne'er let the memory fade
> Of their brave deed.[30]

In spite of the teasing jabs at women's pretense to military strength, the women gradually earned respect as a professionally drilled and trained company, and one IAC writer even related women's entrance into military activity to their rights for suffrage.

The first IAC women's battalion in 1886 was called Company G, for "girls," and by 1888 a second company was formed, called Company L, for "ladies." Women cadets earned officer ranks within these companies. In 1890 the two companies were formally organized as the Third Battalion, or Ladies Battalion, of the IAC regiment. In that position, the ladies also earned the privilege of marching, drilling, and presenting formation in front of Old Main with the entire body of student-soldiers. Photographs from around 1890 show the women as a legitimate and included part of the full IAC regiment. The separation of women into their own battalion seemed a natural gender division. The women were also included in official lists of all regimental members and officers in the IAC yearbook, the *Bomb*, in 1894 and 1895. Although IAC catalogs outlined the requirements for "Military Science" for male students in the early 1880s, no mention was ever made regarding women's military companies, indicating its status as an

23. IAC men and women cadets in front of Old Main, ca. 1890s. Iowa State University Library/Special Collections Department.

extracurricular activity. Still, this military drill experiment had great importance to women's progress within the land-grant culture. The Iowa State women eventually developed great proficiency in saber drilling, and they found early success in performance exhibitions. In contrast to the Nebraska women's embarrassing experience in 1888 and the first IAC female battalion's success at chasing rats, the 1890s IAC women showed incredible precision and capability under the leadership of Gen. James Rush Lincoln. In fact, these women were so accomplished that in 1893 they earned the right to travel with male IAC battalions to the World's Columbian Exposition, or Chicago World's Fair, as part of the Iowa delegation to that event. General Lincoln had trained intensely with the student-soldiers, and their presence in Chicago received much attention.

All members of the IAC military company, including male and female officers and cadets, band, artillery, and hospital corps, took the train from Ames to Chicago. This trip must have been an expensive venture, but General

24. IAC women military officers, 1894, from the *IAC Bomb* (1895). Iowa State University Library/Special Collections Department.

Lincoln brought "twelve hundred sandwiches." With those and the "fruit we bought on the way, we were kept from suffering." They arrived in Chicago, and after getting off the trains, they

> immediately formed into companies, and marched to the busses [*sic*] which took us to the elevated railway, this took us within three blocks of the hotel, which distance we marched. . . . We had four apartments on the corner of 65th St. and Woodlawn Avenue. There being two floors in each. The rooms were large and without partitions. The girls had cots arranged after the fashion that one usually sees in the insane asylum. There was one looking glass, about six by eighteen inches in area, and two sinks for the hundred girls and women. Some were inclined to "kick," but after a short time all began to make to best of things, and the inconveniences only added to the fun.

This excursion had turned into a grand, overnight field trip for the students, with all of the "niceties" of boarding together in large rooms, sightseeing, and experiencing the big city. The cadets spent extra time in drill practice, and "some thought it hard, but General did all in his power to make things comfortable and agreeable for us, and we were willing to do our best for him."[31]

The women's battalion especially was the subject of great curiosity and intrigue at the World's Fair. The uniqueness of land-grant women's military companies is very apparent in the reactions issued by spectators and journalists alike. Immediately upon their arrival, a reporter "was on the spot to find out all he could and make up the rest." The next morning's edition of the *Chicago Tribune* contained the reporter's account of "a unique military organization, the young ladies' spear brigade of the [Iowa] Agricultural College."[32] The reporter gave a detailed, although somewhat exaggerated description of the lady cadets. Indeed, he made a point of noting how these women behaved in public. The most "glaring incident" of misbehavior was "when one of the girls in a standing jump leaped over one of the stools that had been left unoccupied by the musicians."[33] One IAC girl responded to the accusation with, "It probably was intended to compliment us as we had marched about eight miles, and were still able to jump." Still, if he was going to exaggerate, he should have done a better job: "Why didn't they make it a table or some thing worth while?"[34] In other words, if the reporter wanted to draw attention to their unladylike and athletic behavior, why not make their feats even more amazing?

The reporter adequately noted the public's wonder and amazement at seeing the young Iowa women cadets. During the Grand Parade along Cottage Grove Avenue, the Iowa State band marched and played at the front, followed by the cadet band, and then the "column of cadets from the Iowa State Agricultural College. . . . Sandwiched between the first and last battalions marched the spear-brigade of forty-four girls, in blue uniform, armed with spears." This was followed by the cadet artillery division with one "Gatling gun drawn by two horses, and the Hospital Corps, carrying strapped on their backs the different parts of army stretchers." This whole spectacle made quite an impressive sight, but the women drew the most attention. When they arrived at the plaza near the (Iowa?) State Building, they found an enclosed drilling field guarded by police officers. "Even with this protection the eagerness of the crowd to witness the drills was so great that they were with difficulty controlled." Imagine the scene, as a congested Chicago crowd pushed against the ropes to get a better look at these women soldiers. The women cadets' spear performance, together with "the chivalry of the men present," was received with "great applause." When at the end of the display, "the girls marched out of the arena it was with a storm of hand-clapping that they will never forget."[35]

One of the lady cadets, an anonymous chronicler of the students' experiences in Chicago, recalled the various reactions, comments, and curious inquiries they received while in the big city. The Chicago public's reaction lacked no amount of shock at seeing this ladies' battalion. "Without a doubt we astonished the natives . . . for we were only ordinary human beings but they made us everything under the sun but that." As they marched in the Grand Parade, observers called them many names, including a Salvation Army, Columbian Guards, Relief Corps, and other types of "freaks." The women cadets were most disturbed when someone remarked "What big feet they have," and another thought they were "walking ads for Spear-head tobacco"—in a likely reference to the spear used to advertise one brand of tobacco popular in the 1880s and 1890s. One day, as they rushed out from dinner, a "wonder striken [sic] crowd on the streets asked the land lord what he had there. He told them nothing dangerous, only a gang going for the Cherokee Strip."[36] These references to the cadets' masculine qualities indicates observers' difficulties in accepting these challenges to gender separation and associating women military cadets as males. Overheard on the streets of Chicago, one bystander asked, "Do those girls fight with those spears?" and another: "Are you from West Point?"[37] and "Oh! Ain't they pretty?" Crowds accosted the young women wanting to know "what we were? Who we were? What we represented? When the next performance would take place?"[38] In a poem called "A Trip to the 'White City,'" the students recalled:

> Then through the streets we marching went,
> While people stared in wonderment.
> Even the buildings stern and tall,
> Seemed to think us mystical.[39]

The Columbian Exposition proved the most appropriate place in the world to highlight the land-grant women's military regimentation. A display of U.S.

military prowess by college students—combined with some progressively unique activities for young college women—fit well within the Exposition's purpose of showcasing American ingenuity, strength, and aggressive nationalism. The Chicago World's Fair also marked an important transition for American women who used this major event to challenge traditional gender expectations. Historians have highlighted the importance of women's fair participation and displays of female advancements in architecture, music, science, industry, and woman suffrage. However, the Fair represented mixed messages for women—on the one hand, most displays highlighted women's domesticity and feminine artistry, but on the other hand, fairgoers attended talks on suffrage activism. Judy Sund has described this conflict between True Womanhood and New Womanhood at the Fair, suggesting that the "emphases on housework, cookery, child care, and nursing—ratified rather than revised standard notions of women's potential to contribute to society, even as growing ranks of well-educated, affluent 'New Women' rejected conventional roles."[40] Thus the public presence of the Iowa State women's military regiment marked an important symbol of the larger gender transitions taking place for women in the 1890s to a New Womanhood that was educated, athletic, militaristic, but still feminine.

Regarding women students' foray into this public patriotic display at the Chicago World's Fair, one illustration from the *Bomb* captured the spirit of militaristic women who challenged traditional gender roles, while still keeping the physical trappings of femininity. "The American Eagle in Bloomers" indicated young women who represented a patriotic soldiering attitude, but used their bodily and clothing markings to stay womanly while doing so. Just as with earlier women's physical culture classes, these cadets sought to negotiate their femininity even while wearing military uniforms. The uniforms came complete with the decorative regalia of any man's uniform, including swords, caps, buttons, cords, stripes, and belts, but the women still dressed in skirts and feminine sleeves. Further, they ornamented their uniforms with feminine trimmings like jewelry, bows, and broaches (shaped like arrows and sabers!). By using masculine military clothing with feminine adornments, these women successfully entered male space while still maintaining their femininity.

At the Fair, as a true display of their desires to be womanly, the women had made certain to curl their hair before leaving for the dress parade that

The American Eagle in Bloomers..

25. "The American Eagle in Bloomers," from the IAC *Bomb* (1895). Iowa State University Library/ Special Collections Department.

morning. In a crowded hotel room, more than forty women frantically tried to get ready, and the girls, competing for mirror space, "doubled up like jack-knives or tied themselves into double bow-knots, trying to curl their hair before anything which gave a shadow of a reflection."[41] These land-grant women cadets succeeded in representing military efficiency, while still exhibiting Victorian femininity, beauty, and delicacy. Women's military regimentation was a unique aspect of the land-grant university experience.

At OAC, on the other hand, the idea of a women's military company never caught on, and there is no record of any organization of that type in Corvallis, although in the early 1900s, "military and fancy marching" was included in a few catalogs as part of women's physical education. UAC, founded in 1888 and opened in 1890, also established women's military companies in the early 1890s. The second annual catalog of UAC (1891–92)

LADY OFFICERS.

1st. Lieut. Ryan,   Bat. Adjt. Mills,
Capt. Hudson,   Major Starr,   2nd. Lieut. Pammell,
    2nd. Lieut. Bigelow,   1st. Lieut. Fleming.   Capt. Radnich,

26. IAC women military officers at the Chicago World's Fair, 1893, from the *IAC Bomb* (1894). Iowa State University Library/Special Collections Department.

outlined the requirements and benefits of military drill: "This department of instruction has become very popular in college life . . . and is found to be a most valuable method of securing physical culture." The reasons for its popularity were universally known: "It gives an erect carriage, ease and grace of bodily movement, and habits of discipline and order." And, like Nebraska and IAC before it, Utah State had decided to extend this activity to women. Prior to World War I, Utah State was the only western land-grant to include a description of women's military activity in its catalog: "The marked advantage of this practice to young men has led several colleges to extend the privilege of military drill to young women with the most happy results. The spear, light rifle, or some other light weapon is usually carried. The young women of this college will have the advantages of this feature of college instruction."[42]

By 1892–93 military drill at Utah State took on a mandatory flavor: "young women of this college are required to take military drill unless

27. UAC military and physical culture class, from the USAC *Bulletin, 1894–1895.* Special Collections & Archives, Merrill Library, Utah State University.

excused by request of their parents."[43] One year later, the parental excuse had to be in writing, and the women had to wear a "neat uniform-dress of dark blue . . . with forage cap." The college would supply "light rifles for drill."[44] A photograph from the 1894–95 bulletin is the only known photo of the UAC "Ladies' Military Organization," dressed in the typical skirt uniforms, with caps, rifles, and feminine bows. Unlike the Iowa State military women, who were either photographed in their own separate group photos or photographed in full parade formation together with the military men of IAC, the Utah State women cadets are here included as part of the women's physical culture department. This setting indicates how women's military drill was gradually being merged into the physical education classes by the late 1890s. In 1896–97, the college offered physical culture classes for the first time, but women still had the option for "Ladies' Military Drill," which included "Regular Infantry tactics with light rifles." This drill for women would occupy "the same time . . . as with young men."[45] That was the last time that separate women's military drill was mentioned in any UAC catalog, and by 1898 all women's physical activity was taught under Physical Culture, with "military and fancy marching" taught only as part of the general calisthenic regimen. By 1899 the era of women's separate and organized military regiments had ended at UAC, IAC, and Nebraska.

Why did almost all women's military regiments end around 1898? First, military drill for women became swallowed up within the expanding physical culture departments; by the late 1890s, women had more opportunities for team and individual sports participation. Most land-grants had women's basketball teams and also track-and-field activities, which drew the attention of the more active women students away from military drill and toward the excitement of team sports. Another possible reason for decline in women's military participation was the Spanish-American War; this saw some young male cadets leave campuses to take part in real military activity. The war depleted campus battalion numbers, since young soldiers and officers left to join the regular U.S. forces. There had never been any intention of preparing female cadets for real fighting, in spite of all the showy military training and rifle practice. During wartime, then, women students retreated from their earlier challenges to the male sphere and returned to more traditional feminine methods of supporting military economy, service, and production.

LAND-GRANT WOMEN'S SUPPORT ROLES DURING THE GREAT WAR

Women students' participation in both the Spanish-American War and World War I again reverted to something akin to traditional female activities in the Civil War. Just like the 1861–65 conflict, women during World War I supported the war effort through domestic production, soldier aid, nursing, and public activity in wartime causes. But World War I was also the first American conflict in which women could enlist as regular military personnel, although not in combat. In 1917 the navy enlisted women as "Yeomen (F)" or "Yeomenettes" to serve in administrative, communication, and other staff positions, so that more men could be freed for combat. Eventually, twelve thousand women enlisted as "Yeomenettes," serving as "clerks, switchboard operators, translators, fingerprint experts, Naval Intelligence, and recruiters." In 1918 the marines followed the navy's example by enlisting just over three hundred women as "Marinettes," also performing support duties.[46] The army never allowed for women's enlistment during World War I, even though General Pershing had asked for women telephone operators to serve in France. It is unknown whether any land-grant women students enlisted as navy or marine personnel.

Nursing was the military support area most open to women during the First World War. In the Spanish-American War, there had been no unified nurse corps, so in 1901 the Army Nurse Corps was created to supply nurses for military personnel stationed in U.S. territories — Hawaii, Guam, and the Phillippines. In 1908 the navy followed suit with the Navy Nurse Corps. By the time the United States entered World War I, the military already possessed an established and experienced nurse corps. College women served as nurses, with women from around the country attending the Vassar Training Camp for nurses in 1918. Land-grant women went to the war as nurses, through either the Army or Navy Nurse Corps. Many served at home or overseas as Red Cross nurses, particularly to care for military and civilian victims of the 1918 influenza epidemic. Ina Gittings, the director of women's athletics at Nebraska, left the university to serve in the Army Nurse Corps and later went to the Near East with the American Red Cross.[47] Of the almost twenty-two thousand American women who served as army nurses, only about half, or ten thousand, went to combat areas in France. Others served on boats or in army hospitals in the territories. During World War I, approximately three hundred nurses died at home or overseas, and most nurses' deaths were caused by disease, particularly typhoid and influenza.[48] Nebraska, OAC, and UAC each suffered at least one woman killed among their student or alumni war casualties, and Iowa State claimed two female casualties, Hortense Elizabeth Ward and Pearl Wesley Yates. One of IAC's earlier graduates, Irene (Jones) Bonnell (1898) also worked in a war hospital in France during the war, but she survived for a long life as a homemaker.[49]

The majority of land-grant women students did *not* serve overseas as nurses in combat hospitals. The students found their niche helping with wartime production of medical materials and volunteering with the local Red Cross, YMCA, and YWCA. Women also volunteered as "Canteen workers" to help entertain troops with music, reading, and conversation. Jeanie Attie's assessment of female Civil War participation can be compared to land-grant students' roles in World War I: the women's "support of the war represented a conscious decision to make unique sacrifices in defense of the nation.... [They] were propelled by the excitement and urgency that marked mobilization drives."[50] To women college students, the sacrifices were even more personal, since a large portion of fighting troops, especially in 1917 and 1918, came from land-grant college campuses, where young men had been militarily trained for more than five decades. At Nebraska, for example, more than 1,000 men joined the army in 1917; by the end of the war, more than 2,300 students had joined the military or support organizations.[51]

With fellow male students gone, young women felt a special need to support the war effort. They made needed items such as socks, bandages, and first-aid kits. Women students assembled weekly in their literary societies, sororities, dormitory clubs, and other organizations to knit, sew, and wrap bandages. One Nebraska student remembered:

> While the men were actively engaged in battle or in training for it, the women contributed their share. Miss Alice Howell and Miss Blanche Grant of the faculty went overseas as canteen workers. Professor Sarka Hrbkova, as chairman of the Women's Committee of the State Council of Defense, played a conspicuous part in the work throughout the state. An alumna, Helen Sargent, Red Cross nurse, died in the service. During the flu epidemic student nurses were recruited from the S.A.T.C. hospitals. Almost every girl on the campus worked at making surgical dressings in the Red Cross rooms under Mrs. Samuel Waugh. Many became war brides—the number of engagements and marriages skyrocketed to a new high.[52]

At Utah State during World War I, the Faculty Women's League took on major projects in support of the war effort. Beginning in 1914 the FWL, which was composed of both female faculty members and wives of male professors, began some activist efforts by discussing the plight of war-victimized children in Europe. On December 11, 1914, they voted to send a train carload of condensed milk for Belgian babies. They also began collaborating with the local Red Cross organization in Logan and after U.S. entrance into the war in 1917, the Faculty Women founded their own Red Cross unit that would meet every other Friday afternoon for four hours. In the spirit of wartime scarcity and sacrifice, the women served "punch and war wafers."[53] In 1918 the women formed a hospital committee and a "Committee on Soldiers' Welfare." The Utah State faculty women led the way in trying to mentor the young women students in war service. They formed a college women's unit of National Service for helping with wartime production and service. This group would concern itself with the "mending of soldiers, convalescent diets, convalescent comforts, and . . . entertainments."[54] In June of 1918 UAC hosted many soldiers from Utah, Wyoming, Nebraska, and California, who came for military and mechanical training. While these soldiers stayed in

Logan, the FWL provided newspapers, magazines, books, "records for the Victrola," and recreational games. The women also collected donated items for the recreation room, including an "easy chair and couches, pictures, rugs & plants . . . and the men made themselves at home from the first moment the room was opened." Every night during the two-month stay of the soldiers, three Faculty Women and one student volunteered to serve as hostesses.[55]

Every Wednesday evening, the Faculty Women's League sponsored dances for the soldiers and the college girls; these were strictly chaperoned, "thus our control was complete, & the tone of the dances was above question." When the numbers of resident soldiers increased late in the summer of 1918, the FWL stepped up their efforts in providing support to the soldiers and their families. For the women volunteers, even though the growing number of men "increased our responsibility . . . we accepted them gladly, since this seemed a direct part in the activities of the war."[56] The FWL held weekly sewing clubs for the soldiers' wives, appointed a hospital committee to help care for the sick, and also arranged a volunteer "automobile committee" that tagged local cars so that "any Soldier or Sailor 'going my way' saw at a glance an invitation to ride." Sunday outings, potluck dinners, farewell concerts when detachments left for the war, and cafeteria services on the days of departure were some of the services offered by the FWL in the final months of the war. The faculty women felt a great urgency to carry on this work "unabated" because "the men for whom we were going to be doing & planning, the members of the S.A.T.C. [Student Army Training Corps] were our own sons, brothers, and friends."[57] Women felt the need to do whatever they could to support the sacrifice of the young soldiers.

Five months after the November 1918 armistice, the FWL reported on its "war work," both in production and in assisting with recuperating soldiers. Besides entertaining soldiers and their families, the women had wrapped gauze bandage rolls, collected donated clothing, and led Liberty Bond drives. They had the free use of the sewing machines in the Women's Building of the Agricultural College, and they sewed hospital garments for the Red Cross. For months, "knitters were present in full force at every regular meeting of the League . . . and the number of sweaters, socks and mufflers turned in by our unit made a creditable showing."[58] The women continued their benevolent work with children's causes, especially for European children injured during the war. Throughout this time, the Faculty Women held no recorded discussions regarding woman suffrage, but they participated in other political activism, including the protection of migratory birds in Utah, the support of the standardization of textile production and handling in American factories, and the protection of the American dyestuff industry. This type of activism reflected the continuing expansion of the political sphere of women's organizations before, during, and after the war.

Not all land-grant women heartily supported the war effort. At Nebraska, for example, the campus became embroiled in a four-year conflict over the loyalty of German professors and the antiwar sentiment of some faculty. Much of the tension in Nebraska was particularly intense because of the state's substantial German immigrant populations, with their German language, churches, and newspapers. Non-German Nebraskans feared the possible anti-American sympathies that might come from the German professors. Some of the women professors became involved in this campus war; on April 1, 1917, a group of professors issued a resolution of support for President Wilson and his "strong foreign policy" toward Germany. The signers included Chancellor Samuel Avery, a few male professors, and "Mrs. Minnie Throop England, assistant professor of economics."[59] Besides England, another female professor, Sarka Hrbkova also supported the war effort and served on a committee to assess professor loyalty. Eva Miller Grimes remembered Professor Hrbkova as a "sincere patriot."[60] One day following the passage of the war resolution, a group of antiwar professors signed a "peace petition," and among the signers were assistant professor of chemistry Mary L. Fossler and Miss Annis S. Chaikin, secretary of the University Alumni Association. The conflict over professor loyalty to the war effort continued over the next year, with many professors accused of anti-American sentiment. Parents feared that students were being influenced by these professors, and heated debates and letters were exchanged over the war cause.[61]

The university instituted a general housecleaning in April of 1918 by putting some professors on trial for "philosophic pacifism" or "negative, halting or hesitant" support of the war. Twelve professors and staff, including Mary Fossler and Annis Chaikin, were accused in May 1918. An instructor in German, Madelen Wupper, was also questioned by the hearing committee. Women students and professors participated in these hearings as witnesses, testifying about any statements or conversations overheard in classes regarding the war or American versus German loyalties. Against Professor Fossler and Secretary Chaikin, the testimony given was not substantial. Chaikin was supposedly sympathetic to the Industrial Workers of the World (IWW), a radical union popular among western miners, loggers, and farm workers that opposed U.S. entrance into World War I. She was also questioned for not marching in the loyalty parades sponsored by the university. Professor Fossler had been overheard by some students to say that she "would rather be any woman sweeping the streets of Berlin than to be an old woman in America" and other statements that had been misconstrued as pro-German or anti-American.[62] Fossler and Chaikin were the first of the accused faculty to be absolved of any guilt, and eventually the charges against the other faculty were also dropped, since the university had failed to prove any blatant and dangerous disloyalty.

The Nebraska controversy over faculty loyalty showed some of the political activism assumed by women professors and students during wartime, both for and against the war.[63] When the OAC cadets were called up to active duty, Bernice Forest expressed disagreement with the United States' entrance into the war in her diary. On April 8, 1917, she announced, "the biggest and most dreadful reality right now is *War*! We are at last actually at war with Germany."[64] And the reason, she felt, seemed almost trite: "just because a few ships have been submarined out on the Atlantic, the people—I guess it is the people altho [*sic*] I can't discover *which* people—say we must 'uphold our honor' by *war*." Bernice's frustration portrays the frustration that many felt at entering an unpopular, foreign war, and the fact that someone far away in Washington—"the people"—had made this decision without a democratic consultation. Bernice felt that a declaration of war on Germany was an extreme reaction to some minor foreign relations squabbles.

> Now Pres. Wilson is calling for an army of 500,000 men at once and is planning a militarism as big as Germany's. They are going from one extreme to the other. It is dreadful to think of. Some of our boys have gone already and are on their way some where—the destination is unknown—to do parole duty, I suppose altho [*sic*] no one seems to know just what they will have to do. Probably they will go to the Mexican border to prevent invasion there. That isn't bad—I think, that is policy, but this thing of

invading Germany, I think is foolish. By the time they get started over there some submarine will come along and sink the ships. Besides — I don't think we have any business to go over to Germany. It is alright to protect our own interest here at home — but that is enough.[65]

Bernice Forest's antiwar sentiments stemmed not only from the fear at seeing her fellow male students go to war but also from a somewhat thoughtful and pragmatic approach to American isolationism. It may be necessary to defend one's own borders, but not to fight a foreign war on another continent. And perhaps her disapproval was even more personal: "I hope all of the boys here won't have to go anyway. I say I don't like 'l—— but I'd miss him anyway."[66]

Although not involved directly in military activities, women expanded their social and political influence during these years. For the most part, women demonstrated loyalty to the American war cause, and they participated in loyalty parades and Liberty Bond drives. Student women organized into their own campus Red Cross divisions and helped with nursing duties locally and abroad. Mostly, women gave patriotic and moral support to the men fighting overseas. The students who stayed behind gave up their traditional campus activities, such as athletics, theater productions, University Week, and Homecoming. Katherine Coffee remembered, "'Dates' were scarce on the campus for not only were eligibles lacking, but also funds were scarce. 'Spending' was curtailed. . . . Student money went for Liberty Bonds."[67]

One cartoon from a Nebraska student newspaper in 1918 adequately portrayed the role of female student support of the military and the war cause during the First World War. A young woman, dressed in patriotic attire, leans upward toward her soldier in an affectionate and supportive stance. The woman represented in this cartoon is a far cry from the independent, saber-carrying women cadets who marched in the Chicago World's Fair in 1893. But, even as wartime opened new avenues for women's public service, so it also retrenched women and men into traditional gender roles. That meant that male students signed up to fight the Germans, and women either stayed behind to cheer them on or followed them to battlefield hospitals to nurse their wounds. At Nebraska, each male company of cadets had a female "sponsor" — a pretty, finely dressed, and seemingly elegant woman

28. University of Nebraska World War I–era cartoon, ca. 1918. Archives & Special Collections, University of Nebraska–Lincoln Libraries.

student who acted as a kind of mascot or cheerleader. The responsibility of these sponsors is not clearly defined, but perhaps soldiers kept pictures of their sponsors while away at war or received letters from them. At any rate, women students during wartime returned to traditional feminine serving and support roles. Both women and men felt the harsh impact of World War I on campus life. Katharine Newbranch Coffee assessed that "lives and morale of many were broken. Others disillusioned, thwarted, confused, drifted into paths of least resistance. . . . The glory of soldiering was forgotten in the economic and social problems that promptly settled upon us."[68]

Perhaps the greatest impact of women's participation in the 1917–18 war effort was the escalation of the woman suffrage movement across the United States. In 1918 Harriet Stanton Blatch called for an expansion of women's military service and linked female war contributions to the need to give women "an equal share in the right to self-government." Theodore Roosevelt, in his introduction to Blatch's book, called 1918 a "new day in the great epic march of the age" for women's rights.[69] Critics of woman suffrage had long argued that because women could not serve in the military, they should not vote, but this criticism now came under attack.

Even land-grant students had linked women's military participation with the expansion of women's political rights. When the IAC women had lobbied for a military regiment back in 1884, the *Aurora* made a direct connection to women's rights: "Lady believers in Woman Suffrage have resolved to remove the last objection to their voting. They have subjected themselves to military duty."[70] As women had solidified their public and private wartime contributions, in the workforce, in the medical professions, and in the political realm, they added a more vocal emphasis to their demands for universal suffrage. (The direct connections between women's military activity and woman suffrage will be elaborated more thoroughly in the following chapter.) Still, female students very importantly used the foundation of their military activity — either in actual military drilling or in wartime support work like Liberty Bond drives and Red Cross work — to challenge gender separation on land-grant campuses and to call for further progress for women. Women did eventually see the passage of a national woman suffrage amendment soon after the war, but female military service remained controversial, with all military enlistment ended by the War Department until the reestablishment of separate women's military corps units in World War II.

CONCLUSION

Military training for women was one of the truly unique contributions of the western land-grant atmosphere. In almost every case, women students themselves lobbied for and gained the privileges of participating in this event. For around twenty years, between 1878 and 1899, women's military regiments were a significant part of land-grant culture for women students, and the impact was important. Military drill gave women additional opportunities for healthy physical activity — they marched, fenced, and drilled with rifles, and most of this they performed outdoors. Through military drill, women students once again found a method of broadening their social, political, and physical space. Besides providing successful leadership skills, military drill for women students also appeared to lead to other careers and activism outside of the traditional women's sphere. Louise Pound participated with Nebraska's Company D in 1888, and she also succeeded in tennis, basketball, and later as a professor of English at the university. Ethel B. Rundall was a first lieutenant in the 1895 IAC Ladies' Battalion. She also played in intercollegiate tennis championships in the state of Iowa in the 1890s. Elmina Wilson was a member of the Iowa State Ladies' Battalion from 1888 to 1892 and served successively as sergeant, captain, and major. After graduation and subsequent graduate work in civil engineering, Wilson became the first female civil engineering professor at Iowa State in 1893.[71] Of the eight women officers from IAC who went to the Chicago World's Fair in 1893, one died after graduation — Maj. Evelyn Starr. Of the surviving seven, four married and became homemakers — 1st Lt. Edith Ryan, Battle Adjt. Grace Mills, 2nd Lt. Emma Elsie Pammell, and Capt. Helen Radnich. But 2nd Lt. Cassie Pearl Bigelow became an accountant; Capt. Jessie Hudson became a physician; and 1st Lt. Annie Wilson Fleming became a college math professor. All but two of the surviving officers are known to have participated in women's club work and some activism in their postgraduation lives.

At UAC, Blanche Cooper, of the class of 1901, took military drill from 1895 to 1897, which the Alumni Association reported "accounts for her upright and sprightly carriage." She took the teachers' course at Columbia University in New York and later taught domestic science at the University of Utah and UAC.[72] Sabina Hermoine Hart graduated in 1897 from UAC, and she remembered that "I took military drill both years and liked it very much." She taught school and was the first woman elected Cache County Superintendent of Schools in 1909.[73] Rose Homer Widtsoe, of the class of 1900, was a "member of the girls' company of cadets" while at UAC. After postgraduate work in food chemistry and organic chemistry, she founded the department of domestic science at Brigham Young College in Logan, Utah, and later published articles on sanitation and household decoration.[74] These few examples portray some of the successes that women student cadets had in later life. While no direct correlation can be made between students' professional fulfillment and early military participation, it seems apparent that young women who took military drill possessed the energy, motivation, and organizational skills to achieve collegiate and professional success.

Military drill for women had no real and direct precedent prior to its 1870s land-grant invention; even during the Civil War, most of the more than four hundred women who served in the military did so disguised as men. During World War I, the navy and marine enlisted women performed primarily support and clerical roles in administration. At no time in American experience had women organized into official military companies that drilled in marching and combat skills with rifles and sabers. The land-grant experience showed how women students could successfully invade the male sphere, even during a time of strict gender separation. By taking some of the typically masculine activities and redefining them for their own feminine pursuits, women opened avenues to greater freedom of expression. Even when women were fulfilling traditional gender support roles during World War I, such as nursing, home production, entertaining troops, and clerical work, these activities helped women students and faculty to increase their political and social awareness, and led to a greater urgency in the national women's rights movement. Military activity for women students both as "student-soldieresses" and in wartime support roles was an important way in which women challenged gender separation and expanded their public, social, and political influence within the land-grant culture.

8

Challenging Political Separation

Women's Rights Activism at
Land-Grant Colleges and Universities

All I ask for woman is that the opening sentence of the declaration [sic] of Indepen-
dence be made broad enough to include her.
ALMA BENEDICT, *LINCOLN* [NE] *DAILY JOURNAL*, June 15, 1888

On November 12, 1916, Bernice Forest, a student at Oregon Agricultural
College, recorded in her diary that she had voted for Charles Evan Hughes
in the presidential election. When Pres. Woodrow Wilson beat Hughes,
Forest expressed a tempered disappointment: "Maybe my choice was ill
advised," she said. However, she had thoughtful reasons for voting against
Wilson, believing "any kind of a change ought to be better than these hard
times with everything we eat and wear soaring so high we can't get them."[1]
Forest's single ballot, cast on Tuesday, November 7, 1916, represented a
culmination of almost fifty years of feminine political action at western land-
grant colleges. Forest was a beneficiary of the legacy of political activism
practiced by land-grant students since the 1860s, and she had what most
women before her did not have—the right to political franchise. In the midst
of a post–Civil War movement to secure political, social, and legal rights for
women, land-grant students actively contributed to the progress of women's
rights, especially suffrage. From the earliest years of land-grant education,
students discussed, debated, wrote, protested, and argued about feminist
activism. Women students challenged gender separation on a political level
of suffrage and other women's rights. This land-grant culture of feminist
reform and political inclusion successfully contributed to a larger national
culture of gender reforms.

Women's rights activism after the Civil War achieved new heights, especially as feminist leaders sought advancements for women in legal rights, property rights, and woman suffrage.[2] The 1870s growth of the woman suffrage movement accompanied the growth of women's higher education in America. When leaders of the National Woman Suffrage Association failed to see the passage of a federal equal suffrage amendment after the Civil War, they took their battle to the individual states, where much potential for success lay in the western United States.[3] Women land-grant students contributed a necessary energy and momentum for the women's rights movement in the West.

Coeducational land-grants are significant for an examination of women's rights feminist activism, for a few important reasons. First, the mixed-gender environment of land-grant colleges showed how men and women in a small campus community could work together for a cause. Because women and men were educated together, political activism on behalf of women went beyond the "women-only" distinction of eastern and urban women's clubs and organizations. Further, through campus elections, women students often achieved elected positions of leadership, although some historians have shown how women students more often were elected to "second-in-command" positions to men rather than full leadership roles. Still, with males and females running for editorial and class positions, students observed the successful workings of a relatively progressive democracy on a small scale. Historians have correlated women's educational progress with their access to political rights. However, only a few have examined the impact of women students on women's activism, and most of that emphasis has been on eastern women's colleges.[4] Scholars have ignored the impact of western women college students on the culture of feminist political activism. Finally, land-grants proved excellent climates for the promotion of feminine activism because of what women already did as students. Journalism, literary debating, and leadership on newspaper staffs and in literary societies gave women students the experience to further expand their political realm.

Women's rights flourished in coeducational environments that already favored the progress of women in higher education, journalism, military activity, and physical culture. Women students had opportunities for public performance and oration in many venues, including literary exhibitions and commencement exercises. Susan A. Glenn has examined the impact of women's public performance on their new roles as activists in the late nineteenth century. Regarding the growing phenomenon of women "making spectacles of themselves" through theater and other types of exhibitions, Glenn argued that "on stage and off, turn-of-the-century women were increasingly drawing attention to themselves, asserting their rights to education, to political participation, to employment, to sexual expressiveness, to a voice as cultural critics."[5] As land-grant women presented themselves and their ideas to the public, they gained more freedom to defend and support women's issues.

Land-grant women students furthered the cause of women's reform and the progress of political rights through various activist methods. First, on-campus activism supported a variety of women's issues, including education, dress and clothing reform, legal rights, and temperance. Women students also encouraged a feminist awareness by writing and debating about issues particular to women, including women in history, women authors, women's clubs, and women's work. Participation in these rhetorical activities helped move women onto the larger field of suffrage activism. Second, students at coeducational universities were able to experience firsthand what it was like to practice equal suffrage. Both men and women voted for and were elected to positions on the newspaper staffs, literary societies, and class leadership; in these smaller worlds of campus communities, students saw how equal suffrage could succeed in practice among an educated and literate electorate of both sexes. Third, students took the national issue of woman suffrage and applied this debate to their campus environment. Woman suffrage became one of the most important political causes of land-grant students between 1868 and 1918. The fight over suffrage played out in literary societies and even in campus brawls. The land-grant actors in the suffrage debate included both men and women, who added themselves to the growing armies of pro-suffrage activists. A few of these students even became important national figures in the woman suffrage cause. Carrie Chapman Catt, the only female IAC graduate in 1880, represents the land-grant community's greatest contribution to the national woman suffrage cause. Her ideas developed their roots during her collegiate years in Ames. Catt stands as the foremost land-grant activist. Her leadership helped bring about the passage of the Nineteenth Amendment to the Constitution.

THE LAND-GRANT REFORM CLIMATE: WOMEN'S ISSUES

The whisperings of "women's rights" began early on land-grant campuses and caused no small amount of student conflict. As talk of women's rights entered oac in 1869, the *Student Offering* editor gave a sound warning to those professing women's rights: "Avoid advocating any of the isms of the day.... Remember [that] the advocate of false doctrines and dogmatic isms shall surely fall.... Women's Rights don't pay in this age of the world. Avoid this rock upon which it split for there is danger in that direction."[6] And the Nebraska *Hesperian* in 1872 noted the growing interest in women's reform movements: "Now there are some questions which agitate the country at present and prominent among these is what is termed 'Women's Rights.' And as this idea has diffused itself throughout the land and seems to have possessed the minds of some of our lady students, I may be pardoned for referring to it here."[7] The writer did not know quite what to make of women's rights but recognized its potential: "It may be, then, that some good is to grow out of this woman question, although we will not attempt to say what that good is." Land-grant students found themselves in the middle of a budding college culture of social reform, and students took advantage of this reform climate to fight for many issues specific to the women's rights movement. Women's education, dress reform and physical culture, legal rights, and temperance—each of these issues found willing and eager student activists at western land-grant colleges and universities.

In the 1870s women's educational progress was an issue that grew naturally out of the land-grant environment. Male and female student writers seemed especially concerned with the progress of women's education, because of the democratizing effects that public higher education could have on civilization. Not only did students support and promote coeducation as a favorable system to the monastic gender segregation in the East, but they also promoted the ideal of women's practical and scientific training. Student writers often criticized the frivolous finishing education for eastern elite women, which, they felt, taught young females to be useless and shallow ornament-wives. The language of educational reform for women, while promoting the development of women's intellectual talents, continued to ring with a language of separation that emphasized women's elevated, civilizing roles. Women's education should help to establish civilized homes, where proper republican virtues could be taught. Perhaps the best-articulated expression of this move to reform women's education came from the pen of a male Nebraska student, G. A. Watson, in May of 1873. Watson considered the importance of women's education for civilization and the home:

An educated woman will not make herself ridiculous by talking Latin and quoting the Greek Anthology. . . . What women need is not less accomplishments, but more of the solid education, through training which serves as the proper foundation for all graces and refinements. To-day women are accomplished to death. They have been taught to think that graces, and refinements, and elegances are everything. They waste their lives in adornments. It is all ruffle and no garment. To sing and play the piano, and dance, and knit, and sketch, and chaff and dress, and entertain company, and visit, and the thousand other nothings that we have not the patience to enumerate.

These make up the sum of a fashionable woman's existence: and underneath it all there is the weakness of undeveloped powers, the vacuity of an unstored mind, the listlessness and frivolity of an immature soul—a woman in years but a child in everything that pertains to the real.[8]

Male writers were not the only ones to demand a higher standard of women's education. Women reformers continually worked for an education that included scientific and philosophical study. When Sarah Baker Eddy spoke at the opening of UAC in 1890, she emphasized the importance of women's equal education, because women "should have the constant aid of a well disciplined and well stored mind." Eddy soundly echoed the plan of land-grant education: "I hold that every girl ought thoroughly to fit herself for some definite calling aside from the home."[9] Amid this spirit of educational reform emerged the strong demands for women's domestic economy training, and many educators hearkened to the nobilizing and civilizing effects that a sensible education could have on women as homemakers and mothers. Many land-grant writers, both men and women, subscribed to the ideas of domestic feminism, which rolled women's political and social influence into their maternal domesticity.

Complaints against useless feminine adornment went beyond educational reform to include the frivolity and vain ornamentation in women's dress. The women's rights movement spoke much about clothing reform, particularly in the midst of a growing awareness about women's physical health and the negative impact of restrictive corsets on lungs, posture, and blood circulation.[10] Land-grant women felt the importance of the women's dress reform movement. The all-female Cliolian Society at IAC in the 1870s devoted a few of their debating sessions to whether "the present mode of dress is detrimental to the health of women," and "that the late 'Dress Reform' movement is practicable and conducive to the health of the American woman."[11] And one 1873 IAC graduate spoke on women's dress reform in her commencement speech. Ena Edson claimed that both men and women "were answerable for woman's frivolities and wickedness in the matter of dress."[12]

Women's dress reform had a willing audience at land-grants, where students eschewed the elitism and absurdity of what was perceived as eastern behavior, dress, and attitudes. The *Aurora* editor complimented Edson: "This young lady's oration would certainly justify the opinion that the teaching of Iowa State Agricultural College is promotive of good sense, and a commendable reform in female attire."[13] And the Nebraska *Hesperian* in 1872 printed Elizabeth Cady Stanton's famous argument for women's education, which also portrayed how women leaders viewed ridiculous clothing styles. Said Stanton: "I would like to see you take thirteen hundred young men and lace them up and hang ten or twenty pounds weight of clothes on their waists, perch them up on three inch heels, cover their heads with ripples, chignon, rats and mice, and stick ten thousand hairpins into their scalps."[14] Most land-grant women understood the importance of elegant and stylish dress, without ridiculous vanity. Mary Welch's advice to IAC women in the 1870s exhibited the importance of sensible and tasteful dress:

> The art of dressing is a fine art. It does not consist in spending large sums of money on personal adornment or long days of toil in making elaborate trimming. . . . If she be cultivated, refined, and have the true innate womanly grace and taste that are inborn in many, [a woman's] dress will evince it all. From the tip of the well-made shoe—and such a woman can tolerate no other—to the crown of the symmetrical head she will be altogether a thing of beauty. . . . Never wear, if you can possibly help it, ugly shoes, untidy underclothing, soiled gloves, and above all avoid tawdry and dirty finery. The first essential of a well dressed woman is exquisite neatness. Her collar and cuffs are always spotless, her ribbons are fresh, her ornaments are real, her lace is genuine.[15]

What was offensive to dress reformers was the elaborate physical trappings of ridiculous fashion, and Welch's advice certainly suggested a sense of restraint.

Corset reform in the late nineteenth century received the most attention from dress reformers, including women students like Helen Aughey, a
Nebraska student in the 1880s. Aughey attended a lecture given by Dr. Dio
Lewis at the University of Nebraska in 1884, when he spoke about women's
culture and dress reform. Women students showed great interest in what Dr.
Lewis had to say, and the Lincoln newspaper noted that "the ladies were
in large preponderance."[16] Students took interest in Lewis's remarks on
women's health and posture, the need for women to have physical activity,
but most especially, the urgency of corset reform in America. He complained
that among the women he had seen in New York, every one "had her waist
compressed at least eight inches less than its normal circumference, and
some as much as sixteen." He was amazed that designers tried to squeeze
women into unnatural shapes, thus "declaring that God had no taste and no
style." Lewis's solution for the physical and intellectual progress for women
found welcoming listeners among land-grant students, including Aughey,
who kept a report of the talk in her college scrapbook: "When [a woman]
is unshackled and untrammelled [*sic*] by senseless devices of fashion and
frivolity, when she can breathe and digest to her heaven-designed capacity,
she will be stronger than man, and do more with her finely tempered brain
than he can with his more coarse grained. When woman is once free she will
enter upon a grander career than her most enthusiastic friend ever dreamed
of. Now she is so pinched out that she cannot start upon it."[17] Women's
corset reform found willing sympathizers among land-grant women, especially in the 1890s, as students took to the streets on drop-frame bicycles
and participated in team sports.

Reformers in the later nineteenth and early twentieth centuries condemned overly restrictive corsets, frilly and superfluous dress styles, ridicu-
lously large and ornate women's hats, and impractical high heels. Physical
culture instructors especially led the fight against corsets and high heels,
and through the physical education movement, women students began to
understand the importance of practical and healthy dress. Some students
even showed a willingness to breach propriety in order to preserve their
comfort and freedom. Bernice Forest at OAC wore tennis shoes to a dance
instead of high heels, and while waltzing with the dean of women, she
reported, "I stepped on her feet once and she looked down at my feet. I
know I burned clear to my ears, for I had on white tennis shoes and they

didn't look as beautiful as dainty high heel slippers. She always wears such high heeled things that she made me feel, just by looking, that I was very inappropriately dressed."[18] Bernice defended her actions, however, for a reason that most dress reformers would have cheered: "I wore them for comfort, for I remembered my experience of last year and I didn't want any sore feet like them again."[19]

Women's hats also became the objects of dress reform. Critics viewed hat decoration as frivolous and unnecessary. According to Jennifer Price, "Women's elite fashions—which achieved such byzantine dimensions in the late nineteenth century, when they became the stuff of Edith Wharton novels—mandated a devotion to hats that can now seem wondrous in a more hat-free age." Hats in the 1890s became "fashion's major feminine accessory and its superego."[20] Further, since women's hats used exotic and rare birds and their feathers as ornamentation, the conservation movement of the 1890s played on the conservationist sympathies of American women to encourage hat reform.[21] Groups such as the Audubon Society demanded a revolution in women's head apparel. Hat reform found an even more willing audience at land-grant colleges for mostly practical reasons—students could not see over the hats in front of them during classes. In 1898, when the Oregon State YWCA asked the women to remove their hats for a meeting, the *Barometer* heralded the move because "it seems that a change might be hoped for in this aggravating and inappropriate custom of making public gatherings largely exhibitions of head dress."[22] Big hats affected men and women students alike: "A neatly trimmed, handsome little hat is very becoming on a feminine head under proper conditions, but to sit behind it for a whole evening vainly trying to see what might be transpiring beyond will cause anyone to lose his admiration for it. The new woman may have many imperfections but if she can reform this evil fashion she will have done a good deed for humanity."[23] That the *Barometer* editors gave the responsibility of hat reform to the "New Woman" shows the important linkage between clothing reform and women's rights activism.

Women students also found themselves in the midst of legal changes for women. The late nineteenth century saw the expansion of women's prerogatives to purchase and retain their own property and to seek divorces and retain child custody.[24] That land-grant women were keenly aware of important changes in feminine legal rights was evidenced by the many literary society discussions, debates, and mock trials on the topic. In 1873 the mixed Crescent Society at IAC held a mock divorce trial between "Jennie Kent and David A. Kent" in which the judge ruled in favor of the wife's divorce suit.[25]

Land-grant students also understood the changing practices of courtship and marriage. In April 1880 Carrie Lane (later Chapman Catt) participated in a mock "breach of promise" suit in the Crescent Literary Society. The society hall was "crowded with visitors, eager to witness the trial." Lane played "Miss Victoria Hardfist" with Tom Burke as "Mr. Benjamin Butterface." The plaintiff "claimed the small sum of $10,000 with which to heal her broken heart." Due to "the pitiful expression on Benjamin's face," the jury ruled in favor of Mr. Butterface.[26] But even more likely, the decision showed the students' awareness of the loosening of rigid courtship rituals in late nineteenth-century America.[27] Students also understood the movement for changes in property rights, especially for married women. In 1873 the Cliolian Society decided to debate the revolutionary issue that "the financial affairs of husband and wife should be separate."[28]

As they felt the significance of women's reform movements, many women students employed a common feminist tool of the nineteenth century by showcasing famous (and not-so-famous) women's educational, literary, and historical achievements. Called "contribution studies," students focused on the accomplishments of female political and military leaders, writers, and novelists. For example, in 1877, when May Fairfield wrote an essay for the *Hesperian* regarding goal-setting and personal achievement, she used only female examples of individual success. She cited no biographies of famous men, but instead offered Florence Nightingale and Harriet Beecher Stowe, "Mrs. Browning," George Sand, and Margaret Fuller as the subjects for aspiration.[29] Women students most often wrote about Joan of Arc, Madame De Stael, George Elliot, Queen Elizabeth, and Mary, Queen of Scots. Female characters in Shakespeare's plays were common essay subjects, especially Portia in *The Merchant of Venice*. In March of 1883 Agatha West of IAC presented a speech at the Iowa State Oratorical Contest on Charlotte Corday, a martyr for the French Revolution.[30] Women highlighted historical female heroines to combat outdated notions about women's weakness, ignorance, and sexual nature. The famous activist-lawyer, Phoebe Couzins, came to Ames in 1883 and gave a lecture, "Some Mistakes about Eve." The

TABLE 2. OAC Sorosis Literary Society and UAC Sorosis Society debates:
Women's topics presented in society meetings, 1897–1908

Date	OAC debate topics	Date	UAC debate topics
January 19, 1897	Elizabeth is deserving of admiration		
November 9, 1897	Women should go to the Klondike		
November 30, 1897	Are women hurting the chances of men in business?		
May 17, 1898	Women's position in France		
		May 10, 1899	Gabriel and Evangeline
		May 22, 1899	The importance of domestic science
November 3, 1899	Women prominent in Oregon literature		
		February 12, 1900	Women and home
		February 26, 1900	Suffrage for women
		March 21, 1900	The dream of fair women
April 20, 1900	Women in the hospital, women in music, and Club women		
		October 10, 1900	Club women of today
		October 17, 1900	Mrs. Gladstone as seen at home
		October 31, 1900	How perfume is made
		November 7, 1900	The women of China
November 9, 1900	Origins of women's colleges, athletics at women's college, and dormitory life of girls		
		November 28, 1900	Women who have improved the world
December 4, 1900	The founding of Vassar and Wellesley colleges, the influence of these colleges, and pretty customs there		

Date	OAC debate topics	Date	UAC debate topics
		December 5, 1900	Women's work in charity, from *Good Housekeeping*
		January 16, 1901	Women workers in France, from *Harper's Bazaar*
		January 23, 1901	What Woman has done
		January 30, 1901	Biographical sketch of Queen Victoria
October 11, 1901	Women as masqueraders		
		November 14, 1901	A history of women's clubs
May 2, 1902	Dormitory life is not beneficial to young ladies		
		October 15, 1903	The possibilities of women's work
January 8, 1904	Girls should not marry before they are 33 years old		
		April 6, 1905	Mark Twain's "Woman—God Bless Her"
February 14, 1908	Women should receive the same wages for the same work as men		

Source: Sorosis Literary Society, "Minutes, 1895–1901" and "Minutes, 1910–1912," OSUA, Corvallis; Sorosis Society, "Minute Book, 1899–1920," USUA, Logan.

Aurora's coverage made a specific point about Couzins's experience in "court practice," showing the necessity of legal experience for challenging outdated notions about female nature.[31]

The most likely environment for discussing and highlighting women's roles in history and literature were the all-female literary societies, the Cliolian at IAC, the Sorosis at UAC, and the Sorosis at OAC. By 1900 women's societies devoted much attention to women's issues and famous women biographies. Between 1898 and 1908 both the OAC and the UAC Sorosis focused on similar themes particular to women. At OAC topics varied from literary essays about George Elliott to feminist issues such as suffrage and women's wages. Society women expanded their interest in women's problems to an international scale, dealing with the conditions of women around the world. Societies held theme meetings with entire sessions devoted to multiple feminine topics; in 1900 the OAC Sorosis held feminine-themed meetings on three occasions. Table 2 demonstrates the frequency of women's issues presented in the Sorosis Societies of OAC and UAC between 1897 and 1908.

Women students in all-female societies recognized the significance of presenting topics important to women in a comfortable forum. By highlighting social and political issues, biographies, success stories, and women's history, students showed themselves as worthy activists. Society work also gave female students the opportunities for examining women's roles in nontraditional ways, as in 1904, when the OAC Sorosis discussed whether "Girls Should Not Marry Before They are 33 Years Old." And in 1908 the Sorosis women celebrated Valentine's Day with a discussion of women's equal pay for equal work. Society women at land-grants used their female sociality and political awareness to further their understanding of women's lives and work.

The study of history provided an especially empowering tool for increasing feminist understanding at land-grant institutions. Women drew attention to the fact that the goddess of history was a female, and the Cliolian Society at IAC took its name from Clio, one of the nine Greek muses. One essayist reminded students to "follow the Goddess of History . . . to show you the history of noble women of the past."[32] Clio could teach students about "Coriolanus, whose fidelity to country overcame all selfish loves and saved her native city and nation. She will direct you to the bloody fields of the Crimea, and point out the angelic form of Florence Nightingale, who through her undying love for suffering humanity, transformed the . . . hospital into a place of comfort for the wounded soldier." And in the most commonly cited example of feminine historical greatness, "You can read of a Joan of Arc, who, upheld by the inspiration of her own fidelity, rescued her sinking nation." Clio offered others less well-known, including "Josephine, whose untiring energies assisted Napoleon to gain the hearts of his countrymen." She also "points with pride to the mothers of Washington, Sumner and Lincoln."[33]

Interestingly, women's historical and literary achievements were highlighted by both supporters and opponents of woman suffrage—by the former to show how far women could go with the ballot, and by the latter to show that women's influence had no need of the ballot, because of her more elevated and noble impact on the home and family. According to the above-mentioned women's historian, Clio "turns with indifference from the woman whose . . . chief ambition is to gain a throne of power and wave a scepter over a jeering, vulgar, deceitful crowd of politicians." Instead, "she takes pride in recording the acts of women whose love is for home, truth and beauty, and who devote their lives to the work of instilling these holy loves into the hearts of others." Clio will tell you: "The best right of a woman is to be a household queen / Where her power is unbroken, her sway is full and supreme."[34] And in one essay on "The Women of History," the author called for students to look primarily to those women of history who exhibited "patriotism, motherly love, wifely devotion, and the desire for the advancement of the good and the true." For the other, "unveiled half" of woman, we "see woman only in her baser form."[35] Indeed, because Lady Macbeth was so evil, "we hesitate to apply the name of *woman*," and "Catherine de Medechi [*sic*] is truly characterized by the appellation *fiend*."[36] This linkage of women's historical greatness with righteousness and nobility shows how those in the nineteenth century associated women's influence with their innately virtuous, maternal, and moral character. Once Lady Macbeth descended into evil, she completely lost her feminine identity. Although a blanket characterization of all women as virtuous and moral was used to elevate society's regard for women, feminist reform activists would eventually reject this stereotype, because it only served to reinforce the traditional "separate spheres" ideology.

For most feminist writers, the leap from women as great historical figures to the move for woman suffrage was not a huge one. Even if some student historians held to the belief that women's greatest power lay in the home and not the ballot, still most recognized that "women's greatness is not alone . . . in the blessing which her children shower on her head," but also in "her greatness as a legislator, and executive, a warrior."[37] Women's right to vote was a natural outgrowth of their place in history, and student writers and speakers had successfully drawn greater attention to women's historical contributions. Whether the motivation was to reinforce women's domestic influence or to offer her political rights, the land-grant students' use of literary and journalistic feminism portrayed the female contributions of history and thus served as a powerful tool in reform activism of the land-grant culture.

Land-grant colleges and universities served as important laboratories for women's reform movements in the nineteenth and early twentieth centuries. Encouraged by the liberal-minded newspapers and literary societies, women students found an academic climate favorable to a spirit of progressive feminist reform. Verbal and written discussions of women's education, legal rights, dress reform, and female historical achievements all added to a growing spirit of land-grant women's political power. Both male and female students would translate this reform spirit to student activism in favor of the most far-reaching goal of women's rights activism — equal suffrage. Land-grant students contributed in remarkable and unique ways to the woman suffrage movement in the West and in the United States as a whole. Although the students and citizens of Iowa, Nebraska, Utah, and Oregon endured long and hard-fought battles regarding the female franchise, the patient reform activism of land-grant students — both men and women — helped to further the cause of woman suffrage in America.

THE STAGE FOR WOMAN SUFFRAGE: STUDENT POLITICAL ACTIVITIES

Land-grants provided a climate conducive to woman suffrage activism. Students participated in a campus-level form of republicanism, as men and women together voted for class officers, newspaper editorial staffs, and literary society officers. These were important positions, especially in the 1870s and 1880s when student populations were small and all their attention centered around newspapers and literary societies. That women students in the early

1870s secured elected offices is no small matter, especially when viewing campuses as microcommunities with similar social and political structures. Students were able to experience the direct impact of equal suffrage, and one must not assume that they failed to see the significance of this localized democracy. On the contrary, students understood very well how campus elections translated to a wider view of women's political rights in the United States. One *Hesperian* editor remarked that because women "have, and excercise [*sic*] the right of voting in the paper association, and on more than one occasion have determined into whose hands the paper should be placed," then they should show greater responsibility regarding paper contributions.[38]

For the most part, women students earned second-in-command positions, subordinate to male heads of organizations; that is, a female associate editor to a male editor and female vice presidents to male presidents, both in the literary societies and in class leadership. Women also served as secretaries, thus reinforcing this position as a traditionally female role. These elected relationships reflected the dynamics apparent in the Victorian culture of marriage, where husbands were expected to act as heads over their wives. When Henry H. Wilson was elected the *Hesperian* editor in chief in 1878, the associate editor was Emma Parks. Interestingly, the two later married, and Wilson recognized the connection between their elected positions and their marital relationship: "I found her assistance so valuable that in 1880 I offered her a permanent job which she accepted and has been assisting me ever since."[39] The notion of a woman as an assistant in both personal and professional life marked how far the women's rights movement still had to go in pursuing true equality, in spite of small suffrage victories.

These elections were usually accomplished by public and vocal voting within individual society meetings. In the case of Wilson's and Parks's December 1877 elections to the *Hesperian*, the proceedings were no calm affair: "For a month preceding the event the two factions were on the ragged edge of expectation, each party feeling quite sure that they were destined to be successful. At last everything was in readiness, and the day was appointed. Both sides were eager for the fray, and got down to their work with the energy of desperation." After meeting for "a stormy session of four hours' duration," the election results were announced, with Wilson and Parks victorious, along with "Officers of the *Hesperian* Student Association," including a female vice president, Miss Elma Hawley.[40]

Public elections were exactly the environments that nineteenth-century Americans hoped women would never have to enter. Since polls were often scenes of vulgarity, drunkenness, and even physical violence, anti-suffragists sought to keep "the fair sex" away from election debauchery. Even though women were considered too virtuous for public elections, still, land-grant women entered that public sphere, if only at the campus level. Granted, student voters were sober, and professors or administrators supervised society elections. However, to twenty-year-old students in the 1870s, a literary election was just as important as one that might determine the state of the union. Students put body and soul into their opportunities for democratic action, and pro-suffrage activists believed that women voters could morally cleanse the voting environment and political sphere. In July 1885 the IAC *Aurora* printed this exchange between two eastern university newspapers regarding suffrage: the *Vanderbilt Observer* argued, "there has never been upon earth a government whose reins were white enough to be held by the hand of a woman." The *Fayette Collegian* responded, "True, 'Zero' but you know what a hatred of dirt mother has? Well, she wouldn't have hold of the reins very long ere they would be purified and father wouldn't dare soil them again either."[41] In other words, once women got their morally clean hands on the election culture, corruption and graft would inevitably cease.

Campus elections also reinforced anti-suffragists' positions regarding the dangers of women's vote. In September of 1876 the IAC students held an impromptu presidential vote in the dining room of University Hall. The vote was "Hayes 104, Tilden 42, Cooper 4," with Hayes winning because "the ladies wouldn't vote for Tilden because he was an old bachelor!" To the observer, this was a repudiation of woman suffrage: "That shows, the sympathy and prejudice of woman, and shows how she would use them had she her 'rights.'" If women did get to vote, "few men then would risk their political preferment by remaining bachelors."[42]

Sometimes women did achieve election to the highest position in a society, newspaper, or class. May Fairfield was elected president of the Palladian Literary Society at Nebraska in 1877—the first woman to hold that office. Following her election, the *Hesperian* recorded this poignant conversation: "One of the students, who is opposed to female suffrage, was arguing last term with his chum, when he broke out in this strain: 'What would become of us poor men, if the women were allowed to vote, and one were to be elected President of the United States?'" A female president of the United States? To editor Wilson, the thought was not so hard to accept, because "we have an example right here in the Palladian Society."[43] Since literary societies dominated student life in the 1870s, May Fairfield essentially acted in the highest executive office for college student participation. Women as elected officers on land-grant campuses translated easily to their rights as future political voters and representatives.

Women also gained political experience through other literary and election activities, especially since society procedures occurred according to strict parliamentary procedure. Women read and practiced *Robert's Rules of Order* and other procedure manuals; they served on ways and means committees, kept minutes of meetings, and most important, exercised their political voice through orations and debates. As women debated and presented oration, they gained abilities in political discourse.

Female elected officers at land-grants usually had earned their positions because at one time they had portrayed talent in oration and debating skills. For example, Pres. May Fairfield was a common contributor to Palladian and *Hesperian* exercises as a speaker and writer, and associate editor Emma Parks began her journalistic career with early successes in public oration and essay writing. Nine months before her election to the *Hesperian* staff in 1877, Parks debated the "Electoral Commission—Is It Politic?" and received worthy compliments: she "exceeded the expectations of her most sanguine friends. Her argument was forcible, to the point and conclusive. . . . The University should feel proud that it possesses within its walls a young lady of rare oratorical attainments."[44] Carrie Lane Chapman Catt began her activist career as a nervous orator in front of a jeering audience of students at IAC. When she had finally delivered her speech, the crowd cheered her success, and she soon gained respect as a skilled orator.[45] Many students recognized that women who excelled in oratory and debating had ventured beyond what was expected of their gender. In 1885, when Cora Fisher argued against Frank Wheeler on the subject of "Shall our National Banking System be Abolished," the Lincoln newspaper marveled that "her debate on a question that is supposed to belong to the opposite sex was as successful as it was unusual."[46] Whether women gave debates and speeches in their separate female organizations or in the less-familiar territory of mixed-debating, they gained valuable experience in political action.

In the 1870s students participated in a local and national movement that included opportunities for more impassioned activism. The temperance movement was widespread and volatile in the early 1870s; as women students entered this important realm of public protest, the experiences gained would help to launch them into later suffrage politics.[47] Students often debated the cause of temperance in literary societies and attended temperance lectures. As early as 1872 a female student at Nebraska argued the temperance cause in a mixed Palladian debate. In the spring of 1874 temperance activism reached intense and exciting levels in Lincoln, Nebraska, when temperance workers entered saloons in downtown Lincoln and women students also joined the fray. The dramatic events of 1874 were reported with excitement by the *Hesperian* editors: "Some of the University girls are going around to the saloons with the Crusaders." Because the campus lay so close to downtown Lincoln, the students had more visible interaction with the saloon culture, thus prompting a more vigorous activism by the younger crusaders. Students raided the saloons, gave stump speeches, and circulated petitions for securing prohibition in Nebraska. Because of the women's work, "we guess that is the reason so many of the boys are signing the pledge."[48] One observer defended the students' rights to extreme forms of protest. Without the vote, women had no other alternative but to use public agitation: "Woman has been driven to this step. She has long wept over this terrible evil. She has appealed to legislators for the ballot. They were afraid she would disgrace her delicate self by mingling with the riff-raff and rabble at the polls. Hopeless of gaining the ballot to right this evil, she has been forced to the present alternative which, though it may not be 'clean' enough to suit her noble Lord, is the only resort he has left her."[49]

The women became known as "Women Crusaders," and antitemperance Nebraskans heaped criticisms on the movement. The *Hesperian* editors overwhelmingly supported the movement and bristled when an editor from a Nebraska City newspaper questioned "the character of the ladies engaged in the temperance movement in this city." Even as women students "daily beseig[ed] the saloons," they had the approval of the university administration. On March 13, 1874, Chancellor Allen Benton gave a speech at the Lincoln Opera House expressing his favor for the movement. The *Hesperian* noted at the success of women students among the men, "for almost all of the boys have signed the National Pledge . . . and one of the Freshies made a temperance speech on the street a few days ago."[50]

The temperance revolution was an important step for Nebraska women students' eventual entry into suffrage politics. Because the "Woman's Whiskey War" represented the "pent-up rumblings of an approaching tempest," this movement would require the highest political action by women. Embroiled in this female temperance action, students easily made the connection to the need for women's right to vote. "The ballot is undoubtedly the only engine which can overthrow the distillery and the dram shop," said one editor.[51] Similar fervent temperance activism hit Iowa in 1874, causing conservatives to fear the kind of exuberant and unladylike behavior often wielded by women temperance activists. An IAC *Aurora* essayist in 1879 remembered the temperance brawl of 1874. Due to the rough excesses of the activists, the cause lost its validity, because "when a woman becomes unwomanly, all her influence ends." For political persuasion, true feminine influence should only include "the steady, quiet, patient teachings of the example, which each true woman gives to those around her, rather than, as in the temperance reform some years ago, by the uprising of a mob, which had a good end in view but chose the wrong means to accomplish it."[52] Echoing the sentiments of other anti-suffragists, this editor drew on women's moralizing and civilizing role to repudiate woman suffrage: "Men are what women make them! The good or the bad influence which a woman can exert is beyond all estimate. . . . It is not our object to plead 'woman's rights.' We believe in division of labor, and are willing to grant men the privilege of managing the legal affairs, exclusively, for to women is left the more glorious part of softening the asperities and quickening the graces of social intercourse."[53]

Even though temperance was seen by some as a sure-fire path for securing women's suffrage, the liquor question actually hindered the women's movement in the long run, and state suffrage amendments often suffered defeat because of the opposition of anti-Prohibition men. Through the late nineteenth century, the Prohibition Party favored woman suffrage because of the acknowledged power of the female vote in passing temperance and prohibitory laws. In Nebraska, for example, an 1881 suffrage amendment was defeated partly because of the opposition of the "wets," and in Iowa, the 1916 woman suffrage amendment failed to pass because of "the male voters of the four 'wet' counties of eastern Iowa—Clinton, Des Moines, Dubuque, and Scott—who feared that if women received the right to vote men would lose the right to drink alcoholic spirits. A vote for woman suffrage was in their minds a vote for Prohibition."[54] Temperance activism of the early 1870s led to later activism through the Women's Christian Temperance Union (WCTU), organized on land-grant campuses in the 1880s and 1890s. This activity offered women their first taste of direct activism and set the stage for transition into wider spheres of political participation.

WOMAN SUFFRAGE ACTIVISM AT
LAND-GRANT COLLEGES AND UNIVERSITIES

Land-grant students employed many activist methods for furthering the cause of female suffrage. Newspaper editorials and essays often showed sympathy to the woman suffrage cause, and journalistic activism was practiced by many college paper editors. When Emma Parks served as the associate editor of the *Hesperian* in 1878, the paper published pro-suffrage essays in three separate issues—February, April, and May. Newspaper editors helped to solidify information favorable to the suffrage cause. Literary societies also served as appropriate climates for suffrage discussions and debates. The suffrage question was a common debate topic in the land-grant societies of the 1870s and 1880s, at times ranking as one of the top five issues besides temperance, the restriction of Chinese immigration, presidential elections, and the regulation of the railroads. Literary societies at IAC in the 1870s debated woman suffrage two or three times a year, if not more. Societies sometimes held joint sessions of males and females, specifically for the purpose of discussing suffrage. Literary societies were the most important venues for promoting student awareness of women's issues.

While debating woman suffrage in the 1880s, the Adelphian Literary Society at OAC portrayed some interesting gender dynamics among debaters and judges. Every suffrage debate except one was argued by male debaters only, but judging teams often consisted of both men and women. That the debate teams were gender-segregated at OAC—with men only debating against men and women only against women—shows how gender separation on campus limited the opportunities for mixed debating. Still, teams of judges were made up of both men and women. Table 3 portrays the diversity of debate participation and also the diversity of decisions by judges and members.

TABLE 3. OAC Adelphian Society: *Woman suffrage debates, 1885–1889*

Date	Debate teams		Judges		Decisions	
	Negative	*Affirmative*	*Males*	*Females*	*Judges*	*Society*
March 13, 1885	2 men	2 men	0	3	Negative	Negative
February 26, 1886	2 men	2 men	2	1	Aff. (reversal) Neg.	
January 27, 1887	2 men	2 men	3	0	Aff. (reversal) Neg.	
October 21, 1887	2 women	2 women	3	0	Neg. (reversal) Aff.	
December 23, 1887	1 man	1 man	?	?	Split—no decision	
June 1, 1888	2 men	2 men	2	1	Split—no decision	
February 22, 1889	2 men	1 man	0	3	Split—no decision	

Source: ALSC, *"Meeting Minutes, 1884–1887" and "Meeting Minutes, 1887–1889," OSUA, Corvallis.*

What strikes the observer is the variation shown in decisions by judges and general society membership. Rulings were based on the skill of the presenters and the substance of their arguments, but after every decision, the debate went to the house floor for open discussion and vote. Note that the first suffrage debate achieved a negative vote by the judges that was upheld by the house, but in the next three debates, the house reversed the judges' decisions. It is especially interesting that the only time suffrage was argued by two teams of women, the house members ruled in favor of suffrage, perhaps indicative of the sympathy women speakers could generate when they argued for their own political rights.

Considering the divisive nature of woman suffrage, house debates often produced intense conflict and sometimes ended in "no decision" rulings. The final three Adelphian debates on suffrage ended in "split" or "no decisions." That the suffrage question caused great conflict in societies should cause no surprise; on January 27, 1887, when the debate intensified, some debaters and members were "referred to the tribunal" for disorder and fined twenty-five cents each; one female student, Carrie Baldwin, was also fined for disorder, although her punishment was suspended.[55] After one particularly intense debate in 1886, some professors had to step in to mediate. The society thanked the professors "for their attendance under such trying circumstances."[56] When the Nebraska Palladian women debated suffrage in April 1888, the women came to no decision—"the evening was too short to admit of bringing the discussion to a close." The meeting adjourned, and the

TABLE 4. Woman suffrage and land-grant education in western states

State	Territory	Statehood	Land-grant	Suffrage
Wyoming	1868	1890	1886, University of Wyoming (Laramie)	1869 (territory) 1890 (state)
Utah	1850	1896	1888, Utah State University (Logan)	1870–87 (territory, revoked) 1896 (state, restored)
Colorado	1861	1876	1879, Colorado State University (Fort Collins)	1893
Idaho	1863	1890	1889, University of Idaho (Moscow)	1896
Washington	1853	1889	1890, Washington State University (Pullman)	1883–87 (territory) 1910 (state)
California	1848	1850	1868 (coed in 1870), University of California (Berkeley)	1911
Kansas	1854	1861	1863, Kansas State University (Manhattan)	1912
Oregon	1848	1859	1868, Oregon State University (Corvallis)	1912
Arizona	1863	1912	1885, University of Arizona (Tucson)	1912
Alaska	1863	1959	1917, University of Alaska (Fairbanks)	1913 (territory) 1959 (state)
Montana	1864	1889	1893, Montana State University (Bozeman)	1914
Nevada	1861	1864	1874, University of Nevada (Reno)	1914
Iowa	1833	1846	1868, Iowa State University (Ames)	1920
Nebraska	1854	1867	1869, University of Nebraska (Lincoln)	1920

Source: Beck and Haase, Historical Atlas of the American West, maps 41 and 42; and Myres, Westering Women and the Frontier Experience, 219–30.

society members decided to "consider the question again this afternoon," after which the topic would be "brought up in the regular debate tonight."[57] Debate proceedings stirred some of the most emotional reactions among students and further engendered their activist tendencies.

Campus suffrage activism often corresponded with political fervor on the state level. The failure of a national woman suffrage amendment prompted women's rights leaders to take the battle to individual states. In the late 1870s suffrage activism in the West increased, especially as various states considered passing suffrage amendments. Between 1870 and 1910 "there were seventeen state referenda held in eleven states—all but three of them west of the Mississippi."[58] By 1900 four states had granted women the right to vote, all of them in the West. Table 4 shows the progress of coeducation and suffrage in a selection of western states.

The progress of woman suffrage in the western United States has been an important topic of study for historians, and the successful state suffrage amendments in four western states have often been held up as examples of American enlightenment and western progress in the nineteenth century. Sandra Myres has considered the cause of woman suffrage in the West and responded to some historians' arguments about various causes, including western males' chivalrous attitudes and suffrage as a way to "advertise and attract additional population." Others have argued that western men "voted for women's suffrage to reward their wives for working beside them through the difficult pioneering years."[59] A closer examination of western suffrage portrays a more complex picture. Voters were influenced by a multiplicity of factors, both in support of and in opposition to woman suffrage. These included questions over the educational and economic rights of women, religious and social values that preferred or questioned traditional gender roles, temperance and prohibition activism, and finally, as in the case of Mormon voters in Utah Territory, the desires to enfranchise women for the preservation of an isolated and theocratic order. All of these factors certainly had an impact on the women's movement, but what really made the West unique in the suffrage fight was, according to Myres, "because the trans-Mississippi states were relatively new, . . . [they] had no deeply entrenched tradition of restriction, [and] it was easier to convince Western legislators to pass women's rights legislation."[60]

Any attempt to make connections between the progress of education in western states and the success of woman suffrage must be done with caution. One might try to attribute the coeducational progress for women in the West to their eventual political rights as equal voters. However, an examination of the above information shows the link between education and suffrage to be ambiguous, at best. Indeed, the states where coeducational colleges and universities were first chartered—Iowa, Nebraska, Kansas, and Oregon—were also among the last to grant women the right to vote. For this study, only Utah had passed woman suffrage prior to 1900, and that act had more to do with Mormon power structures and fears of federal government intrusion than women's educational progress. In spite of the success of equal education in states like Iowa, Nebraska, and Oregon, suffrage was defeated largely due to the votes of social conservatives who sought to entrench women in their separate, nonpolitical sphere, or by "wets"—anti-temperance men who feared that a vote for woman suffrage would empower the Prohibition movement. But the belated successes of woman suffrage in these states were not without lack of trying during the four decades prior to World War I.

During times of increased suffrage fervor in western states in the late nineteenth century, land-grant students—both men and women—also stepped up their activist tendencies. Because a national woman suffrage amendment had failed, suffrage leaders instead took their battle to the individual states in the West. In response to this widening culture of western suffrage activism, land-grant students experienced their own bursts of activist energy. For instance, although Colorado's first attempt to pass an equal suffrage bill in 1877 failed, it led to a flood of suffrage fervor culminating in passage in 1893. In Oregon equal suffrage came before the state legislature in 1884, 1896, 1905, and 1910.[61] Nebraska had the most difficult road to equal suffrage—amendments came before the legislature in 1856, 1867, 1871, 1875, 1882, and 1887; and when the 1887 attempt failed, suffrage leaders subsequently toned down their goals to demand only the passage of a few municipal suffrage bills between 1889 and 1909. State suffrage was again considered in 1913 and was finally passed in 1919, when the state adopted the federal government's Nineteenth Amendment.[62] After numerous attempts in Iowa between the 1860s and 1910s, suffragists there also had to wait until 1919 to see woman suffrage adopted.[63] During these moments of increased suffrage flurry, land-grant women students added their voices and energy to the cause.

A second factor that affected land-grant student suffrage activities were the nationally circulating suffrage newspapers established in western states. Suffrage newspapers began in Colorado, California, Oregon, Nebraska; lesser-circulating journals were published in states like Iowa and Utah. These periodicals served as journalistic centers of a regional suffrage culture, around which students in those states could build their own activities. For example, in Portland, Oregon, Abigail Scott Duniway founded the *New Northwest*, which served as an important vehicle for women's rights activism in the Pacific Northwest between 1871 and 1887. In Nebraska Clara Bewick Colby edited the *Women's Tribune* out of Beatrice; the paper helped in Nebraska's suffrage fight between 1883 and 1889, until it moved to Washington DC in 1889 and later to Portland, Oregon, from 1904 to 1909.[64] Although Iowa did not have a nationally known women's rights periodical, in 1885 Carrie Lane Chapman coedited the *Mason City Republican* with her husband, Leo Chapman. Their paper included a daily column on the progress of women's rights and suffrage. And in Des Moines in 1886 Mary J. Coggeshall founded the *Women's Standard*, "a radical *woman's right* sheet, containing contributions from many prominent ladies of Iowa." Its purpose was "to materially change the political ideas of the present to a condition where their 'rights' will be realized."[65] Mormon women in Utah also had a women's rights periodical, the *Women's Exponent*, established in 1872 in Salt Lake City. Between 1877 and 1914 the editorship was taken over by Emmeline B. Wells, a leader of the Utah suffrage movement and also the general president of the Church's women's organization. The *Exponent* sought to defend polygamy but also promoted the status of Mormon women and the cause of suffrage. The pro-suffrage journalism in the West helped to further women's rights, and land-grant newspapers contributed to this culture with their own writings and by reprinting editorials from women's rights papers.

A final influence on land-grant student activism was the speaking circuit of national suffrage leaders, who frequently traveled to the West to encourage the suffrage cause and to meet with local and state leaders. Land-grant students attended many of these lectures and felt the speakers' influence; during the 1870s and 1880s students added their public voices to the important cause of woman suffrage. The national woman suffrage movement and the land-grant women's activism grew together, especially as students benefited from hearing the suffrage leaders; these in turn fed off student energy and interest. Elizabeth Cady Stanton, Susan B. Anthony, and others traveled in the West, speaking on behalf of proposed state amendments.[66] Land-grant students felt this fervor. In May 1878 one suffrage debate in the IAC Crescent Literary Society yielded an affirmative decision in favor of woman suffrage, and afterward, the members suggested: "Wouldn't it be a good idea to have Elizabeth Cady Stanton come here and lecture before the societies? Without a doubt she would give some of us many new ideas about the 'sphere of woman.'"[67] One year later, in 1879, a group of Iowa State students decided to travel to nearby Boone, Iowa, to hear Susan B. Anthony's lecture on "Woman Wants Bread, Not the Ballot." Anthony argued that "bread and almost all other comforts and luxuries of life would be rendered more accessible by the ballot; that women will not be recognized in their true capacity, nor be granted equal remuneration with men for the same work, till they are enfranchised." Anthony's lecture left a good impression on the IAC students, and the editor asked, "Can we not secure her for the College during the summer?"[68] During the previous winter of 1878 Anthony had given the same speech in Hebron, Nebraska, on a visit to that state.[69] When the national convention of the National Woman Suffrage Association was held in Lincoln, Nebraska, in 1887, a few Nebraska students attended Anthony's speech, and student Helen Aughey included a transcript of the speech in her college scrapbook.[70]

In 1887 a group of IAC students, including "some of the ladies," heard that Belva Lockwood, the famous and eccentric female lawyer, women's rights activist, and presidential candidate, was scheduled to speak in Ames. Because of her controversial nature, the university president forbade students from attending the lecture. About fifty students — mostly men — defied the president and went to hear Lockwood anyway. She spoke about the social and public life of Washington DC but said nothing about "women as voters nor anything the least unrefined." Still, when they returned to campus, the president caught them, and "it was rumored the next morning that there was talk of expulsion at the president's office." He forced them to sign a petition, "full of penitence."[71] One male student said, "'I won't sign it, I'll be expelled first,' making other remarks about the injustice of forbidding the excursion to Ames." The students involved were "some of the best-behaved, most assiduous and brightest boys of the college," and each eventually agreed to sign the petition. According to Clem Kimball, although the students were "wrong and deserved punishment," still they had shown their willingness to defy university authority for the cause of women's rights.[72]

The most significant display of land-grant student activism in the midst of a state suffrage battle occurred in Nebraska in 1882. A suffrage amendment was being considered in the legislature, and national leaders arrived in droves to support the movement. Henry Blackwell and Lucy Stone, Susan B. Anthony, Phoebe Couzins, and Elizabeth Cady Stanton all arrived in Nebraska in the autumn of 1883 and traveled to more than a hundred different towns.[73] The fervor in Lincoln was unprecedented—speeches, debates, stump lectures, and meetings of suffrage leaders all dominated the preelection activities. The Nebraska students threw themselves into the fray. Amos G. Warner of the class of 1885 remembered that "the literary societies were full of the discussion, and the supply of speakers overflowed into the country school houses round about." One society held a women-only program in the university chapel, and another lecture "drew an equally large crowd. . . . One of the features was a conversational debate between Mr. C.C. Chase and myself."[74] The general house discussion that followed "was vigorous enough so that one speaker was called upon to apologize, but declined to do so."

Student debaters participated in the public and legislative proceedings in Lincoln and tried to show that the "balance of opinion at the University was or was not in favor of the amendment." Some anti-suffrage students endeavored to prove that most students were opposed: they read a long list of students opposed to suffrage, only to discover that "some of the persons named were on the other side, and others had been converted during the convention." In truth, the university was a "hot-bed of woman suffrage," and students extended an overwhelming sense of support to the national suffrage leaders in Lincoln.[75]

When the 1882 suffrage bill failed to pass in Nebraska, the anti-suffrage male students "yearned for some public demonstration of delight." They first decided to "burn Miss Anthony in effigy," but instead decided to have a "bonfire on the public square . . . [and] a mock funeral procession, to cremate the defunct bill with suitable orations." After several days of growing tension, the anti-suffragists purchased a coffin (which they stored in the *Hesperian* office) and recruited band members to march in a mock funeral parade. The "antis" planned a march from campus through the Eleventh Street entrance, and the pro-suffrage men went to hide there in waiting: "It is a chilly business to wait under nervous tension on a November night, but we crouched and waited." With scouts poised to report the movements of the enemy, the pro-suffrage men prepared to stop the anti-suffrage parade. Acting Chancellor Henry E. Hitchcock even tried to "dissuade the antis from their attempt." But with a band, the coffin pulled by mules, and students carrying lighted torches, the procession began to make its way from campus. The group passed through the stile at the campus entrance, and as the "coffin had to be lifted waist high over it," the pro-suffrage students rushed the procession. Students fought over the coffin, "in a confused mass of legs, fists, clubs, torch sticks, and musical instruments." One student cocked a revolver and "found himself courageous enough to swear."[76] The pro-suffrage men sent the mules running home with the coffin, but without the lid that had fallen to the ground.

The discarded lid became the new symbol of dominance, as the anti-suffrage mob "decided to go on with the funeral," and carried it to their place of orations, which "fell rather flat (perhaps because some of the orators had done so a short time before)." A few of Warner's pro-suffrage crowd took the original coffin and, in the middle of the night, managed to secure the box over the entrance of Old Main, with a placard that read "Truth crushed to earth will rise again." The coffin hung over the door without a lid, and its "lidlessness seemed symbolic of a happy resurrection for the sometime occupant [the woman suffrage bill]."[77] Warner's group nailed the upstairs windows of Old Main shut to prevent the antis from removing the coffin from its perch, "and there the trophy of victory remained through the day."

How did Nebraska's female and male pro-suffrage students respond to this suffrage battle by the "antis"? Warner and his friends felt victory in "the smiles of fair women." The "sympathizing co-eds" held a victory reception at the home of "Mrs. H.H. Wilson"—formerly Emma Parks of *Hesperian* associate editor fame! Party-goers gave speeches, broke up the coffin, and divided its pieces as mementos for the pro-suffrage crowd. A group of boys wrote their names on one piece and gave it to Mrs. Wilson as a present.[78] Indeed, Nebraska had proven itself a "hot-bed of woman suffrage," but the impact of the intense student activism of 1882 eventually withered away as students pursued their postcollegiate lives. And the women students who had participated in the early 1880s activism? As of 1895, "many of the girls who were present at the reception are now tired and happy with the care of their children, and perhaps care less, or at least think less, about voting than when they debated something or other that began with the word 'Resolved.'" In spite of suffrage failures in the nineteenth century, student activists clung to the hope often expressed by suffrage leaders in the 1882 campaign: "The sun of progress rises in the West."[79]

THE MILITARY ARGUMENT:
CHALLENGING THE FINAL SEPARATION

Land-grant student activists benefited from a collegiate environment that promoted a pro-suffrage culture. Students' electoral and political experience was bolstered by the energy of national suffrage leaders, women's rights periodicals, and intense political action by western states. All of these factors together created a land-grant culture of woman suffrage activism, but the land-grants had an additional tool for claiming women's right to vote. What Alice Stone Blackwell would one day call "the military argument" might be considered an important land-grant contribution to the national woman suffrage cause. In the 1870s and 1880s anti-suffragists used military policy as a tool against equal suffrage, arguing that, all other factors aside, women still should not vote simply because they could not serve in the military. Pro-suffragists contradicted this argument in two ways. First, they noted the number of male voters who had no experience in the military, nor had they fought in any war. Second, they drew attention to great historical examples of women soldiers, spies, and military leaders. This connection between women's political rights and women's military activity was especially potent in the land-grant environment, particularly because women students served in campus military regiments for two decades at the end of the century.

The story has been told like this: At the beginning of the school year in 1879 the IAC commandant gave a lecture to the students about the benefits of military training. According to Carrie Chapman Catt's biographer, when Catt heard the speech, she "was so moved by his presentation of the subject that she went with a delegation of girls to ask the Commandant to give the girls the same drill he gave the boys!" General Geddes "was so flattered and amused by this tribute to his persuasive oratory that he consented to drill the girls."[80] Thus began the women's military regiment at IAC. Perhaps the women made no direct connection to woman suffrage on that occasion, but when the company was remustered in 1884, the *Aurora* made the connection for them: "Lady believers in Woman Suffrage have resolved to remove the last objection to their voting. They have subjected themselves to military duty."[81] And in 1887, when the Iowa State Suffrage Association held its annual meeting in Ames, the association members made a visit to the IAC campus and were privileged to view "an exhibition drill of Company G, which is composed entirely of girls."[82] Directly or indirectly, women's military companies became important symbols for the progress that women students made as they expanded their political sphere.

Women writers and speakers employed the important tool of feminizing history to draw attention to female military achievements. In April of 1878 the Nebraska *Hesperian* published an essay that favored woman suffrage. After listing some women's achievements in history and literature, the author, "E.C.A.," also suggested the military accomplishments of women: "Even in war, for which it is admitted that woman has no taste, because her finest capacities and faculties are spontaneously put forth to save and not to destroy — even in war, however, woman has displayed so often the most commanding abilities that it is demonstrated that this tallent [*sic*] is not exceptional, but exists there as potent as man. I need to refer only to Joan of Arc."[83]

Because of some women's impact on history, literature, and war, "such women demonstrate that their sex has as fine a capacity and ability to cast a vote intelligently as man. If woman can be a statesman she is competent to cast a ballot. If she can guide the helm of state in calamitous times she can vote intelligently. If she can lead armies and win battles she has also sufficient firmness to maintain her convictions."[84] The military argument, as it was called, also translated to women's patriotic role in society. In the 1890s literary societies often discussed women and patriotism, and where else had women more fully shown their patriotic and military spirit than in all-female military companies?

In the Junior Exhibition of 1879 Mary DeVoss presented a talk titled "Women of the War," which described "the heroism of women who aided in the war of the rebellion [Civil War]; many of them by caring for the wounded and dying, others by serving as soldiers." DeVoss also mentioned Joan of Arc, who "was equaled [to men] in heroism and devotion to country."[85] Because men who serve in war "can hardly fail of receiving due honors, and their names go into history," then women's military service deserves all the more "full appreciation" and "equal honor with man."[86] Perhaps it was no accident that following DeVoss's talk, Carrie Lane Chapman Catt gave her first recorded speech on women's rights.

And perhaps it was also no accident that one of Catt's first suffrage publications was called *The Ballot and the Bullet*, arguing for women's right to suffrage because of their long history of military participation. According to Catt, "women of physical strength and courage, under the influence of ardent devotion to their respective causes, braved both the dangers of war and discovery, and served with honor in the ranks of soldiers."[87] The essays in Catt's collection included "Female Warriors" by D. P. Livermore (the husband of Civil War veteran Mary A. Livermore; "The Right of Woman to the Ballot" by Charles H. Chapman (no relation to Catt); and "The Military Argument," by Alice Stone Blackwell (activist daughter of Lucy Stone and Henry Blackwell). Livermore argued that "all we have attempted to show, is, that women are as patriotic as men, have quite as much power of endurance, and can fight as well as men, and from this point of view, are quite as much entitled to the ballot as men."[88] Chapman also offered that "given universal suffrage, in the event of war woman would occupy the same place that she has in the past, except that she would be more fitted by practice and experience to take the place of the soldier called to the field."[89] As editor of *The Ballot and the Bullet*, Catt showed the impact of her military experience—both as one who organized and marched in a military company and as one who supported feminist rhetoric regarding women's military activities. Catt's land-grant experience left a definite mark on her future role as a national woman suffrage leader.

WOMEN STUDENT SUFFRAGISTS:
VOCALIZING THE CAUSE OF WOMAN SUFFRAGE

It might have been Carrie Lane's first public speech on women's rights, but it certainly would not be her last. At the IAC Junior Exhibition in 1879, members of the class of 1880 presented their orations before a crowd of students, professors, and local Ames residents. As a twenty-one-year-old

29. Carrie C. Lane (later Chapman Catt), 1880 graduate of IAC. Iowa State University Library/Special Collections Department.

college junior, the future president of the National American Woman Suffrage Association already had an activist reputation among her fellow students. The IAC *Aurora* recorded Lane's speech as the "best of the evening." "Miss Carrie C. Lane was the next speaker, with the topic *Social Inertia*. . . . She maintained that creeds and doctrines, deemed enlightened and infallible in one age, are proven false and barbarous in the next: they are all doomed by the law of progress. . . . Yet, after all the progress of the past, prejudice and oppression stalk abroad, in different form, but as tyrannical as ever. Here the speaker made a strong plea for 'Woman's Rights.'"[90]

The year 1879 was still a bit early for a suffrage speech to win the complete sympathy of an audience, and the editor thought "perhaps her picture was a little overdrawn." Nevertheless, she spoke convincingly, and "there is much truth in her representations and justice in her demands. She claimed that revolution must follow oppression, and therefore we look for better days in the future." A final compliment perhaps foreshadowed her later life as a national and international lecturer: "Miss Lane is a fine speaker and has the gift of expressing her thoughts in the most pleasing manner."[91]

Other women student speakers at both IAC and Nebraska used literary and graduation podiums to promote the cause of suffrage. In November 1882 Helen Rice, an IAC and Cliolian alumnus of 1878, spoke to her graduating sisters at a meeting of all literary society seniors. Rice "seemed to be a champion advocate of women's rights, and she advised her Clio sisters to keep abreast with our progressive age."[92] A few days later at commencement exercises, Lizzie Perrett spoke on "Educational Qualifications for Suffrage," and assured the audience that "women will soon be granted suffrage."[93] And at Nebraska in 1888 Alma Benedict gave a commencement address on woman suffrage that covered all of the basic tenets of the national suffrage cause: "All I ask for woman is that the opening sentence of the declaration [sic] of Independence be made broad enough to include her." Further, Benedict demanded the rights of citizenship, plus the freedom for each woman to enter "any occupation to which she may feel she has a calling." In choosing a profession, women should also have "protection from innuendo in so doing." Finally, Benedict offered important legal arguments for women's equal suffrage. First, "they are subject to laws they have had no part in making, and this in a government which boasts, that it derives its just powers from the consent of the governed," and second, "there shall be no taxation without representation. The taxed women of the land are not represented. Contradictions like these should not be tolerated." Benedict even had a response for those women who "do not want the ballot." She stated, "If justice demands that they have it, give it to them whether they want it or not. No special privileges are asked, nothing but what is granted to all human beings except women. . . . Whatever she has done in the past has been in the face of the bitterest prejudices and opposition. See what she can do when she has a chance with man in professional, civil and social life."[94]

Benedict wondered how anyone could deny women the ballot: "Does her sex render her deaf and blind to the interests common to humanity? Does she not love her country?"[95] The questions, similar to President Welch's early IAC inaugural address, seemed to evoke a Shylock tone, and appropriately so, since the most important argument for equal suffrage referred to women's prerogatives as citizens and as human beings.

Women students like Carrie Lane and Alma Benedict took the cause of equal suffrage to the college podiums; by using opportunities for public oratory, these women employed their skills as well-informed political speakers to defend the legal and social reasons for equal suffrage. Women student speakers added legitimacy to the equal suffrage movement, and through the use of convincing argumentation, they could help to bring others to the cause of suffrage. Influenced by the speeches and activism of national and local suffrage leaders, students gained greater awareness of women's political rights and then added their own voices to the cause of women's political liberation.

CONCLUSION

When Bernice Forest voted in November of 1916, the women of Oregon had been enfranchised for only four years. Bernice benefited from an important tradition of suffrage activity at Oregon State University. Women's groups like the Sorosis had supported feminist issues since the 1890s, and individual women added their voices to the cause. In 1908 senior Faye Roadruck declared her graduation goal to be an "imitator of Susan B. Anthony," and when junior Mattie Winford was asked her life's ambition, she simply said, "to vote." Her classmate Ella Dunlap listed her college hobby as "Woman's suffrage."[96] In 1911 senior Leona Leonora Kerr, a "devout Sorosis leader," described her life's hope "to be a leader in the movement for woman's suffrage." She was not alone: her classmate Ruby I. Starr most wanted to be remembered for "advocat[ing] women's suffrage."[97] And less than a year after the Oregon State Legislature passed the equal suffrage bill in 1912, OAC held an intercollegiate debate with McMinnville (Oregon) College, with a topic that reflected the spirit of the times: "That equal suffrage be granted the women of Oregon."[98]

Land-grant students contributed to a vibrant culture of collegiate woman suffrage activism. As debaters, orators, protesters, and especially voters, students added their voices and political actions to a movement that needed the energy and education of American college youth. As one Nebraska essayist recognized as early as 1878, "the friends of female suffrage are the most numerous among the younger classes of all communities. The opponents of female suffrage are dying off, and an equal number are not taking their place." Led by a youthful leadership and brightened with the hopes for a kind of cleansing of antiquated suffrage opponents, the Nebraska author prophesied that "sooner or later this cause will have leavened the whole nation, and the period of [woman's] disfranchisement will be viewed as a barbarous or undeveloped form or period of history."[99]

With the pro-suffrage attitudes gained during their collegiate experience, land-grant students went out into the world to vote, teach, and convert. The graduating class of 1873 at IAC boasted five "advocates of 'Woman's Suffrage'"—"two ladies and three gentlemen"—out of a class of fifteen.[100] The percentages increased in later years, and in 1880 IAC announced that out of 103 graduates from between 1873 and 1880 who had reported to the IAC Alumni Association, there were "fifty-three woman suffragists with an opposition of thirty-seven."[101] A decade later, in 1890, the association reported 117 graduates in favor of suffrage and 104 against.[102] That the pro-suffrage count was only a little over 50 percent in the early 1890s shows how divisive the suffrage question continued to be through the end of the century. But those who did favor suffrage went back to their communities with a vocal experience gained in the literary societies and debating sessions of their college days. A sampling of IAC graduates from the 1890s showed their continued pursuit of suffrage causes: Kate (Stevens) Harpel (class of 1890) served as the chairman of Iowa's Equal Suffrage Association and was vice president when the Nineteenth Amendment passed in 1920.[103] Sisters Elmina and Alda Heaton Wilson (1892 and 1894 respectively), discussed in chapter 5, became "ardent worker(s) for woman suffrage." Alda, in fact, was a "companion to Carrie Chapman Catt" from 1928 to 1947.

One of Elmina's classmates was also a Wilson but not related—Flora Hazel Wilson, who was a musician, writer, and the daughter of Secretary of Agriculture James Wilson. He served under Presidents McKinley, Roosevelt, and Taft as the longest-serving U.S. cabinet member from 1897 to 1913. Flora acted as cabinet hostess for her father during his tenure and "took an active part in politics and made political speeches during the twenties."[104] IAC graduate Ella (Morton) Kearney (1893) was a homemaker but very active in women's club work, and she was a member of the League of Women Voters. Mary Josephine (Maguire) Thomas (1896), also a home-maker in South Dakota, "wrote and delivered lectures on equal suffrage and prohibition."[105] Many of the IAC's women graduates also participated in membership in the Women's Christian Temperance Union as well as the General Federation of Women's Clubs, both of which declared official support for woman suffrage in the 1890s.

Mary B. Welch of IAC retired to California and participated in her local woman suffrage group – she had also been an important influence on many IAC women for almost fifteen years. Three of her graduates went on to suf-frage leadership in western or national organizations. Emma McHenry of the IAC class of 1878 married and moved to Montana where she "introduced into the Montana legislature the first bill for a law allowing kindergartens in public schools in that state." Later Emma and her husband "moved to Seattle, where she was president of the Equal Suffrage Club for Seattle."[106] One of McHenry's classmates was Ida Twitchell Blochman, who had taught chemistry at IAC. She also married and moved to California, where she "served 10 years on the county board of education in Santa Barbara." She worked in temperance and suffrage activism, and later served eight years as president of the League of Women Voters.[107]

Many land-grant women graduates also took their reform ideologies into the world and participated in other women's club activities, mission-ary work, temperance activism, philanthropy, public education, and pro-gressive reform. Mary Welch's most memorable IAC woman graduate was Carrie Lane Chapman Catt, destined to become one of the most important woman suffrage leaders in American history. Catt was proudly boasted by her alma mater in the 1939 "Biographical Directory" as "one of I.S.C.'s most distinguished graduates; [and] one of 12 greatest women leaders in last 100 years of American history."[108] Catt achieved renown at IAC as a debater, orator, organizer of a women's political club, and the first woman to demand a military regiment for women students. Catt represented the "New Woman" at IAC – one who expanded her political and public sphere and then helped to do the same for other women.

The land-grant experience of woman suffrage activism challenges tra-ditional notions about this movement in the United States. According to Sandra Myres, "the impetus for change [in the West] came not from the women in the Western states but from male leaders in Western state governments and Eastern women who came to campaign on behalf of women's rights."[109] The experience of student activism certainly challenges that statement. While it may be true that many "women on the Western frontiers did not have the time or the means of organizing their far-flung neighbors in order to become an effective lobby," western land-grant students possessed other talents and opportunities for establishing pro-suffrage environments in the West. Land-grant campuses served as microcommunities, complete with the political and organizational structures of a small population center and often overcome by political activism in favor of women's rights that influenced citizens around them. Students may not have organized formal activist groups in the traditional sense, but campus activities helped to promote the suffrage cause through newspaper editorials, public orations, debates, and other forms of activism.

Typically seen as an eastern, urban, and female-dominated movement, woman suffrage activism on the campuses of land-grant universities featured major players who were male and female college students taken from rural farm areas and small communities. Land-grant woman suffrage activism was very much a combined effort of men and women students fighting together either for or against the cause of female franchise. Although a significant number of students sought to oppose suffrage by limiting women to a separate domestic culture of "moral influence," many other students favored suffrage and recognized the possibilities for women's equal participation in the American political sphere. In the suffrage cause, men and women students often worked as comrades, and men also actively contributed to "votes for women." When Tom Kerr of the IAC Crescent Society presented an oration, "Why Am I a Woman Suffragist?" in 1888, he vocalized the support that so many male students gave to women's political rights in the late nineteenth century.[110] Men and women voted together in class, newspaper, and literary elections and held joint public debates regarding controversial political issues. Land-grant students practiced an active microcosm of democracy that showed the realistic possibility of an inclusive political culture supported by a vocal and intelligent female electorate.

Conclusion

Bright Epoch

WHEN THE FAIR DAUGHTERS JOINED THE RANKS

What is the ultimate legacy of coeducational experience for land-grant women students between 1870 and 1918? Rather than an example of strict gender exclusion and discrimination in a male-dominated environment, the land-grant experience is a story of the negotiation of gendered spaces—at times toward greater inclusion for women, and at times toward separation. Women took an active part in the process of achieving inclusion, but sometimes they chose to segregate themselves from the male sphere. They also met both acceptance and resistance from their male peers, faculty, and leaders. This shifting process of coeducational inclusion and separation occurred in many contested areas of the land-grant environment, including literary societies, hetero-and homosocial interactions, academic course work, individual and competitive team athletics, military activities, and feminist reform such as political and editorial leadership, dress reform, and suffrage activism.

Between 1870 and 1900 these first three decades of land-grant experience for women might be considered a "bright epoch" for gender inclusion during the history of coeducational practice. This term was used by University of Nebraska's *Hesperian Student*.[1] Although women students were small in numbers during the early years, perhaps the newness of the land-grant experience allowed for more liberal gender experimentations prior to 1900. Rosalind Rosenberg has shown how a surge of women's enrollment in early years did not go unnoticed by education leaders at the time, who acknowledged "the widespread perception that the women students coming to college [after 1900] were distinctly less serious than

GRAPH 1. OAC male and female student enrollments, 1888–1905

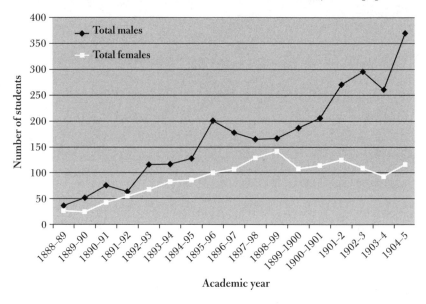

earlier women students had been."[2] A sampling from Oregon Agricultural College from 1888 through 1905 shows a steady increase in female numbers through the beginning of the century. Even more striking, whereas IAC's women students held at around 21 percent of the total student body, OAC's women numbered much higher. For example, women's enrollments at OAC between 1889 and 1899 averaged 40 percent of total student enrollments for the period. Women reached their highest numbers in the 1898–99 school year, at 46 percent of the class, or 142 women students to 167 male enrollees. These numbers of women students prior to 1900 indicate perhaps a more serious approach to educational goals among young women in Oregon at the end of the century.

A similar sampling of student enrollment numbers from IAC from 1879 through 1904 shows how the enrollment of women students remained smaller than at OAC but steady from the late 1870s through 1900, with a couple of slight increases in the late 1880s and the mid-1890s. Between 1880 and 1882 women students had an enrollment of fifty-nine each year, or around 27 percent of total students. Those female enrollments dropped drastically in 1883–84 and 1884–85 to thirty and thirty-five per school year respectively,

GRAPH 2. IAC male and female student enrollments, 1879–1904

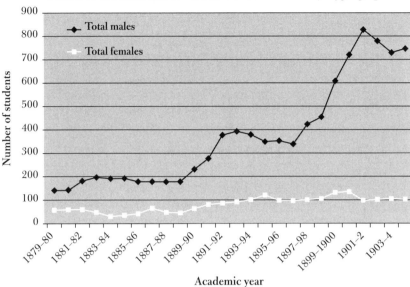

or 15 percent of students. By 1886–87, a recovery showed 64 female students to 178 male students, or 26 percent of the total. The numbers dropped back down to 21 percent in the 1887–88 year, and women students then averaged 21 percent of total IAC students from 1889 through 1899. Women reached their highest numbers in 1894–95 at 26 percent, or 121 women to 350 men. Although overall female enrollments in both raw numbers and percentages were not as high as at OAC during the same period, still IAC numbers of women held steady from the late 1880s through 1900.

Even more striking as an example of female successes in these early years are the persistence rates of female students, or the percentage of entering female enrollees who continued from their freshman year through all four years to their graduation. The persistence rates at both IAC and OAC show that at various times, women matched and even surpassed the persistence rates of men. While larger numbers of men attended, and their numbers continued to increase over time, higher percentages of entering women were able to complete their degrees at various times. From 1882 through 1915, persistence rates for female students at IAC surpassed males in approximately ten different years. OAC shows thirteen times between 1894 and 1914 where women either matched or passed male graduation rates.

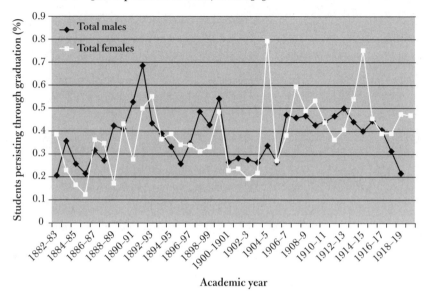

GRAPH 3. IAC persistence rates, 1882–1919

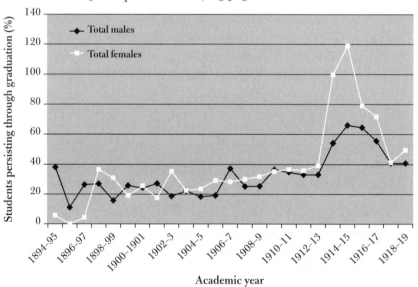

GRAPH 4. OAC persistence rates, 1894–1918

Why did so many entering freshman males discontinue their land-grant education after only one or two years of enrollment? Answers could include numerous motives, from economic pressures that prohibited the cost of education, to young men's needed presence on family farms, to time off from education spent teaching school. Whatever the reason, persistence statistics indicate strongly that even though larger overall numbers of men attended land-grant colleges, higher percentages of entering freshman women tended to actually complete their educations. The reasons for women students' higher persistence rates are due to numerous possible factors. Perhaps because of the newness of land-grant coeducational experience, women did not enroll casually or on a whim. Instead, those women who actually took advantage of regional higher educational opportunities did so with serious intentions. These women students were still a minority, and thus perhaps felt a higher pressure to make the educational sacrifice worthwhile, especially in these early years.

Women's enrollment and persistence rates showed a natural increase during the war years of World War I, especially in the context of male students' wartime absence. However, those percentages would dramatically change as men came home and returned to college in large numbers by 1919 and 1920. Both IAC and OAC showed a marked spike in total male students in the 1918–19 post–World War I recovery. The accompanying graphs show a comparison over time between male and female enrollments at both colleges. Note how both colleges' enrollments of men and women ran roughly parallel through the 1890s, and then began to separate, as male enrollments jumped way ahead of female enrollments around the turn of the century. Both IAC and OAC showed a trend of the recovery of female student numbers around 1912, after a decade-long decline.

As both male and female enrollments increased after 1905, and especially when World War I ended in 1918, female enrollments became more closely tied with marital expectations and vibrant collegiate social atmospheres of the sexual revolution and the Jazz Age. In other words, as land-grant education—indeed, as higher education in general—became more widely available to women, and as the newness and significance of coeducational opportunity wore off in American society, more women pursued higher education as a route toward greater sociality and the possibility of marriage. Rosalind Rosenberg has noted this change in female students' academic

GRAPH 5. IAC male and female student enrollments, 1879–1918

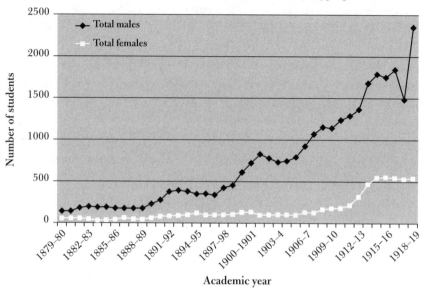

interests from the first decade after 1870, that the "first generation of women who attended such [coeducational] institutions . . . were strongly committed to careers, at the expense, if necessary, of family life, the next generation represented a broader group of young women, many of whom regarded college not simply as an avenue to work but also as preparation for marriage."[3] Although the "strong commitment to careers" among earlier female students is a somewhat debatable point, especially at land-grant colleges where companionate marriage had been so heavily emphasized, the enrollment numbers and persistence rates among female students show steady successes before 1900 and declines afterward.

The stereotype of women attending college to receive their "Mrs." degree emerged in the mid-twentieth century as part of the reinforcement of women's traditional roles and the pressure to eschew higher education in favor of younger marriage and childbirth. Although this work has not offered any comparative statistics of female persistence or graduation rates between the pre-1918 period and the post-1918 period, that would be a fascinating and important study for other historians of women and higher education. Rosenberg has tried to dispel some of the myths associated with women's

GRAPH 6. OAC male and female student enrollments, 1888–1919

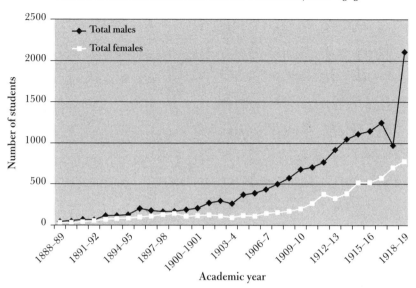

disinterest in higher education during the Roaring Twenties. She argues:

> Some historians have argued that after 1920 college-educated women
> traded the desire to have a career for the desire to have a family life,
> but this does not square with the available evidence. College-educated
> women married in greater numbers, but their commitment to careers did
> not diminish, even after the decline in feminist enthusiasm had robbed
> them of valuable political support. Each generation of college gradu-
> ates proved more ready than the last to pursue a career after marriage,
> despite widespread public opposition to the practice, especially during
> the Great Depression.[4]

Still, a comparison between nineteenth-century and post–World War I coeducational numbers and experience—including women's enrollments and
graduation rates—has yet to be done. When completed, these studies will
add to historians' understanding of gender negotiations in mixed-gender
higher education. Sarah Barnes's promising work examining land-grant
coeducation between 1920 and 1960 will further deepen our comprehension

of how negotiations for gender inclusion and separation at land-grant colleges have shifted over time in response to cultural factors like economic depression and world wars.[5]

Regardless of the recoveries in female student numbers and professional interests in the 1920s and beyond, Rosenberg and other historians have acknowledged an abrupt decline around 1900 in both female enrollment numbers and the overall enthusiasm for coeducation. Historians have tried to outline various reasons for what appeared to be a reaction against women's education, and especially coeducation, from around 1900 through World War I. First, because so many institutions saw huge growth in female numbers from the late 1880s through the 1890s, female students experienced increasing hostility and resentment from male students who feared they were taking over, both in numbers and in cultural influence. Rosenberg suggests that "by 1900 the popularity of higher education among women had become so great that female enrollment at many colleges and universities outstripped male enrollment. There swept through the country a growing fear that if nothing were done to prevent it, within a few years many coeducational institutions would become women's schools."[6] Leslie Miller-Bernal has also noted this tension, that "the early twentieth century was a period of anxiety in the country at large about the feminization of American culture, which manifested itself in part by an opposition to coeducation."[7] Some universities actually backpedaled from earlier acceptance of coeducation, claiming that "they had never really favored coeducation in the first place but had agreed to it merely for economic reasons." Rosenberg provides other poignant examples of this anti-coeducation fervor: Stanford's "founder's widow so feared that the university . . . would become a female seminary that she froze female enrollment permanently at 500." Others, such as Boston University, actually tried to recruit more male students—especially away from the all-male Ivy League institutions—so that increases in male numbers could counter the threat of feminization.[8]

Elisabeth Israels Perry and Jennifer Ann Price have described a similar downturn in female student numbers at the University of Michigan after 1900 and attributed that to men's preference for the "scientific, technical, and professional fields such as law and medicine," whereby women "comprised about 47 percent in literary studies." Thus, coeducation opponents feared that women might begin "'taking over' fields in the humanities," and so must be directed toward "fields more 'suitable' to them, such as domestic science or 'home economics.'"[9] That redirection resulted in many women students turning more toward degrees in domestic science. These examples bear up a distinct cultural reaction against coeducation around 1900 that stemmed from the fears of feminization of education, but also related to other national anxieties.

By 1900 Americans began to fear declining birth rates for middle-and upper-middle-class whites, and especially "among college-educated women," that these groups might be overtaken by the higher population growth of immigrants and other so-called lower orders. According to Perry and Price, "census data were suggesting that less well-educated peoples, including immigrants and people of color, were reproducing at much faster rates. Concerned that 'the old native American stock' would soon lose its ascendancy, President Theodore Roosevelt warned of 'race suicide.'"[10] Roosevelt's demands for upper-class white American women to increase their reproduction were well known, especially as part of his 1902 "Strenuous Life" call for man to "be glad to do a man's work, to dare and endure and to labor," and for woman to "be the housewife, the helpmeet of the homemaker, the wise and fearless mother of many healthy children." Although Roosevelt did not particularly "blame higher education for women's failure to reproduce," he did recognize a cultural "fear of maternity, the haunting terror of the young wife of the present day." He warned that, "when men fear work or fear righteous war, [and] when women fear motherhood, they tremble on the brink of doom."[11]

G. Stanley Hall took Roosevelt's warnings about American women's role in race suicide to the next level. Hall's 1904 work, *Adolescent Girls and Their Education*, argued that marriage and motherhood should be the ultimate goal and "greatest fulfillment" of every American young woman. That many women had chosen education and spinsterhood over young marriage and motherhood he considered a grave danger to the health of the American civilization. "He despaired of an educational system that persisted in training women for 'independence and self-support,' leaving matrimony and motherhood to 'take care of itself.' As periodicity, or the menstrual cycle, was 'perhaps the deepest law of the cosmos,' he argued that women of high-school age ought to be educated in separate schools 'primarily and chiefly for motherhood.'"[12]

What were the results of this larger cultural discouragement of coeducation in America? Many institutions took different steps to limit or discourage coeducation where before it had been allowed and encouraged. For instance, a few schools reinforced the separate course work expectation (usually domestic science or home economics) for women students. In the case of sociology professor Marion Talbot, in 1902 the University of Chicago turned down her request for a sanitary science area of study that "could become the central focus of the social and physical sciences in the reform or urban society." Even more important, Talbot's proposed sanitary science program would invite both male and female students. By 1904 the Sociology Department completely discarded Talbot's hopes for sanitary science and even carved out a separate department of "household administration, under Talbot's direction" from the larger sociology department. Relegated to the lower status of a home economics professor, Talbot's experiences showed how "the dramatic rise in women students' enrollment merged with the trend toward specialization to reinforce traditional attitudes about women's role in American society and to cut short the curricular reforms that some of the more farsighted female academics sought to foster."[13]

Perry and Price describe how some schools like Michigan actually "set up a quota on women's admission to some programs," while a few placed caps on women's admission altogether.[14] Still other institutions reacted against their own earlier coeducational practice by creating separate women's colleges or rescinding coeducation entirely.[15] A few eastern coed schools actually formed societies "for discouraging coeducation," and at Middlebury College, for example,

> the (male) student government sent a petition to each trustee urging them to do something about the situation. And so the trustees did. Among themselves they quickly came to "a tacit understanding that, for the present, the number of girls should be limited," and they began working on separating women from the men by establishing an annex or coordinate institution, using the models of Barnard at Columbia and Pembroke at Brown. By the end of the year the trustees had obtained from the state of Vermont a charter to establish the Women's College of Middlebury.[16]

Most often, however, the vehement reaction against coeducation played out in a marked decrease in female enrollments that lasted about a decade.

GRAPH 7. Female students by institution, 1879–1920 (%)

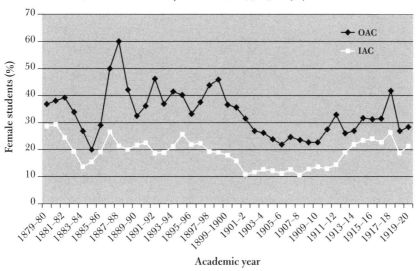

Academic year

The effects of anti-coeducation fervor on western land-grant institutions first and most significantly can be seen in the marked drop in their female enrollments from around 1900 to 1910. A sampling of student enrollment numbers from both IAC and OAC between 1879 and 1920 reveal the same downturn in women's numbers at both colleges that support a similar national decline. Even more striking is that corresponding drops and rises in percentages of women students are the same at both IAC and OAC over a forty-year period. For instance, the overall percentage of female students at both IAC and OAC reached its highest peak from the late 1880s through the late 1890s. The two colleges also experienced the same corresponding drops, as in the years around 1885, when there was a parallel decline in student numbers, and IAC and OAC female percentages dropped to 15 percent and 20 percent respectively. This decline likely corresponded with the national economic depression in the mid-1880s, which pushed down overall student enrollments, and especially for women. But both colleges also saw a similar resurgence in their student numbers during the late 1880s national economic recovery. The biggest decline occurred after 1900, when both IAC and OAC experienced enormous drops in their percentages of women from the end of the century through about 1912.

The reasons for these land-grant enrollment declines around 1900 are not clear, but they are likely related to similar national patterns of anti-coeducation feelings and fears of the feminization of education as described by other historians. Some land-grants may have placed restrictions on female admissions. But more likely, women students appear to have removed themselves while the numbers of their male colleagues increased, perhaps due to more intense cultural pressures on men to become middle-class providers in the late industrial age. Land-grant women likely felt the same nationwide social pressures to reject earlier advances in higher education in favor of renewed emphasis on marriage, family, and higher childbirth rates. The effects of these anti-coeducation declines are noticeable in numerous areas of land-grant education.

With the decline in the enthusiasm for coeducation, many former women's student activities also came to rather abrupt ends. For instance, military activity for women was effectively extinct by 1898. Mixed-gender literary societies and debating activities also gave way to gender-segregated and class-based fraternities and sororities. In addition, land-grants incorporated stricter programs of physical gender segregation, especially with the construction of new separated dormitories and women's gymnasiums. Further, most land-grants around 1900 created the position of "dean of women," similar to the "official chaperones" for young women that were common at other institutions. These deans of women acted in supervisory, maternal roles for increasing numbers of young women students who were experiencing the decline of rigid Victorian social rules. The supporting ideology was that female students needed strong figures to protect their virtue against the pressures of loosening relations between the sexes. Finally, like other colleges, land-grants added renewed emphasis to domestic science or economy programs as the preferred course of study for their female students. Since so many other educational institutions demanded domestic science and instructors for their college faculties, and governmental institutions needed domestic scientists to work in county extension programs, this only served to boost the demand for land-grant women students to pursue these studies after 1900. While the University of Nebraska had successfully postponed a separate domestic economy department for women for four decades, it finally relented in 1908—likely a result of the renewed national emphasis on traditional women's roles.

These declines might support the assessments of some historians that the coeducational experience in the United States was ultimately negative. According to Rosenberg, "despite women's success within coeducation, they remain subordinate figures within it. That subordination stems from the legacy of women's restricted access to coeducation as well as from the limited nature of what access can accomplish by itself."[17] Many would see this subordination in the reemphasis on women's domestic economy course work that limited women's experimentation with other nontraditional areas of study. In many ways coeducation kept women students marginalized through the expectations of "separate spheres" ideology. The emphasis on women's femininity and appearance at times portrayed women students as no more than distractions to more serious men, or it firmly required women to refine and civilize their fellow male students. It was also apparent in women's secondary service to male positions of authority — women as coeditors or assistant editors to male managing editors, or female vice presidents to male presidents. Still, the successes of western land-grant coeducation "gave women the opportunity to be more like their brothers. This was a laudable goal in a society that had long reserved its richest prizes for males."[18] Thus, in spite of the culture of separation that kept women student sometimes subordinated to men in the land-grant atmosphere, women students still achieved great gains and found themselves on equal playing fields with men, in many important ways.

Thus, in spite of disclaimers about the limited successes of early coeducation, the experiences of four western land-grants draw attention to the overwhelming benefits that both men and women felt from mixed-gender political, social, and intellectual interactions on land-grant campuses. The advancements of women's higher education achieved in later years could not have been possible without the successes of early coeducational experimenting. Regarding the debate between the successes of single-sex versus mixed-sex education, Rosenberg has argued that neither type of institution could have reinforced "so extreme a pattern of sex segregation" as much as "the society from which it grew." Still, early successes must be recognized, and "despite the continuing tendency of women and men to concentrate in different kinds of work, higher education greatly broadened women's opportunities."[19] For instance, whereas a majority of land-grant women were well entrenched in domestic economy programs by the turn of the century, enough women ventured into degree programs in journalism, science, commerce, and pharmacology by World War I to show a larger positive effect that the land-grants had on expanding women's opportunities in nontraditional activities.

In this context of coeducational opportunities, women of early land-grant years successfully navigated new gendered inclusion and found successes, often challenging the male sphere and making male activities their own. Early mixed-gender literary societies and debating clubs in the 1870s and 1880s became microcosms for resisting marginalization and exclusion. In military societies, women students successfully restructured a male activity for their own use through displays of athleticism and patriotism. Athletic activities had mixed successes and failures, with women athletes becoming at once sexual objects of curiosity for male students while also negotiating their own displays of aggressiveness to achieve greater respect. The challenges of defining women's course work at land-grant colleges partly enforced women's traditional roles through domestic science or economy courses, while at the same time opening up possibilities for exceptional women students to pursue the sciences, law, medicine, journalism, and pharmacology. The coeducational environment also allowed both men and women to challenge their social relations, toward the end goal of more equal interactions and achieving companionate marriages and friendships. For some women students, this meant embracing forms of homosociality that challenged traditional expectations of marriage and family. Finally, women's political activity at land-grants allowed that men and women together saw mixed-gender democracy in action. Although the land-grant version of that democracy often meant that men served in presiding or head positions and women served in secondary or assistant positions, both men and women took ideals of democracy and expanded suffrage learned during their land-grant experiences into the wider world. Coed land-grant colleges were places of challenging traditional expectations for women toward more equal gendered successes.

Coeducational land-grant colleges and universities offered opportunities for women students to determine new areas of participation and inclusion for themselves within traditionally male environments. As a result, women students were able to effect change on many fronts of feminist reform, by challenging gender restrictions both on campuses and in the larger nation.

From Carrie Chapman Catt's suffrage discussions and activism gained at IAC to Willa Cather's tenure as editor of the *Hesperian Student* newspaper at the University of Nebraska, and from the OAC champion women's basketball team that played in front of mixed-gender crowds to the Iowa State women's military regiment that marched at the Chicago World's Columbian Exposition in 1893, these female students introduced new areas of inclusion for women and helped to push for greater feminist changes in late-nineteenth-century America. This framework of examining gender relations through forms of both separation and inclusion will hopefully serve as a model for understanding gender negotiations in higher education and other historical contexts. The failures and successes of early coeducational practice at western land-grant colleges and universities might invite historians to rethink those same successes and failures of coeducation in today's systems of public and higher education.

Notes

ALSC   Adelphian Literary Society Collection

CLSHC   Cliolian Literary Society, "History" Collection

CLSC   Crescent Literary Society Collection

ISUL/SC   Iowa State University Library/Special Collections

OSUA   Oregon State University Archives

UNASC   University of Nebraska Archives and Special Collections

USUA   Utah State University Archives

INTRODUCTION

1. Clarke, *Sex in Education.*
2. Welch, *Inaugural Address*, 23.
3. Welch, *Inaugural Address*, 23.
4. Welch, *Inaugural Address*, 32.
5. Rosenberg, "The Limits of Access"; Miller-Bernal, *Separate by Degree*, 51–52.
6. Jeffrey, *Frontier Women*, 233.
7. Jeffrey, *Frontier Women*, 233.
8. Myres, "Suffering for Suffrage," 213–37.
9. Gunn, "Industrialists Not Butterflies," 5.
10. "Kansas Ahead," *The Industrialist* (Manhattan), September 18, 1875, quoted in Gunn, "Industrialists Not Butterflies, 6.
11. Dzuback, "Gender and the Politics of Knowledge," 171–95.
12. Bederman, *Manliness and Civilization*, 32–35.
13. Rosenberg, "The Limits of Access," 112; see also Miller-Bernal, *Separate by Degree*; Solomon, *In the Company of Educated Women*; and Gordon, *Gender and Higher Education.*
14. Wharton, "Gender, Architecture," 179.
15. Wharton, "Gender, Architecture," 180. For another interesting study of women's architectural place at Victorian women's colleges in England, see Vickery, *Buildings for Bluestockings.*

16. Bederman, *Manliness and Civilization*, 24.
17. Miller-Bernal, *Separate by Degree*, 3; see also Miller-Bernal and Poulson, *Going Coed*; Miller-Bernal and Poulson, *Challenged by Coeducation*.
18. Anderson, *An American Girl*.
19. Crawford, *The College Girl of America*; Olin, *The Women of a State University*. See also Horowitz, *Alma Mater*.
20. Woody, *A History of Women's Education*, 2:256.
21. Conable, *Women at Cornell*.
22. Rosenberg, "The Limits of Access," 110.
23. Solomon, *In the Company of Educated Women*, 44–61.
24. Gordon, *Gender and Higher Education*, 8.
25. Miller-Bernal, *Separate by Degree*. Especially useful is Table 4.1 on pages 88 and 89, which provides an overview of comparisons among the three colleges of her study.

1. MAKING A WELCOME FOR WOMEN STUDENTS

1. "Discourse" means the "set of ideas and practices which, taken together, organize both the way a society defines certain truths about itself and the way it deploys social power," thus representing those ideas and practices that formulate and reinforce certain societal ideals; in other words, discourse is not just the journalistic language used to spread an idea, but also the physical and material practices of gender-specific behavior. See Bederman, *Manliness and Civilization*, 24.
2. Greene, "Social and Cultural Capital," 153. Italics added.
3. Greene, "Social and Cultural Capital," 158.
4. Welch, *Inaugural Address*, 23.
5. Welch, *Inaugural Address*, 29.
6. Welch, *Inaugural Address*, 30. Italics added.
7. Welch, *Inaugural Address*, 33.
8. Adonijah S. Welch, "Plan of Organization, 1868," 10–11, Adonijah S. Welch Papers, ISUL/SC.
9. For a discussion of the influences on Anderson's views on women and education, see Gunn, "Industrialists Not Butterflies," 2–17.
10. John A. Anderson, "President's Report to the Board of Regents, 1873," *Report of the Kansas State Agricultural College, 1873* (no imprint), 16, quoted in Gunn, "Industrialists Not Butterflies," 6.
11. Fairfield, "Chancellor's Address," 22.
12. Fairfield, "Chancellor's Address," 23.
13. *Aurora* [Iowa Agricultural College, Ames, Iowa], July 1879, 4, ISUL/SC [hereafter cited as *Aurora* with date].

14. *Hesperian Student* [University of Nebraska, Lincoln], March 1872, UNASC [hereafter cited as *Hesperian Student* with date].

15. *Aurora*, April 1871.

16. The male pronoun is employed here because all but one of the editors were men. The first female editor of Nebraska's *Hesperian Student* was Willa Cather, elected in 1894.

17. Miller-Bernal, *Separate by Degree*, 50.

18. Harris, ed., "Introduction," in *Blue Pencils and Hidden Hands*, xxv and xxxiv.

19. Schultz, "Editing *The Jabberwock*: A Formative Experience for Nineteenth-Century Girls," in Harris, ed., *Blue Pencils and Hidden Hands*, 7.

20. Garvey, "Foreword," in Harris, ed., *Blue Pencils and Hidden Hands*, xii.

21. *Student Offering* [Oregon Agricultural College], December 15, 1869, 15, microfilm, OSUA [hereafter cited as *Student Offering* with date].

22. *Hesperian Student*, October 1871.

23. *Hesperian Student*, October 1871.

24. *Hesperian Student*, January 1878, 286.

25. "A Birthday Party: The University Celebrates Its Eighteenth Anniversary," *Hesperian Student*, February 16, 1887, copied in Helen Aughey Fulmer, "Scrapbook, 1884–1889," UNASC [hereafter cited as Fulmer, "Scrapbook, 1884–1889"].

26. "A Birthday Party" in Fulmer, "Scrapbook, 1884–1889."

27. "Annual Meeting of the State Historical Society," *Lincoln Journal*, January 1889, copied in Fulmer, "Scrapbook, 1884–1889."

28. "Annual Meeting of the State Historical Society," *Lincoln Journal*, December 1877, 254, in Fulmer, "Scrapbook, 1884–1889."

29. "Annual Meeting of the State Historical Society," *Lincoln Journal*, December 1877, 254, in Fulmer, "Scrapbook, 1884–1889."

30. "Annual Meeting of the State Historical Society," *Lincoln Journal*, May 1873, in Fulmer, "Scrapbook, 1884–1889."

31. "Annual Meeting of the State Historical Society," *Lincoln Journal*, October 1878, 447, in Fulmer, "Scrapbook, 1884–1889."

32. *The Gem* [Oregon Agricultural College, Corvallis], April 1883, 3, OSUA [hereafter cited as *The Gem* with date].

33. *Hesperian Student*, January 1878.

34. *Hesperian Student*, June 1872.

35. *Hesperian Student*, October 1871.

36. *Hesperian Student*, April and May, 1872.

37. *Hesperian Student*, October 1872 and December 1877, 253.

38. *Hesperian Student*, June 1873.

39. *Hesperian Student,* January 1875 and February 1875.

40. *Hesperian Student,* April 1877, 119.

41. *Hesperian Student,* December 1877, 252.

42. *Hesperian Student,* February 1878, 310.

43. *Hesperian Student,* October 1878, 447.

44. *Hesperian Student,* March 1875, 5.

45. *Hesperian Student,* March 1875, 8.

46. *Hesperian Student,* March 1874, 3.

47. *Aurora,* August 1877, 4.

48. *Aurora,* May 1879, 6.

49. *Hesperian Student,* March 1872.

50. *Hesperian Student,* October 1876, 17–18.

51. *Hesperian Student,* October 1876, 18.

52. *Hesperian Student,* April 1877.

53. Crescent Literary Society Collection, "Meeting Minutes, 1871–1877," April 15, 1871, 59, ISUL/SC [hereafter cited as CLSC, "Meeting Minutes" with date].

54. CLSC, "Meeting Minutes," November 1, 1873, and March 21, 1874, 198–99.

55. *Hesperian Student,* May 1872.

56. *Hesperian Student,* June 1873.

57. Adelphian Literary Society Collection, "Meeting Minutes, 1884–1887, "OSUA [hereafter cited as ALSC, "Meeting Minutes, 1884–1887" with date]; and Adelphian Literary Society Collection, "Book Two: Meeting Minutes, December, 1887–1889," OSUA [hereafter cited as ALSC, "Meeting Minutes, 1887–1889" with date].

58. ALSC, "Meeting Minutes, 1884–1887," November 27, 1885, 90.

59. ALSC, "Meeting Minutes, 1884–1887," January 15, 1886, 110.

60. ALSC, "Meeting Minutes, 1884–1887," September 23, 1887, 212.

61. ALSC, "Meeting Minutes, 1884–1887," November 4, 1887, 220.

62. ALSC, "Meeting Minutes, 1887–1889," November 9, 1888, 77.

63. *Hesperian Student,* November 1, 1893.

2. THE PLACE OF WOMEN STUDENTS

1. *Aurora,* May 1878.

2. Solomon, *In the Company of Educated Women,* 53.

3. Solomon, *In the Company of Educated Women,* 53.

4. *Student Offering,* December 15, 1869.

5. *Fifth Annual Catalogue of Officers and Students of Corvallis College, 1869–1870,* 16.

6. Henry H. Wilson, "Remembering Those First Years," *Reminiscences,* February 1941, 4, General Histories of the University Collection, UNASC.

7. *Hesperian Student*, December 1877.

8. *Tenth Annual Catalogue of the Oregon Agricultural College . . . 1874–1875.*

9. *Eighteenth Annual Catalogue of the Oregon Agricultural College . . . 1882–1883.*

10. *Hesperian Student*, November 1877, 203.

11. *Hesperian Student*, November 1877, 203.

12. *Hesperian Student*, November 1, 1893. For more information on the practices of gender separation at Cornell University, see Conable, *Women at Cornell.*

13. *Aurora*, April 1877, 7.

14. Eppright and Ferguson, *A Century of Home Economics*, 57.

15. *Hesperian Student*, October 1875.

16. "Floorplan of University Hall," Report of the Board of Regents of . . . Nebraska, December 1, 1888, reprinted in Ronning and Turner, *Willa Cather's University Days*, 12. For another relevant discussion on the uses of gendered space and separation on college campuses, see Wharton, "Gender, Architecture," 175–217.

17. My conclusion is similar to Wharton's findings about Duke University's separate campuses for men and women, especially in the expectations for male and female students, that "learning is experienced on West [male] Campus; decorum is learned on East [female]." See Wharton, "Gender, Architecture," 204.

18. *Hesperian Student*, November 1877.

19. *Hesperian Student*, November 1877.

20. *Catalogue of the Utah Agricultural College, 1901–02*, 28.

21. Eppright and Ferguson, *A Century of Home Economics*, 72.

22. *Aurora*, April 1883, 33.

23. *Fifth Annual Catalogue*, 17.

24. *Fifth Annual Catalogue*, 17.

25. Gertrude Tomson Fortna, "Lincoln Has Changed Much in Fifty Years," *Nebraska Alumnus*, January 1927, 16, UNASC.

26. *Annual Catalogue of the State Agricultural College of the State of Oregon for 1894–1895*, 29.

27. *Hesperian Student*, January 1875.

28. *Second Annual Catalogue of . . . Corvallis College, 1867–68*, 16.

29. *Hesperian Student*, April 1877, 92–93.

30. *Hesperian Student*, April 1877, 93.

31. *Aurora*, July 1886, 109.

32. *Catalogue of the Oregon Agricultural College, 1909–1910*, 53–54.

33. "The Way We Are Separated," *The Sombrero* [University of Nebraska] (1895), UNASC [cited hereafter as *Sombrero* with date].

34. E. H. Barbour, "They Were the Gay '90's," *Nebraska Alumnus*, February 1936, 11, UNASC.

35. *Hesperian Student*, April 1874.

36. *Hesperian Student*, April 1874. Italics added.

37. *Hesperian Student*, November 1877.

38. *Hesperian Student*, February 1874.

39. *Student Offering*, December 15, 1869, 12.

40. *Hesperian Student*, February 1874.

41. *Hesperian Student*, April 1872.

42. *Hesperian Student*, November 1875.

43. *Hesperian Student*, December 1877.

44. *Hesperian Student*, October 1876.

45. *Student Offering*, December 15, 1869, 20.

46. *Hesperian Student*, October 1871.

47. Gaylord, "The Agricultural College," *Student Offering*, December 15, 1869, 6.

48. *Hesperian Student*, October 1876.

49. *Hesperian Student*, April 1877.

50. Contrast this nineteenth-century feminist tool with modern feminism, which sought to equalize males and females by eliminating gendered language differences. For example, nineteenth-century feminism would have likely embraced the word *stewardess* as a reaction against the male assumption in "steward," whereas modern feminists would remove all gender distinction in favor of the more neutral "flight attendant."

51. *Hesperian Student*, November 1875.

52. *Hesperian Student*, May 1872.

53. *Hesperian Student*, May 1872.

54. "N.U. Graduations Were Lavender and Lace Affairs in the Old Days," in *Lincoln Sunday Journal and Star*, March 1939, UNASC.

55. *Aurora*, November 1873.

56. *Hesperian Student*, June 1875.

57. *Hesperian Student*, November 1875.

58. *Hesperian Student*, November 1875.

59. *Hesperian Student*, November 1875.

60. *Hesperian Student*, March 1872.

61. *Aurora*, May 1879.

62. *Aurora*, May 1879.

63. *Aurora*, May 1879.

64. *Hesperian Student*, June 1874.

65. *Hesperian Student*, October 1871.

66. *Hesperian Student*, May 1874.

67. *Hesperian Student*, March 1878, 367.

68. *Hesperian Student*, February 1877.

69. *Hesperian Student*, April 1877, 115.

70. *Hesperian Student*, September 1874.

71. *Hesperian Student*, April 1874.

72. *Aurora*, August 1878.

73. *Aurora*, August 1878.

74. *Aurora*, May 1878.

75. *Hesperian Student*, June 1873.

76. "Grad of '06 Tells of Life in His Era," *Daily Nebraskan*, February 17, 1953, UNASC.

77. Edna Bullock, "My Alma Mater: Reminiscences of an '89er," *Nebraska Alumnus*, November 1942, UNASC.

78. Ronning and Turner, *Willa Cather's University Days*, 28.

79. Ronning and Turner, *Willa Cather's University Days*, 28.

80. Ralph S. Mueller, "The Gay Nineties: Being a Reminiscence of the Campus and Its Affairs Thirty Years Ago," *Nebraska Alumnus*, November 1928, 421, UNASC.

81. *Aurora*, November 1873.

3. THE EARLY PRACTICE OF COEDUCATION

1. CLSC, "Meeting Minutes," Book 2.

2. *Hesperian Student*, October 1871.

3. *Hesperian Student*, October 1871.

4. CLSC, William J. Roudabush (president, Crescent Literary Society, 1920), "A Brief History of the Crescent Literary Society," ISUL/SC.

5. CLSC, Roudabush, "A Brief History."

6. Cliolian Literary Society, "History" Collection [hereafter cited as CLSHC], "The Rise and Development of Literary Societies at ISC," *Alumnus* 1909, ISUL/SC.

7. CLSHC, "Minutes, 1871–1880," May 25, 1872, ISUL/SC, 59.

8. CLSHC, "Minutes, 1871–1880," April 21, 1873, 93.

9. CLSHC, "Minutes, 1871–1880," September 30, 1873, 126.

10. CLSC, "Meeting Minutes," August 24, 1872.

11. CLSC, "Meeting Minutes," April 2, 1873.

12. CLSC, "Meeting Minutes," April 2, 1873.

13. CLSC, "Meeting Minutes," April 5, 1873.

14. CLSC, Roudabush, "A Brief History," 6.

15. *Hesperian Student*, March 1873.

16. *Hesperian Student*, March 1873.

17. *Hesperian Student*, October 1871.

18. *Hesperian Student*, February 1872.

19. *Hesperian Student*, November 1872.

20. *Hesperian Student*, November 1872.

21. *Hesperian Student*, April 1873.

22. *Hesperian Student*, June 1873.

23. *Hesperian Student*, September 1875.

24. *Hesperian Student*, September 1875.

25. *Hesperian Student*, October 1876.

26. *Hesperian Student*, June 1873.

27. *Hesperian Student*, April 1873.

28. *Hesperian Student*, February 1874.

29. *Hesperian Student*, February 1874.

30. *Hesperian Student*, June 1874.

31. *Hesperian Student*, September 1874.

32. *Hesperian Student*, November 1874.

33. *Student Offering*, December 15, 1869, 21–22.

34. *Student Offering*, December 15, 1869, 25.

35. *Student Offering*, December 15, 1869, 25–26.

36. *The Gem*, April 1883, 6.

37. *The Gem*, April 1883, 6.

38. *The Gem*, April 1883, 6.

39. *The Gem*, April 1883, 6.

40. *Hesperian Student*, April 1872.

41. *Hesperian Student*, September 1874.

42. *Hesperian Student*, September 1874.

43. *Hesperian Student*, September 1874.

44. *Hesperian Student*, September 1874.

45. *Hesperian Student*, October 1874.

46. *Hesperian Student*, October 1874.

47. *Hesperian Student*, January 1877.

48. *Hesperian Student*, January 1877.

49. "Palladian Year Book, 1884–1885," 6 and 10, Alice Tuttle Clark Collection, 1883–1928, UNASC.

50. CLSC, "Meeting Minutes," June 3, 1871.

51. CLSC, "Meeting Minutes," April 27, 1872.

52. CLSC, "Meeting Minutes," April 12, 1873, and May 31, 1873.

53. CLSC, "Meeting Minutes," September 20, 1873.

54. ALSC, "Meeting Minutes, 1884–1887," March 6, 1885, 46; and April 24, 1885, 53.

55. ALSC, "Meeting Minutes, 1884–1887," February 26, 1886, 111.

56. ALSC, "Meeting Minutes, 1884–1887," February 26, 1886, 115–16.

57. ALSC, "Meeting Minutes, 1884–1887," February 26, 1886, 119.

4. WOMEN STUDENTS' SOCIALITY

1. Woody, *A History of Women's Education*, 2:269. See also Solomon, *In the Company of Educated Women*.

2. Woody, *A History of Women's Education*, 2:224.

3. Woody, *A History of Women's Education*, 2:261.

4. Woody, *A History of Women's Education*, 2:271.

5. Woody, *A History of Women's Education*, 2:261.

6. Woody, *A History of Women's Education*, 2:264–65.

7. Woody, *A History of Women's Education*, 2:264–65.

8. Woody, *A History of Women's Education*, 2:302.

9. Woody, *A History of Women's Education*, 2:301–2.

10. Woody, *A History of Women's Education*, 2:272.

11. *Hesperian Student*, October 16, 1893, 11.

12. Parker, "The Ideal Farmer and His Wife," 47. Cornell began as an all-male institution in 1868, but in 1874, one donor gave a conditional $250,000 donation, if the college admitted female students.

13. *Aurora*, August 1885, 143.

14. *Hesperian Student*, September 1874.

15. *Hesperian Student*, October 1876.

16. *Hesperian Student*, November 1876.

17. *Hesperian Student*, January 1875.

18. Leverett, *IAC Bomb* (1897), 139.

19. *Aurora*, August 1880, 98.

20. *Aurora*, September 1885, 148.

21. Woody, *A History of Women's Education*, 2:226.

22. Eppright and Ferguson, *A Century of Home Economics*, 57.

23. *IAC Bomb* (1895), 120.

24. *Aurora*, May 1883, 54.

25. *Aurora*, May 1883, 54.

26. Eppright and Ferguson, *A Century of Home Economics*, 65.

27. Eppright and Ferguson, *A Century of Home Economics*, 65.

28. Wilson, "Remembering Those First Years," *Reminiscences*, February 1941, 4.

29. *Hesperian Student*, November 1876.

30. *Hesperian Student*, May 1874.

31. Anna Felber, "January 'Old Timer' Attended School in 1870," *Nebraska Alumnus*, January 1927, 10, UNASC.

32. Bullock, "My Alma Mater," *Nebraska Alumnus*, November 1942.
33. Eppright and Ferguson, *A Century of Home Economics*, 65.
34. Bullock, "My Alma Mater," *Nebraska Alumnus*, November 1942.
35. Bullock, "My Alma Mater," *Nebraska Alumnus*, November 1942.
36. Bullock, "My Alma Mater," *Nebraska Alumnus*, November 1942.
37. Davis, "Women on Top," 141.
38. Eason, "Floralia."
39. *The Ladies Bureau* [Iowa Agricultural College], May 13, 1876, ISUL/SC [hereafter cited as *Ladies Bureau* with date].
40. *Ladies Bureau*, May 13, 1876.
41. Davis, "Women on Top," 144.
42. *Ladies Bureau*, May 14, 1876.
43. *Ladies Bureau*, May 14, 1876.
44. Davis, "Women on Top," 142.
45. Bailey, "Sexual Revolution(s)," 235–36. See also Bailey, *From Front Porch to Back Seat*.
46. Bailey, "Sexual Revolution(s)," 241.
47. *Aurora*, July 1884, 113.
48. *Hesperian Student*, October 1874.
49. Edna Bullock, "My Alma Mater: Reminiscences of an '89er," *Nebraska Alumnus*, January 1943, 6, UNASC.
50. Bullock, "My Alma Mater," *Nebraska Alumnus*, January 1943, 6.
51. *Hesperian Student*, May 1874.
52. *Hesperian Student*, October 1876.
53. *Hesperian Student*, December 1877.
54. *Hesperian Student*, April 1877.
55. *Hesperian Student*, April 1877.
56. *Hesperian Student*, November 1877.
57. *Aurora*, August 1884, 135.
58. *Aurora*, August 1884, 135.
59. "Your Loving Pet" to Henry, October 1, 1892, in *IAC Bomb* (1897), 91.
60. *Hesperian Student*, December 1877.
61. *Hesperian Student*, September 1874.
62. *Hesperian Student*, February 1877.
63. *Hesperian Student*, October 1877.
64. *Hesperian Student*, November 1876.
65. "Your Loving Pet" to Henry in *IAC Bomb* (1897), 91.
66. "Your Loving Pet" to Henry in *IAC Bomb* (1897), 91.
67. "Your Loving Pet" to Henry in *IAC Bomb* (1897), 91.

68. Barbour, "They Were the Gay '90's," 11.

69. Barbour, "They Were the Gay '90's," 11.

70. Bailey, "Sexual Revolution(s)," 239.

71. Higham, "The Reorientation of American Culture in the 1890s," 77.

72. Higham, "The Reorientation of American Culture in the 1890s," 77.

73. Higham, "The Reorientation of American Culture in the 1890s," 77.

74. Pound, "Organizations," 62.

75. Mueller, "The Gay Nineties," *Nebraska Alumnus*, November 1928, 422.

76. Flexner, *I Hear America Talking*, 102.

77. Mueller, "The Gay Nineties," *Nebraska Alumnus*, November 1928, 422.

78. Flexner, *I Hear America Talking*, 102.

79. "Mashemology Club," IAC *Bomb* (1895).

80. "Mashemology Club," IAC *Bomb* (1895).

81. Flexner, *I Hear America Talking*, 102.

82. Alvin Johnson, quoted in Manley, *Centennial History of the University of Nebraska*, 1:240.

83. Bailey, "Sexual Revolution(s)," 242.

84. Brown, *Memories*, 59, USUA.

85. Brown, *Memories*, 70.

86. Brown, *Memories*, 70.

87. Brown, *Memories*, 70.

88. Alberta Larson Jacobs Diary, 1898–1901, USUA, 108.

89. Bob Parson, USUA Archivist, interview by author, February 22, 2002, e-mail letter from Logan, Utah. Tanner worked for the Mormon Church in Salt Lake City after his resignation from UAC, but when Congress again instigated anti-polygamy proceedings, the Church had to act. Tanner lost his employment but was never excommunicated. He later moved to southern Alberta and died in Lethbridge in 1927.

90. Parson, interview, February 22, 2002.

91. Parson, interview, February 22, 2002. Only Kerr's first wife accompanied him to Corvallis, where they both abandoned Mormonism.

92. See Crew, *Brides of Eden*. Creffield suffered a sound tarring and feathering by Corvallis townspeople. Creffield's only legal widow starved herself to death in jail in 1906; Linda Crew, Corvallis, Oregon, telephone interview by author, February 27, 2002.

93. Billy Sunday, quoted in Manley, *Centennial History of the University of Nebraska*, 280.

94. Bernice Forest Diary, 1916–17, OSUA, 26.

95. Jacobs Diary, 1898–1901.

96. Jacobs Diary, 1898–1901, 44–45.

97. Jacobs Diary, 1898–1901, 34.

98. Forest Diary, 1916–17, 5.

99. Forest Diary, 1916–17, 7.

100. Forest Diary, 1916–17, 8, 12.

101. Forest Diary, 1916–17, 72–73.

102. Forest Diary, 1916–17, 96, 72.

103. Forest Diary, 1916–17, 88. Italics added.

104. Forest Diary, 1916–17, 104.

105. Smith-Rosenberg, "The Female World," 53.

106. Smith-Rosenberg, "The Female World," 60.

107. *Hesperian Student*, March 1880, 13.

108. *Aurora*, April 1883, 33.

109. Smith-Rosenberg, "The Female World," 60.

110. Brown, *Memories*, 66.

111. Smith-Rosenberg, "The Female World," 63.

112. Brown, *Memories*, 61.

113. Brown, *Memories*, 61.

114. Brown, *Memories*, 65.

115. Smith-Rosenberg, "The Female World," 53.

116. Jacobs Diary, 1898–1901, 102.

117. Forest Diary, 1916–17, 69.

118. Forest Diary, 1916–17, 68.

119. Forest Diary, 1916–17, 78–79.

120. Sahli, "Smashing," 17–27.

121. Alice Stone Blackwell to Kitty Barry Blackwell, March 12, 1882, Blackwell Family Papers, Manuscript Division, Library of Congress, quoted in Sahli, "Smashing," 22.

122. Alice Stone Blackwell to Kitty Barry Blackwell, March 12, 1882.

123. Alice Stone Blackwell to Kitty Barry Blackwell, March 12, 1882.

124. Smith-Rosenberg, "The Female World," 63.

125. Forest Diary, 1916–17, 99–100.

126. Acocella, *Willa Cather & the Politics of Criticism*, 10.

127. Acocella, *Willa Cather & the Politics of Criticism*, 9.

128. O'Brien, *Willa Cather: The Emerging Voice*, 121.

129. O'Brien, *Willa Cather: The Emerging Voice*, 124.

130. O'Brien, *Willa Cather: The Emerging Voice*, 123.

131. Kaye, *Isolation and Masquerade*, 186.

132. O'Brien, *Willa Cather: The Emerging Voice*, 125.

133. O'Brien, *Willa Cather: The Emerging Voice*, 120.
134. O'Brien, *Willa Cather: The Emerging Voice*, 136.
135. O'Brien, *Willa Cather: The Emerging Voice*, 131.
136. O'Brien, *Willa Cather: The Emerging Voice*, 131.
137. Kaye, *Isolation and Masquerade*, 3.
138. Smith-Rosenberg, "The Female World," 68.
139. Smith-Rosenberg, "The Female World," 75.
140. Rosenberg, "The Limits of Access," 108.

5. WOMEN'S COURSE WORK

1. For feminist criticism of the retrenchment of women's roles through domestic economy, see Conway, "Perspectives," 1–12; and Fritschner, "Women's Work and Women's Education," 209–304.
2. For discussions of domestic economy at these institutions, see Gunn, "Industrialists Not Butterflies," 2–17; and Eppright and Ferguson, *A Century of Home Economics*.
3. Woody, *A History of Women's Education*, 2:224.
4. Quoted in Gunn, "Industrialists Not Butterflies," 6.
5. Parker, "The Ideal Farmer and His Wife," in Welch, *Inaugural Address*, 46.
6. Welch, "Plan of Organization, 1868," Adonijah S. Welch Papers, ISUL/SC.
7. Mary B. Welch Papers, 1871–1900, ISUL/SC; also quoted in Eppright and Ferguson, *A Century of Home Economics*, 1–2.
8. *Iowa Agricultural College Catalogue for the Year 1880.*
9. "Lectures on Domestic Economy," Mary B. Welch Papers, 1871–1900, ISUL/SC; also quoted in Ross, *A History of Iowa State College*, 155.
10. *Catalogue of the Oregon Agricultural College, 1910–1911*, 141.
11. Advertisement for Kansas State Agricultural College, *The Industrialist*, April 22, 1876, quoted in Gunn, "Industrialists Not Butterflies," 6.
12. Welch, *Inaugural Address*, 31.
13. Welch, *Inaugural Address*, 40.
14. *Aurora*, November 1879.
15. Beckert, "Propertied of a Different Kind," 287.
16. Beckert, "Propertied of a Different Kind," 288.
17. Beckert, "Propertied of a Different Kind," 289
18. Beckert, "Propertied of a Different Kind," 290.
19. *Fifth Annual Catalogue*, 16.
20. M. Welch, lecture (1875), quoted in Eppright and Ferguson, *A Century of Home Economics*, 28.
21. *Annual Catalogue of the State Agricultural College of the State of Oregon for 1892–93 and Announcements for 1893–94*, 17.

22. Mary Cleaver Faville, quoted in Eppright and Ferguson, *A Century of Home Economics*, 36.
23. M. Welch, lecture (1875), quoted in Eppright and Ferguson, *A Century of Home Economics*, 30.
24. M. Welch, lecture (1875), quoted in Eppright and Ferguson, *A Century of Home Economics*, 30.
25. M. Welch, lecture (1875), quoted in Eppright and Ferguson, *A Century of Home Economics*, 33.
26. *Annual Catalogue of the Agricultural College of Utah, 1893–1894*, 40; and *Annual Catalogue of the Agricultural College of Utah, 1901–1902*, 67.
27. Riley, *The Female Frontier*, 115.
28. Eppright and Ferguson, *A Century of Home Economics*, 24. See also Fink, *Agrarian Women*.
29. Riley, *The Female Frontier*, 114 and 127.
30. *Annual Catalogue of the State Agricultural College of the State of Oregon for 1892–93 . . .*, 15.
31. *The Utah Agriculture College Announcement of Its Opening Year, 1890–91*, 22.
32. *Annual Catalogue of the Agricultural College of Utah, 1893–1894*, 25.
33. *The Utah Agriculture College Announcement of Its Opening Year, 1890–91*, 22.
34. *The Utah Agriculture College Announcement of Its Opening Year, 1890–91*, 22.
35. *Annual Catalogue of the Agricultural College of Utah, 1896–1897*, 40.
36. *Annual Catalogue of the Agricultural College of Utah, 1898–1899*, 57.
37. *Annual Catalogue of the Agricultural College of Utah, 1891–1892*, 32.
38. Hansen, *Democracy's College in the Centennial State*, 79.
39. Burgoyne, "Our University as I Know It," lecture presented to the Utah State University Faculty Women's League, November 7, 1958, USUA.
40. Faville, quoted in Eppright and Ferguson, *A Century of Home Economics*, 36.
41. Riley, *The Female Frontier*, 89–90 and 195–96; and Fink, *Agrarian Women*, 68–69.
42. *Catalogue of the Oregon Agricultural College, 1896–1897*, 41. Italics added.
43. *Catalogue of the Oregon Agricultural College, 1899–1900*, 57.
44. *The Utah Agriculture College Announcement of Its Opening Year, 1890–91*, 21–22. Italics added.
45. *Annual Catalogue of the Agricultural College of Utah, 1893–1894*, 25.
46. *Annual Catalogue of the Agricultural College of Utah, 1898–1899*, 64–65.
47. *Student Life*, October 1903, 34. Emphasis added.
48. *Aurora*, May 1884.
49. *Aurora*, September 1875.
50. *Catalogue of the Oregon Agricultural College, 1892–93*, 7–10.

51. Gunn, "Industrialists Not Butterflies," 17.

52. Eppright and Ferguson, *A Century of Home Economics,* 48.

53. *The Buzzer,* 1909.

54. Conway, "Perspectives," 9.

55. Rossiter, *Women Scientists,* 65.

56. Rossiter, *Women Scientists,* 9–10.

57. Brown, *Memories,* 62.

58. Brown, *Memories,* 62.

59. Brown, *Memories,* 63.

60. *Aurora,* November 1879.

61. *Aurora,* May 1880 and October 1880.

62. *Iowa Agricultural College Catalogue for the Year 1887,* 29.

63. *Iowa Agricultural College Catalogue for the Year 1892,* 65.

64. *Aurora,* June 1878.

65. IAC *Bomb* (1897), 254.

66. Tiernan, *Iowa State College Graduates . . . 1890 through 1899* , 24.

67. Tiernan, *Iowa State College Graduates . . . 1890 through 1899,* 44.

68. *University of Nebraska Catalogue 1884–85 and Register,* 83–86.

69. *Hesperian Student,* January 1878.

70. Rossiter, *Women Scientists,* 78.

71. Tiernan, *Iowa State College Graduates . . . 1890 through 1899,* 43.

72. See Rossiter, *Women Scientists* for a thorough discussion of institutional discrimination against women scientists.

73. *The Cornhusker* (1917), 417. UNASC, Lincoln.

74. Helen M. Gilkey Papers, 1907–1974, OSUA; see also Gilkey, ed., *Dr. Helen Margaret Gilkey.*

75. Rossiter, *Women Scientists,* 61.

76. Helen M. Gilkey, survey in Alice Edwards's 1924 Survey of Domestic Science Graduates, Alice Edwards Papers, 1892–1956, OSUA.

77. Tiernan, *Iowa State College Graduates. . . 1872 through 1889,* 3.

78. *Aurora,* April 1879.

79. Tiernan, *Iowa State College Graduates . . . 1872 through 1889,* 8 and 11.

80. *Aurora,* November 1879.

81. *Aurora,* March 1879.

82. Tiernan, *Iowa State College Graduates . . . 1872 through 1889,* 41.

83. *Aurora,* September 1885. For a discussion of single women homesteaders in the West, see Lindgren, *Land in Her Own Name.* Lindgren has discovered many women homesteaders, including married, divorced, widowed, and single women, including sister-sister and brother-sister homesteading partnerships. Her data

show numbers of female homesteaders as high as 20 percent in some North Dakota counties. See also Smith, "Single Women Homesteaders," 163–83; and Riley, *The Female Frontier.*

84. *Oregon Agricultural College President's Biennial Report, 1918–1920*, 5–6.

85. *Aurora*, September 1876.

86. *Aurora*, July 1883.

87. Minick, *Omaha World Herald*, October 14, 1911, quoted in Willborn, "Women Law Students at Nebraska."

88. *University of Nebraska Catalogue 1883–84 and Register.*

89. *University of Nebraska Catalogue 1886–87 and Register.*

90. "Women in the Medical Profession," *Aurora*, December 1888, 8.

91. Tiernan, *Iowa State College Graduates . . . 1890 through 1899*, 7.

92. Tiernan, *Iowa State College Graduates . . . 1890 through 1899*, 29 and 33.

93. Tiernan, *Iowa State College Graduates . . . 1890 through 1899*, 67.

94. Alice Edwards Papers, 1892–1956, OSUA.

95. Conway, "Perspectives," 9.

96. Rossiter, *Women Scientists in America*, 63, and 64–65.

97. Rossiter, *Women Scientists in America*, 71.

6. UNDER THE GAZE

1. Squires, "Sport and the Cult of True Womanhood," 109.

2. Oglesby, *Encyclopedia of Women and Sport*, 200.

3. *Hesperian Student*, April 1877, 108.

4. Clarke, *Sex in Education.*

5. Rader, *American Sports*, 91.

6. Rader, *American Sports*, 207. For discussions of how women's athletics affected gender boundaries and expectations at the turn of the century, see also Cahn, *Coming on Strong.*

7. See Wilke, "The History of Physical Education"; and Deweese, "Life and Times of a Physical Education Major, 1897–1909," UNASC.

8. *Hesperian Student*, May 1877.

9. Bullock, "My Alma Mater," *Nebraska Alumnus*, November 1942.

10. Bullock, "My Alma Mater," *Nebraska Alumnus*, January 1943, 9.

11. *Hesperian Student*, December 1878, 508.

12. *Student Offering*, December 15, 1869.

13. *Hesperian Student*, December 1874.

14. *Hesperian Student*, November 1876.

15. Bullock, "My Alma Mater," *Nebraska Alumnus*, January 1943, 7.

16. Gordon, "'Any Desired Length,'" 24.

17. Gordon, "'Any Desired Length,'" 26.

18. Adrian and Monplaisir, "Fencing," in Oglesby, *Encyclopedia of Women and Sport*, 92–93. Fencing was one of ten original events at the first modern Olympics in 1896, and female fencers first appeared in the 1924 Olympics, but only in foil fencing. Not until 1996 did women compete in epee.

19. *Hesperian Student*, December 1878, 507.

20. *Aurora*, May 1878. Archery was the first Olympic sport for women—introduced in the 1904 games, after which the sport was canceled in Olympic competition until 1972.

21. Cahn, *Coming on Strong*, 15.

22. *The Sombrero* (1895).

23. *IAC Bomb* (1896).

24. Guy E. Reed, "Athletics," in *The University of Nebraska 1869–1919*, 98.

25. *Lincoln State Journal*, October 15, 1922, UNASC, Lincoln. For other contemporary accounts of 1890s women bicyclists, see Willard, *Wheel within a Wheel*; and Willard, *How I Learned to Ride the Bicycle*.

26. *Lincoln State Journal*, October 15, 1922, UNASC, Lincoln.

27. Tiernan, *Iowa State College Graduates . . . 1872 through 1889*, 36.

28. Tiernan, *Iowa State College Graduates . . . 1872 through 1889*, 36.

29. Higham, "The Reorientation of American Culture," 77.

30. Higham, "The Reorientation of American Culture," 97.

31. Quoted in Manley, *Centennial History of the University of Nebraska*, 291.

32. Lee, "Historical Information," UNASC.

33. The term *female spectacle* comes from Glenn, *Female Spectacle*.

34. *Aurora*, October 1880, 141.

35. Bullock, "My Alma Mater," *Nebraska Alumnus*, January 1943, 7.

36. *Student Life*, December 1902, 35.

37. Jennie Pentzer Bruce, "We Caught the Vision: Reminiscences," *Nebraska Alumnus*, May 1939, 10, UNASC.

38. Manley, *Centennial History of the University of Nebraska*, 291.

39. Mueller, "The Gay Nineties," *Nebraska Alumnus*, November 1928, 420.

40. Fred Williams and Adelloyd (Whiting) Williams, "By the Way," *Nebraska Alumnus*, November 1943, UNASC.

41. "'Silhouettes Only' Taken Local Co-eds: Used for Posture Study at Colleges," *Lincoln Journal Star*, September 14, 1950. UNASC, Lincoln.

42. "Washington U. Will Quit Photographing Co-Eds in Nude after Protest," *Lincoln Journal Star*, September 14, 1950.

43. Cahn, *Coming on Strong*, 84.

44. "'Silhouettes Only,'" *Lincoln Journal Star*, September 14, 1950.

45. Rader, *American Sports*, 91.
46. Rudolph, *The American College and University* (New York: Vintage Books, 1962), 393, quoted in Rader, *American Sports*, 91.
47. "Ladies' Base Ball Club," in *IAC Bomb* (1896).
48. Brown, *Memories*, 66.
49. Jacobs Diary, 1898–1901, 65.
50. Spencer, "Nebraska's Best Basketball Record," in "Scrapbook, 1899–1952," from 1934–35 (23/18/9, Box 8), UNASC.
51. Emery, "The First Intercollegiate Contest for Women," 418.
52. Emery, "The First Intercollegiate Contest for Women," 421.
53. *San Francisco Examiner*, April 5, 1896, 11, quoted in Emery, "The First Intercollegiate Contest for Women," 421.
54. Emery, "The First Intercollegiate Contest for Women," 420.
55. Emery, "The First Intercollegiate Contest for Women," 421.
56. *San Francisco Examiner*, April 5, 1896, quoted in Emery, "The First Intercollegiate Contest for Women," 421.
57. Emery, "The First Intercollegiate Contest for Women," 421.
58. *The Berkleyan* [University of California], March 20, 1896, quoted in Emery, "The First Intercollegiate Contest for Women," 422.
59. *College Barometer* [Oregon Agricultural College], March 1897, 14, microfilm, Oregon State University Library, Corvallis [hereafter cited as *College Barometer* with date].
60. *College Barometer*, February 1899, 14. Italics added.
61. For another look at early Indian women's basketball teams, see Peavy and Smith, "World Champions."
62. *College Barometer*, February 1899.
63. *Souvenir Barometer* [Oregon Agricultural College], June 1900, microfilm, Oregon State University Library, Corvallis.
64. *College Barometer*, May 1900.
65. *College Barometer*, May 1898.
66. Manley, *Centennial History of the University of Nebraska*, 304.
67. *College Barometer*, March 1900.
68. *College Barometer*, October 1900.
69. *College Barometer*, November 1900.
70. Spencer, "Nebraska's Best Basketball Record," in "Scrapbook, 1899–1952."
71. Manley, *Centennial History of the University of Nebraska*, 304.
72. Spencer, "Nebraska's Best Basketball Record," in "Scrapbook, 1899–1952."
73. Spencer, "Nebraska's Best Basketball Record," in "Scrapbook, 1899–1952."
74. "Nebraska Co-eds in Athletics on Larger Scale," *Lincoln Daily Star*, October 19, 1913.

75. "Nebraska Co-eds," *Lincoln Daily Star*, October 19, 1913.
76. "Nebraska Co-eds," *Lincoln Daily Star*, October 19, 1913.
77. "Nebraska Co-eds," *Lincoln Daily Star*, October 19, 1913.
78. "Nebraska Co-eds," *Lincoln Daily Star*, October 19, 1913.
79. Mrs. Joel E. McLafferty, in "Histories and Historic Items," Teachers College, Physical Education for Women, Memoirs, Theses, and Histories, UNASC.
80. Forest Diary, 1916–17, 19–20.
81. Forest Diary, 1916–17, 21–22.
82. Forest Diary, 1916–17, 22.
83. Forest Diary, 1916–17, 24–25.
84. Cahn, *Coming on Strong*, 8.
85. Cahn, *Coming on Strong*, 54.

7. "THE AMERICAN EAGLE IN BLOOMERS"

1. Attie, *Patriotic Toil*, 5.
2. Attie, *Patriotic Toil*, 24–25.
3. Attie, *Patriotic Toil*, 23.
4. Higham, "The Reorientation of American Culture in the 1890s," 83.
5. *Hesperian Student*, October 1876.
6. *Aurora*, May 1878.
7. *Aurora*, June 1878
8. *Aurora*, June 1878.
9. *Aurora*, May 1878, 397.
10. Kaye Askey, "Physical Education Reunion, 6-12-64," Histories and Historic Items collection (23/18/7, Box 2), UNASC.
11. Women students to the "Honorable Board of Regents of the State University, December 17, 1883," Histories and Historic Items collection (23/18/7, Box 2), UNASC.
12. Women students to the "Honorable Board of Regents of the State University, December 17, 1883," Histories and Historic Items collection (23/18/7, Box 2) UNASC.
13. *Lincoln Daily Journal*, May 11, 1888, in Fulmer, "Scrapbook, 1884–1889."
14. *Lincoln Daily Journal*, April 20, 1888, in Fulmer, "Scrapbook, 1884–1889."
15. Pound, "Penthesílea Redívíva," *Sombrero* (1895), 54.
16. Pound, "Penthesílea Redívíva," *Sombrero* (1895), 54.
17. "Lady Cadets at N.U.!" November 29, 1951, UNASC. When Pershing later served as the commander of the American Expeditionary Forces in Europe during World War I, he supported the service of women in civilian staff positions such as telephone operators, but not as formally enlisted army personnel.
18. Pound, "Penthesílea Redívíva," *Sombrero* (1895), 54.

19. *Lincoln Daily Journal*, May 18, 1888, in Fulmer, "Scrapbook, 1884–1889."
20. Pound, "Penthesílea Redivíva," *Sombrero* (1895), 54.
21. Pound, "Penthesílea Redivíva," *Sombrero* (1895), 54.
22. *Lincoln Daily Journal*, May 26, 1888, in Fulmer, "Scrapbook, 1884–1889."
23. *Lincoln Daily Journal*, May 26, 1888, in Fulmer, "Scrapbook, 1884–1889."
24. *Lincoln Daily Journal*, June 12, 1888, in Fulmer, "Scrapbook, 1884–1889."
25. Pound, "Penthesílea Redivíva," *Sombrero* (1895), 54.
26. Pound, "Penthesílea Redivíva," *Sombrero* (1895), 54.
27. *IAC Bomb* (1897), 304.
28. *Aurora*, June 1883, 70.
29. *Aurora*, April 1884, 49.
30. *Aurora*, September 1886, 178.
31. "One of the girls to the Editors of 'The Bomb,' World's Fair, September 23, 1893, *IAC Bomb* (1894), 180. Italics added.
32. From the *Chicago Tribune*, reprinted in the *IAC Bomb* (1894).
33. *Chicago Tribune*, reprinted in *IAC Bomb* (1894).
34. "One of the girls," 181. Italics added.
35. *Chicago Tribune*, reprinted in the *Bomb* (1894). Italics added.
36. "One of the girls," 181.
37. "One of the girls," 190.
38. "One of the girls," 181.
39. "One of the girls," 193.
40. Sund, "Columbus and Columbia in Chicago, 1893," 447. For more on women's participation in the Chicago World's Fair of 1893, see also Muccigrosso, *Celebrating the New World*; Weimann, *The Fair Women*.
41. Sund, "Columbus and Columbia in Chicago, 1893," 180.
42. *Annual Catalogue of the Agricultural College of Utah, 1891–1892*, 26–27.
43. *Annual Catalogue of the Agricultural College of Utah, 1892–1893*, 30.
44. *Annual Catalogue of the Agricultural College of Utah, 1893–1894*, 36.
45. *Annual Catalogue of the Agricultural College of Utah, 1896–1897*, 57.
46. For histories or references of women in World War I, see Friedl, *Women in the United States Military, 1901–1905*; Rustad, *Women in Khaki*; Schneider, *Into the Breach*; and Gavin, *American Women in World War I*.
47. Wilke, "A History of Physical Education," 39.
48. For a detailed history of the U.S. Army Nurse Corps, see Sarnecky, *A History of the U.S. Army Nurse Corps*.
49. Tiernan, *Iowa State College Graduates . . . 1890 through 1899*, 78.
50. Attie, *Patriotic Toil*, 22.
51. Katharine Newbranch Coffee, "Years of War," *Nebraska Alumnus*, May 1939, 11, UNASC.

52. Coffee, "Years of War," *Nebraska Alumnus*, May 1939, 11.

53. Faculty Women's League, "Minutes, 1910–1921," 93 (24/4:35, Box 1), USUA.

54. Faculty Women's League, "Minutes, 1910–1921," 93.

55. Faculty Women's League, "Minutes, 1910–1921," 109–12.

56. Faculty Women's League, "Minutes, 1910–1921," 109–12. Italics added.

57. Faculty Women's League, "Minutes, 1910–1921," 111.

58. Faculty Women's League, "Minutes, 1910–1921," 104 and 108.

59. Manley, *Centennial History of the University of Nebraska*, 214.

60. Eva Miller Grimes, "Our Four Years," *Nebraska Alumnus*, May 1938, 5, UNASC.

61. For a lengthier discussion of the Nebraska conflict over faculty loyalty during World War I, see Manley, *Centennial History of the University of Nebraska*, 212–26.

62. Manley, *Centennial History of the University of Nebraska*, 221–22.

63. For a discussion of the linkage between women's antiwar activism and the feminist movement of the 1910s, see Berkman, "Feminism, War, and Peace Politics."

64. Forest Diary, 1916–17, 110–11.

65. Forest Diary, 1916–17, 111–12.

66. Forest Diary, 1916–17, 113.

67. Coffee, "Years of War," *Nebraska Alumnus*, May 1939, 11.

68. Coffee, "Years of War," *Nebraska Alumnus*, May 1939, 11.

69. Blatch, *Mobilizing Woman-Power*, 6–7, quoted in Rustad, *Women in Khaki*, 26.

70. *Aurora*, April 1884, 49.

71. *IAC Bomb* (1894), 83.

72. "Blanche Cooper, '01," in *Utah Agricultural College Alumni Association Report* (1909), 58, USUA, Logan.

73. "Sabina Hermoine Hart, '97," in *Utah Agricultural College Alumni Association Report* (1909), 88.

74. "Mrs. Osborne J.P. Widtsoe, '00," in *Utah Agricultural College Alumni Association Report* (1909), 232 and 235. Brigham Young College in Logan is not to be confused with Brigham Young Academy, later Brigham Young University, located in Provo, Utah. BYC lasted until the 1920s, when the Mormon Church ended the Logan school's charter and made Brigham Young University the main Latter-day Saint university.

8. CHALLENGING POLITICAL SEPARATION

1. Forest Diary, 1916–17, 31.

2. For a general background of the American woman suffrage movement, see Flexner, *Century of Struggle*.

3. Myres, "Suffering for Suffrage," 213–37.

4. See especially Rosenberg, *Beyond Separate Spheres*; and Kerber, *Toward an Intellectual History of Women*. For women's colleges, see Horowitz, *Alma Mater*.

5. Glenn, *Female Spectacle*, 2–3.

6. *Student Offering*, December 15, 1869, 26.

7. *Hesperian Student*, March 1872.

8. *Hesperian Student*, May 1873.

9. Sarah Baker Eddy, quoted in Simmonds, "Women's Lib Comes to Logan," *The Herald Journal* [Logan UT], August 18, 1980, 9, USUA.

10. Fields, "'Fighting the Corsetless Evil,'" 109–40.

11. CLSHC, "Minutes, 1871–1880," August 27, 1874, and June 19, 1875, ISUL/SC, 171–72 and 208–9.

12. *Aurora*, November 1873.

13. *Aurora*, November 1873.

14. *Hesperian Student*, October 1871.

15. Welch, "Lectures on Domestic Economy," quoted in Eppright and Ferguson, *A Century of Home Economics*, 33.

16. *Lincoln Daily Journal*, November 13, 1884, in Fulmer, "Scrapbook, 1884–1889."

17. *Lincoln Daily Journal*, November 13, 1884, in Fulmer, "Scrapbook, 1884–1889."

18. Forest Diary, 1916–17, 30.

19. Forest Diary, 1916–17, 31.

20. Price, "When Women Were Women," 75.

21. Price, "When Women Were Women," 76–79.

22. *College Barometer*, March 1898.

23. *College Barometer*, March 1898. Italics added.

24. Grossberg, *Governing the Hearth*.

25. CLSC, "Meeting Minutes," September 20, 1873, 195.

26. *Aurora*, May 1880, 51.

27. Grossberg, *Governing the Hearth*, 58–59.

28. CLSHC, "Minutes, 1871–1880," May 17, 1873, ISUL/SC, 102.

29. *Hesperian Student*, April 1877.

30. *Aurora*, March 1883.

31. *Aurora*, July 1883, 86–87.

32. *Aurora*, October 1876.

33. *Aurora*, October 1876.

34. *Aurora*, October 1876.

35. *Aurora*, May 1882, 37.

36. *Aurora*, May 1882, 38.

37. *Aurora*, May 1882, 37.

38. *Hesperian Student*, October 1876, 18.

39. Henry H. Wilson, "H. H. Wilson Watched the University Develop," *Nebraska Alumnus*, December 1926, 487, UNASC.

40. *Hesperian Student*, December 1877, 259.

41. *Aurora*, July 1885, 110.

42. *Aurora*, September 1876.

43. *Hesperian Student*, January 1878.

44. *Hesperian Student*, April 1877, 117.

45. Fowler, *Carrie Catt*, 7.

46. *Lincoln Daily Journal*, June 7, 1885, in Fulmer, "Scrapbook, 1884-1889."

47. See Bordin, *Women and Temperance*; and Mattingly, *Well-Tempered Women*.

48. *Hesperian Student*, March 1874.

49. *Hesperian Student*, March 1874.

50. *Hesperian Student*, March 1874.

51. *Hesperian Student*, April 1874.

52. *Aurora*, May 1879.

53. *Aurora*, May 1879.

54. Wilhite, "Sixty-Five Years Till Victory," 154; and Osbun and Schmidt, *Issues in Iowa Politics*, 22.

55. ALSC, "Meeting Minutes, 1884-1887," January 28, 1887, 179.

56. ALSC, "Meeting Minutes, 1884-1887," February 26, 1886, 111.

57. *Lincoln Daily Journal*, April 20, 1888, in Fulmer, "Scrapbook, 1884-1889."

58. Myres, "Suffering for Suffrage," 219.

59. Myres, "Suffering for Suffrage," 232.

60. Myres, "Suffering for Suffrage," 233.

61. Myres, "Suffering for Suffrage," 233.

62. Wilhite, "Sixty-Five Years Till Victory," 150-57.

63. Horack, "Equal Suffrage in Iowa," in Shambaugh, *Applied History*, II: 298-305. See also Osbun and Schmidt, *Issues in Iowa Politics,* 21-22.

64. Butcher, *Education for Equality*, xiii-xiv and 6-8.

65. *Aurora*, September 1886, 152.

66. See Wilhite, "Sixty-Five Years Till Victory," 149-63; and Horack, "Equal Suffrage in Iowa," 277-313.

67. *Aurora*, May 1878.

68. *Aurora*, March 1879.

69. Wilhite, "Sixty-Five Years Till Victory," 153.

70. *Lincoln Daily Journal*, January 8, 1887, in Fulmer, "Scrapbook, 1884–1889."

71. Kimball, in *IAC Bomb* (1897), 131.

72. Kimball, in *IAC Bomb* (1897), 132.

73. Wilhite, "Sixty-Five Years Till Victory," 155.

74. Warner, "Make Way for the Women," *Sombrero* (1895), 51.

75. Warner, "Make Way for the Women," *Sombrero* (1895), 51.

76. Warner, "Make Way for the Women," *Sombrero* (1895), 52.

77. Warner, "Make Way for the Women," *Sombrero* (1895), 52.

78. Warner, "Make Way for the Women," *Sombrero* (1895), 53.

79. Warner, "Make Way for the Women," *Sombrero* (1895), 53.

80. Peck, *Carrie Chapman Catt*, 34.

81. *Aurora*, April 1884, 49.

82. Peck, *Carrie Chapman Catt*, 34.

83. E.C.A., "The True Status of Woman," *Hesperian Student*, April 1878, 356.

84. E.C.A., "The True Status of Woman," *Hesperian Student*, April 1878, 357.

85. *Aurora*, July 1879.

86. *Aurora*, July 1879.

87. Catt, *The Ballot and the Bullet*, 7–8.

88. Livermore, "Female Warriors," in Catt, *The Ballot and the Bullet*, 29.

89. Chapman, "The Right of Woman to the Ballot," in Catt, *The Ballot and the Bullet*, 51.

90. Chapman, "The Right of Woman to the Ballot," in Catt, *The Ballot and the Bullet*, 51.

91. Chapman, "The Right of Woman to the Ballot," in Catt, *The Ballot and the Bullet*, 51.

92. *Aurora*, November 1882, 131.

93. *Aurora*, November 1882, 139.

94. *Lincoln Daily Journal*, June 15, 1888, in Fulmer, "Scrapbook, 1884–1889."

95. *Lincoln Daily Journal*, June 15, 1888, in Fulmer, "Scrapbook, 1884–1889."

96. *The Orange* (1908) [Oregon Agricultural College], OSUA [cited hereafter as *The Orange* with date].

97. *The Orange* (1911), 97 and 113. Today McMinnville College is called Linfield College.

98. *The Orange* (1913), 171.

99. E.C.A., "The True Status of Woman," *Hesperian Student*, April 1878, 356.

100. *Aurora*, November 1973.

101. *Aurora*, August 1880, 98.

102. *Aurora*, June 1891, 23.

103. Tiernan, *Iowa State College Graduates . . . 1890 through 1899*, 7.

104. Tiernan, *Iowa State College Graduates . . . 1890 through 1899*, 24 and 44.
105. Tiernan, ed., *Iowa State College Graduates . . . 1890 through 1899*, 32 and 60.
106. Tiernan, *Iowa State College Graduates . . . 1872 through 1889*, 19; see also Eppright and Ferguson, *A Century of Home Economics*, 54.
107. Tiernan, *Iowa State College Graduates . . . 1872 through 1889*, 20; and Eppright and Ferguson, *A Century of Home Economics*, 54.
108. Tiernan, *Iowa State College Graduates . . . 1872 through 1889*, 26.
109. Myres, "Suffering for Suffrage," 219.
110. *Aurora*, May 1888.

CONCLUSION

1. *Hesperian Student*, June 1874.
2. Rosenberg, "The Limits of Access," 116.
3. Rosenberg, "The Limits of Access," 116.
4. Rosenberg, "The Limits of Access," 126–27.
5. Barnes, "Moving Beyond Home Economics."
6. Rosenberg, "The Limits of Access," 115.
7. Miller-Bernal, *Separate by Degree*, 52.
8. Rosenberg, "The Limits of Access," 116.
9. Perry and Price, "Introduction," in Anderson, *An American Girl*, 18.
10. Perry and Price, "Introduction," in Anderson, *An American Girl*, 18.
11. Perry and Price, "Introduction," in Anderson, *An American Girl*, 18–19; Roosevelt, "Theodore Roosevelt Links War in the Philippines to the Ideal of the Strenuous Life, 1899," in Fink, *Major Problems in the Gilded Age*, 266.
12. Perry and Price, "Introduction," in Anderson, *An American Girl*, 19; see also Hall, *Adolescence*, vol. 2.
13. Rosenberg, "The Limits of Access," 119–20.
14. Perry and Price, "Introduction," in Anderson, *An American Girl*, 19.
15. Rosenberg, "The Limits of Access," 116.
16. Miller-Bernal, *Separate by Degree*, 52–53.
17. Rosenberg, "The Limits of Access," 127–28.
18. Rosenberg, "The Limits of Access," 128.
19. Rosenberg, "The Limits of Access," 121–22.

Bibliography

ISUL/SC Iowa State University Library/Special Collections
OSUA Oregon State University Archives
UNASC University of Nebraska Archives and Special Collections
USUA Utah State University Archives

ARCHIVAL SOURCES

Adelloyd (Whiting) Williams Papers and Scrapbook. University of Nebraska Archives and Special Collections, Lincoln.

Adelphian Literary Society Collection. Oregon State University Archives, Corvallis.

Adonijah Strong Welch Papers, 1868–85. Iowa State University Library/Special Collections, Ames.

Alberta Larsen Jacobs Diary, 1898–1901. Utah State University Archives, Logan.

Alice Edwards Papers, 1892–1956. Oregon State University Archives, Corvallis.

Alice Tuttle Clark Collection, 1883–1928. University of Nebraska Archives and Special Collections, Lincoln.

Aurora. Iowa State University Library/Special Collections, Ames.

Bernice Forest Diary, 1916–17. Oregon State University Archives, Corvallis.

Burgoyne, Allie Peterson. "Our University as I Know It." Lecture presented to the Utah State University Faculty Women's League, November 7, 1958. Utah State University Archives, Logan.

The Buzzer. Utah State University Archives, Logan.

Cliolian Literary Society. "History" Collection. Iowa State University Library/Special Collections Department, Ames.

College Barometer. Microfilm. Oregon State University Library, Corvallis.

Crescent Literary Society Collection. Iowa State University Library/Special Collections Department, Ames.

Deweese, Alice Towne. "Life and Times of a Physical Education Major, 1897–1909." University of Nebraska Archives and Special Collections, Lincoln.

Faculty Women's League. "Minutes, 1910–1921." Utah State University Archives, Logan.

Fulmer, Helen Aughey. "Scrapbook, 1884–1889." University of Nebraska Archives and Special Collections, Lincoln.

Helen M. Gilkey Papers, 1907–74. Oregon State University Archives, Corvallis.

Histories and Historic Items. University of Nebraska Archives and Special Collections, Lincoln.

The IAC Bomb. Iowa State University Library/Special Collections Department, Ames.

"Lady Cadets at N.U.!" November 29, 1951. University of Nebraska Archives and Special Collections, Lincoln.

Lee, Mabel. "Historical Information on Departments of Physical Education for Women in American Colleges and Universities." University of Nebraska Archives and Special Collections, Lincoln.

Mary B. Welch Papers, 1871–1900. Iowa State University Library/Special Collections, Ames.

McLafferty, Mrs. Joel E. "Histories, and Historic Items." Teachers College, Physical Education for Women, Memoirs, Theses, and Histories, University of Nebraska Archives and Special Collections, Lincoln.

Nebraska Alumnus. University of Nebraska Archives and Special Collections, Lincoln.

"N.U. Graduations Were Lavender and Lace Affairs in the Old Days." *Lincoln Sunday Journal and Star*, March 1939. University of Nebraska Archives and Special Collections, Lincoln.

The Orange. Oregon State University Archives, Corvallis.

Reminiscences. General Histories of the University Collection. University of Nebraska Archives and Special Collections, Lincoln.

The Sombrero. University of Nebraska Archives and Special Collections, Lincoln.

Sorosis Literary Society. "Minutes, 1895–1901." Oregon State University Archives, Corvallis.

———. "Minutes, 1910–1912." Oregon State University Archives, Corvallis.

Sorosis Society. "Minute Book, 1899–1920." Utah State University Archives, Logan.

Souvenir Barometer. Oregon State University Archives, Corvallis.

Spencer, Merlin B. "Scrapbook, 1899–1952." University of Nebraska Archives and Special Collections.

PUBLISHED SOURCES

Acocella, Joan. *Willa Cather & the Politics of Criticism.* Lincoln: University of Nebraska Press, 2000.

Anderson, Olive San Louie. *An American Girl, and Her Four Years in a Boys' College,* edited by Elisabeth Israels Perry and Jennifer Ann Price. Ann Arbor: University of Michigan Press, 2006.

Annual Catalogue of the Agricultural College of Utah, 1891–1892. Logan: Smith, Cummings and Col., 1892. USUA, Logan.

Annual Catalogue of the Agricultural College of Utah, 1892–1893. Logan: Utah Agricultural College, 1893. USUA, Logan.

Annual Catalogue of the Agricultural College of Utah, 1893–1894. Logan: Utah Agricultural Printing Office, 1894. USUA, Logan.

Annual Catalogue of the Agricultural College of Utah, 1896–1897. Logan UT: Press of Smith, Cummings, and Co., 1896. USUA, Logan.

Annual Catalogue of the Agricultural College of Utah, 1898–1899. Salt Lake City UT: Tribune Job printing, 1898. USUA, Logan.

Annual Catalogue of the Agricultural College of Utah, 1901–1902. Logan: Utah Agricultural Printing Office, 1902. USUA, Logan.

Annual Catalogue of the State Agricultural College of the State of Oregon for 1892–1893 and Announcements for 1893–1894. Corvallis: Agricultural Printing Office, 1893. OSUA, Corvallis.

Annual Catalogue of the State Agricultural College of the State of Oregon for 1894–95. Corvallis: Agricultural College Printer, 1895. OSUA, Corvallis.

Attie, Jeanie. *Patriotic Toil: Northern Women and the American Civil War.* Ithaca NY: Cornell University Press, 1985.

Bailey, Beth L. *From Front Porch to Back Seat: Courtship in Twentieth-Century America.* Baltimore: Johns Hopkins University Press, 1988.

———. "Sexual Revolutions(s)." In *The Sixties: From Memory to History*, edited by David Farber, 235–62. Chapel Hill: University of North Carolina Press, 1995.

Barnes, Sarah. "Moving Beyond Home Economics: Women at Midwestern and Western Land-Grants, 1920–1960." Paper presented at the History of Education Society Annual Meeting. Pittsburgh PA, November 2, 2002.

Beck, Warren A., and Ynez D. Haase. *Historical Atlas of the American West.* Norman: University of Oklahoma Press, 1989.

Beckert, Sven. "Propertied of a Different Kind: Bourgeoisie and Lower Middle Class in Nineteenth-Century United States." In *The Middling Sorts: Explorations in the History of the American Middle Class*, edited by Burton J. Bledstein and Robert D. Johnston, 285–95. New York and London: Routledge, 2001.

Bederman, Gail. *Manliness and Civilization: A Cultural History of Gender and Race in the United States, 1880–1917.* Chicago: University of Chicago Press, 1995.

Berkman, Joyce. "Feminism, War, and Peace Politics: The Case of World War I." In *Women, Militarism and War: Essays in History, Politics, and Social Theory*, edited by Bethke Elshtain and Sheila Tobia, 141–60. Savage MD: Rowman and Littlefield, 1990.

Bishop, Morris. *A History of Cornell*. Ithaca NY: Cornell University Press, 1962.

Bordin, Ruth Birgitta Anderson. *Women and Temperance: The Quest for Power and Liberty, 1873–1900*. Philadelphia: Temple University Press, 1981.

Brown, Almeda Perry. *Memories*, ed. Charles F. Brown. Downey CA: Self-published, 1993. USUA, Logan.

Bushman, Richard L. *The Refinement of America: Persons, Houses, Cities*. New York: Vintage Books, 1992.

Butcher, Patricia Smith. *Education for Equality: Women's Rights Periodicals and Women's Higher Education*. Westport CT: Greenwood Press, 1989.

Cahn, Susan K. *Coming on Strong: Gender and Sexuality in Twentieth-Century Women's Sport*. New York: The Free Press, 1994.

Catalogue of the Oregon Agricultural College, 1892–1893. Corvallis: Agricultural College Printer, 1893. OSUA, Corvallis.

Catalogue of the Oregon Agricultural College, 1896–1897. Corvallis: Agricultural College Printer, 1897. OSUA, Corvallis.

Catalogue of the Oregon Agricultural College, 1899–1900. Corvallis: Agricultural College Printer, 1900. OSUA, Corvallis.

Catalogue of the Oregon Agricultural College, 1909–1910. Corvallis: Agricultural Printing Office, 1910. OSUA, Corvallis.

Catalogue of the Oregon Agricultural College, 1910–1911. Corvallis: Agricultural Printing Office, 1911. OSUA, Corvallis.

Catalogue of the Utah Agricultural College, 1901–02. Logan: College Printing Office, 1902. USUA, Logan.

Catt, Carrie Chapman, and the National American Woman Suffrage Association, eds. *The Ballot and the Bullet*. Philadelphia: A. J. Ferris, 1897.

Clarke, Dr. E. H. *Sex in Education*. Boston: James R. Osgood, 1874.

Clifford, Geraldine Jonçich. *Lone Voyagers: Academic Women in Coeducational Universities, 1870–1937*. New York: Feminist Press at the City University of New York, 1989.

Conable, Charlotte Williams. *Women at Cornell: The Myth of Equal Education*. Ithaca NY: Cornell University Press, 1977.

Conway, Jill K. "Perspectives on the History of Women's Education in the United States." *History of Education Quarterly* 14 (Spring 1974): 1–12.

Crawford, Mary Caroline. *The College Girl of America*. Boston: L. C. Page, 1905.

Crew, Linda. *Brides of Eden: A True Story Imagined*. New York: HarperCollins, 2001.

Cross, Coy F., II. *Justin Smith Morrill: Father of the Land-Grant Colleges*. East Lansing: Michigan State University Press, 1999.

Davis, Natalie Zemon. *Society and Culture in Early Modern France*. Stanford CA: Stanford University Press, 1975.

Dzuback, Mary Ann. "Gender and the Politics of Knowledge." *History of Education Quarterly* 43 (Summer 2003): 171–95.

Eason, Jason. "Floralia," at http://penelope.uchicago.edu/~grout/encyclopaedia_romana/calendar/floralia/html. Accessed February 19, 2008.

Eighteenth Annual Catalogue of the Oregon Agricultural College . . . 1882–1883. Corvallis: Benton Leader Print, 1882. OSUA, Corvallis.

Emery, Lynne. "The First Intercollegiate Contest for Women's Basketball, April 4, 1896." In *Her Story in Sport: A Historical Anthology of Women in Sports*, edited by Reet Howell, 417–23. West Point NY: Leisure Press, 1982.

Eppright, Ercel Sherman, and Elizabeth Storm Ferguson. *A Century of Home Economics at Iowa State University*. Ames: Iowa State University Press, 1971.

Fairfield, Chancellor Edmund B. "Chancellor's Address to the Board of Regents, Inaugural Ceremony, June 1876." In *Fifth Annual Register and Catalogue of the University of Nebraska, 1875–76*. Lincoln: Journal Company, 1876. UNASC, Lincoln.

Faragher, John Mack, and Florence Howe, eds. *Women and Higher Education in American History: Essays from the Mount Holyoke College Sesquicentennial Symposia*. New York: W. W. Norton, 1988.

Fields, Jill. "'Fighting the Corsetless Evil': Shaping Corsets and Culture, 1900–1930." In *Beauty and Business: Commerce, Gender, and Culture in Modern America*, edited by Philip Scranton, 109–40. New York: Routledge, 2001.

Fifth Annual Catalogue of Officers and Students of Corvallis College, 1869–1870. Corvallis: Willamette Valley Mercury Book and Job Office, 1870. OSUA, Corvallis.

Fink, Deborah. *Agrarian Women: Wives and Mothers in Rural Nebraska, 1880–1940*. Chapel Hill: University of North Carolina Press, 1992.

Fink, Leon, ed. *Major Problems in the Gilded Age and the Progressive Era*, 2nd ed. Boston and New York: Houghton Mifflin, 2001.

Flexner, Eleanor. *Century of Struggle: The Woman's Rights Movement in the United States*. Cambridge MA: Belknap Press, 1975.

Flexner, Stuart Berg. *I Hear America Talking: An Illustrated History of American Words and Phrases*. New York: Simon and Schuster, 1976.

Foley, Neil. *The White Scourge: Mexicans, Blacks, and Poor Whites in Texas Cotton Culture*. Berkeley: University of California Press, 1997.

Fowler, Robert Booth. *Carrie Catt: Feminist Politician*. Boston: Northeastern University Press, 1986.

Friedl, Vicki L. *Women in the United States Military, 1901–1905: A Research Guide and Annotated Bibliography*. Westport CT: Greenwood Press, 1996.

Fritschner, Linda Marie. "Women's Work and Women's Education: The Case of Home Economics, 1870–1920." *Sociology of Work and Occupations* 4 (May 1977): 209–304.

Gavin, Lettie. *American Women in World War I: They Also Served*. Niwot: University of Colorado Press, 1997.

Gilkey, Beulah, ed. *Dr. Helen Margaret Gilkey: Her Life, Her Family and Her Poems*. Oxenhill MD: Silesia Printing, 1973.

Glenn, Susan A. *Female Spectacle: The Theatrical Roots of Modern Feminism*. Cambridge MA: Harvard University Press, 2000.

Gordon, Lynn D. *Gender and Higher Education in the Progressive Era*. New Haven CT: Yale University Press, 1990.

Gordon, Sarah A. "'Any Desired Length': Negotiating Gender Through Sports Clothing, 1870–1925." In *Beauty and Business: Commerce, Gender and Culture in Modern America*, edited by Philip Scranton, 24–51. New York: Routledge, 2001.

Graves, Karen. *Girls' Schooling during the Progressive Era: From Female Scholar to Domesticated Citizen*. New York: Garland Publishing, 1998.

Greene, Jack P. "Social and Cultural Capital in British America." In *Patterns of Social Capital: Stability and Change in Historical Perspective*, edited by Robert I. Rotberg, 153–71. Cambridge: Cambridge University Press, 2001.

Grossberg, Michael. *Governing the Hearth: Law and the Family in Nineteenth-Century America*. Chapel Hill: University of North Carolina Press, 1985.

Gunn, Virginia Railsback. "Educating Strong Womanly Women: Kansas Shapes the Western Home Economics Movement, 1860–1914." PhD dissertation, University of Akron, 1992.

———. "Industrialists Not Butterflies: Women's Higher Education at Kansas State Agricultural College, 1873–1883." *Kansas History* 18 (Spring 1995): 2–17.

Hall, G. Stanley. *Adolescence: Its Psychology and Its Relations to Physiology, Anthropology, Sociology, Sex, Crime, Religion and Education*, vol. 2. New York: D. Appleton, 1904.

Hansen, James E., II. *Democracy's College in the Centennial State: A History of Colorado State University*. Fort Collins: Colorado State University Press, 1977.

Horack, Frank E. "Equal Suffrage in Iowa." In *Applied History*, 6 vols., edited by Benjamin F. Shambaugh, 2:277–314. Iowa City: State Historical Society of Iowa, 1914.

Harris, Sharon, ed. *Blue Pencils and Hidden Hands: Women Editing Periodicals, 1830–1910*. Boston: Northeastern University Press, 2004.

Higham, John. *Writing American History: Essays on Modern Scholarship*. Bloomington: Indiana University Press, 1970.

Horowitz, Helen Lefkowitz. *Alma Mater: Design and Experience in the Women's Colleges from Their Nineteenth-Century Beginnings to the 1930s*, 2nd ed. Amherst: University of Massachusetts Press, 1993.

Howell, Reet, ed. *Her Story in Sport: A Historical Anthology of Women in Sports*. West Point NY: Leisure Press, 1982.

Iowa Agricultural College Catalogue for the Year 1880. Ames: Iowa Agricultural College, 1880. ISUL/SC, Ames.

Iowa Agricultural College Catalogue for the Year 1887. Ames: Iowa Agricultural College, 1887. ISUL/SC, Ames.

Iowa Agricultural College Catalogue for the Year 1892. Ames: Iowa Agricultural College, 1892. ISUL/SC, Ames.

Jeffrey, July Roy. *Frontier Women: "Civilizing" the West? 1840–1880*, rev. ed. New York: Hill and Wang, 1998.

Kasson, John F. *Rudeness and Civility: Manners in Nineteenth-Century Urban America*. New York: Hill and Wang, 1990.

Kaye, Frances W. *Isolation and Masquerade: Willa Cather's Women*. New York: P. Lang, 1993.

Kerber, Linda. *Toward an Intellectual History of Women: Essays by Linda Kerber*. Chapel Hill: University of North Carolina Press, 1997.

Knewtson, Katrina Anne. "The Experience of Women's Higher Education at Oregon Agricultural College, 1870–1916." Master's thesis, Oregon State University, 1995.

Knoll, Robert E. *Prairie University: A History of the University of Nebraska*. Lincoln: University of Nebraska Press, 1995.

Lindgren, H. Elaine. *Land in Her Own Name: Women as Homesteaders in North Dakota*. Fargo: The North Dakota Institute for Regional Studies, North Dakota State University, 1991.

Manley, Robert N. *Centennial History of the University of Nebraska. Volume I: Frontier University, 1869–1919*. Lincoln: University of Nebraska Press, 1969.

Mattingly, Carol. *Well-Tempered Women: Nineteenth-Century Temperance Rhetoric*. Carbondale and Edwardsville: Southern Illinois University Press, 1998.

McClelland, Averil Evans. *The Education of Women in the United States: A Guide to Theory, Teaching, and Research*. New York: Garland Publishing, 1992.

Milam, Ava Clark. *Camp Cookery, A Cookery and Equipment Handbook for Boy Scouts and Other Campers*. Portland OR: J. K. Gill, 1918.

Milam, Ava Clark, and J. Kenneth Mumford. *Adventures of a Home Economist*. Corvallis: Oregon State University Press, 1969.

Miller-Bernal, Leslie. *Separate by Degree: Women Students' Experiences in Single-Sex and Coeducational Colleges*. New York: Peter Lang, 2000.

Miller-Bernal, Leslie, and Susan L. Poulson, eds. *Challenged by Coeducation: Women's Colleges Since the 1960s*. Nashville: Vanderbilt University Press, 2007.

——, eds. *Going Coed: Women's Experiences in Formerly Men's Colleges and Universities*. Nashville: Vanderbilt University Press, 2004.

"The Morrill Act of July 2, 1862, Providing for the endowment, support and maintenance of colleges of agriculture and mechanic arts." In *The Land Grant*

Tradition, by the National Association of State Universities and Land-Grant Colleges. Washington DC: National Association of State Universities and Land-Grant Colleges, 1995.

Muccigrosso, Robert. *Celebrating the New World: Chicago's Columbian Exposition of 1893*. Chicago: Ivan R. Dee, 1993.

Myres, Sandra L. "Suffering for Suffrage: Women and the Struggle for Political, Legal, and Economic Rights," in *Westering Women and the Frontier Experience, 1800–1915*, 213–37. Albuquerque: University of New Mexico Press, 1982.

Nevins, Allan. *The State Universities and Democracy*. Urbana: University of Illinois Press, 1962.

Newcomer, Mabel. *A Century of Higher Education for American Women*. New York: Harper & Brothers, 1959.

O'Brien, Sharon. *Willa Cather: The Emerging Voice*. New York: Oxford University Press, 1987.

Olin, Helen R. *The Women of a State University: An Illustration of the Working of Coeducation in the Middle West*. New York: G. P. Putnam's Sons, 1909.

Oglesby, Carole A., et al., eds. *Encyclopedia of Women and Sport in America*. Phoenix: The Oryx Press, 1998.

Osbun, Lee Ann, and Steffen W. Schmidt, eds. *Issues in Iowa Politics*. Ames: Iowa State University Press, 1990.

Parker, Professor H. W. "The Ideal Farmer and His Wife," in *Inaugural Address* by A. S. Welch. ISUL/SC, Ames.

Peavy, Linda, and Ursula Smith. "World Champions: The 1904 Girls' Basketball Team from Fort Shaw Indian Boarding School." *Montana: The Magazine of Western History* 51 (Winter 2002): 2–25.

Peck, Mary Gray. *Carrie Chapman Catt: A Biography*. New York: H. W. Wilson, 1944.

Pound, Louise. "Organizations," in *The University of Nebraska, 1869–1919*. Lincoln: University of Nebraska, 1919.

Price, Jennifer. *Flight Maps: Adventures with Nature in Modern America*. New York: Basic Books, 1999.

Rader, Benjamin G. *American Sports: From the Age of Folk Games to the Age of Televised Sports*, 3rd ed. Englewood Cliffs NJ: Prentice Hall, 1996.

Riley, Glenda. *The Female Frontier: A Comparative View of Women on the Prairie and the Plains*. Lawrence: University Press of Kansas, 1988.

Ronning, Kari, and Elizabeth Turner, eds. *Willa Cather's University Days: The University of Nebraska, 1890–1895*. Lincoln: Center for Great Plains Studies, 1995.

Rosenberg, Rosalind. *Beyond Separate Spheres: Intellectual Roots of Modern Feminism*. New Haven CT: Yale University Press, 1982.

———. "The Limits of Access: The History of Coeducation in America." In *Women and Higher Education in American History: Essays from the Mount Holyoke College Sesquicentennial Symposia*, edited by John Mack Faragher and Florence Howe, 107–29. New York: W. W. Norton, 1988.

Ross, Earle D. *Democracy's College: The Land-Grant Movement in the Formative State*. New York: Arno Press & The New York Times, 1969.

———. *A History of Iowa State College*. Ames: Iowa State College Press, 1942.

———. *The Land-Grant Idea at Iowa State College: A Centennial Trial Balance, 1858–1958*. Ames: Iowa State University Press, 1958.

Rossiter, Margaret. *Women Scientists in America: Struggles and Strategies to 1940*. Baltimore: Johns Hopkins University Press, 1982.

Rustad, Michael. *Women in Khaki: The American Enlisted Woman*. New York: Praeger Press, 1982.

Sahli, Nancy. "Smashing: Women's Relationships Before the Fall." *Chrysalis* (Summer 1979): 17–27.

Sarnecky, Mary T. *A History of the U.S. Army Nurse Corps*. Philadelphia: University of Pennsylvania Press, 1999.

Schneider, Carl J., and Dorothy Schneider. *Into the Breach: American Women Overseas in World War I*. New York: Viking, 1991.

Second Annual Catalogue of . . . Corvallis College, 1867–68. Portland OR: A. G. Walling and Co., 1867.

Smith, Sherry L. "Single Women Homesteaders: The Perplexing Case of Elinore Pruitt Stewart." *Western Historical Quarterly* (May 1991): 163–83.

Smith-Rosenberg, Carroll. "The Female World of Love and Ritual: Relations between Women in Nineteenth-Century America," in *Disorderly Conduct: Visions of Gender in Victorian America*, 53–76. New York: Oxford University Press, 1986.

Solomon, Barbara Miller. *In the Company of Educated Women: A History of Women and Higher Education in America*. New Haven CT: Yale University Press, 1985.

Squires, Mary-Lou. "Sport and the Cult of True Womanhood: 'Paradox at the Turn of the Century.'" In *Her Story in Sport: A Historical Anthology of Women in Sports*, edited by Reet Howell, 101–6. West Point NY: Leisure Press, 1982.

Stadtman, Verne A. *The University of California, 1868–1968*. New York: McGraw-Hill, 1970.

Stock, Phyllis. *Better than Rubies: A History of Women's Education*. New York: G. P. Putnam's Sons, 1978.

Sund, Judy. "Columbus and Columbia in Chicago, 1893: Man of Genius Meets Generic Woman." *The Art Bulletin* 75 (Sept. 1993): 443–66.

Tenth Annual Catalogue of the Oregon Agricultural College . . . 1874–75. Salem: E. M. Waite, Book and Job Printer, 1875. OSUA, Corvallis.

Thorne, Alison Comish. "Visible and Invisible Women in Land-Grant Colleges, 1890–1940." 72nd Faculty Honor Lecture, October 8, 1985. Logan: Utah State University Press, 1985.

Tiernan, Elizabeth, ed. *Iowa State College Graduates: Biographical Directory, A Who's Who of the Graduates from 1872 through 1889*. Ames: Collegiate Press, Inc., 1939.

——, ed. *Iowa State College Graduates: Biographical Directory, A Who's Who of the Graduates from 1890 through 1899*. Ames: Iowa State College Press, 1952.

The University of Nebraska, 1869–1919. Lincoln: University of Nebraska, 1919. UNASC, Lincoln.

University of Nebraska Catalogue 1883–84 and Register. Lincoln: Journal Company, Printers, 1884. UNASC, Lincoln.

University of Nebraska Catalogue 1884–85 and Register. Lincoln: University of Nebraska, 1885. UNASC, Lincoln.

University of Nebraska Catalogue 1886–87 and Register. Lincoln: Journal Company, Printers, 1887. UNASC, Lincoln.

The Utah Agriculture College Announcement of Its Opening Year, 1890–91. Logan: J. P. Smith Printer, 1891. USUA, Logan.

Vickery, Margaret Birney. *Buildings for Bluestockings: The Architecture and Social History of Women's Colleges in Late Victorian England*. Newark: University of Delaware Press and Associated University Presses, 1999.

Weimann, Jeanne Madeline. *The Fair Women*. Chicago: Academy Press, 1981.

Welch, Adonijah Strong. *Inaugural Address Delivered at the Opening of the Iowa State Agricultural College, March 17, 1869*. Davenport IA: Gazette Premium Book & Job Printing Establishment, 1869. ISUL/SC, Ames.

Wharton, Annabel. "Gender, Architecture, and Institutional Self-Presentation: The Case of Duke University." *South Atlantic Quarterly* 90 (Winter 1991): 175–217.

White, Kevin. *The First Sexual Revolution: The Emergence of Male Heterosexuality in Modern America*. New York: New York University Press, 1993.

Wilhite, Ann L. Wiegman. "Sixty-Five Years Till Victory: A History of Woman Suffrage in Nebraska." *Nebraska History* 49 (Summer 1968): 148–63.

Wilke, Phyllis Kay. "The History of Physical Education for Women at the University of Nebraska from the Early Beginnings to 1952." Master's thesis, University of Nebraska, 1973.

Willard, Frances. *How I Learned to Ride the Bicycle: Reflections of a 19th-Century Woman*, edited by Carol O'Hare. Fair Oaks CA: Fair Oaks Publishing, 1991.

——. *Wheel within a Wheel*. Grand Rapids MI: Fleming H. Revell, 1895.

Willborn, Steve. "Women Law Students at Nebraska: The First Woman and the First

100 Years of Women." *Nebraska Transcript*. University of Nebraska College of
Law, 1991. UNASC, Lincoln.

Woody, Thomas. *A History of Women's Education in the United States*, 2 vols. New
York: The Science Press, 1929.

Wyman, Walker D. *History of the Wisconsin State Universities*. River Falls WI: River
Falls State University Press, 1968.

Index

*The Colonel's Lady on the Western Frontier: The Correspondence of
Alice Kirk Grierson*
Edited by Shirley A. Leckie

*Their Own Frontier: Women Intellectuals Re-Visioning
the American West*
Edited by Shirley A. Leckie and Nancy J. Parezo

*A Stranger in Her Native Land: Alice Fletcher and
the American Indians*
By Joan Mark

*So Much to Be Done: Women Settlers on the Mining and
Ranching Frontier*, second edition
Edited by Ruth B. Moynihan, Susan Armitage, and Christiane Fischer
Dichamp

Women and Nature: Saving the "Wild" West
By Glenda Riley

The Life of Elaine Goodale Eastman
By Theodore D. Sargent

"Give Me Eighty Men": Women and the Myth of the Fetterman Fight
By Shannon D. Smith

Bright Epoch: Women and Coeducation in the American West
By Andrea G. Radke-Moss

Moving Out: A Nebraska Woman's Life
By Polly Spence
Edited by Karl Spence Richardson

Eight Women, Two Model Ts, and the American West
By Joanne Wilke